Directory
of
Rural Organisations

Directory
of
Rural Organisations

Elizabeth M Powell
Derek Taylor

FARMING PRESS

First published 1997

ISBN 0 85236 349 4

A catalogue record for this book is available from the British Library

Published by Farming Press
Miller Freeman plc
Wharfedale Road, Ipswich IP1 4LG, United Kingdom

Distributed in North America
by Diamond Farm Enterprises,
Box 537, Alexandria Bay, NY 13607, USA

Cover design by Andrew Thistlethwaite
Typeset by Galleon Typesetting
Printed and bound in Great Britain by
St Edmundsbury Press Limited, Bury St Edmunds, Suffolk

Contents

Foreword

No one doubts the importance of the countryside, as shown by government in Rural White Papers for England and Wales. It is increasingly understood that the countryside is neither just a food factory nor simply to provide recreation for town and city dwellers. It is a dynamic synthesis of these and other interests. Many people depend on rural Britain for their livelihood, others value it for recreation – all need information about rural organisations to help their work, or to improve the quality of their lives. This directory helps people identify those sources of information.

The directory does not just list those organisations which operate purely in the rural environment, but also those which overlap in function between the urban and rural environments. Organisations which may be useful to those individuals and companies who work and live in the countryside have also been included, even if they are not directly rural.

Recent events in agriculture, major environmental concerns, water shortages and climate change, the disappearance of wildlife species, loss of rural services and traditional farming methods all point to the need to provide timely and accurate information. In listing government departments, trade and professional bodies, pressure groups and societies the

directory reminds us of the multitude of different, and sometimes conflicting, interests which are at work in the countryside. It will prove invaluable both to individuals and professionals who operate within the rural environment.

One group of professionals dedicated to serving the rural property markets are chartered surveyors who seek practical policies and solutions for a thriving rural economy. This means more diverse business relying on agriculture and forestry as an economic cornerstone. It also means conserving countryside and wildlife habitats, thereby offering an attractive environment to people seeking employment, affordable homes or beautiful places to visit.

The many organisations listed in this directory have their part to play – but they cannot operate in isolation. This directory builds on earlier information provided by the Royal Institution of Chartered Surveyors and enables contact to be made with other organisations serving rural interests.

Edward Perkins, OBE, FRICS, FAAV, ACIArb
President, Rural Practice Division
The Royal Institution of Chartered Surveyors

Preface

It became apparent while working in the Learning Resources Department at Harper Adams Agricultural College that it was often extremely difficult to obtain accurate and up-to-date information about rural organisations. Many excellent directories do exist, but cover specialist subject areas, in education and the environment in particular. It was to fill this gap that the idea of a directory to assist those seeking information about organisations which are important to the rural community was born.

We have used our combined 20 years of experience as librarians at one of the leading agricultural colleges in the UK to identify those subjects and organisations about which those interested in the rural community of the UK need information.

We have worked hard to ensure that the information contained in the directory is accurate. Over 2,300 organisations were initially identified from a variety of sources and all were sent a letter and profile form to complete. The majority replied promptly and many addresses were corrected. Defunct and merged organisations were identified. A second letter was sent to those who had not responded to the initial request for information. Organisations who still did not reply were phoned to check their details. Directory entries for organisations whose existence was confirmed, but who did not reply to our letters have a note to that effect in the profile section. Organisations whose existence could not be confirmed have been omitted from the directory. Despite thorough checking it is inevitable that there will be some errors and we take full responsibility for these. After checking and editing, some 1,800 organisations have been included.

Without the support of Harper Adams College and, in particular, Dr Wynne Jones, Principal, this directory could not have been completed and we would like to express our sincere thanks to the college for its support. We wish to thank all the organisations who took the time to complete the profile forms and returned them so promptly. Within the limitations of space, the organisation profile has been reproduced as supplied by the organisation. We are happy that Farming Press shared our view that this directory was a worthwhile venture and we trust that it will fulfil its aim.

Elizabeth M Powell and Derek Taylor

Alphabetical List of Rural Organisations

Aberdeen Angus Cattle Society
Pedigree House
6 King's Place
Perth
PH2 8AD
Tel: 01738 622477
Fax: 01738 636436
Contact: Robert Anderson, Secretary
Founded: 1879
Membership: 1437
Publications: The Aberdeen-Angus Review, The Aberdeen-Angus Herd Book
Profile: In 1879 the Aberdeen Angus Cattle Society was established with objectives of maintaining the pedigrees of Aberdeen Angus cattle and preserving and publishing these, along with relevant information, in the herd book and promoting the breeding of Aberdeen Angus cattle. Aberdeen Angus is recognised worldwide as the brand leader for quality beef – heifers making ideal suckler cows with long, productive lives and steers being sought for their ability to finish on natural, home-produced feed. The society's Certified Aberdeen Angus Beef Scheme has been in existence for over fourteen years.

Abergavenny and Border Counties Agricultural Society
Show Office
Lewis's Lane
Abergavenny
Monmouthshire
NP7 5BA
Tel: 01873 853152
Contact: Joyce Davies-Griffiths, Secretary
Founded: 1844
Membership: 600
Publications: Schedules and catalogues
Profile: The encouragement of agricultural enterprise, to promote improvements in the breeding, rearing and health of livestock, the improvement of agricultural produce, invention and improvement of agricultural implements, the encouragement of skill and industry in husbandry by the holding of an annual show.

Action with Communities in Rural England
Somerford Court
Somerford Road
Cirencester
Gloucestershire
GL7 1TW
Tel: 01285 653477
Fax: 01285 654537
Contact: Information Officer
Founded: 1987
Publications: Publications list available
Previous names: Standing Conference of Rural Community Councils
Profile: ACRE is the national association of rural community councils whose shared purpose is to improve the quality of life of local communities, and particularly of disadvantaged people in rural England.

ADAS
Oxford Spires Business Park
The Boulevard
Langford Lane
Kidlington
Oxfordshire
OX5 1NZ
Tel: 01865 842742
Fax: 01865 845055
Contact: Phillip Needham, Chief Executive
Previous names: Agricultural Development and Advisory Service
Profile: ADAS is the leading consultancy to land-based industries in the UK, with over 2,000 staff and a turnover of £76 million. They provide independent, impartial advice to both government and private sector companies involved in food, farming and environmental

management. Based throughout England and Wales, their 1,400 consultants provide up-to-date consultancy to over 40,000 businesses, ranging from small rural enterprises to major corporations and they are unequalled in the depth and breadth of their expertise.

ADAS is organised through a range of consultancy and statutory centres which are listed in MAFF's free publication 'At the Farmer's Service' or by contacting ADAS headquarters. ADAS also runs a range of research centres which are listed separately in this directory.

ADAS Arthur Rickwood
ADAS
Mepal
Ely
Cambridgeshire
CB6 2BA
Tel: 01354 692531
Profile: The ADAS horticultural research centre.

ADAS Boxworth
ADAS
Boxworth
Cambridge
CB3 8NN
Tel: 01954 267666
Email: Jenny-Allder@adas.co.uk
Contact: JH Clarke, Team Manager
Founded: 1948
Profile: ADAS Boxworth is located 18 km north west of Cambridge and is the operational base of the ADAS Arable Research Centre, and one of ten research centres operated by ADAS. Current research projects include work on appropriate levels of crop inputs, integrated farming and alternative land use (including set-aside). The research programme is 70% funded by MAFF, the remainder being funded by levy bodies, commercial companies, other government departments and the EU.

ADAS Bridgets Dairy Research Centre
ADAS
Martyr Worthy
Winchester
Hampshire
SO21 1AP
Tel: 01962 779765
Fax: 01962 779739
Contact: B Drew, Centre Manager
Founded: 1946
Previous names: Bridgets Experimental Husbandry Farm until 1992
Profile: The ADAS Bridgets Dairy Research Centre is the main ADAS centre for dairy research. Research is based on a herd of 600

Holstein cattle. Research is also conducted on crop and environmental topics as part of the national ADAS research and development programme.

ADAS Drayton
ADAS
Alcester Road
Stratford Upon Avon
Warwickshire
CV37 9RQ
Tel: 01789 293057
Profile: An ADAS dairy research centre.

ADAS Gleadthorpe
ADAS
Meden Vale
Mansfield
Nottinghamshire
NG20 9PF
Tel: 01623 844331
Profile: An ADAS land research centre.

ADAS High Mowthorpe
ADAS
Duggleby
Malton
North Yorkshire
YO17 8BP
Tel: 01944 738646
Fax: 01944 738434
Email: Sue_Ogilvey@adas.co.uk
Contact: Mrs Sue Ogilvey, Research Team Manager
Founded: 1949
Previous names: MAFF ADAS High Mowthorpe Experimental Husbandry Farm until 1992
Profile: ADAS High Mowthorpe is the most northerly arable research centre in the network of ten ADAS research centres providing research services and facilities for government, levy and commercial funders in the arable, livestock, environment and horticulture sectors. The centre is based on a 436ha arable farm and has a large beef suckler herd. The research programme includes a wide range of work across relevant fields.

ADAS Pwllpeiran
ADAS
Cwmystwyth
Aberystwyth
Ceredigion
SY23 4AB
Tel: 01974 282261
Profile: The ADAS research centre in Wales.

ADAS Redesdale
ADAS
Rochester
Otterburn
Northumberland
NE19 1SB
Tel: 01830 520608
Profile: An ADAS livestock research centre.

ADAS Rosemaund
ADAS
Preston Wynne
Hereford
HR1 3PG
Tel: 01432 820444
Fax: 01432 820121
Contact: RW Clare, Research Centre Manager
Founded: 1946
Publications: ADAS Research
Previous names: NAAS until 1974
Profile: ADAS Rosemaund Research Centre is one of ten ADAS research centres in England and Wales. Research is carried out on a wide range of arable crops concentrating on cost effective use of pesticides and the physiology of crop growth and development in cereals and breakcrops, including variety exploitation. Work on hops, cider fruit and other horticultural crops is targeted towards integrated pest and disease management. The emphasis within the four livestock enterprises: beef cattle, sheep, veal and red deer, is an efficient utilisation of feed inputs, meat quality and welfare issues.

ADAS Terrington
ADAS
Terrington St Clement
Kings Lynn
Norfolk
PE34 4PW
Tel: 01553 828621
Profile: An ADAS arable research centre.

Advisory Committee on Dangerous Pathogens
Health and Safety Commission/Department of Health
Health and Safety Executive
Room 703 Rose Court
2 Southwark Bridge
London
SE1 9HS
Tel: 0171 717 6230
Fax: 0171 717 6199
Email: Jillian.Deans@HSE.GOV.UK
Contact: Mr P Lister, Joint Secretary
Founded: 1981

Publications: Publications list available
Previous names: Dangerous Pathogens Advisory Committee until 1981
Profile: The ACDP is an advisory committee of the Health and Safety Commission and also advises the Departments of Health and Agriculture. Terms of reference are to advise the Health and Safety Commission, the Health and Safety Executive and Health and Agriculture Ministers, as required, on all aspects of hazards and risks to workers and others from exposure to pathogens.

Advisory Committee on Novel Foods and Processes
Room 235 Ergon House
c/o Nobel House
17 Smith Square
London
SW1P 3JR
Tel: 0171 238 6377
Fax: 0171 238 6382
Email: ntomlinson@csf.gov.uk
Contact: Mr Nick Tomlinson, Grade 7
Founded: 1980
Publications: Annual Report; press releases; reports on products cleared; reports on the use of antibiotic resistance markers in genetically modified food organisms.
Previous names: Food and Drink Industries Council (FDIC) until 1980; Advisory Committee on Irradiated and Novel Foods until 1986
Profile: The Advisory Committee on Novel Foods and Processes (ACNFP) is an independent body of experts whose remit is 'to advise Health and Agriculture Ministers of Great Britain and the Heads of the Departments of Health and Social Services and Agriculture for Northern Ireland on any matters relating to the irradiation of food or to the manufacture of novel foods or foods produced by novel process, having regard where appropriate to the views of relevant expert bodies'.

Advisory Committee on Pesticides
c/o Pesticides Safety Directorate
Room 309 Mallard House
Kings Pool
3 Peasholme Green
York
YO1 2PX
Tel: 01904 455701
Fax: 01904 455733
Contact: DPE Williams, Secretary
Founded: 1954
Publications: Advisory Committee on Pesticides Annual Reports (from HMSO)

Previous names: Advisory Committee on Poisonous Substances used in Agriculture and Food Storage until 1968
Profile: The Advisory Committee on Pesticides was established under the Food and Environment Protection Act 1985 to advise ministers in the regulatory departments on all matters relating to the safe and effective control of pests. Its membership provides a wide range of medical and environmental expertise independent of the government and the agrochemical industry.

Advisory Committee on Releases to the Environment
c/o The Department of the Environment
Room B351
Romney House
43 Marsham Street
London
SW1P 3PY
Tel: 0171 276 8187
Fax: 0171 276 8333
Contact: Dr Firoz Amijee, ACRE Secretrary
Founded: 1990
Profile: The Advisory Committee on Releases to the Environment (ACRE) was first established as an advisory committee by the Secretary of State for the Environment in April 1990. The present committee, under the chairmanship of Professor Beringer, was appointed in June 1993 as a statutory advisory committee of independent experts under the Environmental Protection Act 1990. The committee is composed of scientific experts from the public and private sectors including environmental groups. The main activity of the committee is to provide advice on whether an application for consent to release or market a genetically modified organism should be granted. The decision to grant a consent is taken by the Secretaries of State for the Environment, Scotland and Wales, the Minister of Agriculture, Fisheries and Food, and the Health and Safety Executive as appropriate.

Advisory Committee on Sites of Special Scientific Interest
c/o Scottish Natural Heritage
12 Hope Terrace
Edinburgh
EH9 2AS
Tel: 0131 447 4784
Contact: Mr Angus Lane

Advisory Committee on the Microbiological Safety of Food
c/o J Heath
Room 515a Ergon House

17 Smith Square
London
SW1P 3JR
Tel: 0171 238 5572
Profile: We have been unable to contact this organisation. The details given are unconfirmed.

Advisory Committee on Toxic Substances
Health and Safety Executive
Rose Court
2 Southwark Bridge
London
SE1 9HS
Tel: 0171 717 6184
Fax: 0171 717 6299
Contact: Ms J Stephens, HSO
Founded: 1977
Profile: The Health and Safety Commission has appointed the Advisory Committee on Toxic Substances (ACTS) to advise the Commission on matters relating to the prevention, control and management of hazards and risks to the health and safety of person arising from the supply or use of toxic substances at work, with due regard to any related risks to consumers, the public and the environment and to other associated matters referred to it by the Commission/Executive.

Advisory Council for the Education of Romany and other Travellers
Moot House
The Stow
Harlow
Essex
CM20 3AG
Tel: 01279 418666
Contact: Bill Forrester, Chairman
Founded: 1973
Membership: 100
Profile: ACERT was one of the pioneer agencies in providing good practice concerning the education of traveller children. ACERT works for equal access to education for gypsies and travellers, safe and secure accommodation, equal access to health and other community services. ACERT works for good community relations, endeavouring to eliminate discrimination on racial or other grounds. ACERT also runs a Planning Help Line for use by the public giving information on planning applications, objections, site rules and local authority planning policies available on 01279 418666 between 10am and 4pm, Mon–Fri.

Advisory, Conciliation and Arbitration Service
Department of Trade and Industry
Clifton House

83–117 Euston Road
London
NW1 2BR
Tel: 0171 396 0022
Fax: 0171 396 5159
Contact: ACAS Public Enquiry Point
Founded: 1974
Publications: Publications list available
Previous names: Conciliation and Arbitration
Service until 1973
Profile: The ACAS mission is to improve the
performance and effectiveness of organisations
by providing an independent and impartial service
to prevent and resolve disputes and to build
harmonious relationships at work. The key ACAS
services are: preventing and resolving industrial
disputes; resolving individual disputes over
employment; providing impartial information and
advice on employment matters and the
improvement of the understanding of industrial
relations.

Advocates for Animals
10 Queensferry Street
Edinburgh
EH2 4PG
Tel: 0131 225 6039
Fax: 0131 220 6377
Contact: Reg Ward, Director
Founded: 1912
Membership: 10,000
Publications: Annual Pictorial Review;
newsletters; numerous leaflets.
Profile: Advocates for Animals is one of Britain's
leading animal protection organisations. They
campaign against all forms of animal abuse and in
particular the use of animals in experiments. The
society campaigns for parliamentary legislation to
protect animals. They campaign for the abolition
of animal experimentation, for humane slaughter,
opposing the use of animals in circuses, opposing
intensive farming methods and the exploitation of
marine life.

AEA
Samuelson House
Paxton Road
Orton Centre
Peterborough
Cambridgeshire
PE2 5LT
Tel: 01733 371381
Fax: 01733 370664
Contact: J Vowles, Director General
Founded: 1873
Membership: 200
Publications: OPE Directory and Price Guide;
British Farm and Outdoor Power Equipment

Previous names: Agricultural Engineers
Association
Profile: A trade association representing
manufacturers and sole importers of machines
and equipment used on the land in agriculture,
horticulture, forestry, amenity and leisure areas.
AEA provides statistical and market information,
technical and safety support, export instruction
and assistance.

Agenda
ATB-Landbase (Training Services) Ltd
National Agricultural Centre
Stoneleigh Park
Warwickshire
CV8 2LG
Tel: 01203 696511
Fax: 01203 696723
Contact: Helen Beard, Office Manager
Founded: 1976
Publications: Annual brochure
Previous names: ATB-Management Training
Centre until 1992
Profile: Provision of in-house consultancy
helping to improve business performance;
scheduled open courses to meet the needs of
individuals and tailored course designed to
specific requirements.

Agenda 21 Network
The Observatory
36–41 Clerkenwell Close
London
EC1R 0AU
Tel: 0171 251 6455
Fax: 0171 251 6466
Contact: Andrea Cronin

Agricultural Co-operative Training Council
Plunkett Foundation
23 Hanborough Business Park
Long Hanborough
Oxford
OX8 8LH
Tel: 01993 883577
Fax: 01993 883576
Contact: Anne Watson Jones, Manager
Founded: 1988

Agricultural Credit Corporation Ltd
Agriculture House
25–31 Knightsbridge
London
SW1X 7NJ
Profile: We have been unable to contact this
organisation. The details given are unconfirmed.

Agricultural Economics Society

Dept of Agricultural & Food Economics
The Queen's University of Belfast
Newforge Lane
Belfast
BT9 5PX
Tel: 01232 255204
Fax: 01232 668384
Contact: Dr John Davis, Hon Secretary
Founded: 1926
Membership: 750
Publications: Journal of Agricultural Economics;
newsheet
Profile: The society aims to promote the study
and teaching of all disciplines relevant to
agricultural economics as they apply to the
agricultural, food and related industries and rural
communities. The society operates as a learned
society rather than as a pressure group or
professional association. Membership is drawn
largely from academia, the civil service,
agribusiness, consultancy, marketing firms,
farmers' organisations and environmental bodies.

Agricultural Economics Unit (Exeter)

University of Exeter
Lafrowda House
St Germans Road
Exeter
Devon
EX4 6TL
Tel: 01392 263839
Fax: 01392 263852
Email: J.P.McInerney@exeter.ac.uk
Contact: Professor John P McInerney, Director
Founded: 1955
Publications: AEU Occasional Reports Series
Farm Management Handbook; Farm Incomes in
South West England; discussion papers and
briefing papers
Profile: An academic department of the
University of Exeter researching all aspects of
the economics of food, agriculture, natural
resources and the environment at BSc level, plus
research degrees. Responsible for the Farm
Business Survey in South West England,
collecting and analysing data on farm technical
and financial performance and enterprise
profitability. AEU undertakes a range of research
studies in agricultural policy and rural
development.

Agricultural Extension and Rural Development Department

University of Reading
3 Earley Gate
The University
White Knights Road
Reading
RG6 2AL
Tel: 01734 318119
Fax: 01734 261244
Email: c.j.garforth@reading.ac.uk
Contact: Chris Garforth, Head of Department
Founded: 1965
Publications: Rural extension bulletins; rural
extension and education research reports;
AERDD working papers.
Previous names: Agricultural Extension and
Rural Development Centre until 1989
Profile: AERDD runs postgraduate and in-service
courses for rural development professionals,
both in Europe and developing countries. They
conduct research on issues of agricultural
extension and rural development policy. Eight
postgraduate diploma and masters courses are
run each year, and up to 20 short courses and
study tours. Forty research students are
registered for MPhil and PhD degrees. The
department works closely with ADAS to provide
training for agricultural advisory services in the
countries of Eastern Europe and the former
Soviet Union.

Agricultural Futures Exchange

ATA UK Representative Office
PO Box 6947
London
E14 8BL
Tel: 0171 515 2264
Fax: 0171 515 2264
Email: 100670.614@compuserve.com
Contact: Peter Sceats, UK Representative
Founded: 1958
Publications: Contributes data to the Weekly
Tribune
Profile: The Agricultural Futures Exchange is the
EU's largest agfutures exchange, listing
potatoes, pigs, weaner and wheat futures
contracts. It has offices in the UK, Germany,
Belgium and Holland. Certificated training
courses are available free of charge to farmers,
merchants and processors.

Agricultural Land Tribunals

Ministry of Agriculture, Fisheries and Food
Room 721
Nobel House
17 Smith Square
London
SW1P 3JR
Tel: 0171 238 6991
Fax: 0171 238 6591
Contact: Miss C A Brittan, ALT Secretary
Founded: 1947

Profile: Agricultural Land Tribunals (ALTs) are courts of first instance and settle certain disputes and other issues between agricultural landlord and tenant under the Agricultural Holdings Act 1986. ALTs also deal with cases under the Land Drainage Act 1991 and the Hill Farming Act 1946. There are a series of tribunals for the counties and regions of England and Wales and each tribunal is an independent statutory body with jurisdiction in its own area. ALT procedures are contained in the Agricultural Land Tribunals (Rules) Order 1978 and, for succession cases, The Agricultural Land Tribunals (Succession to Agricultural Tenancies) Order 1984. Details of the individual tribunals are available in the ministry's free publication 'At the farmer's service' or may be obtained by phoning the MAFF Helpline on 0645 335577.

Agricultural Law Association
63 Palmer Avenue
Cheam
Surrey
SM3 8EF
Tel: 0181 644 8041
Fax: 0181 641 7328
Contact: Miss ED Pinfold, Hon Secretary
Founded: 1972
Membership: 400
Publications: The Bulletin
Profile: It is a body of persons professionally interested in the law related to agriculture and the countryside. It is strictly non-political. It has strong commitment of encouraging legislation which is technically workable and to promoting a wider and more up-to-date knowledge of the often very complex law. It offers advice and assistance on questions of legislative reform.

Agricultural Lime Producers' Council
156 Buckingham Palace Road
London
SW1W 9TR
Tel: 0171 730 8194
Fax: 0171 730 4355
Contact: Fred Leitch, Secretary

Agricultural Manpower Society
Farm Management Unit
Department of Agriculture
Reading University
Earley Gate
Reading
RG6 2AT
Tel: 01734 875123 ext 8479
Fax: 01734 847813
Contact: GA Hill, Treasurer and Editor
Founded: 1970

Membership: 100
Publications: Agricultural Manpower
Profile: Founded in 1970 AMS is a voluntary organisation of individuals and representatives of organisations and services with an interest in the rural environment. It is concerned with all that contributes to the health, safety, welfare, performance and development of those at work, including their management, training and education and the improvement and safety of the work environment.

Agricultural Mortgage Corporation plc
AMC House
Chantry Street
Andover
Hampshire
SP10 1DD
Tel: 01264 334344
Fax: 01264 334614
Contact: Information Officer

Agricultural Policy Resources Division
Ministry of Agriculture Fisheries and Food
Nobel House
17 Smith Square
London
SW1P 3JR
Tel: 0171 238 6348
Fax: 0171 238 6553
Profile: The Agricultural Resources Policy Division is divided into three branches. Branch A deals with organic food standards, horses, supply of agricultural machinery, fertiliser and lime, and energy. Branch B is responsible for labour, training, voluntary bodies, taxation and finance. Branch C is concerned with deregulation, open government, health and safety liaison, metrication and summer time.

Agricultural Produce Exchange Ltd
The Cattle Market
Craven Road
Rugby
Warwickshire
CV21 3HX
Tel: 01788 550000
Fax: 01788 550622
Contact: E Barratt, Secretary

Agricultural Research Institute of Northern Ireland
Large Park
Hillsborough
County Down
BT26 6DP
Tel: 01846 682484
Fax: 01846 689594

Contact: Mr G Troughton, Institute Secretary
Founded: 1927
Publications: Annual Report and various other publications
Profile: The remit of the Agricultural Research Institute of Northern Ireland is primarily to strengthen the agriculture and food industries in Northern Ireland so that they may make their maximum contribution to the rural and total Northern Ireland economy, taking account of the needs of the community for conservation of the environment, welfare of animals and quality of food. This remit is fulfilled through strategic and applied research, technology transfer and inputs into undergraduate and postgraduate teaching through Queens University, Belfast.

Agricultural Show Exhibitors Association
7 Nursery Close
Chadwell Heath
Romford
Essex
RM6 4LB
Tel: 0181 220 0552
Contact: Fred Cater, Secretary
Founded: 1948
Membership: 55
Publications: Quarterly news bulletin; annual list of show dates and venues
Profile: The Agricultural Show Exhibitors Association is the premier trade association representing the interests of agricultural, commercial and industrial companies and traders who regularly take trade stand space at agricultural shows and other outdoor events. The association offers a free advice and support service to cover all aspects of outdoor show representation for both large and small exhibitors.

Agricultural Wages Board for England and Wales
Room 320D Nobel House
17 Smith Square
London
SW1P 3JR
Tel: 0171 238 6540
Fax: 0171 238 6553
Contact: Miss H Baker, Secretary
Founded: 1917
Publications: Agricultural Wages Order
Profile: The main responsibility of the AWB under the Agricultural Wages Act 1948, as amended, is to fix the minimum rates of wages and holiday entitlement of workers employed in agriculture and determine any other terms or conditions of employment. Under powers contained in the Agriculture Act 1967, the board

fixes minimum rates to be paid to workers while they are sick or injured.

Agricultural Wages Board for Northern Ireland
Department of Agriculture
Dundonald House
Upper Newtownards Road
Belfast
BT4 3SB
Tel: 01232 524567
Fax: 01232 525015
Contact: Margaret Hood, Secretary of the Board
Founded: 1977
Profile: The Agricultural Wages Board for Northern Ireland operates under the Agricultural Wages (Regulations) (Northern Ireland) Order 1977. Under this legislation it fixes minimum rates of wages for workers employed in agriculture in Northern Ireland. It also fixes minimum rates of wages for periods of sick leave and determines the holiday entitlement for workers so employed.

Agriculture Advisory Panel for Wales
Welsh Office
Agriculture Department (ESU)
Cathays Park
Cardiff
CF1 3NQ
Tel: 01222 823740
Fax: 01222 823352
Contact: Mrs A Noyes, Secretary to Agriculture Advisory Panel for Wales
Founded: 1980
Profile: The panel exists to advise the Secretary of State on agricultural issues and problems, to determine possible trends and to provide independent and objective views of the industry.

Agroforestry Research Trust
46 Hunters Moon
Dartington
Totnes
Devon
TQ9 6JT
Contact: Mr M Crawford, Director
Founded: 1991
Publications: Agroforestry News; numerous technical publications
Profile: The Agroforestry Research Trust was set up to conduct research into temperate agroforestry systems and tree, shrub and perennial crops for temperate climates, and to disseminate the results of such research for the public benefit. The trust has several trial sites in Devon, including a forest garden.

Akhal-Teke Society of Great Britain

Bodare Cottage
Daymer Lane
Trebetherick
Wadebridge
Cornwall
PL27 6SA
Tel: 01208 862964
Fax: 01208 862964
Contact: Sue Waldock, President
Founded: 1990
Membership: 70
Publications: Annual newsletter
Profile: The Society has three basic objectives:
to act in the best interests of the Akhal-Teke; to
guide breed development in Great Britain; and,
ultimately, to offer a complete service, covering
breed activities at home and abroad. They can
translate and check pedigrees as they have
Russian stud books and partbred registers. They
are sent current lists of stallions at stud,
performance tests and young stock from Russia.
They have in operation a purebred and a partbred
register. They hold an annual Akhal-Teke horse
awards competition, and with only 14 pure and
10 partbred Akhal-Tekes in Great Britain, they
also have a members competition, both are run
on a points system from 1st January to 31st
December.

Alcoholic Drinks Division

Ministry of Agriculture, Fisheries and Food
Nobel House
17 Smith Square
London
SW1P 3JR
Tel: 0171 238 6470
Fax: 0171 238 5962
Profile: The Alcoholic Drinks Division of MAFF is
divided into two branches. Branch A deals with:
the English and Welsh wine industry; the pilot
quality wine scheme; oenological practices; and
EU wine legislation. Branch B is responsible for
spirit drinks, beer and cider.

All Wheel Drive Club

PO Box 6
Fleet
Hampshire
GU13 9YE
Contact: Secretary
Founded: 1968
Membership: 2,500
Publications: All Wheel Driver members
newsletter
Profile: A club operating nationwide with the aim
of promoting responsible and fun use of off road
vehicles. About 120 motor sport events
organised annually. Also concerned with green
laning. Always keen to hear from land owners
who have rough land available for hire at
weekends.

Allerton Research and Educational Trust

Game Conservancy Trust
Loddington House
Main Street
Loddington
East Norton
Leicestershire
LE7 9XE
Tel: 01572 717220
Fax: 01572 717408
Email: 100631.1625@compuserve.com
Contact: Dr Nigel Boatman, Head of Research
Founded: 1992
Publications: Publications list available
Profile: The Allerton Research and Educational
Trust (ARET) aims to demonstrate the integration
of profitable modern farming and the
conservation of wildlife, particularly game
species. It is based on a 333 ha mixed farming
estate at Loddington in Leicestershire. In addition
to its role as a demonstration farm, monitoring of
the effects of management on fauna and flora,
and research into the interactions between
farming methods and wildlife are carried out.
ARET is run in partnership with the Game
Conservancy Trust.

Alternative Crops Unit

Ministry of Agriculture, Fisheries and Food
Profile: Please contact the MAFF Helpline on
0645 335577 for details of the Alternative Crops
Unit.

Alternative Technology Association

Centre for Alternative Technology
Llwyngwern Quarry
Machynlleth
Powys
SY20 9AZ
Tel: 01654 702400
Fax: 01654 702782
Email: cat@gn.apc.org
Internet: http://www.foe.co.uk/cat
Contact: Steven Jones, Administrator
Founded: 1975
Membership: 4000
Publications: Publications list available
Profile: The ATA is a network of over
4,000 members from many countries and walks
of life, striving to reduce their impact on the
Earth's natural systems. The ATA supports them

with practical advice, a forum for discussion and a range of member benefits.

Amateur Jockeys Association of Great Britain
Croft Cottage
29 Main Road
Farnley Tyas
Huddersfield
West Yorkshire
HD4 6UL
Tel: 01484 667335
Fax: 01484 666507
Email: jgreenall@nettec.co.uk
Contact: Sandy Brook, Hon Secretary
Founded: 1960
Membership: 300
Publications: Bumper
Previous names: Amateur Riders Association until 1995
Profile: Represents and protects the status and interests of amateur jockeys who ride under National Hunt and flat rules. Promotes amateur racing by sponsorship and arranging sponsorship.

Amateur Motor Cycling Association
28 Mill Park
Hawks Green Lane
Cannock
Staffordshire
WS11 2XT
Tel: 01543 466282
Fax: 01543 466283
Contact: Miss CA Davis, Secretary
Founded: 1932
Membership: 5,500
Profile: The AMCA was founded in 1932 and today is the largest organiser of adult motocross events in Europe.

Amenity Grass Marketing Association
Irene House
Kirkby Underwood
Bourne
Lincolnshire
PE10 0SD
Tel: 01778 440669
Fax: 01778 440066
Contact: Anthony D Andrews, Secretary
Founded: 1980
Membership: 36
Publications: AGMA News (members newsletter)
Profile: AGMA is a marketing association focusing on amenity grass seed to ensure that the consumer/user is aware of all relative merits of individual cultivars, and that high quality product is available. By independent audit or records, AGMA members ensure consumer/user

receives the goods requested to the specifications offered.

American Saddlebred Association of Great Britain
Uplands
North Road
Alfriston
East Sussex
BN26 5XE
Tel: 01323 870295
Fax: 01323 870295
Contact: Cheryl R Lutring

Ancient Monuments Board for Scotland
Longmore House
Salisbury Place
Edinburgh
EH9 1SH
Tel: 0131 668 8764
Fax: 0131 668 8765
Contact: Ronald A J Dalziel, Board Secretary
Founded: 1913
Publications: Annual Report
Profile: The Board advises the Secretary of State for Scotland on the exercise of his functions, under the Ancient Monuments and Archaeological Areas Act 1979, of providing protection for monuments of national importance. Protection may be provided by including a monument in a statutory list of protected monuments by acquisition or by guardianship in which the Secretary of State assumes responsibility for maintenance.

Ancient Monuments Board for Wales
Brunel House
2 Fitzalan Road
Cardiff
CF2 1UY
Tel: 01222 500207
Fax: 01222 500300
Contact: Simon Morris, Secretary
Publications: Annual Report (from HMSO)

Ancona Club
Leckby House
Flaxton
York
North Yorkshire
YO6 7QZ
Tel: 01904 468387
Contact: Mr PE Smedley, Secretary
Profile: A breed society for the promotion of the Ancona breed of poultry.

Anglers' Conservation Association
23 Castlegate
Grantham
Lincolnshire
NG31 6SW
Tel: 01476 61008
Fax: 01476 60900
Contact: Ms Jane Brett, Director
Founded: 1948
Membership: 16,000
Publications: ACA Review
Previous names: Anglers' Co-operative
Association until 1994

Anglesey Agricultural Society
Ty Glyn Williams
Anglesey Showground
Gwalchamai
Holyhead
Anglesey
LL65 4RW
Tel: 01407 720072
Fax: 01407 720880
Contact: Mr Aled W Hughes, Show
Administrator
Founded: 1808
Membership: 1,150
Publications: Society Annual Report; Annual
County Show Schedules and Show Catalogue;
Winter Fair Schedule and Catalogue
Previous names: The Anglesey Agricultural
Society 1808–1846; The Caernarvonshire and
Anglesey Society 1851–1912
Profile: The society organises the largest
two-day agricultural county show in Wales and
attracts an average of 52,000 people. The Winter
Fair is a one day event held in December. The
objects of the society are to promote agriculture,
horticulture and forestry, and to advance science
and research in connection with these subjects
for the benefit of the public and to promote the
improvement of livestock and the prevention and
eradication of diseases in animals useful to man
– in particular in the Isle of Anglesey and Wales.

Anglian Water plc
Anglian House
Ambury Road
Huntingdon
Cambridgeshire
PE18 6NZ
Tel: 01480 443000
Fax: 01480 443115
Contact: Richard Iwanicki, Conservation
Scientist – East
Founded: 1989

Publications: Manual of Good Practice for
Utilisation of Sewage Sludge in Agriculture;
numerous technical reports
Previous names: Anglian Water Authority until
1989
Profile: Anglian Water provides water services to
3.9 million customers, and sewerage services to
5.2 million. They run 1,072 sewage works and
159 water treatment works. Involved with annual
'Caring for the Environment' awards.

Angling Foundation
Angling Trade Association
The Federation House
National Agricultural Centre
Stoneleigh Park
Warwickshire
CV8 2RF
Tel: 01203 414999
Fax: 01203 414990
Contact: Dr Bruno Broughton, Executive Director
Founded: 1969
Membership: 36
Profile: To raise money from companies or
individuals earning all or part of their livelihoods
from the sport of angling, to invest in the
'protection and promotion of the sport, in the
present and the future, with special reference to
environmental considerations'.

**Anglo and Part Bred Arab Owners
  Association**
Gosford Farm
Ottery St Mary
Devon
EX11 1LX
Tel: 01404 814998
Contact: Aline Holmes, Secretary
Founded: 1993
Membership: 150
Profile: To look after the interests of Anglo and
Part Arab owners.

Anglo-Dutch Breeders Association
PO Box 61
Tunbridge Wells
Kent

Anglo-Nubian Breed Society
2 Bowling Green Cottages
Old Worcester Road
Albrighton
Wolverhampton
WV7 3EZ
Tel: 01902 373526
Contact: Mrs A Carrier, Secretary
Founded: 1972
Membership: 200

Publications: Members newsletter; Stud Goat Register; publications list available
Profile: The Anglo-Nubian Breed Society was formed in 1972 to bring breeders together with the aims: to foster the Anglo-Nubian breed and to encourage the breeding of Anglo-Nubians to a breed standard. The society enjoys many international members and contacts, as well as being affiliated to the British Goat Society.

Angus College

Keptie Road
Arbroath
Angus
DD11 3EA
Tel: 01241 432600
Fax: 01241 876169
Email: angusfe@mail.on-line.co.uk
Contact: James Menzies

Animal Aid

The Old Chapel
Bradford Street
Tonbridge
Kent
TN9 1AW
Tel: 01732 364546
Fax: 01732 366533
Contact: Andrew Tyler, Director
Founded: 1977
Membership: 19,000
Publications: Outrage (members journal); Youthrage (young supporters newsletter); Humane Scientist (journal); numerous publications and leaflets
Profile: Animal Aid promotes a more compassionate attitude to animals by educating and campaigning against all forms of cruelty. Animal Aid investigates and exposes the suffering that animals face in laboratories, factory farms, the countryside and in captivity. However, it also offers a message of hope, showing how everyone can play their part in making the world a better place for animals, people and the environment. Animal Aid has an active education department sending out over 11,000 student information packs a year and providing an excellent range of teaching resources.

Animal Amnesty

62 Thornton Street
Newcastle upon Tyne
NE1 4AW
Profile: We have been unable to contact this organisation. The details given are unconfirmed.

Animal Breeding Research Institute

Kings Building
West Mains Road
Edinburgh
EH9 3JQ
Tel: 0131 667 6901
Profile: We have been unable to contact this organisation. The details given are unconfirmed.

Animal Concern

62 Old Dumbarton Road
Glasgow
G3 8RE
Tel: 0141 334 6014
Fax: 0141 445 6470
Contact: John Robins, Organising Secretary
Founded: 1876
Membership: 350
Publications: Animal Concern News; various leaflets and pamphlets
Previous names: Scottish Anti-Vivisection Society until 1988
Profile: Animal Concern campaigns against all forms of animal abuse and exploitation. Current campaigns include: misuse of airguns, factory farming, seal shooting, animal circuses and zoos, vivisection, over fishing, blood sports and culling.

Animal Cruelty Investigation Group

PO Box 8
Halesworth
Suffolk
IP19 0JL
Tel: 01986 782280
Contact: Mike Huskisson, Founder
Founded: 1989
Membership: 2,000
Publications: News Bulletin
Profile: The Animal Cruelty Investigation Group was created to acquire the hard evidence of the cruel abuse of our fellow creatures in order to curtail such abuse. ACIG investigators strive to expose all forms of cruelty: bloodsports, vivisection, factory farming, the fur trade, etc. They gather by any lawful means the still pictures, video and audio tapes, and documentary records that will show the truth to the public.

Animal Data Centre

Residuary Milk Marketing Board
Lavrock Lane
Rickmansworth
Hertfordshire
WD3 3AW
Tel: 01932 710852
Fax: 01932 710505
Email: 100560.453@compuserve.com

Contact: Mr G Swanson, Head, Bull & Cow Evaluation Unit
Publications: Publications list available.
Previous names: Bull and Cow Evaluation Unit
Profile: The centre's prime responsibility is to carry out genetic evaluations for dairy production traits for all bulls and cows in the UK; to carry out genetic evaluations for type-minor breeds; to maintain an abnormality database; to carry out data exchanges and results transfers; and to provide services to farmers.

Animal Freedom
Hunt Saboteurs Association
PO Box 127
Kidderminster
Worcestershire
DY10 3UZ
Tel: 0121 643 2445
Contact: Celia Ryan, Organiser
Founded: 1986
Membership: 1,250
Publications: Animal Freedom (magazine)
Previous names: Fox Cubs
Profile: To educate and inform on all aspects of animal abuse. Aimed basically at 6 to 17-year-olds. Animal Freedom is a youth group of the Hunt Saboteurs Association. They promote a meat and dairy free diet, and a non-exploitative life-style.

Animal Health (Disease Control) Division
Ministry of Agriculture Fisheries and Food
Block B Government Buildings
Hook Rise South
Tolworth
Surbiton
Surrey
KT6 7NF
Tel: 0181 330 8084
Fax: 0181 337 3640
Contact: Alison J Reeves, Head of Branch A
Profile: Co-ordinates policy on a number of animal diseases, including foot and mouth disease, rabies, bovine tuberculosis, brucellosis, EBL, SVD, CSF and ASF. It also holds policy responsibility for animal identification and certain movement legislation.

Animal Health (International Trade) Division
Ministry of Agriculture Fisheries and Food
Block C Government Buildings
Hook Rise South
Tolworth
Surbiton
Surrey
KT6 7NF
Tel: 0181 330 8197

Profile: This division of MAFF deals with animal health import controls and export procedures for live animals and genetic material; approval for bulls in AI; licensing of AI centres for cattle; and approval of boars for use in AI.

Animal Health (Zoonoses) Division
Ministry of Agriculture Fisheries and Food
Block B Government Buildings
Hook Rise South
Tolworth
Surbiton
Surrey
KT6 7NF
Tel: 0181 330 8007
Profile: The Animal Health (Zoonoses) Division is responsible for control of salmonella in poultry and control of salmonella and other non-notifiable zoonotic diseases in agricultural livestock.

Animal Health and Welfare Veterinary Section
Ministry of Agriculture Fisheries and Food
Block B Government Buildings
Hook Rise South
Tolworth
Surbiton
Surrey
KT6 7NF
Tel: 0181 330 8292
Profile: The section is responsible for veterinary aspects of control and eradication of notifiable diseases, animal health schemes and welfare of animals on farms, in transit and in markets; also the welfare of imported and exported animals.

Animal Health Distributors Association (UK) Ltd
Gable Court
8 Parsons Hill
Hollesley
Woodbridge
Suffolk
IP12 3RB
Tel: 01394 410444
Fax: 01394 410455
Email: ahda@anglianet.co.uk
Contact: Dr Roger Dawson, Chief Executive
Founded: 1985
Membership: 201
Profile: An association of agricultural merchants who are registered and qualified to distribute animal medicines to farmers and horse owners together with several wholesalers of such products. Aims to prevent the EC legislating members out of business and to ensure that an appropriate number of animal medicines are classified for distribution by registered distributors and that new products are so classified.

Animal Health Division
Department of Agriculture for Northern Ireland
Dundonald House
Upper Newtownards Road
Belfast
BT4 3SB
Tel: 01232 524660
Fax: 01232 524982

Animal Health Trust
Balaton Lodge
Snailwell Road
Newmarket
Suffolk
CB8 7DW
Tel: 01638 661111
Fax: 01638 665789
Email: 100546.3713@compuserve.com
Contact: Dr Andrew Higgins

Animal Liberation Front Supporters' Group
BCM1160
London
WC1N 3XX
Email: 100302.1616@compuserve.com
Founded: 1976
Publications: Quarterly newsletter
Profile: Supports all forms of direct action committed against animal abusers and their property. The main business is to support those imprisoned for ALF type activities.

Animal Medicines Training Regulatory Authority
8 Parsons Hill
Hollesley
Woodbridge
Suffolk
IP12 3RB
Tel: 01394 411010
Fax: 01394 411030
Contact: Dr Roger Dawson, Chief Executive
Founded: 1987
Profile: AMTRA is an independent regulatory body whose task is to ensure that the distribution of animal medicines in the UK is undertaken in a responsible manner by qualified persons.

Animal Procedures Committee
c/o Home Office
50 Queen Anne's Gate
London
SW1H 9AT
Tel: 0171 273 2861
Fax: 0171 273 2423
Profile: We have been unable to contact this organisation. The details given are unconfirmed.

Animal Rights Bureau
4 Garden Lane
Bradford
West Yorkshire
BD9 5QJ
Tel: 01274 495847
Profile: We have been unable to contact this organisation. The details given are unconfirmed.

Animal Transportation Association
PO Box 25
Redhill
Surrey
RH1 5FU
Tel: 01737 822249
Fax: 01737 822954
Email: 100257.1720@compuserve. com
Contact: Tim Harris, European Secretary
Founded: 1976
Membership: 400
Publications: AATA Manual for the Transport of Animals by Road; quarterly magazine
Previous names: Animal Air Transport Association until 1989
Profile: AATA is concerned with all modes of animal transportation anywhere in the world. Whilst it was born out of the special problems faced by international airlines, the basic skills and experience are of equal value to road, rail and sea transportation. Membership embraces all associated disciplines from the largest airline to the smallest container manufacturer, as well as academics, boarding facilities, breeders, agents, governments, humane associations, insurers, libraries, port and quarantine facilities involved with the transport of all classes of animals from farm to fur, or feral to fish. There are special classes of membership for students and libraries.

Animal Welfare Division
Ministry of Agriculture Fisheries and Food
Tolworth Tower
Surbiton
Surrey
KT6 7DX
Tel: 0181 330 4411
Profile: The Animal Welfare Division is responsible for animal welfare on farms; animal welfare in markets and in transit; and, acts as secretariat for the Farm Animal Welfare Council.

Animal Welfare Institute
21 Ospringe Road
London
NW5
Tel: 0171 485 6968
Profile: We have been unable to contact this organisation. The details given are unconfirmed.

Animaline
The Lodge
Broadhurst Manor
Horstead Keynes
West Sussex
RH17 7BG
Tel: 01342 810596
Email: Animaline.Falalice@pncl.co.uk
Contact: Peter Wakeham, Manager
Founded: 1990
Membership: 2,600
Publications: Animaline brochure
Profile: To rescue and rear all wild animals, giving talks on animal welfare; to investigate human cruelty and prosecute if necessary; to protect our environment and to encourage the general public to help in wildlife rescue.

Animals (Scientific Procedures) Inspectorate
Home Office
50 Queen Anne's Gate
London
SW1H 9AT
Tel: 0171 273 3000
Fax: 0171 273 2423
Contact: Dr Robert M Watt, Chief Inspector
Founded: 1876
Previous names: Cruelty to Animals Inspectorate until 1986
Profile: The Animals (Scientific Procedures) Inspectorate has a central role within the legal and administrative controls over the use of living animals for experimental or other scientific purposes. Inspectors provide professional medical, veterinary and scientific advice to the Home Secretary and his officials who operate the licensing system under the Animals (Scientific Procedures) Act 1986 and determine policy. They also inspect facilities where work under the Act is carried out to check on the standards of care and accommodation of the animals held and the observance of the controls.

Animals in Distress
1 Rippingham Road
Withington
Manchester
M20 9FX
Tel: 0161 434 4276
Contact: Mrs Dunn, Manageress
Founded: 1967
Membership: 1,700
Profile: Animals in Distress was founded in 1967 to alleviate the suffering of sick and injured animals. They achieve this through a 24 hour ambulance service, veterinary treatment and neutering. Because many animals are passed on by other organisations they feel they are the end of the line and are therefore reluctant to refuse a call. Animals in Distress is looking to the future to prevent long-term suffering.

Animals' Vigilantes
James Mason House
24 Salisbury Street
Fordingbridge
Hampshire
SP6 1AF
Tel: 01425 653663
Contact: Mrs PE Price, Chairman
Founded: 1965
Membership: 2,500
Publications: United Against Cruelty to Animals
Profile: Animals' Vigilantes is an educational trust pledged to fight all cruelty to animals. A major part of their campaign is the education of the young in the care and welfare of animals and to teach respect and reverence for all life. Animals' Vigilantes is a non-militant organisation which seeks by peaceful means to achieve their objectives. The organisation is opposed to hunting and trapping of wildlife and objects to all forms of intensive and unnatural methods of rearing animals for food. They also campaign for the abolition of painful experiments on living animals and the promotion of alternatives.

Antrim Agricultural Society
189 Seven Mile Straight
Loanends
Crumlin
County Antrim
BT29 4YR
Tel: 018494 32914

Apicultural Education Association
Rural Education and Training Centre
Writtle College
Chelmsford
Essex
CM1 3RR
Tel: 01245 420705
Contact: Clive De Brun
Profile: We have been unable to contact this organisation. The details given are unconfirmed.

Appenzeller Breed Society
Oakberrow
2 Stoneyard Green Cottages
Bosbury
Ledbury
Herefordshire
HR8 1JR
Tel: 01531 640289
Contact: Miss D Smillie, Secretary

Profile: A breed society for the promotion of the Appenzeller breed of poultry.

Apple and Pear Research Council
Bradbourne House Stable Block
East Malling Research Station
East Malling
Kent
ME19 6DZ
Tel: 01732 845115
Fax: 01732 844828
Contact: Secretary
Founded: 1989
Profile: The Apple and Pear Research Council is a statutory body set up to administer levy-funded research on all aspects of the production, storage and marketing of apples and pears. It is responsible for collecting the levy from registered growers and approving the allocation of research contracts.

Applied Rural Alternatives
United Nations Association – UK (South East Berkshire Branch)
10 Highfield Close
Wokingham
Berkshire
RG11 1DG
Tel: 01734 783204
Contact: DS Stafford, Secretary
Founded: 1984
Publications: The Pace of Change in Farming – The Organic Option
Previous names: ARA Study Tours until 1990
Profile: ARA exists for the charitable object of advancing the education of the public in rural development in an environmentally sensitive manner with particular reference to underdeveloped countries. ARA organises visits/lectures, etc., in the UK on organic husbandry, environmental problems in farming and appropriate technologies. Details of the current programme are available on receipt of an SAE.

Arab Horse Society
Windsor House
The Square
Ramsbury
Salisbury
Wiltshire
SN8 2PE
Tel: 01672 520782
Fax: 01672 520880
Contact: James Carine, Registrar/Secretary
Founded: 1918
Membership: 4,100
Publications: Stud books; members newsletter; The Arab Horse Society News

Profile: The Society holds the UK stud books for the Arab and its derivatives. It organises a northern breed show and a National Championships Show and flat racing – 22 amateur meetings in 1996 countrywide under Jockey Club regulations. There are 20 regional groups with their own social programmes and shows.

Arable Research Centres
Manor Farm Barn
Manor Farm
Lower End
Daglingworth
Cirencester
Gloucestershire
GL7 7AH
Tel: 01285 652184
Fax: 01285 642561
Contact: Dr M Carver, Director
Founded: 1979
Publications: Information available to members only
Profile: ARC is the largest independent trials organisation in the UK, providing agronomic information on combinable crops to its subscribing members. The network of 16 trial centres provides progressive farmers with the most up-to-date agronomic information available in the UK.

Arable Research Institution Association
IACR – Long Ashton Research Station
Long Ashton
Bristol
BS18 9AF
Tel: 01275 392181
Fax: 01275 394007
Contact: HM Anderson, ARIA Secretary
Founded: 1990
Membership: 400
Publications: Annual newsletter
Profile: The Arable Research Institute Association is the members' association of the Institute of Arable Crops Research which comprises three sites: IACR – Rothamsted, IACR – Long Ashton Research Station and IACR – Broom's Barn. The aim of the association is to forge two-way links between IACR scientists and people involved in the everyday business of arable farming. In this way members gain an insight into current research thinking and future developments. A minimum of three members days and two workshops are held annually.

Araucana Club
Bloomfield Cottage
Oakhill
Bath

Avon
BA3 5BG
Tel: 01749 840431
Contact: Mrs AR Williams, Secretary
Profile: A breed society for the promotion of the Araucana breed of poultry

Arboricultural Advisory and Information Service
The Tree Advice Trust
Alice Holt Lodge
Wrecclesham
Farnham
Surrey
GU10 4LH
Tel: 01420 22022
Fax: 01420 22000
Contact: D Patch, Director
Founded: 1993
Publications: Arboriculture Practice Notes; Arboriculture Research and Information Notes
Profile: The Arboricultural Advisory and Information Service aims to develop the highest possible standards of tree management and practice. It also aims to advance professional development.

Arboricultural Association
Ampfield House
Ampfield
Romsey
Hampshire
SO51 9PA
Tel: 01794 368717
Fax: 01794 368978
Contact: Jonathon Hazell, Technical Director
Membership: 2,000
Publications: Arboricultural Journal; News; directories of approved contractors and registered consultants
Profile: The lead body for amenity tree care professionals, the Arboricultural Association publishes a Directory of Approved Contractors and a Directory of Registered Consultants which are revised each year.

Ardennes Horse Society of Great Britain
Weather Hill
Near Brancepeth
Crook
County Durham
Tel: 01385 780159
Contact: Mr GR Cole

Ark Environmental Foundation
Suite 604–643
Linen Hall

162–168 Regent Street
London
W1R 5TB
Tel: 0171 439 4567
Fax: 0171 734 6042

Arkleton Centre for Rural Development Research
Geography Department
University of Aberdeen
St Mary's
Elphinstone Road
Aberdeen
AB9 2UF
Tel: 01224 273901
Fax: 01224 272331
Contact: Professor John Bryden, Director
Founded: 1995
Previous names: Arkleton Trust (Research) Ltd until 1995
Profile: The main focus of work is on the non-agricultural dimensions of rural development; looking at issues such as community involvement in rural development, problems of rural poverty and disadvantage, including those of access to housing, training and transport; and problems and opportunities arising from technological changes, particularly the development of the Information Highway.

Arkleton Trust
Enstone
Chipping Norton
Oxfordshire
OX7 4HH
Tel: 01608 677255
Fax: 01608 677276
Contact: Libby Hollinshead, Administrative Officer
Founded: 1977
Publications: Publications list available
Profile: The Arkleton Trust was set up in 1977 to study new approaches to rural development and education and to improve communication between policy makers, academics and practitioners on rural issues.

Arthur Rank Centre
National Agricultural Centre
Stoneleigh Park
Warwickshire
CV8 2LZ
Tel: 01203 696969
Fax: 01203 696900
Contact: Reverend John Clarke, Director
Founded: 1972
Publications: Publications list available

Profile: The ARC was established at the NAC in 1972 as a joint venture by the churches, the Royal Agricultural Society of England and the Rank Foundation. It is an Ecumenical Chaplaincy Centre concerned with farming and countryside matters, dedicated to serving the rural church and community. It has a permanent staff with library and resource unit. There are five main areas of work: the rural church; the rural community; agriculture; environment; and international matters incorporating the Farmers World Network.

Askham Bryan College
Askham Bryan
York
North Yorkshire
YO2 3PR
Tel: 01904 702121
Fax: 01904 702629
Email: MKTG@ASKHAM-BRYAN.AC.UK
Contact: Peter Corker, Director
Founded: 1948
Publications: Prospectus
Profile: One of the largest colleges of agriculture and horticulture in the UK, offering full-time and part-time training in all aspects of the land-based industries. Operations include dairy, arable and sheep farms.

Asparagus Growers Association
133 Eastgate
Louth
Lincolnshire
LN11 9QG
Tel: 01507 602427
Fax: 01507 600689
Contact: Mrs JA Dyas, Co-Secretary
Founded: 1980
Membership: 110
Profile: Marketing and agronomy advice.

Association de Criodores de Caballas Falabella
1 Hambrook Hill Farm
Hambrook Hill
Hambrook
West Sussex
PO18 8UJ
Tel: 01243 573469
Fax: 01243 574416
Contact: AF Shepherd, Director
Membership: 25
Profile: To promote the breed of the Falabella horse.

Association for Biomass and Biofuels
PO Box 7
Southend

Reading
EG7 6AY
Tel: 01635 862131
Profile: We have been unable to contact this organisation. The details given are unconfirmed.

Association for Crop Protection in Northern Britain
c/o SAC
Bush Estate
Penicuik
Midlothian
EH26 0PH
Tel: 0131 535 33076
Fax: 0131 535 3070
Email: acpnb@ed.ac.uk
Contact: Dr DHK Davies, Secretary
Founded: 1983
Publications: Crop Protection in Northern Britain – (conference series)
Profile: ACPNB is a non-profit making registered charity with the principal objective of promoting the understanding of crop protection with the aim of promoting and encouraging improvements in agriculture and horticulture in northern Britain. The association is managed by a small committee drawn from statutory, official, voluntary and commercial bodies concerned with crop protection in northern Britain. The principal activity of the association is to organise the triennial conference, Crop Protection in Northern Britain ('The Dundee Conference'). This conference brings together agricultural and horticultural advisers, technical staff of the crop protection trade and all concerned with developments in crop protection, including advisory, research and government organisations.

Association for the Advancement of British Biotechnology
1 Queen Anne's Gate
London
SW1
Profile: We have been unable to contact this organisation. The details given are unconfirmed.

Association for the Protection of Rural Scotland
3rd Floor
Gladstone's Land
483 Lawnmarket
Edinburgh
EH1 2NT
Tel: 0131 225 7012
Fax: 0131 225 6592
Contact: Mrs EJ Garland, Manager

Founded: 1926
Membership: 1,050
Publications: Annual Report; members newsletter
Profile: Founded in 1926, The Association for the Protection of Rural Scotland (APRS) works to protect Scotland's countryside from unnecessary or inappropriate development. It recognises the needs of those who live and work there and the necessity to reconcile these with the sometimes competing requirements of tourism and recreation. APRS works through the town and country planning legislation and seeks to promote policies to further countryside protection. Practical conservation work includes a repair programme for historic masonry bridges. An award is presented annually in recognition of good practice in the renovation or construction of new buildings/structures in rural areas.

Association for the Study of Animal Behaviour

School of Biological and Medical Sciences
Bute Building
University of St Andrews
St Andrews
Fife
KY16 9TS
Tel: 01334 463506
Fax: 01334 463600
Email: aem1@st-andrews.ac.uk
Contact: Dr A Magurran, Honorary Secretary
Founded: 1936
Membership: 1,500
Publications: Animal Behaviour Journal, ASAB Newsletter and Feedback
Profile: The aim of the ASAB is to promote the study of animal behaviour.

Association of Animal Behaviour Psychologists

5 Pepperscoombe Lane
Upper Beeding
Steyning
West Sussex
BN44 3HS
Tel: 01903 879336
Profile: We have been unable to contact this organisation. The details given are unconfirmed.

Association of Applied Biologists

Horticulture Research International
Wellesbourne
Warwickshire
CV35 9EF
Tel: 01789 470382
Fax: 01789 470234

Contact: Dr FA Langton, Hon Secretary
Founded: 1914
Membership: 1,150
Publications: Publications list available
Profile: The aim of the association is to promote the study and enhancement of biology with special reference to its applied aspects. Residential and one day meetings are held throughout the year with emphasis usually on agricultural aspects.

Association of British Primary Breeders and Exporters

Imperial House
15–19 Kingsway
London
WC2B 6UA
Tel: 0171 240 9889
Fax: 0171 240 7757

Association of British Riding Schools

Queen's Chambers
38–40 Queen Street
Penzance
Cornwall
TR18 4BH
Tel: 01736 69440
Fax: 01736 51390
Contact: Mrs J Packer, General Secretary
Founded: 1954
Membership: 600
Publications: ABRS Official Handbook
Profile: The association is the UK's longest established approval scheme for riding schools. It is the only organisation solely representing the interests of the professional riding school proprietor. Although the horse has changed little, the environment in which we ride and the attitude of the general public has changed enormously making the provision of safe riding more demanding than ever. By choosing an ABRS school, the public will be assured of sound instruction on suitable horses where safe, well kept saddlery is used.

Association of British Veterinary Acupuncture

East Park Cottage
Handcross
West Sussex
RH17 6BD
Tel: 01444 400213
Contact: Mrs Jill Hewson, Secretary
Founded: 1987
Membership: 70
Publications: Newsletter
Profile: To further advancement of veterinary acupuncture in the UK, developing and encouraging the appropriate study and use of

acupuncture and assisting with training of veterinary surgeons in the subject. To achieve representation of national and international bodies associated with veterinary medicine and acupuncture and to consider the implications of relevant legislation.

Association of Chartered Physiotherapists in Animal Therapy

The Chartered Society of Physiotherapy
Morland House
Salters Lane
Winchester
Hampshire
SO22 5JP
Tel: 01962 863801
Fax: 01962 863801
Contact: The Secretary
Founded: 1985
Membership: 115
Publications: ACPAT Magazine
Profile: ACPAT has been formed for chartered physiotherapists wishing to work, or working within the field of animal therapy. It aims to educate and ensure that members practising (category A) are constantly improving their knowledge and maintaining standards within the profession. ACPAT runs courses and has a magazine which is distributed twice per year. Practising ACPAT members work with referrals from veterinary surgeons and can treat a wide range of conditions using joint and soft tissue mobilisation and manipulation. They also use electrotherapy techniques and are able to advise owners regarding rehabilitation.

Association of Cheese Processors

Dairy Industry Federation
19 Cornwall Terrace
London
NW1 4QP
Tel: 0171 486 7244
Fax: 0171 487 4734
Contact: Robert McKeith, Secretary
Membership: 8
Profile: To represent the interests of suppliers of processed cheese.

Association of Chief Estates Surveyors and Property Managers in Local Government

23 Athol Road
Bramhall
Cheshire
SK7 1BR
Tel: 0161 439 9589
Fax: 0161 439 9589
Previous names: Local Authority Valuers Association

Association of County Councils

Eaton House
66a Eaton Square
London
SW1W 9BH
Tel: 0171 201 1500
Fax: 0171 235 8458
Contact: MR Baker

Association of Deer Management Groups

Dalhousie Estates Office
Brechin
Angus
DD9 6EL
Tel: 01356 624566
Fax: 01356 623725
Contact: RMJ Cooke, Secretary
Founded: 1992
Membership: 37
Profile: The association was formed to represent those involved in deer management in Scotland, and in particular to promote the development of the Scottish wild venison industry. It is involved in establishing good management practice, promoting training and representing its 37 group members at a political level to UK and EU Governments. The Association of Deer Management Groups purpose is to co-ordinate the management of wild deer, particularly red deer, in a manner which is suitable in terms of their natural habitat.

Association of District Councils

26 Chapter Street
London
SW1P 4NP
Tel: 0171 233 6868
Fax: 0171 233 6551
Contact: Mr Crispin Moor, Principal Policy Officer
Founded: 1974
Membership: 296
Publications: Publications list available
Profile: The Association of District Councils represents the interests of the English shire district councils to Westminster and Whitehall.

Association of Drainage Authorities

(The Mews) 3 Royal Oak Passage
High Street
Huntingdon
Cambridgeshire
PE17 6EA
Tel: 01480 411123
Fax: 01480 431107
Contact: Mr David Noble, Secretary
Founded: 1937
Publications: ADA Gazette

Profile: ADA is a body representing flood protection and water level management interests in England and Wales. The membership includes Internal Drainage Boards and the Flood Defence Committees of the Environmental Agency. Associate membership is open to local authorities, companies and organisations with an interest in flood protection issues.

Association of Environmental Consultancies
2 Manchuria Road
London
SW11 6AE
Tel: 0171 978 4347
Fax: 0171 924 6848
Contact: Fiona Hoffman, Executive Secretary
Founded: 1991

Association of Fellows and Instructors of the British Horse Society, The
Burton Dassett Vicarage
Northend
Leamington Spa
Warwickshire
CV33 0TH
Tel: 01295 770400
Fax: 01295 651190
Contact: Mrs Phillipa Francis, Secretary
Founded: 1986
Membership: 150
Profile: An association formed from Fellows and Instructors of the British Horse Society to act as a professional body within the industry. The main aims are to ensure high standards amongst members, to represent the views of instructors to the British Horse Society, to communicate between members and to arrange training days for all involved.

Association of Heads of Outdoor Education Centres
Pendarren House
Llangenny
Crickhowell
Powys
NP8 1HE
Tel: 01873 810694
Fax: 01873 811986
Contact: Glyn Thomas, Secretary
Founded: 1963
Membership: 155

Association of Independent Crop Consultants Ltd
Agriculture House
Station Road
Liss

Hampshire
GU33 7AR
Tel: 01730 895354
Fax: 01730 895535
Contact: Sarah Swatton, Executive Administrator
Founded: 1981
Membership: 150
Profile: The 150 members are independent agronomists from throughout the UK. The association aims to maintain professional standards and re-enforce the independence of its members. It provides training and conferences.

Association of Independent Forest Managers
Perth Agricultural Centre
East Huntingtower
Perth
PH1 3JJ
Tel: 01738 627655
Fax: 01738 474160
Contact: DE Carter, Chairman
Founded: 1990
Membership: 8
Profile: The Association of Independent Forest Managers is a network of chartered foresters throughout the UK. Each member has a long and successful track record in UK forest management. AIFM has a policy of complete disclosure so that its clients can be reassured that its members are working in their best interests: practical work is put out to tender to ensure the most competitive rates.

Association of Landscape Management
Wiltshire Direct Services
Brook House
Bythesea Road
Trowbridge
Wiltshire
BA14 8JH
Tel: 01225 771670
Fax: 01225 751325
Contact: Matthew Smith, General Secretary
Publications: Journal; conference report
Previous names: Association of Playing Fields and Landscape Management

Association of Librarians in Land-based Colleges and Universities
Agriculture and Biological Sciences Library
University College Dublin
Belfield
Dublin 4
Ireland
Tel: 00 353 1 7067541
Email: Mary.Flynn@ucd.ie
Contact: Mary Flynn, Honorary Secretary
Founded: 1978

Membership: 50
Publications: Newsletter, Annual Conference Proceedings, Directory
Previous names: Agricultural Librarians in Colleges and Universities (ALCU) until 1994
Profile: ALLCU unites librarians working in academic institutions in Britain and Ireland. The association holds an annual conference, rotating between member's libraries, where issues of common concern relating to agricultural and rural information are debated. Knowledge of each library's strengths encourages the informal interchange of information and loan of stock between libraries.

Association of Local Authorities of Northern Ireland
123 York Street
Belfast
BT15 1AB
Tel: 01232 249286
Fax: 01232 326645
Contact: Raymond McKay, Secretary

Association of Malt Product Manufacturers
1 Surrey Road
Felixstowe
Suffolk
IP11 7SB
Tel: 01394 271713
Fax: 01394 271713
Contact: Richard EA Holt

Association of Masters of Harriers and Beagles
Craven Lodge
Portchester Road
Newbury
Berkshire
RG14 7QJ
Tel: 01635 41320
Fax: 01635 582936
Contact: CJ Austin, Director
Founded: 1891
Membership: 650
Publications: Year Book; Annual Stud Book
Profile: The governing body of hare hunting covering the packs of beagles and harriers in the UK.

Association of Meat Inspectors
44 Parkfield Road
Taunton
Somerset
TA1 4SF
Tel: 01823 333201
Fax: 01823 333201
Contact: Peter Comrie

Profile: We have been unable to contact this organisation. The details given are unconfirmed.

Association of Metropolitan Authorities
35 Great Smith Street
London
SW1P 3BJ
Tel: 0171 222 8100
Fax: 0171 222 0878
Contact: Rodney G Brooke
Publications: Municipal Review

Association of National Park and Countryside Voluntary Wardens
60 Defoe Drive
Parkhall
Stoke on Trent
Staffordshire
ST3 5RS
Tel: 01782 316046
Contact: Jay Burkinshaw, Vice-Chairman/Secretary
Founded: 1967
Membership: 300
Publications: Members newsletter
Profile: Their aim is to promote effective and enjoyable wardening by volunteers throughout the countryside. The association aims to complement the work of the voluntary warden's own service by bringing together those with similar interests, by enabling information and experience to be exchanged.

Association of National Park Authorities
Ponsford House
Moretonhampstead
Newton Abbot
Devon
TQ13 8NL
Tel: 01647 440245
Fax: 01647 440187
Contact: Professor Ian Mercer, Secretary General
Founded: 1992
Publications: Annual Review, technical reports
Previous names: Association of National Parks until 1996
Profile: The association is the corporate voice of the ten National Park Authorities and the Broads Authority. It exists to facilitate the sharing of information and experience between the member authorities, and to represent their shared interests to government, it's agencies, peer organisations and the public.

Association of Nature Reserve Burial Grounds
Natural Death Centre

20 Heber Road
London
NW2 6AA
Tel: 0181 208 2853
Fax: 0181 452 6434
Email: rhino@dial.pipex.com
Internet: http://dspace.dial.pipex.com/town/
square/ac026/sites.html
Contact: Mr Nicholas Albery, Co-ordinator
Founded: 1994
Membership: 18
Profile: There is now a growing movement for
farmers, local authorities and wildlife charities to
establish woodland or nature reserve burial
grounds. The association sets criteria for green
burial grounds – woodland sites run by farmers,
local authorities and wildlife trusts – where the
body is buried with a tree rather than a
headstone marking the spot.

Association of Noise Consultants, The
6 Trap Road
Guilden Morden
Royston
Hertfordshire
SG8 0JE
Tel: 01763 852958
Contact: David Fleming, Hon Secretary
Founded: 1973
Membership: 49
Publications: Membership List
Profile: The range of expertise available from
members of the association is comprehensive
including such subject areas as: architectural
acoustics, environmental noise; hearing
conservation; industrial noise control; expert
testimony in court hearings and planning enquiries
noise nuisance evaluations; transport noise and
vibration assessments; product development and
vibration control. Some members additionally
specialise in certain areas such as educational
courses or test laboratory facilities.

Association of Pole Lathe Turners
11 Bridge Street
Brigstock
Northamptonshire
NN14 3ET
Tel: 01536 373738
Contact: Olvin Smith, Secretary
Founded: 1990
Membership: 180
Publications: The Bodgers Gazette
Profile: The association was formed in
September 1990 by a group of enthusiasts who
believe the pole lathe has an exciting future as
well as a fascinating past. It was the increasing

public interest in pole lathes that prompted the
formation of an association to act as a forum for
the interchange of information about this ancient
craft and its modern revival. The association's
aims are: to find out what they can about the
history of pole lathe turning; to promote a high
standard of pole lathe turning in the present; and,
to explore and develop new applications of the
pole lathe in the future.

Association of Private Market Operators
4 Worrygoose Lane
Rotherham
Yorkshire
S60 4AD
Tel: 01709 700072
Fax: 01709 703648
Contact: Mr DJ Glasby, Secretary
Founded: 1990
Membership: 20
Publications: Handbook
Profile: APMO is the sole voice of the private
sector of the British market industry. APMO's
main aims are to increase awareness of private
markets, raise standards and to generally seek to
improve the business opportunities of members
by political lobbying and unified action. APMO
members currently operate markets on around
300 sites in the UK and Eire with around
1,000 market days per week.

**Association of Professional Foresters of Great
Britain**
7–9 West Street
Belford
Northumberland
NE70 7QA
Tel: 01668 213937
Fax: 01668 213555
Contact: Jane Karthaus, Secretary/Editor
Founded: 1960
Membership: 1,200
Publications: Quarterly News; information
leaflets; diary
Profile: The APF is an association for those who
derive their livelihood from forestry. It was
started to meet the need for an organisation for
the practical side of the industry and its
endeavours to promote and contribute to the
future of employment in the many aspects of the
home based forest industry. In 1973 the APF
became the first British forestry body to join the
Union of European Foresters.

**Association of Scottish District Salmon
Fishery Boards**
The Stables
Cargill

Perth
PH2 6DS
Tel: 01250 883365
Fax: 01250 883342
Contact: GDB Keelan, Director
Founded: 1932
Membership: 53
Publications: Occasional newsletters and handbooks
Profile: The association was established in 1932 to protect, preserve and develop salmon fisheries in Scotland. It co-ordinates the work of boards and districts providing an interchange of views as appropriate; it takes action as may be competent in connection with any legislation or Bills before Parliament and it assists in the initiation and process of any litigation or prosecution connected with the salmon fisheries of Scotland. It exists to promote, safeguard and protect the interests of the wild salmon fisheries of Scotland and in achieving this it seeks to co-operate with any other association or society in the furtherance of these objectives.

Association of Scottish Shellfish Growers

Overton
2a Manse Road
Roslin
Midlothian
EH25 9LF
Tel: 0131 440 2116
Fax: 0131 448 2461
Email: jbuchanan@sc.uhi.ac.uk
Contact: Dr JS Buchanan, Executive Director
Founded: 1986
Membership: 65
Publications: Members newsletter
Previous names: Scottish Shellfish Growers' Association until 1987
Profile: To represent and promote the Scottish Shellfish cultivation sector for the production of farmed mussels, oysters and scallops and to be the point of contact for the industry for local and national government and other organisations.

Association of Show and Agricultural Organisations

The Showground
Shepton Mallet
Somerset
BA4 6QN
Tel: 01749 822200
Fax: 01749 823169
Profile: A body that consists of agricultural shows, breed societies and other organisations involved with the promotion of British agricultural breeding and excellence in the countryside.

Association of Stillwater Game and Fishery Managers

Packington Fisheries
Packington Hall
Meriden
Coventry
CV7 7HF
Tel: 01676 222754
Fax: 01676 523399
Contact: Penny Wigley, Secretary
Founded: 1984
Membership: 100
Publications: Newsline
Profile: The ASGFM represents still water trout fisheries throughout the UK.

Association of Veterinary Anaesthetists

Royal Veterinary College
Hawkshead Lane
Worth Mynns
Hatfield
Hertfordshire
SS48 8XS
Tel: 01717 666216
Fax: 01717 660621
Contact: Dr Clarke, Hon Secretary
Founded: 1965
Membership: 320
Publications: Journal of Veterinary Anaesthesia
Profile: The association promotes study of and research into veterinary anaesthesia. It holds regular meetings and refresher courses. Full membership is open to veterinary surgeons, but animal nurses may become 'technical members'. The association promotes the teaching of the subject and has an Educational Trust Fund.

Association of Veterinary Teachers and Research Workers

Department of Pathology and Infectious Diseases
Royal Veterinary College
Royal College Street
London
NW1 0TY
Contact: Dr M Fox

ATB-Landbase

National Agricultural Centre
Stoneleigh Park
Warwickshire
CV8 2LG
Tel: 01203 696996
Fax: 01203 696732
Contact: Nigel Snook, Chief Executive
Founded: 1967
Publications: Publications list available
Previous names: Agricultural Training Board until 1994

Profile: ATB-Landbase is closely involved in every aspect of training in the landbase sector. From broad strategic issues, such as the future direction of training across the whole sector, to the detailed requirements of National and Scottish Vocational Qualifications, and from representing the sectors views to government to ensuring the remotest areas of the country can gain access to high quality training.
ATB-Landbase is a Limited company which, through its charitable status, is owned by the industry it serves. It is recognised by the Department for Education and Employment as the Industry Training Organisation for agriculture and commercial horticulture and the Industry Lead Body responsible for setting the occupational standards for the sector. It works closely with other organisations which have complementary interest in the rural economy including TECs, LECs, FE colleges and other rural agencies.

Atlantic Salmon Trust
Moulin
Pitlochry
Perthshire
PH16 5JQ
Tel: 01796 473439
Fax: 01796 473554
Contact: Rear Admiral DJ Mackenzie, Director
Founded: 1967
Publications: Publications list available
Profile: The Atlantic Salmon Trust was formed in 1967 to encourage the conservation of Atlantic salmon and sea trout. It aims to ensure that the Atlantic salmon is preserved for the good of the community and to promote enlightened fishery management at local, national and international level, so that wild stocks may be maintained and developed. The Trust argues the need for a UK salmon policy based on the principle that salmon stocks should be managed and harvested in their native river systems.

Aubrac Cattle Society of the UK Ltd
Quarles
Wells next the Sea
Norfolk
NR23 1RY
Tel: 01328 738105
Fax: 01328 738134
Contact: BR Basset, Director
Founded: 1990
Membership: 4
Profile: Breed society for the promotion of the Aubrac cattle breed.

Australorp Club
Dover
Main Road
Nutbourne
Chichester
West Sussex
PO18 8RL
Tel: 01243 373295
Contact: Mr I Turner, Secretary
Profile: A breed society for the promotion of the Australorp breed of poultry.

Aylesbury College
Department of Agriculture and Horticulture
Hampden Hall
Stoke Mandeville
Aylesbury
Buckinghamshire
HP22 5TB
Tel: 01296 434111
Fax: 01296 614175
Contact: Y Richardson, Agricultural Lecturer
Profile: Hampden Hall has a mixed farm totalling 320 acres. On offer are both full and part-time courses at NVQ levels 1, 2 and 3 and BTEC First Diplomas in agriculture, equine studies, animal care, countryside management, agricultural mechanisation and a varied programme of short courses. The horticultural department offer NVQ 1 and 2 and BTEC First Diploma in RHS general floristry and flower arranging, plus a wide range of short courses.

Ayrshire Agricultural Association
9 Miller Road
Ayr
Strathclyde
KA7 2AX
Tel: 01292 266600
Fax: 01292 610464
Contact: Mr Ronald JG Jamieson, Secretary
Founded: 1,837
Membership: 2,275
Publications: Annual show catalogue and show schedule
Profile: The Ayrshire Agricultural Association was formed in 1837 to promote agriculture in Ayrshire and achieves this by organising on an annual basis the Ayrshire Agricultural Show which is the second biggest agricultural show in Scotland.

Ayrshire Cattle Society of Great Britain and Ireland
1 Racecourse Road
Ayr
Strathclyde
KA7 2DE
Tel: 01292 267123

Fax: 01292 611973
Contact: Stuart Thomson, Chief Executive
Founded: 1877
Membership: 1,000
Publications: Ayrshire Journal; Ayrshire Dairyman; Herd Directory; Semen Brochure
Profile: Ayrshire Cattle Society involved in the promotion of the Ayrshire breed as a quality dairy cow and the recording of pedigree stock. Cattle Services Ayr Ltd is a commercial company marketing semen, embryos and livestock and funds a future bulls' progeny testing scheme.

Backpackers Club
49 Lyndhurst Road
Exmouth
Devon
EX8 3DS
Tel: 01395 265159
Contact: Mr and Mrs WJ Beed, Joint Secretaries
Founded: 1972
Membership: 800
Publications: Backpacker Magazine, camp site directories
Profile: A relatively small national club with a membership who enjoy travelling with lightweight camping equipment. Its aim is to encourage this activity while remaining friendly and informal.

Badger Face Welsh Mountain Sheep Society
Hafan
Tynlon
Tregarth
Bangor
Gwynedd
LL57 4BB
Tel: 01248 601380
Contact: Mrs M Pritchard, Secretary
Founded: 1976
Profile: A breed society for the promotion of the Badger Face Welsh Mountain sheep.

Bagot Goat Breed Society
Ramshill Farm
Mockley
Tamworth in Arden
Warwickshire
B94 5BA
Tel: 01564 742354
Contact: Peter Evans, Secretary
Founded: 1987
Publications: Quarterly newsletter and promotional material
Previous names: Bagot Goat Breeders Study Group until 1996
Profile: The group was set up by breeders who wished to help the breed and themselves at the same time. Membership is open to anybody

interested in this rare and historic breed of goat which at present has no commercial attraction. It is kept because of its fine looks and its long history of well over 700 years. It is a most interesting and attractive goat to keep, both male and female carry large horns. The Bagot Goat Breeders Study Group became the Bagot Goat Breed Society in late 1996.

Balwen Welsh Mountain Sheep Society
Tynewydd
Cefn Coch
Welshpool
Powys
SY21 0AY
Tel: 01938 810358
Contact: Mrs N Owen, Secretary
Profile: We have been unable to contact this organisation. The details given are unconfirmed.

Barley Futures and Options Contracts
London Commodity Exchange
1 Commodity Quay
St Katharine's Dock
London
E1 9AX
Tel: 0171 481 2080
Fax: 0171 702 9923
Email: info@lce.co.uk
Contact: Doug Thow, Product Business Manager

Barn Owl Trust
Waterleat
Ashburton
Newton Abbot
Devon
TQ13 7HU
Tel: 01364 653026
Contact: Sharon Clayborough, Administrator
Founded: 1988
Publications: Annual Report; publications list available
Profile: The Barn Owl Trust is a registered charity which aims to conserve the barn owl and its environment. The main areas of the trust's work are conservation, education, information and research. The trust provides a free national information service on all aspects of barn owl conservation – for details send a large SAE.

Barnevelders Club
113 Collingwood Road
Sutton
Surrey
SM1 2QN
Tel: 01816 435706

Contact: Mr B Clarke, Secretary
Profile: A society to promote the Barnevelder breed of poultry.

Barony College
Parkgate
Dumfries
DG1 3NE
Tel: 01387 860251
Fax: 01387 860395

BASIS (Registration) Ltd
2 St John Street
Ashbourne
Derbyshire
DE6 1GH
Tel: 01335 343945
Fax: 01335 346488
Contact: Mr BK Orme, Chief Executive
Founded: 1978
Membership: 2,860
Publications: Publications list available
Previous names: British Agrochemical Supply Industry Scheme Ltd until 1985; British Agrochemical Standards Inspection Scheme Ltd until 1991
Profile: BASIS was established at the behest of Government in 1978 to independently assess the standards relating to storage, transport and competence of staff in the pesticide supply industry. BASIS carries out annual assessments of distributor pesticide stores and annually audits staff under the statutory Code of Practice under the Control of Pesticides Regulations 1986. All BASIS Certificates of Competence are recognised under the Food and Environment Protection Act 1985. BASIS also runs a Professional Register of pesticide advisers along with a training and certification scheme for fertiliser salesman and advisers.

Bat Conservation Trust
15 Cloisters House
8 Battersea Park Road
London
SW8 4BG
Tel: 0171 627 2629
Fax: 0171 627 2628
Email: batcontrust@gn.apc.org
Contact: Jill Bradley, Administration Officer
Founded: 1991
Membership: 2,160
Publications: Publications list available
Profile: The Bat Conservation Trust is Britain's only organisation solely devoted to the conservation of bats and their habitats. Their major objectives include education, the

development of conservation projects and policies, and research. They provide expert advice and co-ordinate over 90 voluntary groups.

Bee Disease Insurance Association
Pump Cottage
Weatheroak
Alvechurch
Worcestershire
B48 7EQ
Tel: 01564 822059
Profile: We have been unable to contact this organisation. The details given are unconfirmed.

Bee Farmers Association of the UK
Borders Honey Farm
Newcastleton
Scottish Borders
TD9 0SG
Tel: 01387 376737
Fax: 01387 376737
Contact: BA Stenhouse, General Secretary
Membership: 320
Publications: Bulletin; products directory

Beef and Sheep Division
Ministry of Agriculture, Fisheries and Food
Room 418
Whitehall Place West Block
London
SW1A 2HH
Tel: 0171 270 8591
Fax: 0171 270 8762
Profile: The Beef and Sheep Division deals with livestock subsidy schemes and quota allocations, in particular: Beef Special Premium Scheme; Suckler Cow Premium Scheme; Sheep Annual Premium Scheme; Hill Livestock Compensatory Allowances; Moorland Scheme.

Beef Shorthorn Cattle Society
4th Street
National Agricultural Centre
Stoneleigh Park
Warwickshire
CV8 2LG
Tel: 01203 696549
Fax: 01202 696729
Contact: Breed Secretary

Bees and Trees Trust
36 Rock Lane
Ludlow
Shropshire
SY8 1ST
Profile: We have been unable to contact this organisation. The details given are unconfirmed.

Bees for Development
Troy
Monmouth
Monmouthshire
NP5 4AB
Tel: 01600 713648
Fax: 01600 716167
Email: 100410.2631@compuServe.COM
Contact: Helen Jackson, Co-ordinator
Founded: 1993
Publications: Beekeeping and Development:
The Journal for Sustainable Beekeeping
Profile: BFD works to promote understanding of
the vital role of sustainable beekeeping, and to
form links between those who share this
interest. Their network encompasses the globe.
BFD assists people in the poorest places by
making beekeeping information available without
charge wherever possible.

Belgian Bantam Club
West View
Londonderry
Northallerton
North Yorkshire
DL7 9ND
Tel: 01677 425243
Contact: Mr C Gullon, Secretary
Profile: A society to promote the Belgium
Bantam breed of poultry.

Belted Galloway Cattle Society
Rutherford Lodge
Kelso
Roxburghshire
TD5 8NW
Tel: 01835 823757
Fax: 01835 823757
Contact: JMC Rutherford, Secretary/Treasurer
Founded: 1921
Membership: 314
Publications: Belted Galloway News
Profile: Breed society for Belted Galloway Cattle.
The Beltie is a hardy beef breed with the typical
conformation of native British beef breeds.

Beltex Sheep Society
Lawns Farm
Orrell
Wigan
Lancashire
WN5 8UH
Tel: 01695 627626
Fax: 01695 627626
Contact: Helen Ashton, Secretary
Founded: 1989
Membership: 150
Publications: Yearbook

Profile: The Beltex Sheep Society maintains a
flock book of Beltex sheep in the UK. It promotes
the breed for the benefit of its members.

Berkshire College of Agriculture
Hall Place
Burchetts Green
Maidenhead
Berkshire
SL6 6QR
Tel: 01628 824444
Fax: 01628 824695
Contact: Mr Peter Thorn, Principal
Founded: 1948
Profile: A centre of excellence for training for
landbased industries and professions in the
Thames Valley Region. Programmes up to the
equivalent of A levels offered in agriculture,
animal care, arboriculture, floristry, countryside
management, greenkeeping, horticulture,
landscape design, agricultural engineering,
horticultural engineering, marine engineering,
horse management and veterinary nursing on a
full or part time basis. Many short courses are
offered. The college has open days and receives
up to 20,000 visitors each year.

Berkshire Pig Breeders Club
Violetbank
Hawkshead
Ambleside
Cumbria
LA22 0PL
Tel: 01539 436222
Contact: Mr Chris Penrice, Secretary
Profile: A breed society for the promotion of the
Berkshire pig.

Beulah Speckled Face
c/o Russell, Baldwin and Brice
6 Market Street
Builth Wells
Powys
LD2 3AG
Tel: 01982 553614
Fax: 01982 552006

Bicton College of Agriculture
East Budleigh
Budleigh Salterton
Devon
EX9 7BY
Tel: 01395 568353
Fax: 01395 567502
Contact: Helen Lynch, Marketing
Founded: 1947

Profile: Bicton College specialises in vocational training in the following areas: agriculture, horticulture, countryside management, horse studies, animal care, veterinary nursing, engineering and rural business administration. Bicton is set in 212 ha of farmland and forms the ideal environment for training, study and relaxation.

Bio-Dynamic Agricultural Association
Woodman Lane
Clent
Stourbridge
Worcestershire
DY9 9PX
Tel: 01562 884933
Fax: 01562 886219
Contact: Jutta Patterson, Secretary
Founded: 1926
Membership: 550
Publications: Star and Furrow (magazine); members newsheet.
Profile: The association's main objectives are to foster and promote the agricultural impulse started by Rudolf Steiner in 1924 and to help and support those wishing to put into practice the biodynamic method. With these objectives in mind it keeps close touch with biodynamic agriculture abroad, with other aspects of the anthroposophical work (especially on nutrition and other sciences) and with various organisations concerned with a non-chemical approach to soil, environment and health.

Biological Recording in Scotland Campaign
Cramond House
Kirk Cramond
Cramond Glebe Road
Edinburgh
EH4 6NS
Tel: 0131 312 7765
Fax: 0131 312 8705
Contact: Robert Bryson, Development Officer
Founded: 1976
Membership: 157
Publications: Publications list available
Profile: BRISC aims to promote and co-ordinate biological recording in Scotland by designing and running surveys in conjunction with other environmental organisations in Scotland. It acts as an information bureau, it organises an annual conference and exhibition. It aims to raise awareness of the importance of biological recording to environmental conservation. BRISC acts as a central intelligence body, developing and linking a comprehensive network of records, record centres, recorders, and scientific,

environmental and conservation groups covering the whole of Scotland.

Bioregional Development Group
Sutton Ecology Centre
Honeywood Walk
Carshalton
Surrey
SM5 3NX
Tel: 0181 773 2322
Fax: 0181 773 2878
Contact: Pooran Desai, Director
Founded: 1993
Membership: 6
Profile: BDG is an environmental charity developing models of sustainable regional industries supplying local needs from local production. Current projects include producing barbecue charcoal from coppice woodlands and textiles from hemp.

Biotechnology and Biological Sciences Research Council
Polaris House
North Star Avenue
Swindon
Wiltshire
SN2 1UH
Tel: 01793 413200
Fax: 01793 413201
Contact: Sir Alastair Grant, Chairman

Bird Observatories Council
Dungeness Bird Observatory
Dungeness
Romney Marsh
Kent
TN29 9NA
Profile: We have been unable to contact this organisation. The details given are unconfirmed.

Birdlife International
Wellbrook Court
Girton Road
Cambridge
CB3 0NA
Tel: 01223 277318
Fax: 01223 277200
Email: birdlife@gn.apc.org
Contact: Judi James, Head of Marketing
Founded: 1922
Publications: World Birdwatch (journal); Birdlife Conservation Series; publications list available.
Previous names: International Council for Bird Preservation (ICBP) until 1994
Profile: Their aim is to prevent the extinction of birds in the wild and their habitats. Birdlife works with partner organisations around the world to identify global priorities for conservation.

Birkbeck College Biology Department
Malet Street
London
WC1E 7HX
Tel: 0171 631 6238

Bishop Burton College
Bishop Burton
Beverley
East Yorkshire
HU17 8QG
Tel: 01964 553000
Fax: 01964 553101
Contact: Professor Roy Brown, Director of
Research
Founded: 1954
Publications: College prospectus; research
newsletter
Previous names: Bishop Burton College of
Agriculture until 1992
Profile: College in partnership with University
of Humberside offering a wide range of
courses in FE and HE related to agriculture,
countryside management, equine studies,
design and horticulture as well as numerous
short courses in craft areas. Major research
and development initiatives from 1995 with
the focus on integrated crop management,
upland management and rural/environmental
health issues. Links with Eastern Europe, USA
and Africa.

Black and White Pig Association (Berkshires)
Marley Cottages
Bolham
Tiverton
Devon
EX16 7RF
Tel: 01884 252306
Fax: 01884 252306
Contact: Bob Matthews, Secretary
Profile: A breed society for the promotion of the
Berkshire breed of pig.

Black Leicester Longwool
White Alice Farm
Carnmenellis
Redruth
Cornwall
TR16 6PH
Tel: 01209 860634
Profile: We have been unable to contact this
organisation. The details given are unconfirmed.

**Black Welsh Mountain Sheep Breeders
Association**
Brierley House
Summer Lane

Combe Down
Bath
Somerset
BA2 5LE
Tel: 01225 837904
Fax: 01225 834741
Contact: David Child, Secretary
Founded: 1920
Membership: 245
Publications: Annual flock book; Periodic
members newsletters
Profile: The purpose of the association is to
maintain breeding of pure bred Black Welsh
Mountain sheep and registration of flocks,
together with the promotion of this hardy,
attractive, prolific and disease resistant breed
which produces rich, profitable meat.

Black Wyandotte Club
349 Manchester Road
Millhouse Green
Sheffield
South Yorkshire
Tel: 01226 762443
Contact: Mr EG Crossland, Secretary
Profile: A society to promote the Black
Wyandotte breed of poultry.

Blackface Sheep Breeders Association
26 York Place
Perth
PH2 8EH
Tel: 01738 623780
Fax: 01738 621206

**Blonde d'Aquitaine Breeders Society of
GB Ltd**
16 Market Place
Faringdon
Oxfordshire
SN7 7HS
Tel: 01367 242315
Fax: 01367 242963
Contact: Rex Diffey, Breed Secretary
Founded: 1971
Membership: 700
Publications: Annual journal
Profile: The Blonde Society is responsible for the
registration and promotion of the breed within
the UK and Northern Ireland. It is supported in
this work by its nine regional clubs who perform
a most important function.

Blue Albion Cattle Society
Cronkstone Grange
Hurdlow
Buxton

Derbyshire
SK17 9QL
Tel: 01298 83224
Contact: Tanya Fox, Secretary
Founded: 1920
Membership: 100
Publications: Annual herd book
Profile: Blue Cattle were originally popular in Derbyshire and Staffordshire at the turn of the century. Many of these were Welsh Black Cross Shorthorn animals. So great was their appeal that the Blue Albion Cattle Society was formed in 1920. However, for various reasons the society fell into decline until recently when it reformed and published the first modern herd book.

Blue Cross
Shilton Road
Burford
Oxford
OX18 4PF
Tel: 01993 822651
Fax: 01993 823083
Contact: Andrea Fraser, Information Officer
Founded: 1897
Publications: Blue Cross Illustrated (magazine); information packs
Profile: The Blue Cross exists to foster the bond of friendship between animals and people. The society has three hospitals and a clinic, which care for animals belonging to people who cannot afford a private vet, and eleven adoption centres which offer a home-finding service for unwanted cats, dogs and other pets. A horse protection scheme and a limited welfare boarding scheme are also administered by the organisation.

Bluefaced Leicester Sheepbreeders Association
Kirkbeck
Clarencefield
Dumfries
DG1 4NY
Tel: 01387 870671
Fax: 01387 870671
Contact: Mrs Fiona Sloan, Secretary
Founded: 1962
Membership: 1,650
Publications: Looking Ahead (magazine); flock book
Profile: The objects of the Association are: to encourage the breeding and maintain the purity of the Bluefaced Leicester sheep; establishing and publishing a flock book of recognised pure-bred stock of the Bluefaced Leicester sheep; registering the pure-bred progeny of the Bluefaced Leicester sheep; generally advancing the Bluefaced Leicester sheep and maintaining and improving the standard of carcass quality, milking ability and prolificacy of the Bluefaced Leicester sheep and their progeny; doing all such other things as are incidental or conducive to the attainments of the above objects or any of them.

Border Union Agricultural Society
Showground Office
Springwood Park
Kelso
Borders
TD5 8LS
Tel: 01573 224188
Fax: 01573 226778
Contact: Donald S Maclaren, Secretary and Treasurer
Founded: 1813
Membership: 1,100
Publications: Show catalogue; ram sales catalogue; list of prizes
Previous names: Border Agricultural Society 1813–1820; Union Agricultural Society 1820–1866
Profile: Founded in 1813, the Border Union Agricultural Society was instituted to encourage improvements in agriculture and animal husbandry in the Borders area. This precept has been constantly supported by the society through the organisation of exhibitions featuring farm livestock and agricultural machinery, plus sales of quality breeding animals. The society also continues to foster participation in events which actively encourage good stockmanship, efficient land use and the preservation of rural activities.

Borders College Agricultural and Rural Development Centre
Borders College
Newtown St Boswells
Roxburghshire
TD6 0PL
Tel: 01835 823023
Fax: 01835 823649
Contact: Miss L Humble, Senior Manager
Previous names: Borders College Agricultural Centre until 1996
Profile: Borders College Rural Development Centre is situated across two sites, Duns and Newton St Boswells, spanning the Scottish Borders countryside. A range of courses are offered as part of the FE curriculum; agriculture, horticulture, game keeping, countryside skills, agricultural engineering and horse management. Consultancy and short courses are offered to organisations in all of the above vocational areas, drawing on the wealth of expertise and

experience of the staff. The centre works closely with the related industries providing work based training and assessment to meet the needs of employers. The facilities and resources are available as venues for meetings, training courses and conferences.

Boreham
see **Rare Breeds Survival Trust**

Botanical Society of Scotland
c/o Royal Botanic Gardens
Edinburgh
Midlothian
EH3 5LR
Tel: 0131 552 7171
Contact: The General Secretary
Founded: 1836
Membership: 500
Publications: Botanical Journal of Scotland
Previous names: Botanical Society of Edinburgh until 1991
Profile: The society exists to promote the study of plants and to exchange botanical information between members. The activities of the society include: lectures on current botanical research at six venues throughout Scotland; symposia and conferences to discuss major botanical issues; and field meetings to familiarise members with elements of the Scottish flora.

Botanical Society of the British Isles
c/o Department of Botany
Natural History Museum
Cromwell Road
London
SW7 5BD
Contact: Honorary General Secretary
Founded: 1836
Membership: 2,000
Publications: Watsonia; BSBI Abstracts; BSBI News
Previous names: Botanical Society of London; Botanical Exchange Club until 1858
Profile: The society is interested in the structure and distribution of vascular plants in the British Isles. It holds regular field meetings and conferences and continuously undertakes surveys to monitor variation in plant populations to identify those species which become threatened.

Brackenhurst College
Southwell
Nottinghamshire
NG25 0QF
Tel: 01636 812252
Fax: 01636 815404

Contact: Jamie Woolley, Marketing Manager
Founded: 1947
Publications: College prospectus
Previous names: Nottinghamshire College of Agriculture
Profile: Nottinghamshire's only college of further education specialising in environmental and land-based studies. Courses available in: agriculture, animal care, countryside management, engineering, equine studies, floristry, food technology, horticulture and learning support. Qualifications range from First Diploma to Degree level.

Brahma Club
Fair View
Stainton Road
Seamer Stokesley
Middlesborough
Durham
TS9 5NB
Contact: Mrs L Burn, Secretary
Profile: A society to promote the Brahma breed of poultry.

Bramley Apple Information Service
Glen House
125 Old Brompton Road
London
SW7 3RP
Tel: 0171 373 4889
Fax: 0171 244 8385
Contact: Rebecca Hopkins

Brassica Growers' Association
53 High Street
Gosberton
Spalding
Lincolnshire
PE11 4NJ
Tel: 01775 840140
Fax: 01775 840124
Contact: A Whitlock, Secretary
Founded: 1987
Membership: 22
Profile: A federal organisation that represents the interests of brassica growers and packers in all aspects of research, production, packing, marketing and promotion.

Braunvieh Cattle Association (UK)
41 Bank Street
Carlisle
Cumbria
CA3 8HJ
Tel: 01228 34423
Fax: 01228 818022

Contact: FC Culvey, Secretary
Founded: 1993
Membership: 5
Profile: To promote the original Swiss type of Braunvieh cattle in the UK.

Brecknock Hill Cheviot Sheep Society
13 Lion Street
Brecon
Powys
LD3 7HY
Tel: 01874 622488

Brecon Beacons National Park
7 Glamorgan Street
Brecon
Powys
LD3 7DP
Tel: 01874 624437
Fax: 01874 622574
Email: 100070.1353@compuserve.com
Contact: Angela Owens, Public Relations Officer
Founded: 1957
Publications: Publications list available
Previous names: Brecon Beacons National Park Joint Advisory Committee 1957–1974; Brecon Beacons National Park Committee 1974–1996
Profile: The authority has responsibility (under the 1949 National Parks and Access to the Countryside Act, and the 1995 Environment Act, etc.) for conservation and informal recreation, and puts increasing emphasis on working with the local community. The authority is responsible for planning functions within the park.

BRF International
Lyttel Hall
Cooper's Hill Road
Nutfield
Redhill
Surrey
RH1 4HY
Tel: 01737 822272
Fax: 01737 822747
Email: 100627.2315@compuserve.com
Contact: Dr E Denise Baxter, Head of Membership Affairs and Food Safety
Founded: 1941
Membership: 200
Publications: Monthly Industry Review; Quarterly Research Review; Best Practice manuals
Previous names: Brewing Industry Research Foundation until 1976; Brewing Research Foundation until 1991
Profile: BRF International is a private research organisation with an international membership drawn from the malting and brewing industries and allied companies in the alcoholic beverage industries. It provides a comprehensive research and development programme, specialist analytical services, commissioned project work, malting and brewing trials, information and training services and food safety support. Facilities include fully equipped laboratories, pilot malting and brewing plant, library, engineering workshops and conference facilities.

Brinsbury College
West Sussex College of Agriculture and Horticulture
North Heath
Pulborough
West Sussex
RH20 1DL
Tel: 01798 873832
Fax: 01798 875222

British Aggregate Construction Materials Industries
156 Buckingham Palace Road
London
SW1W 9TR
Tel: 0171 730 8194
Fax: 0171 730 4355
Contact: Simon van der Byl, Director General

British Agricultural and Garden Machinery Association
British Hardware Federation
14–16 Church Street
Rickmansworth
Hertfordshire
WD3 1RQ
Tel: 01923 720241
Fax: 01923 896063
Contact: Ian Jones, General Manager
Founded: 1917
Membership: 684
Publications: BAGMA Bulletin; Market Guide to Used Tractors and Farm Machinery; Garden Machinery Price Guide
Previous names: Agricultural Machinery and Tractor Dealer Association until 1976

British Agricultural Export Committee
c/o LCCI
33 Queen Street
London
EC4R 1AP
Tel: 0171 248 4444
Fax: 0171 489 0391

British Agricultural History Society
Department of Historical and Critical Studies
University of Central Lancashire

Preston
Lancashire
PR1 2HE
Tel: 01772 893844
Fax: 01772 892970
Email: R.Hoyle@uclan.ac.uk
Contact: R W Hoyle, Secretary
Founded: 1953
Membership: 700
Publications: Agricultural History Review;
occasional publications
Profile: The object of the Society is to promote
the study of agricultural history, the history of
rural economy and society. It does this chiefly
through the publication of the Agricultural History
Review, by holding conferences, and the
promotion of the teaching of the history of
agriculture, the rural economy and society.

British Agrochemicals Association Ltd
4 Lincoln Court
Lincoln Road
Peterborough
Cambridgeshire
PE1 2RP
Tel: 01733 349225
Fax: 01733 62523
Contact: Dr AH Buckenham, Secretary

British Alliance of Sheep Contractors
Huts Corner
Tilford Road
Hindhead
Surrey
GU21 6SF
Tel: 01234 708877
Fax: 01234 708862
Contact: Tim Wilkinsoney, Chairman
Previous names: British Association of Sheep
Contractors

British Alpine Breed Society
The Old Tanyard
Pound Pill
Corsham
Wiltshire
SN13 9HT
Tel: 01249 701024
Contact: Mrs S C Head, Secretary
Founded: 1979
Membership: 102
Publications: British Alpine Breed Society
handbooks, members newsletter
Profile: The British Alpine Breed Society was
formed to promote interest in the breed. It is a
thriving society producing a quarterly newsletter
and a stud list. It organises national and regional
breed shows. As well as Britain, membership is

drawn from France, Australia and New Zealand.
The British Alpine stud list and information about
stock as well as availability of semen is
obtainable from the secretary, as are
membership forms.

British American Quarter Horse Society
38 Orchards Way
Westend
Southampton
Hampshire
SO3 3FB
Profile: We have been unable to contact this
organisation. The details given are unconfirmed.

British Angora Goat Society
4th Street
National Agricultural Centre
Stoneleigh Park
Warwickshire
CV8 2LG
Tel: 01203 696722
Fax: 01203 696729
Contact: John Wood Roberts, Secretary
Publications: Members newsletter, yearbook
Profile: Aims of the society are to organise
official shows and sales, to register and record all
pedigree animals, to improve the standard of the
national flock, to market the fleeces in
conjunction with British Mohair Marketing and to
keep members informed of current goat health
and market developments through newsletters
and the yearbook.

British Angora Producers Marketing Association
The Dingle
Barnton
Northwich
Cheshire
CW8 4SS
Tel: 01606 76853
Profile: We have been unable to contact this
organisation. The details given are unconfirmed.

British Appaloosa Society
36 Clusterbolts
Stapleford
Hertford
Hertfordshire
SG14 3ND
Tel: 01992 558657
Contact: Mrs Brenda George, Secretary
Founded: 1971
Membership: 480
Publications: Stallion brochure/guide

Profile: The society was formed to promote and improve the Appaloosa horse. They now have over 2,000 animals on the register.

British Arachnological Society
Burns Farm
Cornhill
Banff
Aberdeen
AB45 2DL
Tel: 01466 751231
Fax: 01466 751395
Contact: Secretary

British Association for Biofuels and Oils
St Nicholas Court Farm
Birchington
Kent
CT7 0PT
Tel: 01843 847240
Fax: 01843 847444
Contact: Nick Tapp, Secretary
Founded: 1993
Membership: 85
Publications: Newsletter; reports (list available)
Profile: BABFO is a trade association dedicated to the promotion of fuels and oils of vegetable origin (eg biodiesel).

British Association for Chemical Specialities
The Gatehouse
White Cross
Lancaster
Lancashire
LA1 4XQ
Tel: 01524 849606
Fax: 01524 849194
Contact: Richard J Farn, Director
Founded: 1977
Membership: 160
Publications: Annual review; Choice of Disinfectant; codes of practice
Previous names: British Disinfectant Manufacturers Association and British Polish Manufacturers Association merged to form BACS in 1977
Profile: BACS is the trade association representing manufacturers and formulators of speciality chemicals and intermediates. Major classes of performance and effect chemicals covered by BACS include maintenance products for consumer and industrial use, disinfectants and industrial biocides, including water treatment chemicals and services, waterborne polymers and speciality surfactants.

British Association for Shooting and Conservation
Marford Mill
Rossett
Wrexham
LL12 0HL
Tel: 01244 570881
Fax: 01244 571678
Email: pressoffice@basc.demon.co.uk
Contact: Robin Peel, Head of Public Affairs
Founded: 1908
Membership: 112,000
Publications: Shooting and Conservation; Handbook of Shooting; publications list available
Previous names: Wildfowlers Association of Great Britain and Ireland until 1981
Profile: The national governing body for sporting shooting. An all party lobby for shooting in the UK and Europe.

British Association for the Pure Bred Spanish Horse
High Oaks
The Cwm
Forden
Montgomery
Powys
Tel: 01938 555536
Fax: 01938 552233
Contact: Mrs Jenny Bernard, Chairwoman
Founded: 1982
Membership: 350
Publications: Pura Raza Español
Previous names: British Andalusian Horse Society until 1992
Profile: BAPSH is the only recognised body in the UK affiliated to the Cria de Caballar in Spain. Three types of stud book are held, pure, hispano-arab (Andalusian /Arab) and part breds. They organise and hold shows, clinics and dressage competitions.

British Association of Feed Supplement and Additive Manufacturers
Mill House
The Hill
Cranbrook
Kent
TN17 3AH
Tel: 01580 291425
Fax: 01580 714337
Contact: WH Beaumont, Secretary-General
Founded: 1968
Membership: 32
Previous names: British Association of Feed Supplement Manufacturers until 1994

Profile: The principal objects are to promote, encourage and protect the lawful interests of the members. BAFSAM is consulted by the Ministry of Agriculture on potential EU legislation and its implementation in the UK and on UK legislation affecting the industry by any ministry. BAFSAM is the UK member of its European equivalent (FEFANA) based in Brussels with access to the European Commission.

British Association of Golf Course Constructors

2 Angel Court
Dairy Yard (High Street)
Market Harborough
Leicestershire
LE16 7NL
Tel: 01858 464346
Fax: 01858 434734
Contact: TJ Banks, Honorary Secretary
Founded: 1981
Membership: 20
Profile: The association aims to promote the development of the golf course construction industry and adopt policies ensuring high quality workmanship and working practices. It aims to collect and disseminate information regarding golf course construction to members of the association, allied industries and the general public – to inform same, public and private bodies institutions and organisations of developments within the industry. To promote training/education of personnel within the industry and maintain agreed standards of golf course construction by adhering to contractual procedures and codes of practice.

British Association of Green Crop Driers Ltd

Silverwood
Stone Street
Westenhanger
Hythe
Kent
CT21 4HT
Tel: 01303 267317
Fax: 01303 268270
Email: 100732.3071@compuserve.com
Contact: Mr Roger H Earl, Secretary
Founded: 1963
Membership: 30
Profile: BAGCD represents the interests of all those involved in the production of dried grass and dried lucerne throughout the UK.

British Association of Homeopathic Veterinary Surgeons

Alternative Veterinary Medicine Centre
Chinham House

Stanford in the Vale
Oxfordshire
SN7 8NQ
Tel: 01367 710475
Fax: 01367 718243
Contact: Christopher Day, Hon Secretary
Founded: 1981
Membership: 150
Publications: Members newsletter
Profile: The association was formed in 1981 to advance the understanding, knowledge and practice of veterinary homoeopathy. It aims to stimulate professional awareness of homoeopathy and to encourage and provide for the training of veterinary surgeons in the practice of homoeopathy. The association will provide names and addresses of veterinary surgeons with the homoeopathic qualification and others using homoeopathy who have undergone some of the training.

British Association of Landscape Industries

Landscape House
9 Henry Street
Keighley
West Yorkshire
BD21 3DR
Tel: 01535 606139
Fax: 01535 610269
Contact: Information Officer
Founded: 1972
Membership: 700
Publications: Landscape News (members newsletter); publications list available
Profile: BALI was formed in 1972 and membership currently stands at over 720 companies and individuals. The association's principal objective is to encourage high standards of workmanship in all aspects of landscape contracting. Members' services cover the full spectrum of landscaping – from sports facilities to shopping malls, grounds maintenance to water features and every other landscape requirement.

British Association of Nature Conservationists

c/o The Wildlife Trust
Lings House
Billing Lings
Northampton
NN3 8BE
Contact: Adam Cole-King, Secretary
Founded: 1979
Membership: 1,000
Publications: Ecos; publications list available

Profile: BANC's objective is to advance nature conservation in the UK. It acts as a network for conservationists and people who care about the natural world. BANC exerts pressure on UK Government policy as an active member of Wildlife Link, and has an important voice in world conservation affairs through IUCN, the world conservation union.

British Association of Radio Control Soarers
Langstone
Havant
Hampshire
PO9 1RT
Profile: We have been unable to contact this organisation. The details given are unconfirmed.

British Association of Seed Analysts
3 Whitehall Court
London
SW1A 2EQ
Tel: 0171 930 3611
Fax: 0171 930 3952
Contact: Paul Rooke, Secretary
Founded: 1923
Membership: 127
Publications: Members newsletter
Previous names: British Association of Commercial Analysts until 1950s
Profile: The main objectives of BASA are the advancement of seed testing and the co-operation and mutual advice of its members in matters relating to seed testing. Key functions include liaison with various official organisations and the dissemination of technical information to its members, relating to seeds and seed testing.

British Athletic Federation
Athletics House
225A Bristol Road
Edgbaston
Birmingham
B5 7UB
Tel: 0121 440 5000
Fax: 0121 440 0555
Contact: Bill Adcocks, Information Officer

British Balloon and Airship Club
Hurcott Hall Farm
Kidderminster
Worcestershire
DY10 3PH
Tel: 01562 820421
Fax: 01562 829205
Contact: Peter Vale, National Landowner Relations Officer
Founded: 1968

Membership: 2,200
Publications: Aerostat
Profile: The BBAC represents lighter than air craft pilots. The organisation has delegated powers from the Civil Aviation Authority to train, examine and test pilots for their licence, and inspect balloons and the design of balloons for airworthiness. There are 14 regional clubs and each has a landowner relations officer. Sensitive areas are recorded by an officer of the club who issues these to all pilot members and a map over-printing service. Meetings are held with the National Farmers Union and Country Landowners Association to agree policy.

British Bavarian Warmblood Association
Landesverband Bayerischer Pferdezeuchter e.V., Germany
Sittyton
Straloch
Newmacher
Aberdeen
AB21 0RP
Tel: 01651 882226
Fax: 01651 882313
Contact: Christa Jeffery, Secretary
Founded: 1987
Membership: 96
Profile: The British Bavarian Warmblood Association (BBWA) is an independent working horse breed association. It is affiliated to the Bavarian Horse Breeder's Association in Germany and works according to their breeding rules. The BBWA's objective is to support and improve horse breeding and to produce noble, generously proportioned, good saddle-horses with smooth, far reaching elastic movements which, because of their temperament, character and rideability are eminently suited for all forms of riding. The BBWA holds annually a breed show, mare and stallion gradings, a mare performance test and a stallion 100 day performance test.

British Bazadais Cattle Society
Western Green
Spa Lane
Aylsham
Norfolk
NR11 6UE
Tel: 01263 733508
Fax: 01263 731311
Contact: Corinne Matthews, Secretary
Founded: 1989
Membership: 12
Profile: The society was formed in 1989 to promote the newly introduced Bazadais cattle in Great Britain. The Bazadais has gradually carved a

niche in the AI market and is becoming well known over the whole country.

British Bedding and Potplant Association
164 Shaftesbury Avenue
London
WC2H 8HL
Tel: 0171 331 7281
Fax: 0171 331 7410
Contact: Rachel Moseley, Association Adviser
Publications: News and Views

British Bee-Keepers Association
National Agricultural Centre
Stoneleigh Park
Warwickshire
CV8 2LZ
Tel: 01203 696679
Fax: 01203 690682
Contact: AC Waring, General Secretary
Founded: 1874
Membership: 12,000
Publications: BBKA News, Yearbook
Profile: To further the craft of beekeeping.

British Belgian Blue Cattle Society
Coleshill Lodge
Abbots Bromley
Rugeley
Staffordshire
WS15 3DN
Tel: 01283 840990
Fax: 01283 840885
Contact: Alex JH Fox, Secretary
Founded: 1982
Membership: 420
Publications: Annual herd book
Profile: A cattle breed society established in 1982 to encourage the development, usage and potential for the Belgian Blue in the UK.

British Berrichon du Cher Sheep Society Ltd
The Lodge
Sutton Bassett
Market Harborough
Leicestershire
LE16 8HL
Tel: 01858 462427
Fax: 01858 462427
Contact: Sue Drury, Company Secretary
Founded: 1986
Membership: 150
Publications: Annual flock book; annual magazine
Profile: Sheep breed society.

British Biogen
164 Shaftesbury Avenue
London
WC2H 8HL
Tel: 01435 882228
Fax: 01435 882247
Contact: Mr Peter Billins, Chief Executive
Founded: 1995
Membership: 70
Profile: British Biogen is the government-recognised Trade Association for the UK's biomass industry. It has as its stated mission: 'to promote and co-ordinate the commercial development of biomass as a renewable fuel resource for energy production'. Biomass includes energy crops, short rotation coppice, agricultural wastes and forest residues.

British Bison Association
Bush Farm
West Knoyle
Warminster
Wiltshire
BA12 6AE
Tel: 01747 830263
Fax: 01747 830263
Contact: Colin Ellis, Secretary
Founded: 1991
Membership: 21
Publications: BBA Handbook
Profile: The British Bison Association is a group of people enthusiastic about keeping bison whether for pleasure or for gain. The object of the association is to provide an umbrella organisation for bison breeders in order to foster co-operation and communication for the betterment and development of the species.

British Bleu du Maine Sheep Society
Enville Court
8F Lillington Avenue
Leamington Spa
Warwickshire
CV32 5UJ
Tel: 01926 889923
Fax: 01926 889923
Contact: Jean Barbour, Secretary

British Bloodstock Agency (UK) Ltd
Queensbury House
High Street
Newmarket
Suffolk
CB8 9BD
Tel: 01638 665021
Fax: 01638 660283
Contact: Colin H Bothway, Managing Director

Founded: 1911
Membership: 40
Publications: Annual yearbook

British Boer Goat Society
Layby Farm
Old Risborough Road
Stoke Mandeville
Buckinghamshire
HP22 5XJ
Tel: 01296 612983
Fax: 01296 613063
Contact: M Gaisford, Chairman
Founded: 1987
Membership: 30
Publications: Members newsletter
Profile: A breed society for the promotion of
Boer goats.

British Camargue Horse Society
Valley Farm Riding and Driving Centre
Wickham Market
Woodbridge
Suffolk
IP13 0ND
Tel: 01728 746916
Fax: 01728 746916
Contact: Sarah Ling
Founded: 1992
Membership: 20
Profile: To promote and protect the Camargue
horse in Britain.

**British Camelid Ltd Owners and Breeders
    Association**
Banksway House
Effingham Common
Leatherhead
Surrey
KT24 5JB
Tel: 01372 458350
Fax: 01372 451131
Contact: Mrs Candida Midworth, Honorary
Secretary
Founded: 1987
Membership: 275
Publications: The Camelids Chronicle; Welfare
Guidelines; GALA Sales List
Profile: The aims of the association are to guide
and foster the growing interest in camelids, to
promote good husbandry practices, and the
establishment of sound breeding programmes
for the continued improvement of British stock.
The association holds seminars, a biannual
conference, judges classes for camelids at
agricultural shows and workshops for new
owners.

British Carrot Grower's Association
Whithall Farm
Temple Road
Isleham
Ely
Cambridgeshire
CB7 5RF
Tel: 01638 780087
Fax: 01638 780056
Contact: Mrs Jackie Seddon, Treasurer
Membership: 19
Previous names: Gold Prince Carrot Group
1984–1989
Profile: The British Carrot Grower's Association
consists of 19 UK individual carrot growing
companies, who meet to discuss various aspects
of the industry. BCGA is open to any UK carrot
growing organisation to join.

British Cashmere Society
23 Damhead Holdings
Lothianburn
Edinburgh
EH10 7EA
Tel: 0131 445 3438
Fax: 0131 445 3438
Contact: Mrs D Marsh, Secretary
Founded: 1988
Publications: Information sheets on background
management of goats

British Caspian Society
Rose Cottage
Bromsgrove Road
Clent
West Midlands
Tel: 01562 730483
Profile: We have been unable to contact this
organisation. The details given are unconfirmed.

British Cattle Breeders Club
16 Aswan Street
Loughborough
Leicestershire
LE11 5BL
Tel: 01509 261810
Fax: 01509 610585
Contact: Malcolm Peasnall, Secretary
Founded: 1946
Membership: 500
Publications: Digest
Profile: The British Cattle Breeders Club has held
its winter conference for the last 52 years. A
unique format with farmers, scientists and
industry people meeting to discuss cattle
breeding and new techniques.

British Cattle Veterinary Association
The Green
Frampton on Severn
Gloucestershire
GL2 7ER
Tel: 01452 740816
Fax: 01452 741117
Contact: Chris Watson, President
Founded: 1973
Membership: 1,400
Publications: Cattle Practice
Profile: The provision of education and
information to cattle vets.

British Central Prefix Register
Weston Manor
Corscombe
Dorset
DT2 0PB
Tel: 01935 89466
Fax: 01935 89466
Contact: Mrs ECM Williamson, Secretary
Founded: 1978
Membership: 40
Profile: The register was founded in 1978 to
avoid, as far as humanly possible, any further
duplication of prefixes. The register now serves
40 societies of which seven are in Europe. There
are over 25,000 prefixes on file. The register also
helps to trace breeders of equines whose papers
have been lost, but whose prefix has remained
with them. Prefixes may only be used on an
equine bred by the registered owner of the
relevant prefix.

British Cereal Exports
Home-Grown Cereals Authority
HGCA
Hamlyn House
Highgate Hill
London
N19 5PR
Tel: 0171 263 3391
Fax: 0171 561 6202

British Charolais Cattle Society Ltd
Avenue M
National Agricultural Centre
Stoneleigh Park
Warwickshire
CV8 2RG
Tel: 01203 697222
Fax: 01203 690270
Contact: David Benson, Chief Executive
Founded: 1962
Membership: 3,000
Publications: Charolais News

British Charollais Sheep Society Ltd
Crogham Farm
Wymondham
Norfolk
NR18 8RR
Tel: 01953 603335
Fax: 01953 607860
Contact: Mrs Carroll Barber, Breed Secretary
Founded: 1977
Publications: British Charollais Sheep Society
Year Book; Charollais Times
Profile: The breed society of the British
Charollais sheep.

**British Chemical Distributors and Traders
    Association Ltd**
Suffolk House
George Street
Croydon
Surrey
CR0 0YN
Tel: 0181 686 4545
Fax: 0181 688 7768
Contact: Colin JD Wainwright, Director and
Secretary
Founded: 1923

British Chicken Association
British Poultry Meat Federation
Imperial House
15–19 Kingsway
London
WC2B 6UA
Tel: 0171 240 9889
Fax: 0171 240 7757
Contact: Information Officer

British Chicken Information Service
Bury House
126–128 Cromwell Road
London
SW7 4ET
Tel: 0171 373 7757
Fax: 0171 373 3926
Contact: John Ramuz, Chairman
Founded: 1983
Publications: Chicken Rules (hygiene leaflet);
Market Review (statistical analysis of the market)
Profile: The British Chicken Information Service
was created in 1983 to act as a media information
service for the British Chicken Association (BCA).
Working under the umbrella of the British Poultry
Meat Federation, the BCA is committed to
protecting the interests of Britain's chicken
producers and processors. The association
represents its members' views in consultations
and lobbying with MAFF, the DTI and other

departments, as well as other organisations. It is the role of the BCIS to support the UK chicken industry by promoting the benefits of British chicken to both the consumer and trade press by releasing regular information on the retail market.

British Christmas Tree Growers Association
12 Lauriston Road
Wimbledon
London
SW19 4TQ
Tel: 0181 946 2695
Fax: 0181 947 0211
Contact: Mr Tony Richardson, Secretary
Founded: 1979
Membership: 295
Publications: BCTGA Newsletter
Profile: The association assists and co-ordinates Christmas tree marketing. It carries out market research and advises on market prospects. It represents the interests of British growers. It promotes homegrown trees. It advises on the growing and care of Christmas trees. It organises open days, meetings, overseas visits and publishes a newsletter for members. Its aim is to ensure that British growers produce top quality Christmas trees.

British Coloured Sheep Breeders Association
Avenue Cottage
Cutmill
Bosham
West Sussex
PO18 8PN
Tel: 01243 573516
Contact: Miss PE Cornwell, Secretary
Founded: 1985
Membership: 169
Publications: Members directory; members newsletter
Profile: The Coloured Sheep Breeders Association was set up originally to act as a pressure group towards the legislation of the sale of coloured wool to hand spinners and to act as a forum for the exchange of ideas and mutual support among coloured sheep breeders. Through publications and meetings, members express their views and provide a link between the individual breed societies and give much appreciated support at the various coloured sheep classes at shows locally and nationally. They have a continuing aim to promote the merits and versatility of coloured wools within the trade and to the general public.

British Commercial Rabbit Association
Fairfield House
Sound

Nantwich
Cheshire
CW5 8BA
Tel: 01270 780248
Fax: 01270 780248
Contact: Secretary

British Crop Protection Council
49 Downing Street
Farnham
Surrey
GU9 7PH
Tel: 01252 733072
Fax: 01252 727194
Contact: Dr John Fisher, General Secretary
Founded: 1977
Membership: 28
Publications: Publications list available
Profile: BCPC exists to promote a balanced understanding of crop protection. The work is carried out by volunteers, either representatives of corporate members who are in full-time work, or former senior executives now independent members. The council produces a wide range of publications and organises symposia and conferences on both a UK and international basis. Links with overseas organisations are being strengthened.

British Cycling Federation
National Cycling Centre
Stuart Street
Manchester
M11 4DQ
Tel: 0161 230 2301
Fax: 0161 231 0591
Contact: Pat Clark, Communications and PR
Founded: 1959
Membership: 1,500
Publications: Annual handbook; Slipstream (members newsletter)
Profile: Governing body for cycling.

British Cyclo-Cross Association
14 Deneside Road
Darlington
County Durham
DL3 9HZ
Tel: 01325 482052
Fax: 01325 482052
Contact: Brian Furness, General Secretary
Founded: 1954
Publications: Annual handbook
Profile: The governing body in England and Wales for the sport of cyclo-cross. The original off-road bicycle sport, contested over a variety of surfaces on circuits of 1–2 miles in length. Around 250 promotions are held each year during

the main season which runs from September to February.

British Deer Farmers Association
Holly Lodge
Spencers Lane
Berkswell
Coventry
Warwickshire
CV7 7BZ
Tel: 01203 465957
Fax: 01203 469063
Contact: Anne Dymond, Secretary
Founded: 1978
Publications: Deer Farming Magazine;
Introduction to Deer Farming; Perfect Venison
Profile: The BDFA was formed to further the interests of deer farmers, and membership is open to all interested in deer farming. It is closely involved in the improvement of deer farming methods and helps with the advancement of education and research into deer farming. Although not a marketing organisation, it is responsible for the promotion of farmed venison. The association organises a full programme of activities including an annual conference and regional meetings.

British Deer Society
Beale Centre
Lower Basildon
Reading
RG8 9NH
Tel: 01425 655434
Profile: We have been unable to contact this organisation. The details given are unconfirmed.

British Domesticated Ostrich Association
41 Bank Street
Carlisle
Cumbria
CA3 8HJ
Tel: 01228 34423
Fax: 01228 818022
Contact: C Culley, Secretary
Founded: 1992
Membership: 350
Publications: Ostrich News
Profile: The association was formed to promote the ostrich, emu and rhea industry in the UK. It also lobbies government on legislation and other matters.

British Dragonfly Society
The Haywain
Hollywater Road
Bordon

Hampshire
GU33 0AD
Tel: 01420 472329
Contact: Dr WH Wain, Honorary Secretary
Founded: 1983
Membership: 1,250

British Driving Society
27 Dugard Place
Barford
Warwick
CV8 8DX
Tel: 01926 624420
Fax: 01926 624633
Contact: Jenny Dillon, Executive Secretary
Founded: 1957
Membership: 5,000
Publications: Annual journal; Annual Book of Driving Shows and Events; quarterly newsletter (free to members); B.D.S. Introduction to Driving and Book of Examination Syllabus
Profile: To encourage and assist those interested in the driving of horses and ponies.

British Ecological Society
26 Blades Court
Deodar Road
Putney
London
SW15 2NU
Tel: 0181 871 9797
Fax: 0181 871 9797
Email: general@ecology.demon.co.uk
Contact: Dr Hazel J Norman, Executive Secretary
Founded: 1913
Membership: 5,000
Publications: Journal of Ecology; Journal of Applied Ecology; Journal of Animal Ecology; The Bulletin
Profile: The society's membership is open to all who are genuinely interested in ecology. The BES holds general and special interest meetings and awards grants for ecological projects and expeditions.

British Edible Pulse Association
Smeeth Road
Marshland St James
Wisbech
Cambridgeshire
PE14 8JF
Tel: 01945 430479
Fax: 01945 430328
Contact: Mrs G Fleetwood, Association Secretary
Founded: 1973

Membership: 33
Profile: An association made up of members of different sides of the British dried pea and field bean trade. Their members consist of canners, cleaners, seedsmen and agricultural merchants.

British Egg Association
Suite 101 Albany House
324–326 Regent Street
London
W1R 5AA
Tel: 0171 580 7172
Contact: L Platt

British Egg Industry Council
Suite 101 Albany House
324–326 Regent Street
London
W1R 5AA
Tel: 0171 580 7172
Fax: 0171 580 7082
Contact: Mike Ring, Chief Executive
Profile: The British Egg Industry Council is an inter-professional body to which are affiliated all interested organisations. The BEIC is largely funded by voluntary subscriptions derived from a levy paid by BEIC egg packer or producer subscribers. BEIC also funds research and development. BEIC lobbies government and the European Commission.

British Egg Information Service
Bury House
126–128 Cromwell Road
London
SW7 4ET
Tel: 0171 370 7411
Fax: 0171 373 3926

British Egg Marketing Board Trust
121 Station Road
Withall
Birmingham
B47 6AG
Tel: 01564 824446
Fax: 01564 824446
Contact: Alan M Beckett, Secretary/Administrator
Founded: 1971
Profile: The British Egg Marketing Board Trust was set up on the demise of the British Egg Marketing Board (1969). It has a portfolio of approx £1 million and funds six PhD scholars in egg related poultry research as well as supporting other similar projects and an annual Nuffield Travelling Scholarship.

British Egg Products Association
Suite 101 Albany House
324–326 Regent Street
London
W1R 5AA
Tel: 0171 580 7172
Fax: 0171 580 7082
Contact: L Platt

British Equestrian Federation
British Equestrian Centre
Stoneleigh Park
Warwickshire
CV8 2LR
Tel: 01203 696697
Fax: 01203 696484

British Equestrian Trade Association
Wothersome Grange
Bramham
Wetherby
North Yorkshire
LS23 6LY
Tel: 0113 289 2267
Fax: 0113 289 2267
Contact: Antony Wakeham, Secretary
Founded: 1979
Membership: 550
Profile: BETA helps the equestrian industry. Its members are retailers, manufacturers and suppliers, agents and a small equine section. BETA operates a code of conduct and criteria for membership. It is accepted as the official body for the trade. BETA monitors safety standards within the industry. It chairs the Body Protector Committee and has representation on the BSI Hat Committee and the BHS Safety Policy Committee. It is committed to improving standards within the industry.

British Equine Veterinary Association
Hartham Park
Corsham
Wiltshire
SN13 0QB
Tel: 01249 715723
Fax: 01249 701026
Contact: Mrs Andi Ewen, Administrative Secretary
Founded: 1961
Membership: 1,500
Publications: Equine Veterinary Journal; Equine Veterinary Education

British European Potato Association
31 Keats Road
Copsewood
Coventry
CV2 5JZ

Tel: 01203 650005
Fax: 01203 650005
Contact: ABS Paine, Secretary and Treasurer
Founded: 1990
Membership: 28
Profile: An organisation for those engaged in import or export trading in potatoes of all kinds. A member of Europatat and thus solely responsible for all of the UK in the administration of the rules governing the international potato trade (RUCIP). It represents the UK's potato interests in Europe via Europatat – the European Union of the wholesale potato trade.

British Falconers' Club
Home Farm
Hints
Tamworth
Staffordshire
B78 3DW
Tel: 01543 481737
Fax: 01543 481737
Contact: John R Fairclough, Director
Founded: 1927
Membership: 1,100
Publications: Members newsletter; Falconer
Previous names: The Old Hawking Club until 1926
Profile: The promotion of practical falconry in the British Isles and elsewhere and to promote and maintain observance of the club's code of conduct amongst falconers.

British Farm Turkey Committee
5 Box Mill Lane
Halstead
Essex
CO9 2DR
Tel: 01787 472197
Contact: Gordon Pickering, Secretary
Founded: 1989
Previous names: EEC Draft Regulations Committee (Turkeys) until 1991
Profile: Originally formed to campaign for the retention of traditional farm fresh turkeys and the right of consumers to have freedom of choice in their purchases. Petition launched Christmas 1989 resulted in an audited and certified count of 106,959 signatures. Now it is regarded that the battle has been won and the committee remains in existence for any future political contingencies and to consider financial aid for research, education and product promotions.

British Federation of Hotel, Guest House and Self Catering Associations
5 Sandicroft Road
Blackpool
FY1 2RY

Tel: 01253 352683
Contact: Mrs KM Harris, General Secretary
Founded: 1916
Membership: 500
Publications: Members newsletter
Previous names: British Federation of Hotel and Boarding House Association until 1953; British Federation of Hotel and Guest House Associations until 1975
Profile: Represents the smaller operators, i.e. privately run small hotels, guest houses, bed and breakfast houses and self catering accommodation. Looks after their interests at both local and national level and keeps them informed of any new legislation etc. which might affect the hotel and catering industry.

British Field Sports Society
59 Kennington Road
London
SE1 7PZ
Tel: 0171 928 4742
Fax: 0171 620 1401
Email: 101456.1641@compuserve.com
Contact: Mrs Janet George, Chief Press Officer
Founded: 1930
Membership: 415,000
Publications: Country Sports; numerous leaflets and videos
Profile: For over 60 years, the BFSS has defended all field sports. Field sports provide recreation for some 5 million people in Britain from all walks of life; including anglers, shooters and hunters. The BFSS is the only society representing every field sport with an effective lobby at Westminster and Brussels.

British Fine Wool Sheep Breeders
Lancombe Farm
Higher Chilfrome
Dorchester
Dorset
DT2 0HU
Tel: 01300 320657
Profile: We have been unable to contact this organisation. The details given are unconfirmed.

British Food Export Council
Food From Britain
123 Buckingham Palace Road
London
SW1W 9SA
Tel: 0171 233 5111
Fax: 0171 233 9516
Contact: Information Officer

British Free Range Egg Producers Association
c/o UKL Services Ltd
Cheviot House
71 Castle Street
Salisbury
Wiltshire
SP1 3SP
Tel: 01722 323546
Contact: David Trick, Chair

British Friesian Breeders Club
Holstein Friesian Society of Great Britain and
 Ireland
23 Oakham Drive
Agar Nook
Coalville
Leicestershire
LE67 4SY
Tel: 01530 831491
Contact: Robert J Clay, Secretary
Founded: 1990
Membership: 130
Publications: Members newsletter; annual
brochure
Profile: The club was formed to represent the
interests of those dairy farmers who do not wish
to use North American genetics, but to retain
their British Friesian herds. It is controlled by a
committee of 16, which meets regularly to
decide and implement policy. The club organises
annually a Bull Progeny Competition and the
National British Friesian Show and has embarked
on a long term programme of progeny testing
young bulls. The Holstein Friesian Society to
which the club is affiliated has recently
introduced a classification scheme for cattle to a
British Friesian Standard.

British Friesian Horse Society
Hanstead
Streetlam
Northallerton
North Yorkshire
DL7 0AJ
Tel: 01325 378556
Fax: 01325 378025
Profile: Disbanded 1996.

British Friesland Sheep Society
Fouts Cross Farm
Seavington St Michael
Ilminster
Somerset
TA19 0QA
Tel: 01460 240313
Contact: Mrs BH Tavernor, Honorary Secretary
Founded: 1981

Membership: 60
Publications: Members handbook
Profile: To promote, regulate and develop the
British Friesland breed. To publicise their unique
characteristics. The society maintains a register
of pedigree animals and endeavours to
co-ordinate contact between members and
others in this county and abroad who are seeking
breeding stock.

British Gas plc
Rivermill House
152 Grosvenor Road
London
SW1V 3JL
Tel: 0171 821 1444

British Gelbvieh Cattle Society
Paddock Farm
Taylors Lane
Buckden
Cambridgeshire
PE18 9UW
Tel: 01480 810743
Contact: Mrs B Cade, Secretary
Founded: 1973
Membership: 40
Publications: Members newsletter
Profile: To promote and support the breeding of
the British Gelbvieh cattle and to record and
register pedigree animals.

British Geological Survey
Natural Environment Research Council
Kingsley Dunham Centre
Keyworth
Nottingham
NG12 5GG
Tel: 0115 936 3100
Fax: 0115 936 3200
Internet: http://www.nkw.ac.uk/bgs/home.html
Contact: Mr A D Evans, Enquiries Officer
Founded: 1835
Publications: List of publications and maps
available
Previous names: Geological Survey of Great
Britain until 1965; Institute of Geological
Sciences until 1983.
Profile: The British Geological Survey is the
national centre for earth science information and
expertise. It is one of five centres and surveys of
the Natural Environment Research Council,
which is the lead body in the UK for research,
survey, monitoring and training in the
environmental sciences. BGS's work relates to
mineral, energy and groundwater resources, land
use, and geological hazards.

British Goat Society
34–36 Fore Street
Bovey Tracey
Newton Abbot
Devon
TQ13 9AD
Tel: 01626 833168
Fax: 01626 834536
Contact: Sue Knowles, Secretary
Founded: 1879
Membership: 1,500
Publications: Monthly journal; yearbook; herd book

British Goose Producers Association
Imperial House
15–19 Kingsway
London
WC2B 6UA
Tel: 0171 240 9889
Fax: 0171 240 7757
Contact: Lise Hartmann, Executive Officer
Profile: Membership includes breeders, rearers and processors of geese. Their role encompasses: consideration of legislation; advice to members on the effects of legislation; information on other subjects of interest and the promotion of the goose to the retail trade and consumers.

British Gotland Sheep Society
Roseland Farm
Redmoor
Bodmin
Cornwall
PL30 5AT
Tel: 01208 872448
Contact: Mr James Pedric

British Grassland Society
1 Earley Gate
University of Reading
Reading
RG6 6AT
Tel: 01734 318189
Fax: 01734 666941
Contact: Michael B Helps, Society Secretary
Founded: 1945
Membership: 1,000
Publications: Publications list available

British Growers Look Ahead
Agriculture House
Northgate
Uppingham
Rutland
LE15 9PL
Tel: 01541 565600
Fax: 01541 565601
Contact: Malcolm Taylor, Exhibition Director

Founded: 1965
Profile: The organisers of horticultural exhibitions: BGLA – held in February and the showcase event for the horticultural trade – source of all equipment, supplies and services; IFTEX – the International Flower and Plant Trades Exhibition, the only show of its kind for the cut flower sector in the UK; and, SWRG – the South West Regional Growers exhibition, a specialist trade show for growers in the south west.

British Hanoverian Horse Register
1 Hare Park
Allington Hill
Newmarket
Suffolk
CB8 0UW
Tel: 01638 570288
Contact: Miss JL Connaught-Bone, Registrar
Founded: 1980
Membership: 3,000
Profile: British Hanoverian Horse Register is purely a register of full and crossbred Hanoverians. The purpose of the register is to confirm registration details, aid identification at shows and at times of sale, aid the police should the need arise and provide a comprehensive record of vaccinations.

British Harness Racing Club
Burlington Crescent
Goole
East Yorkshire
DN14 5EG
Tel: 01405 766877
Fax: 01405 766878
Contact: Geraldine Berry, Administrator
Founded: 1969
Membership: 1,200
Publications: Harness Racing Calendar; BHRC Stud Book; BHRC Rule Book; British Racing and Trotting Records
Profile: The BHRC is the governing body for harness racing in this country and also represents Britain at the World Trotting Conference. It also aims to promote harness racing to a wider audience, and to encourage education and training with the NHETC.

British Hay and Straw Merchants Association
52 Park Meadow
Hatfield
Hertfordshire
AL9 5HB
Tel: 01707 268807
Fax: 01707 268807
Contact: Miss AR Dick, Secretary

Founded: 1919
Membership: 40
Profile: A trade association for the hay and straw trade.

British Hedgehog Preservation Society
Knowbury House
Knowbury
Ludlow
Shropshire
SY8 3LQ
Tel: 01584 890287
Contact: Pat Gifford
Founded: 1982
Membership: 10,500
Publications: Twice yearly newsletter; publications list available
Profile: The BHPS aims to encourage and give advice to the public about the care of hedgehogs, particularly when injured, sick, orphaned, treated cruelly or in any other danger; to assist in wildlife education, thereby encouraging the interest of young people in their indigenous wildlife, specifically hedgehogs; to fund serious research into hedgehog ethology and to ascertain the best methods of assisting their survival.

British Herb Trade Association
c/o NFU
164 Shaftesbury Avenue
London
WC2H 8HL
Tel: 0171 331 7281
Fax: 0171 331 7410
Contact: Rachel Moseley, Association Adviser
Founded: 1980
Membership: 75
Publications: Herb News
Profile: The BHTA is the key industrial association for British herb producers. It can help members with particular problems like VAT, pesticide legislation and legal matters or point them in the direction of sound advice. The association represents the interests of herb growers as a whole as well as offering individual benefits.

British Herdsmans Club
9 King's Meadow
Great Cornard
Sudbury
Suffolk
CO10 0HP
Tel: 01787 373137
Contact: Bernard Mulvaney, Honorary Secretary/Treasurer
Founded: 1894

Membership: 300
Publications: News and Views
Profile: Originally started to provide prizes for the winning herdsmen at the London Show. Local branches were formed and educational meetings were held in the winter months and farm walks in the summer. There is an annual rally where members compete in a 'Herdsman of the Year' competition.

British Herpetological Society
c/o Zoological Society
Regent's Park
London
NW1 4RY
Tel: 0181 452 9578
Contact: Mrs M Green, Secretary
Founded: 1947
Membership: 1,000
Publications: Herpetological Journal; Bulletin; Natterjack
Profile: The society was founded with the broad aim of catering for all interested in reptiles and amphibians. Four particular areas of activity have developed – Captive Breeding Committee; Research Committee; Education Committee (which runs the Young Herpetologist Club); and the Conservation Committee. It is the accepted authority on reptile and amphibian conservation in the UK. A number of nature reserves are owned or leased.

British Holstein Society
28 Worcester Road
Malvern
Worcestershire
WR14 4QW
Tel: 01684 565477
Fax: 01684 893290
Contact: Richard Evans, Breed Secretary
Founded: 1946
Membership: 3,000
Publications: British Holstein Journal
Profile: Founded in 1946 for the registration of Holstein cattle. The herd book presently registers approximately 30,000 cows per year. The society promotes the Holstein breed through its publications and show. It organises the National Holstein Show in February each year.

British Horse Society
British Equestrian Centre
Stoneleigh Park
Warwickshire
CV8 2LR
Tel: 01203 696697
Fax: 01203 692351
Email: mark@bhshorse.demon.co.uk

Contact: John Goldsmith, Director of Training and Education
Founded: 1947
Publications: British Horse (journal); BHS Members Yearbook
Profile: A charity for the welfare, care and use of the horse, encouraging horsemanship and the improvement of horse management and breeding and representing all equine interests. The BHS is the national governing body for dressage, eventing, endurance riding, horsedriving trials and vaulting. A major part of the National Equestrian Federation, the BHS is also the national body for qualifications to work in the horse industry.

British Horse Society Endurance Riding Group
British Horse Society
British Equestrian Centre
Stoneleigh Park
Warwickshire
CV8 2LR
Tel: 01203 696697
Fax: 01203 692351
Email: mark@bhhorse.demon.co.uk
Contact: Mrs Sandie Braund, Executive Secretary
Founded: 1976
Membership: 1,300
Publications: Bulletin (members newsletter); Omnibus Schedule (including rules)
Previous names: Long Distance Riding Group until 1990
Profile: In 1984 endurance riding came under the umbrella of the Federation Equestre International, thus giving the discipline full international status. The sport comprises riding over considerable distances (internationally 100 miles) over consecutive days. A test of stamina and courage for horse and rider. For the less ambitious, rides of 15 to 20 miles per day are organised. These are not races but must be ridden at a set speed and awards are made according to the condition of the horse at completion.

British Horseball Association
67 Clifford Road
New Barnet
Hertfordshire
EN5 5NZ
Tel: 0181 441 1799
Fax: 0181 441 1060
Contact: Jim Copeland, Chairman
Founded: 1991
Membership: 100
Publications: Members newsletter

Profile: The BHA is the governing body of horseball in Great Britain. It was formed to develop and regulate the game of horseball. It organises the league, championships, the national team and offers training to new clubs, referees etc.

British Horseracing Board
42 Portman Square
London
W1H 0EN
Tel: 0171 396 0011
Fax: 0171 935 3626
Contact: Simon Clare, Executive Assistant
Founded: 1993
Publications: Annual Report; Thrill of Ownership (brochure); Media Fact File
Profile: The British Horseracing Board is the governing authority for horseracing in Great Britain. Its principal responsibilities include the creation of the fixture list, race planning, marketing, finance, political lobbying, liaison with the betting industry and the development of the sport as a whole.

British Iceberg Growers Association
133 Eastgate
Louth
Lincolnshire
LN11 9QG
Tel: 01507 602427
Fax: 01507 600689
Contact: Mrs JA Dyas, Company Secretary
Founded: 1980
Profile: Marketing advice.

British Ile de France Sheep Society
Reagarth Farm
Helmsley
York
YO6 5HX
Tel: 01439 770284
Fax: 01439 770284
Contact: Christine Thompson, Secretary
Founded: 1978
Membership: 50
Profile: To promote and improve the Ile de France breed.

British Independent Fruit Growers Association
Broad Oak
Brenchley
Tonbridge
Kent
TN12 7NN
Tel: 01892 722080

Fax: 01892 724540
Contact: J Perry, Secretary
Founded: 1988
Membership: 285
Profile: The aims of the association are to enable independent growers to join together and use their collective strength for the benefit of the individual member and the industry as a whole.

British Institute of Agricultural Consultants
The Estate Office
Torry Hill
Milstead
Sittingbourne
Kent
ME9 0SP
Tel: 01795 830100
Fax: 01795 830243
Contact: Anthony Hyde, Chief Executive
Founded: 1957
Membership: 250
Publications: Directory of Members; Directory of Expert Witness Consultants; Directory of International Consultants
Profile: The British Institute of Agricultural Consultants is a professional association of independent qualified specialists. Members' skills and expertise cover a wide range of activities in agriculture, horticulture, forestry and related sciences which have an application in the countryside. Members are bound by the rigidly enforced Code of Professional Conduct of the Institute and also by the codes of conduct of other professional bodies of which they may also be members.

British Institute of Golf Course Architects
Merrist Wood House
Worplesdon
Guildford
Surrey
GU3 3PE
Contact: SR Gidman, Secretary
Founded: 1971
Membership: 45
Publications: Annual yearbook
Profile: The institute was founded in 1971 to encourage the highest standards of golf course design and construction and to encourage a full knowledge and understanding of the historic principles of golf and golf course architecture. It also aims to promote the best interests of members' clients and to support research and development in any matter affecting the practice of golf course architecture, construction and maintenance.

British Isles Bee Breeders Association
11 Thomson Drive
Codnor
Ripley
Derbyshire
DE5 9RU
Tel: 01773 745287
Fax: 01773 570461
Email: aknight@blackgold.win-uk.net
Contact: Albert Knight, Secretary
Founded: 1964
Membership: 480
Publications: Publications list available
Previous names: Village Bee Breeders Association
Profile: BIBBA is an organisation of beekeepers both large and small who seek to improve the standard of beekeeping in the British Isles, by the restoration and improvement of the native bee of the British Isles. Our native honeybee, the Dark European honeybee, is the predominant strain of honeybee in these islands in spite of imports of other European sub-species. This sub-species is preferred to others because of its ability to cope with our damp maritime climate, a character developed over thousands of years by pressures of the environment.

British Kerry Cattle Society
Blair
Achiltibuie
Ullapool
Ross-Shire
IV26 2YW
Tel: 01854 622262
Contact: Miss MRC Leslie, Honorary Secretary
Founded: 1892
Membership: 40
Publications: Members newsletter
Previous names: English Kerry and Dexter Cattle Society until 1924
Profile: The society exists to keep contact among members and breeders and to promote and provide information about the Kerry as a hardy, thrifty, easy calving, smallish dairy animal, suitable as a house cow etc. (since 1966 it keeps no herd book, registrations being made now in the Irish Herd Book).

British Kune Kune Pigs Society
Holly Bank
Duddon Common
Tarporley
Cheshire
CW6 0HG
Tel: 01829 781567
Fax: 01829 261311
Contact: Zoe Lindop, Secretary

Founded: 1993
Membership: 50
Publications: Newsletter
Profile: The society was formed in 1993 by a small group of Kune Kune owners. The aims are to promote the breeding, welfare and interests of the Kune Kune pigs in Britain and to give help and advice to owners and breeders. The society also aims to produce a herd book.

British Lawn Mower Racing Association Ltd
Hunt Cottage
Wisborough Green
Billinghurst
West Sussex
RH14 0HN
Tel: 01403 700220
Fax: 01403 700037
Contact: Jim Gavin, General Secretary
Founded: 1973
Membership: 200
Publications: Cuttings (members newsletter)
Profile: The organisation aims to provide keen, well organised and inexpensive motor sport in a daft sort of way. The association is non-profit making and any monies made are given to charities or good causes. Lawn mower racing is an amateur sport, although Stirling Moss has won the British Grand Prix for mowers and the annual 12 hour race!

British Lichen Society
c/o Department of Botany
Natural History Museum
Cromwell Road
London
SW7 5BD
Tel: 0171 938 8852
Fax: 0171 938 9260
Contact: Dr OW Purvis
Founded: 1958
Membership: 550
Publications: Lichenologist

British Lime Association
BACMI
156 Buckingham Palace Road
London
SW1W 9TR
Tel: 0171 730 8194
Fax: 0171 730 4355
Contact: FN Leitch, Secretary
Founded: 1989
Membership: 7
Publications: Lime Stabilisation Manual; Lime Washes; Quality Building with Lime Mortars
Profile: BLA represents the UK lime industry in discussions with government and on BSI and CEN Standards Committees. BLA is a member of the International Lime Association and the European Lime Association.

British Limousin Cattle Society Ltd
Avenue Q
National Agricultural Centre
Stoneleigh Park
Warwickshire
CV8 2RA
Tel: 01203 696500
Fax: 01203 696716
Contact: Mr Iain Kerr, Breed Secretary
Founded: 1971
Membership: 2,000
Publications: Studbook and Factfinder; newspaper
Profile: To promote the Limousin breed of cattle. Registering 11,500 cattle per year from 2,000 members. Organising society sales at six different markets throughout the UK.

British Lipizzaner Horse Society
Ausdan Stud
Glynarthen
Llandysul
SA44 6PB
Tel: 01239 810433
Fax: 01239 810433
Contact: Miss LD Moran

British Llama Society
37 Ashfield Avenue
Lancaster
Lancashire
Profile: We have been unable to contact this organisation. The details given are unconfirmed.

British Lop Pig Society
Wenfork Farm
Treburley
Launceston
Cornwall
PL15 9NU
Tel: 01579 370503
Contact: Mrs Sue Collins, Secretary
Founded: 1920
Profile: The society aims to promote the British Lop as a pure pedigree breed which possesses all the qualities anyone could ask of a pig.

British Meat Information Service
Meat and Livestock Commission
26 Fitzroy Square
London
W1P 6BT

Tel: 0171 388 7421
Fax: 0171 388 7761
Contact: Vanessa Saull
Publications: Free booklets and leaflets
Profile: A responsive information service on behalf of the Meat and Livestock Commission.

British Meat Manufacturers Association

19 Cornwall Terrace
London
NW1 4QP
Tel: 0171 935 7980
Fax: 0171 487 4734
Contact: Mr PJ Mobsby, Director
Founded: 1908
Membership: 100
Publications: Publication list available
Previous names: Sausage Manufacturers Association until 1976; Bacon and Meat Manufacturers Association until 1989
Profile: BMMA is an experienced and professional organisation dedicated to the protection and advancement of British companies manufacturing meat products and other prepared foods.

British Merino Sheep Society

Merino Centre
Youngman's Road
Wymondham
Norfolk
NR18 0RR
Tel: 01953 601233
Fax: 01953 607626
Contact: Mr Johnathan Barber, Chairman
Founded: 1989

British Milksheep Society

The Row
Roweltown
Carlisle
Cumbria
Tel: 016977 48217
Contact: Chris Parsons, Secretary
Founded: 1970
Profile: The British Milksheep Society aims to promote the breed within the UK and abroad. It aims to assist breeders to continue to breed high performance stock and to monitor these aims.

British Miniature Horse Society

Howick Farm
The Haven
Billinghurst
West Sussex
RH14 9BQ
Tel: 01403 822639

Contact: Mrs Tikki Adorian, Chairman
Founded: 1992
Membership: 250
Publications: Annual booklet; information leaflets
Profile: The BMHS was founded to promote and register British Miniature Horses. The society works with the British Horse Society on giving welfare advice to miniature horse owners. The society arranges exhibits, seminars and lectures.

British Morgan Horse Society

PO Box 155
Godalming
Surrey
GU8 5YE
Tel: 01483 861283
Fax: 01483 861283
Email: Morgans@CIX.compulink.co.uk
Contact: Miss Quita King, Chairman
Founded: 1975
Membership: 170
Profile: The BMHS was founded in 1975 to promote the Morgan Horse in Britain. The BMHS has full reciprocity with the American Morgan Horse Association and all Morgans in Britain must be registered with the BMHS Registry. There are around 400 registered Morgans in Britain and the society is dedicated to promoting the versatility of the breed. The BMHS runs shows, clinics and events throughout the year.

British Mountain Bike Federation

36 Rockingham Road
Kettering
Northamptonshire
NN16 8HG
Profile: We have been unable to contact this organisation. The details given are unconfirmed.

British Mountaineering Council

177–179 Burton Road
Manchester
M20 2BB
Tel: 0161 445 4747
Fax: 0161 445 4500
Email: bmc_hq@cix.compulink.co.uk
Contact: Jeremy Barlow, Access and Conservation Officer
Founded: 1944
Membership: 30,000
Publications: Summit Magazine
Profile: The BMC is a representative body that exists to protect the interests of climbers, hillwalkers and mountaineers. The BMC campaigns for greater rights of access and the protection of the crag and mountain environment.

British Mule Society

Hope Mount Farm
Top of Hope
Alstonfield
Ashbourne
Derbyshire
DE6 2FR
Tel: 01335 310353
Contact: Mrs Lorraine V Travis, Honorary
Secretary
Founded: 1978
Membership: 260
Publications: The Mule (quarterly members
journal); Introduction to the Mule (booklet)
Profile: A small, friendly society whose main aim
is to educate members – and the general public –
about all aspects of mules – practical, historical,
scientific, etc. Besides mule owners, members
include soldiers, historians, vets, smallholders
and many who are solely interested in learning
more about these fascinating animals. Many
contacts with related organisations in the UK and
overseas.

British Mycological Society

PO Box 30
Stourbridge
West Midlands
DY9 9PZ
Tel: 01562 887043
Fax: 01562 887043
Email: mosss@biol.port.ac.uk
Contact: Dr Stephen T Moss, Honorary Secretary
Founded: 1896
Membership: 1,961
Publications: Mycologist; Mycological Research;
members newsletter; symposium volumes
Profile: The British Mycological Society has
members from all over the world. Its objective is
to promote mycology in all its aspects by
publications, meetings and such other means as
it shall deem appropriate. Areas of interest
include macrofungi, microfungi, lichens, yeast,
medical and veterinary fungi, mycorrhizas, plant
pathogenci fungi, arthropophilic fungi, aquatic
fungi, wood decay fungi and conservation. A
library, a fungal database and a photographic
library exist.

British Naturalist's Association

1 Bracken Mews
Chingford
London
E4 7HE
Contact: Mrs June Pearton, General Secretary
Founded: 1905
Publications: Country-Side (members
newsletter)

Previous names: British Empire Naturalist's
Association
Profile: Founded by E.Kay Robinson in 1905
when he published a penny paper called
'Country-Side' to encourage the interests and
bring into contact with each other UK and
overseas nature lovers. Today the association
encourages and supports schemes and
legislation for the protection of the country's
natural resources and organises meetings,
field weeks, lectures and exhibitions to extend
and popularise the study of nature. The
association encourages the furtherance of
education and understanding of the
environment.

British Normandy Cattle Society

Crib Barton
River Corner
Sturminster Newton
Dorset
DT10 2AE
Tel: 01258 472549
Fax: 01258 471212
Contact: Geoffrey E Clacy, Secretary
Founded: 1973
Membership: 29
Publications: Quarterly magazine (French);
quarterly newsletter (English)
Profile: The British Normandy Cattle Society
was formed on 7th March 1973, but
importation difficulties precluded it from
achieving its full potential. Scientific
developments in the cattle breeding industries
and the opening up of the EEC marketing
areas has made it possible for the Society to
make a new start in 1994 to realise its full
potential in developing the breed and offering
herd book facilities to the Normandy breeders
in the UK.

British Nutrition Foundation

High Holborn House
52–54 High Holborn
London
WC1V 6RQ
Tel: 0171 404 6504
Fax: 0171 404 6747
Contact: Mr NS Porter, Company Secretary
Founded: 1967
Publications: BNF Bulletin; briefing papers;
conference proceedings; Task Force reports
Profile: An impartial scientific charity providing
independent balanced information on nutritional
matters with a view to the improvement of the
health of the consumer.

British Oat and Barley Millers Association
6 Catherine Street
London
WC2B 5JJ
Tel: 0171 836 2460
Fax: 0171 836 0580
Contact: Flora A McLean, Executive Secretary
Profile: BOBMA represents millers of oats and barley in the UK. Members of BOBMA are concerned to ensure future steady supplies of home grown oats for the milling industry and are committed to growing contracts with farmers to promote stability and confidence in the market. The association is concerned with the production of oat and barley products, primarily for human consumption.

British Oldenburg Sheep Society
Nackington Farms
Farm Office
Nackington
Canterbury
Kent
CT4 7AF
Contact: MJ Munford, Honorary Secretary
Profile: We have been unable to contact this organisation. The details given are unconfirmed.

British Onion Growers' Association
The Pack House Store
Ringmore Road
Southery
Downham Market
Norfolk
PE38 0NJ
Tel: 01366 377432
Fax: 01366 377432
Contact: Mrs Francis, Secretary

British Onion Producers Association
133 Eastgate
Louth
Lincolnshire
LN11 9QG
Tel: 01507 602427
Fax: 01507 600689
Contact: Mrs JA Dyas, Company Secretary
Founded: 1980
Membership: 80
Profile: Marketing information.

British Organic Farmers
Soil Association
86 Colston Road
Bristol
Avon
BS1 5BB
Tel: 0117 929 9666
Fax: 0117 925 2504
Email: soilassoc@gn.apc.org
Profile: The producers' wing of the Soil Association – they run seminars, farm walks and conferences and represent producer interests to the authorities.

British Orienteering Federation
Riversdale
Dale Road North
Darleydale
Matlock
Derbyshire
DE4 2HX
Tel: 01629 734042
Fax: 01629 733769
Contact: Neil Cameron, Secretary General
Founded: 1971
Membership: 7,000
Publications: BOF Bulletin; Compass Sport; numerous leaflets
Profile: BOF is the British national governing body for the sport of orienteering, a sport requiring high levels of skill and fitness that involves competitors navigating as fast as they can over unfamiliar terrain. BOF has twelve associations and approximately 150 local clubs. Land access is arranged between the local club hosting an event and the relevant land owner(s).

British Ornithologists Union
Zoological Museum
Akeman Street
Tring
Hertfordshire
HP23 6AP
Tel: 01442 890080
Fax: 01442 890693
Contact: Mrs Gwen Bonham, Administrative Secretary
Founded: 1858
Membership: 2,000
Publications: IBIS
Profile: Aims to encourage the study of birds throughout the world, in order to understand their biology and to aid their conservation. In pursuit of this aim the union supports scientific ornithology by providing financial assistance in the form of research grants, by organising conferences, publishing checklists, books and its journal, IBIS.

British Palomino Society
Penrhiwllan
Llandysul
SA44 5NZ

Tel: 01239 851387
Fax: 01239 851040

British Parthenais Cattle Society
Housham Farm
Hives Lane
North Scarle
Lincolnshire
LN6 9HA
Tel: 01522 778359
Contact: Mrs Brenda Popplewell, Honorary
Secretary
Founded: 1988
Membership: 15
Profile: The society promotes the breeding of
high quality, easy calving, docile cattle with a high
killing out percentage. Cattle which produce lean,
yet marbled, meat much in demand in the
restaurants of Paris.

British Percheron Horse Society
The White House
South Harting
Petersfield
Hampshire
GU31 5PZ
Tel: 01730 814185
Fax: 01730 825061
Contact: Miss Beatrice Potter, Secretary
Founded: 1918
Profile: A breed society involved in the
promotion of the Percheron horse.

British Photovoltaic Society
The Warren
Bramshill Road
Eversley
Hampshire
RG27 0PR
Tel: 01734 730073
Fax: 01734 730820
Email: itpower@gn.apc.org
Contact: Jenny Gregory, Secretary General
Founded: 1992
Membership: 40
Publications: Publications list available
Profile: PV-UK was formed in 1992 to further the
development and use of PV both within the UK
and in export markets. Amongst the 40 members
there are companies which manufacture PV
modules, a number of companies representing
overseas module manufacturers and systems
houses supplying mainly the home market.

British Piemontese Cattle Society
41 Bank Street
Carlisle
Cumbria

CA3 8HJ
Tel: 01228 34423
Fax: 01228 818022
Contact: FC Culley, Secretary
Founded: 1988
Membership: 101
Publications: Members newsletter
Profile: The Piemontese society manages its
own herd book of Piemontese cattle as well as
promoting the breed throughout the UK. There
has been some assistance in research of the
breed and further work is expected in the future.

British Pig Association
7 Rickmansworth Road
Watford
Hertfordshire
WD1 7HE
Tel: 01923 234377
Fax: 01923 211924
Contact: GE Welsh, Secretary
Founded: 1882
Publications: Pig Industry; herd book
Previous names: National Pig Breeders'
Association until 1991; British Pig Breeders'
Association until 1995

British Pinzgauer Cattle Society
Manor Farm
Chadwick Lane
Knowle
Solihull
B93 0AS
Tel: 01564 772922
Profile: We have been unable to contact this
organisation. The details given are unconfirmed.

British Polwarth Sheep Breeders Association
Quercus Bluff
Painswick
Gloucestershire
GL6 6SN
Tel: 01452 613433
Contact: DL Murray

**British Poultry Breeders and Hatcheries
  Association**
Imperial House
15–19 Kingsway
London
WC2B 6UA
Tel: 0171 240 9889
Fax: 0171 240 7757
Contact: Lise Hartmann, Executive Officer
Profile: Membership of breeders, hatcheries and
flock farmers. Their role is consideration of
legislation; advice to members on effects of

legislation; information on other subjects of interest.

British Poultry Meat Federation
Imperial House
15–19 Kingsway
London
WC2B 6UA
Tel: 0171 240 9889
Fax: 0171 240 7757
Contact: Peter Bradnock, Director General

British Quality Assured Pig Initiative
Winterhill House
Snowdon Drive
Milton Keynes
Buckinghamshire
MK6 1BE
Tel: 01908 235580
Contact: Tim Green, Administrator
Founded: 1994
Publications: The Standard

British Quarter Horse Association Ltd
2 Tile Farm Road
Orpington
Kent
BR6 9RZ
Tel: 01689 855 021
Fax: 01689 855 021
Contact: Mrs V Copper, Secretary
Founded: 1974
Membership: 500
Publications: Quarterly newsletter
Profile: An organisation set up to promote the breeding of American Quarter Horses in Great Britain. Affiliated to the American Quarter Horse Association in the USA. The society is supported in its premium breeding scheme by the Horse Race Betting Levy Board from which it receives an annual grant. It also supports major Quarter Horse shows throughout the country and holds the largest event – the British Quarter Horse Association Breed Show in July.

British Rabbit Council
Purefoy House
7 Kirkgate
Newark on Trent
Nottinghamshire
NG24 1AD
Tel: 01636 76042
Fax: 01636 611681
Contact: Mrs Jo Jalland, Secretary
Founded: 1934
Membership: 5,000
Publications: Yearbook

Profile: To protect, further and co-ordinate the interests of all British rabbit breeders, to assist and extend the exhibition of rabbits, to influence, advise and co-operate with central and local authorities, departments, education and other committees and schools in promoting the extension of the breeding of rabbits and to promote and encourage education and research of a scientific and/or practical nature for the welfare and benefit of the rabbit.

British Racing School
Snailwell Road
Newmarket
Suffolk
CB8 7NU
Tel: 01638 665103
Fax: 01638 560929
Contact: WR MacDonald, Director
Founded: 1983
Profile: The British Racing School is an Approved Training Provider involved in professional training for the horseracing industry. This includes NVQs in racehorse care and training for professional and amateur jockeys. The school was a winner of a National Training Award in 1994 and achieved recognition as an Investor in People in 1995.

British Reed Growers Association
c/o Francis Hornor and Son
Old Bank of England Court
Queen Street
Norwich
Norfolk
NR2 4TA
Tel: 01603 629871
Fax: 01603 760756
Contact: Charles Cator, Chairman
Founded: 1960
Membership: 50
Publications: Reed Bed Management; leaflets and pamphlets
Previous names: Norfolk Reed Growers Association until 1964
Profile: To promote the production of reed in the UK through sound management guidelines; to produce quality reed for the thatching industry; to provide information to encourage public awareness of conservation and commercial benefits of reed bed management and to co-ordinate the marketing, production and awareness of this rural enterprise.

British Romagnola Cattle Society
26 York Place
Perth
PH2 8EH

Tel: 01738 623780
Fax: 01738 621206

British Rouge de l'Ouest Sheep Society
Yockenthwaite
Buckden
Skipton
West Yorkshire
BD23 5JH
Tel: 01756 760373
Fax: 01756 760373
Contact: Mrs E Hird, Secretary
Profile: A breed society to promote the Rouge de l'Ouest breed of sheep.

British Saanen Breed Society
British Goat Society
The Fisheries
Colesbridge Lane
Chorleywood
Hertfordshire
WD3 5SS
Tel: 01923 282611
Contact: Mrs Claire Barlow, Secretary
Founded: 1980
Membership: 70
Publications: Breed booklet; Stud Male List; quarterly members newsletter
Profile: Objective of the society is to maintain and improve the standards of the British Saanen breed of goat as a high quality milking animal of good conformation.

British Self Catering Federation
6 St Anthony's Road
Bournemouth
Dorset
BH2 6PD
Tel: 01202 295959
Fax: 01202 295959
Contact: Shane Busby, Chief Executive
Founded: 1986
Membership: 80
Publications: Newsletter
Profile: Founded to represent operators of self catering establishments (excluding caravans, houseboats and mobile homes). Consulted by BTA/ETB and government departments, members of Joint Hospitality Industry Congress.

British Sheep Dairying Association
Wield Wood
Arlesford
Hampshire
SO24 9RU
Tel: 01420 563151
Fax: 01420 561018
Contact: Mrs Olivia Mills, Honorary Secretary

Membership: 370
Publications: Sheep Dairy News

British Shooting Sports Council
4 Belgrave Avenue
New Mill
Huddersfield
West Yorkshire
HD7 7DP
Profile: We have been unable to contact this organisation. The details given are unconfirmed.

British Show Hack, Cob and Riding Horse Association
Chamberlain House
Chamberlain Walk
88 High Street
Coleshill
Birmingham
B46 3BZ
Tel: 01675 466211
Fax: 01675 466242
Contact: Mrs P Jones, Secretary
Founded: 1920
Membership: 1,300
Publications: Rule Book, show date booklet, newsletters
Profile: The association aims to improve the standard of hacks, cobs and riding horses and encourage their breeding. Also to encourage shows to affiliate to the association, abide by its rules and to endeavour to safeguard the interests of members in every way possible. There are classes for everyone from the fun rider to the professional. All newcomers are welcomed and encouraged.

British Show Jumping Association
British Equestrian Centre
National Agricultural Centre
Stoneleigh Park
Warwickshire
CV8 2LR
Tel: 01203 696516
Fax: 01203 696685
Contact: Jacky Knightley, Marketing Manager
Founded: 1925
Membership: 14,940
Profile: The BSJA is the governing body of show jumping in Great Britain, formulating the rules and codes of practice for our competitions. Their purpose is to improve and maintain standards of showjumping while encouraging riders of all standards at all levels to enjoy fair competition over safe and attractive courses.

British Show Pony Society
124 Green End Road
Sawtry
Huntingdon
Cambridgeshire
PE17 5XA
Tel: 01487 831376
Fax: 01487 832779
Contact: Breed Secretary

British Simmental Cattle Society Ltd
National Agricultural Centre
Stoneleigh Park
Warwickshire
CV8 2LR
Tel: 01203 696513
Fax: 01203 696724
Contact: DS Gaunt, Chief Executive
Founded: 1970
Membership: 1,800
Publications: Annual Review; commercial and technical literature
Profile: The British Simmental Cattle Society represents the interest of all pedigree Simmental members in the UK. It is one of the country's leading beef breeds. It has a high profile in both the pedigree and commercial beef industry, with an extensive programme of pedigree and commercial breeding sales with major sponsorship and support from leading agricultural companies in the UK. It is an innovative and visionary organisation and has set the trend for many of the pedigree industry's developments.

British Skewbald and Piebald Association
West Fen House
High Road
Little Downham
Ely
Cambridgeshire
CB6 2TB
Tel: 01353 699430
Fax: 01353 699430
Contact: Linda Hutchinson, Secretary
Founded: 1989
Membership: 1,000
Publications: Members' handbook; quarterly newsletter
Profile: Aims to promote interest and pleasure in skewbalds and piebalds; to promote the status of skewbalds and piebalds by helping members to maximise their potential and to promote the welfare of all horses and ponies.

British Small Animal Veterinary Association
Kingsley House
Church Lane

Shurdington
Cheltenham
Gloucestershire
GL51 5TQ
Tel: 01242 862994
Fax: 01242 863009
Contact: P Harvey Locke, Honorary Secretary
Membership: 4,200
Publications: Publications list available

British Snail Farmers Association
Barrow Farm
Rode Hill Road
Somerset
BA3 6PS
Profile: We have been unable to contact this organisation. The details given are unconfirmed.

British Society for Plant Pathology
PBI Cambridge
Maris Lane
Trumpington
Cambridgeshire
CB2 2LQ
Tel: 01223 840411
Fax: 01223 844425
Email: Graham.J.Jellis@PBIGB.Sprint.com
Contact: Professor Graham J Jellis, Secretary
Founded: 1981
Membership: 700
Publications: Plant Pathology; BSPP Newsletter; publications list available
Previous names: Federation of British Plant Pathologists until 1981
Profile: Founded for the study and advancement of plant pathology in the UK and overseas. Meetings (paper-reading, poster sessions, discussions, workshops and visits to research establishments) held regularly. The BSPP fosters the professional interests of plant pathologists and publishes widely. It provides grants for travel, to meetings and to other research establishments and for undergraduate vacation placements.

British Society of Animal Science
PO Box 3
Penicuik
Midlothian
EH26 0RZ
Tel: 0131 445 4508
Fax: 0131 535 3120
Email: BSAS@ed.sac.ac.uk
Contact: Mr MA Steele, Secretary
Founded: 1943
Membership: 1,290
Publications: Animal Science; occasional publications; publications list available

Previous names: British Society of Animal Production until 1994
Profile: The membership is drawn from research, education, advisory work, industry and farming covering a wide range of interests. The main objective is to provide opportunities for those interested in science and its application to animal production to meet and exchange information, ideas and experiences. The society is consulted by the government on various aspects of animal science.

British Society of Dowsers
Sycamore Barn
Hastingleigh
Ashford
Kent
TN25 5HW
Tel: 01233 750253
Fax: 01233 750253
Contact: Deidre Rust, Assistant Secretary
Founded: 1933
Membership: 1,200
Publications: Journal of the British Society of Dowsers
Profile: The society was established to: encourage the study and advancement of the knowledge of the scientific principles of dowsing including the knowledge of its application to the search for subterranean watercourses, cavities, tunnels, ores and other entities, concealed by natural or artificial means; the diagnosis of disease and restoration of health in human beings, trees and plants to the improvement of agriculture; the quest for lost and missing objects animate and inanimate – in so far as such objects may be charitable.

British Society of Plant Breeders Ltd
Woolpack Chambers
Market Street
Ely
Cambridgeshire
CB7 4ND
Tel: 01353 664211
Fax: 01353 661156
Contact: Ms Carol James, Administration Manager

British Society of Soil Science
Department of Soil Science
University of Reading
Whiteknights
PO Box 233
Reading
RG6 6DW
Tel: 01734 316559
Fax: 01734 316660
Email: s.nortcliff@reading.ac.uk

Contact: Dr Stephen Nortcliff, Honorary Secretary
Founded: 1947
Membership: 950
Publications: European Journal of Soil Science; Soil Use and Management
Profile: To promote an understanding of soil and soil processes and an awareness of the importance of soils in many aspects of our lives.

British Sports and Allied Industries Federation
Federation House
National Agricultural Centre
Stoneleigh Park
Warwickshire
CV8 2RF
Tel: 01203 414999
Fax: 01203 414990
Contact: Dr John Hooper, Chief Executive
Founded: 1918
Membership: 450
Publications: BSAIF Update; members newsletter
Profile: BSAIF is Europe's largest and fastest growing sports trade federation and represents the interests of the sports goods and equipment industry in the UK and includes virtually the whole industry within its membership. The federation is the umbrella organisation for 19 trade associations.

British Sports Horse Register
c/o Shorthorn Cattle Society
4th Street
National Agricultural Centre
Stoneleigh Park
Warwickshire
CV8 2LG

British Spotted Pony Society
Hollygate House
Ridlington
Leicestershire
LE15 9AU
Tel: 01572 821781
Fax: 01572 821781
Contact: Julie Allen, Secretary and Registrar
Founded: 1947
Membership: 250
Publications: Tri-annual newsletter
Previous names: British Spotted Horse and Pony Society until 1976

British Standards Institution
British Standards House
389 Chiswick High Street
London

W4 4AL
Tel: 0181 996 9000
Fax: 0181 996 7400

British Stickmakers Guild
44a Eccles Road
Chapel-en-le-Frith
High Peak
Derbyshire
SK12 6RG
Tel: 01298 815291
Contact: Brian Aries, Secretary
Founded: 1984
Membership: 1,200
Publications: The Stickmaker
Profile: The British Stickmakers Guild was formed in 1984 to bring together the many people practising this craft. The BSG stages the British and UK National Open Stickmaking Championship each year holding 35 shows throughout the UK. The Stickmaker magazine is the cornerstone of the BSG and is sent free to all members. The guild provides courses in stickmaking by their experts. The only qualification for membership of BSG is an interest in the subject.

**British Sugar Beet Seed Producers
    Association**
23 New Road
Spalding
Lincolnshire
PE11 1DH
Tel: 01775 722261
Fax: 01775 767525
Contact: Anthony P Withyman, Secretary

British Sugar plc
Associated British Foods plc
Oundle Road
Peterborough
PE2 9QU
Tel: 01733 63171
Contact: Geoff Lancaster, Head of Communications
Founded: 1936
Publications: British Sugar Beet Review
Profile: Until the 1930s Britain's sugar beet crop was processed by 13 autonomous companies in 18 factories throughout the country in an unplanned and unco-ordinated operation. In 1936 those factories were amalgamated by an Act of Parliament to form the British Sugar Corporation to manage the entire domestic crop. British Sugar provides more than half the country's needs from home grown sugar beet.

British Tersk Society
Loch Ness Riding Centre
Dores
Inverness-Shire
IV1 2TX
Tel: 01463 751251
Fax: 01463 751240
Contact: C Cameron

British Texel Sheep Society Ltd
National Agricultural Centre
Stoneleigh Park
Warwickshire
CV8 2LG
Tel: 01203 696629
Fax: 01203 696472
Contact: Mr Steven McLean, Breed Director
Founded: 1974
Membership: 2,700
Publications: Annual journal; Texel Times; Sire Register
Profile: The largest sheep breed society in the UK with a primary objective of expanding the use of Texel terminal sires in the UK's commercial sheep flocks.

British Timber Merchants' Association
Stocking Lane
Hughenden Valley
High Wycombe
Buckinghamshire
HP14 4JZ
Tel: 01494 563602
Fax: 01494 565487
Contact: Sherman Chatha, BTMA Secretariat
Founded: 1917
Membership: 105
Publications: Buyers and Specifiers Guide; members newsletter; advisory notes
Previous names: Federated Home Timber Merchants' Association until 1966; Home Grown Timber Merchants' Association of England and Wales until 1977
Profile: An organisation which claims to have all sides of the timber industry including hardwood and softwood sawmillers, round and sawn timber merchants, specialist fencing producers and paper, board and chipboard mills and agents within its membership. The association has representatives serving on all the committees and institutions affecting the industry and it is therefore able to monitor and influence matters which are of concern to its members and to the British timber trade as a whole.

British Tourist Authority
Thames Tower
Black's Road

Hammersmith
London
W6 9EL
Tel: 0181 846 9000
Fax: 0181 563 0302
Contact: Jonathan Griffin, Director of
Commercial Services
Founded: 1969
Publications: Publications list available
Profile: Government agency responsible for the
promotion of Britain to tourists from overseas.

British Tractor Pullers Association
3 Whittle Close
Henlow
Bedfordshire
SG16 6JB
Tel: 01462 816436
Fax: 01462 816436
Profile: We have been unable to contact this
organisation. The details given are unconfirmed.

British Trout Association Ltd
8/9 Lambton Place
London
W11 2SH
Tel: 0171 221 6065
Fax: 0171 221 6049
Contact: Caroline Sutcliffe, General Secretary
Founded: 1984
Membership: 125
Profile: Trade association for UK trout farmers
covering all aspects of technical, research,
legislation and generic promotion.

British Trout Farmers' Restocking Association
Allenbrook Trout Farm
Lumber Lane
Brockington
Wimborne St Giles
Dorset
BH21 5LT
Tel: 01725 517369
Fax: 01725 517769
Contact: T Whyatt, Honorary Secretary
Founded: 1932

British Trust for Conservation Volunteers
36 St Mary's Street
Wallingford
Oxfordshire
OX10 0EU
Tel: 01491 839766
Fax: 01491 839646
Contact: Emily Mason, Information Officer
Founded: 1959
Membership: 83,000

Publications: The Conserver; Local Action;
Global Action; list of handbooks available
Profile: BTCV is the UK's largest practical
conservation charity, supporting people in steps
to improve their local environment. The
organisation has over 100 offices throughout
England, Wales and Northern Ireland which
organise a wide range of conservation
volunteering opportunities such as conservation
working holidays, weekend and day projects. It
runs over 150 training courses each year
covering all aspects of practical conservation.
BTCV also provides information, advice and
training to support 2,000 affiliated local
community and school groups.

**British Trust for Conservation Volunteers/
Gwarchodwyr Cefn Gwlad**
British Trust for Conservation Volunteers
Wales Regional Office
The Conservation Centre
Forest Farm Road
Whitchurch
Cardiff
CF4 7JH
Tel: 01222 520990
Fax: 01222 522181
Email: BTCV-WALES@dial.pipex.com
Contact: Anne Cowell, Regional Administrator
for Wales
Founded: 1959
Membership: 14,000
Publications: Publications list available

British Trust for Ornithology
National Centre for Ornithology
The Nunnery
Nunnery Place
Thetford
Norfolk
IP24 2PU
Tel: 01842 750050
Fax: 01842 750030
Contact: Claire Forrest, Research Contracts
Assistant
Founded: 1933
Membership: 10,000
Publications: BTO News; Bird Study; catalogue
of books and reports available
Profile: The British Trust for Ornithology is
Britain's foremost bird research organisation. It
has a staff of 60 personnel based in Thetford,
Norfolk who carry out a wide range of research
on Britain's birds with the help of a large network
of volunteers. The BTO's mission is to promote
the wider understanding, appreciation and
conservation of birds through objective scientific

studies. It places great emphasis on sound research which leads to well-informed decisions by developers, planners, conservationists and others.

British Turf and Landscape Irrigation Association

Myerscough College
Bilsborrow
Preston
Lancashire
PR3 0RY
Tel: 01995 640611
Contact: David G Halford, Secretary

British Turkey Federation

Imperial House
15–19 Kingsway
London
WC2B 6UA
Tel: 0171 240 9889
Fax: 0171 240 7757
Contact: Lise Hartmann, Executive Officer
Publications: Market reports; recipe leaflets
Profile: Membership includes breeders, rearers and processors of turkey in the UK. Their role is in the consideration of legislation, advice, information on other subjects of interest, and promotion of turkey to retailers and consumers.

British Turkey Information Service

Glen House
125 Old Brompton Road
London
SW7 3RP
Tel: 0171 244 7701
Fax: 0171 244 8385

British Vendeen Sheep Society

20 Brookfield Drive
Wolvey
Hinckley
Leicestershire
LE10 3LT
Tel: 01455 220456
Fax: 01455 220456
Contact: Adrian Tidswell, Secretary
Founded: 1982
Membership: 75
Publications: Vendeen Vision; flock book
Profile: The society was formed to improve and expand the stocks of Vendeen sheep in the UK. The society is administered by a council of up to 12 elected members. There is a part-time secretary.

British Veterinary Association

7 Mansfield Street
London
W1M 0AT
Tel: 0171 636 6541
Fax: 0171 436 2970
Contact: Rebecca Snow, Company Services
Founded: 1880
Membership: 9,000
Publications: The Veterinary Record; In Practice; Research in Veterinary Science; You and Your Vet
Previous names: National Veterinary Medical Association until 1952
Profile: BVA is the national representative body for the veterinary profession. BVA's chief interests are standards of animal health, veterinary surgeon's working practices, professional standards and quality of service and relationships with external bodies, particularly government. BVA's three main objectives are policy development, protecting and promoting the profession and provision of services to BVA members.

British Veterinary Hospitals Association

Oakbeck Veterinary Hospital
Oakbeck Way
Skipton
Harrogate
North Yorkshire
HG1 3HU
Tel: 01423 561414
Fax: 01423 521550
Contact: RD Partridge, Honorary Secretary
Founded: 1971

British Veterinary Nursing Association Ltd

D12 The Seedbed Centre
Coldharbour Road
Harlow
Essex
CM19 5AF
Tel: 01279 450567
Fax: 01279 420866
Contact: Secretary
Founded: 1965
Membership: 2,500
Publications: Veterinary Nursing Journal
Previous names: British Veterinary Nursing Association until 1995
Profile: The British Veterinary Nursing Association was founded in 1965 and aims to foster and promote the standard of veterinary nursing and provide help and advice to persons wishing to make veterinary nursing their career.

British Veterinary Poultry Association
c/o Royal College of Veterinary Surgeons
32 Belgrave Square
London
Profile: We have been unable to contact this organisation. The details given are unconfirmed.

British Warm-Blood Society
Moorlands Farm
New Yatt
Witney
Oxfordshire
OX8 6TE
Tel: 0199386 8673
Contact: Mrs J Matthews-Griffiths, President
Founded: 1977
Membership: 400
Publications: Members newsletter
Profile: A small organisation run on the strict continental grading system. High quality, judges from Germany, and numerous successful horses now competing internationally.

British Water
1 Queen Anne's Gate
London
SW1H 9BT
Tel: 0171 957 4554
Fax: 0171 957 4565
Contact: David Neil-Gallacher, Chief Executive

British Waterfowl Association
Gill Cottage
New Gill
Bishopdale
Leyburn
North Yorkshire
DL8 3TQ
Tel: 01969 663693
Fax: 01969 663693
Contact: Roz Taylor, Secretary/Treasurer
Founded: 1887
Membership: 1,500
Publications: Yearbook; Spring Waterfowl; Summer Waterfowl; Breeders' Directory
Profile: An association of enthusiasts interested in keeping, breeding and conserving all types of waterfowl including domestic ducks, geese and ornamental wildfowl.

British Waterways
Willow Grange
Church Road
Watford
Hertfordshire
WD1 3QA
Tel: 01923 226422
Fax: 01923 226081

British White Cattle Society
PO Box 35
National Agricultural Centre
Stoneleigh Park
Warwickshire
CV8 2XE
Tel: 01203 696523
Fax: 01203 699716
Contact: Miss E Matheson, Breed Co-ordinator
Founded: 1918
Membership: 270
Publications: Annual herd book; annual journal; quarterly newsletter
Previous names: The Park Cattle Society until 1945
Profile: To preserve the breed's ancient lineage by publishing annual herd books and to promote British White Cattle in modern-day farming.

British Wild Boar Association
Fen End Cottage
30 Fen Road
Milton
Cambridgeshire
CB4 6AD
Tel: 01223 860116
Fax: 01223 860116
Contact: Dr W Derek Booth, Secretary
Founded: 1989
Membership: 43
Publications: The Sounder (members newsletter)
Profile: The British Wild Boar Association is committed to the commercial development, welfare and understanding of husbanded wild boar in Britain and is open to all who are interested in wild boar. The association works for the recognition of the special qualities of the purchased wild boar, by publicity and by running a registration scheme open only to association members with purebred stock.

British Wind Energy Association
89 Kingsway
London
WC2B 6RH
Tel: 0171 404 3433
Fax: 0171 404 3432
Email: bwea@gn.apc.org
Contact: Hugh Babington Smith, Executive Director
Founded: 1979
Membership: 600
Publications: Best Practice Guidelines; Health and Safety in the Wind Industry; Wind Directions (members newsletter)
Profile: The British Wind Energy Association exists to promote excellence in wind energy

research, development and deployment. Formed in 1979 as a professional association and now also acts as a trade association for the wind energy industry. Its membership includes individuals and companies involved in wind energy research, consultancy, manufacture, development, operation and associated services. The association takes an active interest in all issues affecting the wind energy industry, from financing to lobbying and publicity.

British Wool Marketing Board
Oak Mills
Station Road
Clayton
Bradford
West Yorkshire
BD14 6JD
Tel: 01274 882091
Fax: 01274 818277
Contact: Mrs G Humphries, Company Secretary
Founded: 1950
Membership: 90,000
Publications: Wool Price Schedule; Annual Report and Accounts; British sheep breeds booklet
Profile: The statutory wool marketing organisation.

Broads Authority
Thomas Harvey House
18 Colegate
Norwich
Norfolk
NR3 1BQ
Tel: 01603 610734
Fax: 01603 765710
Email: 100070.1364@compuserve.com
Contact: Rob Holman, Chief Administration Officer
Founded: 1989
Publications: Publications list available
Profile: The Broads Authority was established under the Norfolk and Suffolk Broads Act 1988. The general duty of the authority is to manage the Broads for the purposes of: conserving and enhancing the natural beauty of the Broads; promoting the enjoyment of the Broads by the public; and, protecting the interests of navigation. The authority has a membership representing a range of national and local organisations and has a status equivalent to that of national park authorities.

Brogdale Horticultural Trust
Brogdale Farm
Brogdale Road
Faversham

Kent
ME13 8XZ
Tel: 01795 535286
Fax: 01795 531710
Contact: Mrs J Wade, Visitor Centre Manager
Founded: 1990
Membership: 1,400
Profile: The trust was founded in 1990 in order to safeguard the National Fruit Collections and the fruit trial work. The collections hold some 4,000 varieties of temperate fruit and acts as a gene bank for future research and development. The current variety testing programme covers up to 700 new varieties at any one time. The visitor centre enables members of the general public to experience the wealth of diversity within the national collections.

Brooksby College, Leicestershire
Brooksby
Melton Mowbray
Leicestershire
LE14 2LJ
Tel: 01664 434291
Fax: 01664 434572
Contact: John Gusterson, Principal
Founded: 1950
Publications: Prospectus
Previous names: Brooksby Farm Institute; Brooksby Agricultural College
Profile: Brooksby College stands in open countryside between the market town of Melton Mowbray and the city of Leicester. The college estate extends to some 330 ha and provides an excellent resource base for the wide range of land-based curricula delivered at the college. Course programmes at FE and HE level are available in agriculture, countryside and fishery studies, environmental management, animal care, equine studies, horticulture and floristry and business management including farm secretarial studies.

Broomfield College
Broomfield
Morley
Ilkeston
Derbyshire
DE7 6DN
Tel: 01332 831345
Fax: 01332 830298
Contact: Mr JC Field, Principal
Founded: 1946
Previous names: Derbyshire College of Agriculture and Horticulture
Profile: Further education corporation situated just north of Derby city on 180 ha estate of farms, gardens, woodland and parkland. A

section of the college farm is devoted to organic production of crops and livestock. A hill farm is run at Hathersage near Sheffield. Courses include HNDs in organic production and integrated land management, BTEC NDs in agriculture, horticulture, countryside care, animal care and floristry. City and Guilds National Certificates in countryside and horticulture. A full range of day and block release courses are also available. Residential accommodation is available for students plus conference facilities.

Brown Swiss Cattle Society
Lynn House Farm
London Road
Smallwood
Sandbach
Cheshire
CW11 0TX
Tel: 01477 500559
Fax: 01477 500559
Contact: Mrs Jayne Edwards, Secretary
Membership: 124
Publications: Swiss Chimes; newsletter

Buff Orpington Club
Leckby House
Flaxton
York
North Yorkshire
YO6 7QZ
Tel: 01904 468387
Contact: Mr PE Smedley, Secretary
Profile: A society to promote the Buff Orpington breed of poultry.

Butchers and Drovers Charitable Institution
61 West Smithfield
London
EC1A 9EA
Tel: 0171 606 5711
Fax: 0171 600 3094

Butterfly Conservation
PO Box 222
Dedham
Colchester
Essex
CO7 6EY
Tel: 01206 322342
Fax: 01206 322559
Email: butterfly@cix.compulinc.co.uk
Contact: Mrs DJ Scullion, Office Manager
Founded: 1968
Membership: 8,250
Previous names: British Butterfly Conservation Society Ltd

Profile: Butterfly Conservation is dedicated to the saving of wild butterflies and their habitats. By making people aware of their declining numbers, funding research into their life needs and by setting up reserves for the rarer species, the aim is to preserve these insects for future generations to enjoy.

Byways and Bridleways Trust
St Mary's Business Centre
Oystershell Lane
Newcastle upon Tyne
NE4 5QS
Tel: 0191 233 0770
Fax: 0191 233 0775

CAB International
Wallingford
Oxfordshire
OX10 8DE
Tel: 01491 832111
Fax: 01491 833508
Email: cabi@cabi.org

CADW: Welsh Historic Monuments
Brunel House
2 Fitzalan House
Cardiff
CF2 1UY
Tel: 01222 465511
Fax: 01222 500300

Cambridge Sheep Society
Pharm House
Neston Road
Willaston
Wirral
Merseyside
L64 2TF
Tel: 0151 794 6103
Fax: 0151 794 6107
Contact: Alun Davies, Honorary Secretary
Founded: 1979
Membership: 40
Profile: The breed society for Cambridge sheep. The Cambridge breed has outstandingly high prolificacy. The society is concerned with developing the breed and particularly its role in the production of high performance crossbred ewes for commercial use. Flocks have been established throughout the UK. All pedigree sheep are sold with performance records.

Cambridgeshire College of Agriculture and Horticulture
Landbeach Road
Milton

Cambridge
CB4 6DB
Tel: 01223 860701
Fax: 01223 860262
Contact: JPL Whittington, Principal
Founded: 1987
Publications: College prospectus
Profile: CCAH is a further education college specialising in providing education and training for land-based industries. It has centres at Milton near Cambridge and at Wisbech in north Cambridgeshire. Students may attend on a full or part-time basis. Qualification outcomes for vocational programmes may include National Diplomas, First Diplomas, National Certificates, NVQs and others related to professional bodies.

Campaign for the Protection of Rural Wales
Ty Gwyn
31 High Street
Welshpool
Powys
SY21 7JD
Tel: 01938 552525
Fax: 01938 552741
Email: CPRW@mcrl.poptel.org.uk
Contact: Jenny Smith, Assistant Director
Founded: 1928
Membership: 3,800
Publications: Rural Wales Magazine; various subject reports
Previous names: Council for the Preservation of Rural Wales until 1960; Council for the Protection of Rural Wales until 1991
Profile: CPRW is a national charity which organises concerted action to protect the beauty of our coast and countryside. CPRW has branches in every part of Wales, whose aim it is to protect the local environment while encouraging sustainable rural development. Funded by members' subscriptions and supporters' donations, CPRW is an authoritative source of guidance on conservation issues for political leaders, the news media and rural bodies in Wales.

Campden and Chorleywood Food Research Association
Chipping Campden
Gloucestershire
GL55 6LD
Tel: 01386 842000
Fax: 01386 842100
Contact: Mr John Wilkinson, Company Secretary
Founded: 1919
Membership: 1,000

Publications: Research and development reports; quality specifications; guideline documents; computer software
Previous names: Campden Food Preservation RA until 1988; Campden Food and Drink until 1995
Profile: A membership based organisation involved with all aspects of food and drink processing, preservation and storage. Activities include research and development, basic research, analytical services, training courses and publications.

Camping and Caravanning Club
Greenfields House
Westwood Way
Coventry
Warwickshire
CV4 8JH
Tel: 01203 694995
Fax: 01203 694886

Camping for the Disabled
20 Burton Close
Dawley
Telford
Shropshire
TF4 2BX
Tel: 01743 761889
Fax: 01743 761149
Profile: We have been unable to contact this organisation. The details given are unconfirmed.

Cannington College
Cannington
Bridgwater
Somerset
TA5 2LS
Tel: 01278 652226
Fax: 01278 652479
Contact: Mr Mike Smith, Director of Academic Programmes
Founded: 1921
Publications: Prospectus
Previous names: Somerset Farm Institute; Somerset College of Agriculture and Horticulture
Profile: Cannington College offers opportunities to study towards full-time and part-time awards in horticulture, golf course management, arboriculture, sport science (golf studies), agriculture, equitation, countryside management, management, animal care, food and science, environmental sciences at BTEC first, national and higher national levels for most subjects.

Capel Manor Horticultural and Environmental Centre
Bullsmoor Lane
Enfield

Middlesex
EN1 4RQ
Tel: 0181 366 4442
Fax: 0181 01992 717544
Contact: Bruce Taggart, Head of Arboriculture
Founded: 1968
Publications: Course leaflets and prospectus
Previous names: Capel Manor Institute for
Horticulture and Field Studies until 1988
Profile: Capel Manor is Greater London's only
specialist college catering for land-based industry
training and education. A complete range of
full-time and part-time courses are available in
arboriculture, countryside management, equine
and animal studies, horticulture and floristry. The
courses are set amongst 30 ha of mature
gardens and many of the practical elements of
courses take place on site. Fully equipped
classrooms and workshops ensure that an ideal
learning environment is maintained.

Caravan Club Ltd
East Grinstead House
East Grinstead
West Sussex
RH19 1UA
Tel: 01342 326944
Fax: 01342 410258
Contact: John A Bell, Executive Secretary
Founded: 1907
Membership: 285,000
Publications: The Caravan Magazine; Sites
Directory and Handbook – biannual; Supplement
to Sites Directory and Handbook – interim years;
Continental Sites Guide
Profile: The Caravan Club provides facilities and
services related to caravanning for its members.
The club has a network of 200 sites nation wide.
The club caters for those members who wish to
stage rallies. Other services provided are
insurances and site reservations.

Care for the Wild
1 Ashfolds
Horsham Road
Rusper
Horsham
West Sussex
RH12 4QX
Tel: 01293 871596
Fax: 01293 871022
Email: cftw@fastnet.co.uk
Contact: Chris Jordan, Director
Founded: 194
Membership: 20,000
Profile: International wildlife charity dedicated to
protecting animals from cruelty and exploitation.

Careers in Land-based Industries
c/o Warwickshire Careers Service
10 Northgate Street
Warwick
CV34 4SR
Tel: 01926 412427
Fax: 01926 412800
Contact: DK Sharman, Careers Advisor
Publications: Careers in Land-based Industries
(binder)
Previous names: Careers, Education and
Training for Agriculture and the Countryside until
1996
Profile: An information and advice service which
has provided every secondary school, main
careers offices and colleges of agriculture with a
binder of loose-leaf information sheets of advice
on all aspects of careers, education and training
in the land-based industries. A service operated
by Warwickshire Careers Service Ltd and
supported by colleges of agriculture, university
departments and ATB-Landbase Ltd.

Carlisle Old English Game Club
Gale Cottage
Thorganby
York
North Yorkshire
YO4 6DQ
Tel: 01904 448905
Contact: Dr H Bell, Secretary
Profile: A society to promote the Carlisle Old
English Game breed of poultry.

**Carmarthenshire College of Technology and
    Art, Agriculture Department**
Golden Grove Campus
Carmarthen
SA32 8LR
Tel: 01558 668341
Fax: 01558 668748
Contact: Peter Rees, Dean of Faculty
Founded: 1985
Profile: CCTA has long been established as a
centre of excellence providing a broad range of
further and higher education courses for
agriculture and associated land-based industries.
The college offers a complete portfolio of NVQ
and BTEC programmes (First Diploma, Certificate
and National and Higher National) in agriculture,
countryside management, horticulture, equine
studies and small animal care. Programmes are
available on a part-time and full-time basis with
excellent facilities at the Gelli Aur and Pibwrlwyd
campuses. Specialist short courses, exhibitions
and demonstrations are regularly undertaken and

the college is an established location for local variety trials and applied research.

Carnivore Wildlife Trust
35 Church Street
Kidlington
Oxford
OX5 2BA
Tel: 01865 373241
Fax: 01865 373241
Contact: Roger Panaman
Founded: 1991
Membership: 500
Publications: Tails Up (members newsletter)
Profile: The Carnivore Wildlife Trust is for the conservation and welfare of carnivores. Our main project is to facilitate an introduction of wolves to the Scottish Highlands.

Caspian Pony Society
4 The Gassons
Filkins
Lechlade
Gloucestershire
GL7 3HZ
Contact: Mrs S Cumberpatch

Castlemilk Moorit Sheep Society
see Rare Breeds Survival Trust

Castlewellan and District Agricultural Show
Moorcroft
38 Newry Road
Rathfriland
County Down
BT34 5AL
Tel: 018206 30536
Fax: 018206 30536
Contact: Mrs Violet I Bell, Secretary

Catholic Study Circle for Animal Welfare
39 Onslow Gardens
South Woodford
London
E18 1ND
Tel: 0181 989 0478
Contact: Mrs May Bocking, Hon Secretary
Founded: 1929
Membership: 2,000
Publications: The Ark (journal)
Profile: Their purpose is to study and propagate all positive Catholic teaching on questions relating to the non-human creation in general, and the animal kingdom in particular. CSCAW's membership is worldwide and open to persons of all faiths or none. Non-political, non-profit making, CSCAW was launched as a prayer circle.

CSCAW strives by personal and organised prayer and theological research, by propaganda and by co-operation to combat all forms of cruelty and abuse, whether direct or indirect.

Central Association of Agricultural Valuers
First Floor
4 Lord's Hill
Coleford
Gloucestershire
GL16 8BD
Tel: 01594 832979
Fax: 01594 810701
Contact: Jeremy Moody, Secretary
Founded: 1910
Membership: 2,000
Publications: Publications list available
Profile: The CAAV is the specialist professional body representing those practising in agricultural and rural valuations throughout England and Wales. Members provide advice and valuation expertise on issues affecting the countryside to all those who require these services whether owner occupiers, tenants, landlords or public authorities.

Central Association of Bee-Keepers
6 Oxford Road
Teddington
Middlesex
TW11 0PZ
Tel: 0181 977 5867
Contact: Mrs MR English, Honorary Secretary
Founded: 1945
Membership: 300
Publications: Publications list available
Profile: The Central Association of Bee-Keepers acts as a bridge between the bee-keeper and the scientist. Specialists in their field are invited to give lectures on scientific aspects of bees, bee-keeping and related topics, with an emphasis on current research. Meetings are held at the Linnean Society of London. An annual conference takes place in Royal Leamington Spa, visitors are welcome at all meetings. Membership details and a list of current publications are available from the Honorary Secretary.

Central Committee of Fell Packs
Sword House
Eskdale
Holmrook
Cumbria
CA19 1TT
Tel: 01946 723295
Contact: Mr WE Porter, Chairman
Founded: 1967

Membership: 24
Profile: The Central Committee of the fell packs comprises of officials of the six fell packs of foxhounds.

Central Rights of Way Committee
21 The Chase
Abbeydale
Gloucester
GL4 4WP
Tel: 01452 538905
Contact: Alan Seyers, Secretary
Profile: We have been unable to contact this organisation. The details given are unconfirmed.

Central Science Laboratory
Ministry of Agriculture Fisheries and Food
London Road
Slough
Berkshire
SL3 7HJ
Tel: 01753 534626
Fax: 01753 824058

Central Science Laboratory National Bee Unit
Central Science Laboratory
Ministry of Agriculture, Fisheries and Food
Luddington
Stratford upon Avon
Warwickshire
CV37 9SJ
Tel: 01789 750601
Fax: 01789 750957
Contact: Melanie Hughes, Laboratory Technical Manager
Publications: Various pamphlets and leaflets on honey bee diseases
Previous names: Part of ADAS until 1994
Profile: The unit's main responsibility is the statutory implementation of the Bees Act 1980 and its Orders. Under the Orders, a disease diagnosis service is provided free of charge for American Foul Brood, European Foul Brood and Varrosis, all of which are notifiable diseases. The NBU also co-ordinates the MAFF Wildlife Incident Investigation Scheme (WIIS) which monitors the effects of pesticides on wildlife including bees.

Centre for Agricultural Strategy
University of Reading
PO Box 236
Earley Gate
Reading
RG6 6AT
Tel: 01734 318150
Fax: 01734 353423
Email: CASAGRI@reading.ac.uk

Contact: Freda Miller, Research Fellow
Founded: 1975
Membership: 9
Publications: List of papers and reports available
Profile: CAS was established by the Nuffield Foundation, an independent non-profit distributing organisation and is part of the University of Reading within the Faculty of Agriculture and Food. Its objectives are to provide independent and continuing assessment of developments in the agricultural and food industries and the countryside. This facilitates strategic planning by the agricultural, food and ancillary industries, together with relevant government departments and agencies. The centre's expanding field of work and influence now extends over a range of farming, food and countryside issues in the UK, the EU and worldwide.

Centre for Agricultural, Food and Resource Economics
University of Manchester
Dover Street
Manchester
M13 9PL
Tel: 0161 275 4793
Fax: 0161 275 4929
Contact: Dr Trevor Young, Director
Founded: 1994
Publications: Working papers
Previous names: Department of Agricultural Economics until 1994
Profile: CAFRE acts as the focus, within the School of Economic Studies, for research in the areas of agricultural, food, environmental and natural resources economics. It co-ordinates bids for outside research contracts in those areas and manages existing contracts. It also manages the Farm Business Survey contract.

Centre for Alternative Technology
Llwyngwern Quarry
Machynlleth
Powys
SY20 9AZ
Tel: 01654 702400
Fax: 01654 702782
Email: cat@gn.apc.org
Internet: http://www.foe.co.uk
Contact: Paul Allen, Press Officer
Founded: 1975
Publications: Publications list available
Previous names: National Centre for Alternative Technology
Profile: Established in 1975 and now recognised as Europe's leading eco-centre. CAT has a highly

Alphabetical List

C

qualified staff of 30 environmentalists and receives around 80,000 visitors each year, including respected academic, governmental and international institutions. Central to communicating CAT's positive, practical environmental messages, its seven acre display complex reflects ways in which our society is taking seriously the need to adopt sustainable technologies and lifestyles. Many of the centre's employees live on the site and depend on the technologies displayed.

Centre for Aquatic Plant Management

Institute of Arable Crops Research
Broadmoor Lane
Sonning on Thames
Reading
RG4 0TH
Tel: 01734 9690072
Fax: 01734 9441730
Contact: Dr Jonathan Newman, Senior Research Scientist
Founded: 1986
Publications: Annual Reports; quarterly newsletter; information sheets
Previous names: Weed Research Organisation until 1986; Aquatic Weeds Research Unit until 1995

Centre for Dairy Research

Arborfield Hall Farm
Arborfield
Reading
RG2 9HX
Tel: 01734 76094
Fax: 01734 761044
Contact: E Leonard, Business Manager
Founded: 1992
Profile: Established in 1992 by the University of Reading, CEDAR offers dairy producers and the allied industries a unique research facility. The combination of a 400 cow herd, managed on a commercial basis and a 'state of the art' metabolism unit enables both applied and strategic work to be carried out at CEDAR. Located at Shinfield, a site historically associated with dairy research, CEDAR is dedicated to the execution of quality research work and the creation of a two way flow of information between researchers and farmers.

Centre for Environment and Business in Scotland

58–59 Timber Bush
Edinburgh
EH6 6QH
Tel: 0131 555 5334
Fax: 0131 555 5217
Email: info@iem.org.uk
Contact: Anne Caroline Peckham, Director
Founded: 1991
Publications: Various publications
Profile: Scotland's central source of environmental information and advice for business.

Centre for Environment and Land Tenure Studies

University of Reading
PO Box 219
Whiteknights
Reading
RG6 6AW
Tel: 01734 875123
Fax: 01734 318172
Email: s.markwell@reading.ac.uk
Contact: Mrs Susan Markwell, Development Manager
Founded: 1994
Previous names: Publications list available
Profile: CELTS is a specialist education, training and research centre covering the areas of rural land management, development and planning. It runs seminars on a wide range of issues including agricultural law, rural planning and environmental management; it organises training sessions on issues such as information technology and it undertakes research for external bodies.

Centre for Environmental Data and Recording

Ulster Museum Sciences Division
Ulster Museum
12 Malone Road
Belfast
BT9 5BN
Tel: 01232 383000
Fax: 01232 383003
Contact: Dr Damian McFerran, Records Centre Manager
Founded: 1995
Previous names: Northern Ireland Biological Records Centre 1991–1993; Northern Ireland Biological and Earth Sciences Records Centre 1993–1995
Profile: The role of CEDaR is to accumulate, store and supply information relating to the geology and distribution of the flora and fauna of Northern Ireland and its coastal waters whilst ensuring the confidentiality of sensitive records. CEDaR will provide planners, environmental consultants, conservation bodies and amateur and professional naturalists with environmental information.

69

Centre for Environmental Interpretation
Manchester Metropolitan University
St Augustine's
Lower Chatham Street
Manchester
M15 6BY
Tel: 0161 247 1067
Fax: 0161 247 6390
Contact: Information Officer
Founded: 1980
Publications: Interpretation – jointly with the
Society for Interpretation of Britain's Heritage.
Profile: A national charitable unit with remit to
promote and develop good practice in
environmental interpretation in fields of
recreation, conservation, tourism and heritage.
The centre has three main areas of work –
consultancy, advice and information, and projects
and training.

Centre for Environmental Strategy
University of Surrey
Guildford
Surrey
GU2 5XH
Tel: 01483 300800
Fax: 01483 509394
Email: s.sutherland@surrey.ac.uk
Contact: Professor Roland Clift, Director
Founded: 1992
Publications: Publications list available

Centre for European Agricultural Studies
Wye College
Wye
Ashford
Kent
TN25 5AH
Tel: 01233 812181
Fax: 01233 813309
Contact: Professor AE Buckwell, Director

**Centre for Organic Husbandry and
  Agroecology**
University of Wales
Welsh Institute of Rural Studies
Stapledon Building
Aberystwyth
Ceredigion
SY23 3DD
Tel: 01970 622248
Fax: 01970 622238
Email: nhl@aber.ac.uk
Contact: Dr NH Lampkin, Co-ordinator
Founded: 1989
Publications: Publications list available
Profile: The centre is a collaborative initiative
linking the University of Wales, ADAS and the

Institute of Grassland and Environmental
Research. Facilities include three organic
research farms: ADAS Pwllpeiran; IGER,
Trawsgoed and UWA, Frongoch, featuring
dairying, lowland and hill beef and sheep
production.

Centre for Rural Economy
Department of Agricultural Economics and Food
  Marketing
The University
Newcastle upon Tyne
NE1 7RU
Tel: 0191 222 6623
Fax: 0191 222 6720
Email: cre@newcastle.ac.uk
Contact: Hilary Talbot, Research Manager
Founded: 1992
Profile: The Centre for Rural Economy is
committed to applied research of the highest
quality, oriented towards the achievement of a
sustainable rural economy. Its work raises
fundamental questions of social science analysis
but also of considerable policy relevance. It
draws together contributions mainly from policy
and institutional analysis, resource and
environmental economics, rural sociology,
regional geography and countryside planning and
management. The centre disseminates its
results through publications, policy advice and
advanced training activities.

Centre for Rural Studies
Royal Agricultural College
Cirencester
Gloucestershire
GL7 6JS
Tel: 01285 652531
Fax: 01285 642740
Email: wjm@racrelm.demon.co.uk
Contact: Will Manley, Director
Founded: 1987
Publications: Publications list available
Profile: Specialist unit operating from within the
School of Rural Economy and Land
Management. CRS provides the focus for a wide
range of applied research and consultancy
services.

Centre for Rural Studies, Belfast
The Queens University of Belfast
Faculty of Agriculture and Food Science
Newforge Lane
Belfast
BT9 5PX
Tel: 01232 683538
Fax: 01232 668384

C

Contact: Dr John Davis, Director
Founded: 1994
Publications: ADOP Report; Rural Development in Ireland
Profile: The inter-disciplinary centre was established in 1994 with core aims: to expand knowledge of the development of the rural economy in its social and environmental context; to promote and co-ordinate curriculum development in rural studies at both undergraduate and postgraduate levels; to promote and co-ordinate interdisciplinary research programmes and publish the results; to provide an independent forum for discussion and debate of rural development issues, thus forging links between the university and rural society. It will also develop collaborative networks with other institutions with emphasis on the EU, China and Eastern Europe.

Centre for the Study of Rural Society
Bishop Grosseteste College of Education
Lincoln
Lincolnshire
LN1 3DY
Profile: We have been unable to contact this organisation. The details given are unconfirmed.

Centre of Management in Agriculture
Farm Management Unit
University of Reading
PO Box 236
Reading
RG6 2AT
Tel: 01734 351458
Fax: 01734 352421

Cereals and Set Aside Division
Ministry of Agriculture, Fisheries and Food
Whitehall Place East Block
London
SW1A 2HH
Tel: 0171 270 8748
Profile: This division of MAFF is responsible for the arable area payments scheme and for five-year set-aside and environmental set-aside schemes.

Charities Aid Foundation
Kinds Hill
West Malling
Kent
ME19 4TA
Tel: 01732 520000
Fax: 01732 520001
Email: info@caf.charitynet.org
Contact: Vicki Pulman, Press Officer

Founded: 1924
Publications: Directory of Grant Making Trusts; Dimensions of the Voluntary Sector
Previous names: National Council of Social Service Benevolent Fund
Profile: CAF is a registered charity providing services and information which are both charitable and financial. It helps individuals and companies make the most of their giving and charities make the most of their resources. CAF operates a charity account for tax effective giving, provides investment, administrative and loans services to charities and distributes grants enabling registered charities to operate more effectively.

Charity Commission
St Albans House
57–60 Haymarket
London
SW1Y 4QX
Tel: 0171 210 4556
Fax: 0171 210 4545
Contact: Hugh Rogers
Profile: The Charity Commission is a non-ministerial government department with the complementary roles of supporting and supervising registered charities, including rural ones.

Charmoise Sheep Society
1 Crown Square
Denbigh
Clwyd
LL16 3AA
Tel: 01745 812161
Fax: 01745 816120
Contact: Mr Gerald Moulden, Secretary
Founded: 1993
Membership: 16
Profile: Breed society of the Charmoise sheep.

Chartered Institution of Water and Environmental Management
15 John Street
London
WC1N 2EB
Tel: 0171 831 3110
Fax: 0171 405 4967
Contact: Mr RA Bispham, Executive Director
Founded: 1895
Membership: 11,500
Publications: Publications list available
Previous names: Institution of Water and Environmental Management until 1995
Profile: CIWEM is a multi-disciplinary professional and examining body for engineers, scientists and other professionally qualified

personnel engaged in water and environmental management. The main objects of the institution are to advance the science and practice of water and environmental management for the public benefit and to promote education, training, study and research in those areas. CIWEM organises conferences and seminars.

Cheshire Agricultural Society
Clay Lane Farm
Marton
Winsford
Cheshire
CW7 2QH
Tel: 01829 760020
Fax: 01829 760021
Contact: David J Broster, Secretary
Founded: 1838
Membership: 1,100
Publications: Showing schedules; annual show catalogue; Annual Report
Profile: The objects of the society are the encouragement of agricultural enterprise; to promote improvement in the breeding, rearing and health of livestock; the improvement of agricultural produce and invention and improvement of agricultural implements. Also to encourage skill and industry in husbandry by holding of shows or otherwise, and for the benefit of charity. The society organises the annual Cheshire County Show which is agriculturally based with classes for cattle, sheep, goats, rare breeds, shires, light horses, poultry, pigeons, rabbits, cavies, cheese, honey, wine, flowers and dogs.

Cheviot Sheep Society
Holm Cottage
Langholm
Dumfriesshire
DG13 0JP
Tel: 013873 80222
Contact: Mrs IJ McVittie, Secretary
Founded: 1891
Membership: 120

Chianina Cattle Breed Society of Great Britain
Farley Farm
Great Haywood
Stafford
ST18 0RA
Profile: The breed society for Chianina cattle.

Chickens' Lib
PO Box 2
Holmfirth
Huddersfield
HD7 1QT
Tel: 01484 688650

Chillingham Wild Cattle Association
Estate Office
Chillingham
Alnwick
Northumberland
NE66 5NW
Tel: 01668 215250
Contact: Mrs A Widdows, Secretary/Treasurer
Founded: 1939
Membership: 380
Publications: History leaflet; annual President's report
Profile: Formerly the property of the Earls of Tankerville, the wild cattle are now owned and administered by the Chillingham Wild Cattle Association, a registered charity formed for this express purpose. It receives no grants or government sponsorship and is totally dependent for its income upon membership subscriptions and visitors fees. The park is open from 1st April to 31st October on all days except Tuesdays, and visitors, who must be accompanied at all times by the Park Warden, are most welcome.

Christian Rural Concern
2 Curborough Road
Lichfield
Staffordshire
WS13 7NG
Tel: 01543 264074
Contact: Dr Ken Wilkinson, Administrative Secretary
Founded: 1986
Publications: Course material for Certificate in Christian Rural Studies (Units 1 to 6)
Profile: Christian Rural Concern has run courses on rural issues since 1986. They aim to look at rural and environmental issues from a Christian rural viewpoint, based on the belief that God cares about us and the way in which we live on the Earth which He created.

Church and Conservation Project
Arthur Rank Centre
National Agricultural Centre
Stoneleigh Park
Warwickshire
CV8 2LZ
Tel: 01203 696969
Fax: 01203 669600
Contact: David Manning, Project Leader
Founded: 1987
Publications: Publications list available
Profile: The Church and Conservation Project was established to: seek ways and means of promoting the principles and practices of nature

conservation in the management of church owned lands; raise the level of environmental awareness and understanding of conservation more generally in the work and ministry of churches, especially in the rural context; help churches and conservation organisations to interrelate more productively; and to examine the ethical and theological dimensions of the changing countryside and environmental issues.

Church Commissioners
1 Millbank
London
SW1P 3JZ
Tel: 0171 222 7010
Fax: 0171 233 0804,
Contact: The Estates Secretary
Founded: 1948
Publications: Annual Report
Profile: A charity supporting the stipends, pensions and housing of Church of England clergy.

City & Guilds
1 Giltspur Street
London
EC1A 9DD
Tel: 0171 294 2468
Fax: 0171 294 2400
Contact: Customer Services Enquiries Unit
Founded: 1978
Publications: Broadsheet; Annual Report
Previous names: National Examinations Board for Agriculture, Horticulture and Allied Industries (NEBAHAI) until 1995
Profile: City & Guilds is the UK's leading assessment and awarding body for vocational qualifications. NEBAHAI operates as a National Advisory Committee for City & Guilds. Amongst the 500 subjects offered are agriculture and horticulture, environmental conservation, fish husbandry, forestry, game keeping and sea fishing. City & Guilds qualifications follow a clearly defined structure allowing progression from introductory level to graduate and postgraduate equivalents.

Civic Trust
17 Carlton House Terrace
London
SW1Y 5AW
Tel: 0171 930 0914
Fax: 0171 321 0180
Contact: Saskia Hallam, Secretary
Profile: The Civic Trust is the leading charity concerned with improving the built environment in the places where people live and work. It

promotes Heritage Open Days, Civic Trust Awards and undertakes regeneration projects in both rural and urban areas. It administers the Environmental Action Fund and the Local Projects Grant Fund. It campaigns and publishes reports on national environmental issues. A comprehensive reference library is open to all.

Civic Trust for Wales
4th Floor
Empire House
Mount Stuart Square
Cardiff
CF1 6DD
Tel: 01222 484606
Fax: 01222 482086

Clay Pigeon Shooting Association
Earlstrees Court
Earlstrees Road
Corby
Northamptonshire
NN17 4AX
Tel: 01536 443566
Fax: 01536 443438
Contact: Emilio G Orduna, Director
Founded: 1928
Membership: 21,000
Publications: Pull (in-house magazine)
Profile: Membership administration for clay pigeon shoots.

Cleveland Bay Horse Society
York Livestock Centre
Murton
York
YO1 3UF
Tel: 01904 489731
Fax: 01904 489782
Contact: JF Stephenson, Secretary/Treasurer
Founded: 1884
Membership: 350
Publications: Stud Book; annual magazine
Profile: The CBHS is the breed society, formed in 1884, for Britain's only native clean legged horse. All pure horses are registered with the society and included in the stud book. Part-bred Clevelands are also registerable. All stallions are inspected and licenced by the society. Grading/premium schemes operate for stallions and mares.

Clogher Valley Agricultural Society
88–90 Main Street
Lisnaskea
County Fermanagh
BT92 0JD
Tel: 013657 21365

Profile: We have been unable to contact this organisation. The details given are unconfirmed.

Clun Forest Sheep Breeders Society Ltd
c/o McCartneys
The Livestock Market
The Ox Pasture
Overton Road
Ludlow
Shropshire
SY8 4AA
Tel: 01584 872251
Fax: 01584 875727
Contact: David Uffold, Field Officer
Founded: 1935
Membership: 160
Publications: Annual flock book; handbook
Profile: Livestock society breeding Clun Forest sheep and covering the whole of the UK.

Clydesdale Horse Society of Great Britain and Ireland
Castlepart
The Castleton
Auchterader
Perthshire
PH3 1JR
Tel: 01764 664925
Contact: Mrs Fiona Roebuck, Secretary
Founded: 1877
Membership: 800
Publications: Stud Book
Profile: The society's objects are: to maintain unimpaired the purity of the breed of horses known as Clydesdale horses and to promote the breeding of these horses; to collect, verify, preserve and publish the pedigrees of the said horses and other useful information relating to them; to promote the general interests of the breeders and owners of the said horses; to investigate suspicious or doubtful pedigrees or other alleged misrepresentations relating to them and to publish the results of the investigations and to arbitrate upon, investigate and settle disputes and questions relating to Clydesdale horses.

Co-ordinating Animal Welfare
PO Box 589
Bristol
BS99 1RW
Profile: We have been unable to contact this organisation. The details given are unconfirmed.

Coaching Club, The
West Compton House
West Compton
Shepton Mallet
Somerset
BA4 4PD
Tel: 01749 890633
Fax: 01749 890722
Contact: David Clarke, Honorary Secretary
Founded: 1871
Membership: 60
Previous names: Four in Hand Club
Profile: Club founded for those interested and able to drive a team of four horses to a road coach or private drag. A private club, applications for membership invited by committee only.

CoastNET (Coastal Heritage Network)
c/o Centre for Environmental Interpretation
Manchester Metropolitan University
St Augustines
Lower Chatham Street
Manchester
M15 6BY
Tel: 0161 247 1067
Fax: 0161 247 6390
Email: cei-manchester@mcrl.poptel.org.uk
Contact: Kira Gee, Project Officer
Founded: 1995
Publications: CoastNET (journal); publications list available
Previous names: Heritage Coast Forum
Profile: CoastNET links individuals and organisations working for the sustainable management of the coastal and marine environment. CoastNET has the following objectives: to provide a network between coastal managers and field staff on the UK coast; to improve the ways in which the coastal heritage of the UK is managed; to ensure that the practical experience of coastal managers and field staff contributes to the formulation of policy for the coastal zone. CoastNET is being established as an independent charitable trust and will become a membership organisation during the course of 1997.

Cochin Club
Firs Lodge Farm
Much Dewchurch
Hereford
HR2 8DN
Tel: 01981 540645
Contact: Mrs J Sollis, Secretary
Profile: A society to promote the Cochin breed of poultry.

Colbred Sheep Society
Crickley Barrow
Northleach
Cheltenham

Gloucestershire
GL54 3QA
Tel: 01451 860330

Coleg Llysfasi
Ruthin
Clwyd
LL15 2LB
Tel: 01978 790263
Fax: 01978 790468,
Contact: Principal
Founded: 1921
Publications: Prospectus; occasional
investigational reports
Profile: A further education college providing
education and practical training in agriculture,
forestry, conservation and environmental care,
veterinary nursing, animal care, business,
secretarial skills, European languages, Welsh for
adults and Welsh in the workplace.

Coleg Merion Dwyfor Glynllfion
Clynnog Road
Caernarvon
Gwynedd
LL54 5DU
Tel: 01286 830261
Fax: 01286 831597
Contact: E Eurwyn Edwards, Sector Leader
Profile: The sector is concerned with the
land-based industries offering courses from
BTEC 1st diploma to National Diploma in
agriculture, equine and forestry conservation.
Also the NCA and NCMA courses are available
along with NVQ/BHS qualifications. Farm
machinery is a new course which commences in
September 1996. The college extends to 303 ha
with a modern working farm, equine and forestry
facilities.

College of Animal Welfare
King's Bush Farm
London Road
Godmanchester
Huntingdon
Cambridgeshire
PE18 8LJ
Tel: 01480 831177
Fax: 01480 831291
Contact: B Cooper, Principal
Founded: 1989
Publications: Pet Ownership (GCSE resources
document)
Profile: The College of Animal Welfare provides
education and training for the animal care
industry. The college works closely with Wood
Green animal shelters, running a range of

courses including veterinary nursing, national
certificate in animal care, NVQs in animal care,
dog behaviour and feline symposia. Situated
close to the A1 it is easily accessible from all
parts of East Anglia and the Midlands.

College of Estate Management
Whiteknights
Reading
RG6 6AW
Tel: 01734 861101
Fax: 01734 755344
Email: 101574.156@compuserve.com
Contact: Director of Courses
Founded: 1919
Publications: Rural Notes (annual); publications
list available
Profile: The college is the leading international
body providing education and training for
students and members of the land and property
professions. Founded in 1919 and granted its
Royal Charter in 1922 the college today provides
a wide range of highly flexible services including
distance learning courses for professional degree
and postgraduate qualifications, research and
in-house training, books, audio tapes and videos.

Coloured Horse and Pony Society
Red Heights
Duck End
Great Brickhill
Milton Keynes
Buckinghamshire
MK17 9AP
Contact: Secretary
Founded: 1983
Profile: The society was founded in 1983, with
its primary objects to promote and encourage
coloured horses and ponies in all aspects of
equestrian spheres.

Commercial Horticultural Association
PO Box 8
Department M14/H
Harrogate
North Yorkshire
HG2 8XB
Tel: 01423 879208
Fax: 01423 870025
Email: 100450.2631@compuserve.com
Contact: Brian L Dunsby, Secretariat
Founded: 1979
Membership: 90
Publications: CHA Buyers' Guide
Profile: CHA is a trade association of
manufacturers and suppliers of equipment,
products and services used in the commercial

horticultural industry. Operating for over 17 years, the association is particularly active in exhibitions and regional shows, working for a cost effective programme, with the minimum of overlap. Benefits of membership include: regular newsletter; entry in CHA Buyers' Guide which has worldwide circulation; regular appraisal of shows, UK and European: discounts on hotels via block bookings; export information services; opportunities to exhibit at overseas exhibitions with DTI subsidies; forum on topics to the industry.

Committee for Occupational Standards and Qualifications in Environmental Conservation

Environmental Training Organisation
The Red House
Pillows Green
Staunton
Gloucester
GL19 3NU
Tel: 01452 840825
Fax: 01452 840824
Contact: Keith Turner, Secretary Environmental Training Organisation
Founded: 1995
Publications: Newsletter; Occupational Standards and N/SVQs in Environmental Conservation

Committee on Agricultural Valuation

Ministry of Agriculture, Fisheries and Food
Nobel House
17 Smith Square
London
SW1P 3JR
Tel: 0171 238 6713
Fax: 0171 238 5671
Contact: Mark Edwards, Secretary
Founded: 1986
Profile: The Committee on Agricultural Valuation advises the Minister of Agriculture, Fisheries and Food and the Secretary of State for Wales on the content of regulations which prescribe the method of calculating the value of short-term improvements and tenant right matters for compensation purposes. This applies when a tenant quits a holding under a tenancy subject to the provisions of the Agricultural Holdings Act 1986. The current regulations are the Agriculture (Calculation of Value for Compensation) Regulations 1978 (as amended).

Committee on Carcinogenicity of Chemicals in Food, Consumer Products and the Environment

Department of Health
80 London Road

London
SE1 6LW
Tel: 0171 972 5020
Fax: 0171 972 5156
Contact: KN Mistry, Administration Secretary
Founded: 1978
Publications: Publications list available
Profile: To assess and advise government on the toxic risk of substances which are: used or proposed to be used as food additives, or in such a way that they might contaminate food through natural occurrence in agriculture including horticulture and veterinary practice or in the distribution, storage, preparation, processing or packaging of food; used or proposed to be used or manufactured or produced in industry, agriculture, food storage or any other workplace; used or proposed to be used or disposed of in such a way as to result in pollution of the environment. They advise on important general principles or new scientific discoveries in connection with toxic risks, to co-ordinate with other bodies concerned with the assessment of toxic risks and to present recommendations for toxicity testing.

Committee on Medical Aspects of Food Policy

Department of Health
Room 652c Skipton House
80 London Road
London
SE1 6LW
Tel: 0171 972 2000
Fax: 0171 972 5143
Contact: Dr Alison Redfern, Scientific Officer, Secretary of COMA
Founded: 1963
Publications: 46 reports concerning various aspects of food policy
Profile: This independent, non-statutory, committee established in 1963 comprises experts in the field of nutrition and health and other relevant fields, under the chairmanship of the government's Chief Medical Officer. It's terms of reference are 'To consider and advise on: a) the medical and scientific aspects of policy in relation to nutrition, b) at the request of, or in association with, appropriate Advisory Committees, the medical and nutritional aspects of developments in the agricultural and food industries including the production and processing of food, and c) at the request of the Department of Health, matters falling within these terms of reference.'

Committee on Mutagenicity of Chemicals in Food, Consumer Products and the Environment

Department of Health

80 London Road
London
SE1 6LW
Tel: 0171 972 5020
Fax: 0171 972 5134
Contact: KN Mistry, Administration Secretary
Founded: 1978
Publications: Publications list available
Profile: To assess and advise government on the toxic risk of substances which are: used or proposed to be used as food additives, or in such a way that they might contaminate food through natural occurrence in agriculture including horticulture and veterinary practice or in the distribution, storage, preparation, processing or packaging of food; used or proposed to be used or manufactured or produced in industry, agriculture, food storage or any other workplace; used or proposed to be used or disposed of in such a way as to result in pollution of the environment. They advise on important general principles or new scientific discoveries in connection with toxic risks, to co-ordinate with other bodies concerned with the assessment of toxic risks and to present recommendations for toxicity testing.

Committee on Plant Supply and Establishment

c/o HTA
19 High Street
Theale
Reading
RG7 5AH
Tel: 01734 303132
Fax: 01734 323453
Contact: Mrs J Peaple, Committee Secretary
Founded: 1973
Profile: CPSE is a technical committee drawing representation from the member organisations of the Joint Council for Landscape Industries and a few other associations which are not members but have a positive interest in technical matters involving the growing, supply and establishment of plants.

Committee on Toxicity of Chemicals in Food, Consumer Products and the Environment

Department of Health
80 London Road
Elephant and Castle
London
SE1 6LW
Tel: 0171 972 5018
Fax: 0171 972 5134
Contact: Mrs Dionne Davey, Administrative Secretary

Founded: 1978
Publications: Publications list available
Profile: To assess and advise on the toxic risk to man of substances which are: used or proposed to be used as food additives or used in any way which may contaminate food; to be used or manufactured or produced in industry, agriculture, food storage or any other workplace; to be used as household goods or toilet goods and preparations; used as drugs; used or disposed of in such a way as to result in pollution of the environment. Also to advise on important general principles or new scientific discoveries in connection with toxic risks, to co-ordinate with other bodies concerned with the assessment of toxic risk and to present recommendations for toxicity testing.

Common Ground

Seven Dials Warehouse
44 Earlham Street
London
WC2H 9LA
Tel: 0171 379 3109
Fax: 0171 836 5741
Contact: Sue Clifford, Joint Co-ordinator
Founded: 1983
Publications: Publications list available
Profile: Common Ground emphasises the value of our everyday surroundings and the positive investment people can make in their own localities. They forge links between the arts and the conservation of nature and the cultural landscapes, offering ideas and inspiration, information, through publications, exhibitions and projects.

Common Land Cause – The Countryside Society

9 St Anne's Road
Caversham
Reading
RG4 PA
Profile: We have been unable to contact this organisation. The details given are unconfirmed.

Commons Commissioners

Department of the Environment and Lord Chancellor's Department
4th Floor
35 Old Queen Street
London
SW1H 9JA
Tel: 0171 222 0038
Fax: 0171 222 0133
Contact: Miss F A A Buchan, Clerk to the Commons Commissioners
Founded: 1971

Publications: Decisions following public hearings throughout England and Wales
Profile: The commissioners decide disputes arising under the Commons Registration Act 1965 and the Common Land (Rectification of Registers) Act 1989 and enquire into the ownership of unclaimed common land. Commissioners are appointed by the Lord Chancellor.

Commonwealth Association of Surveying and Land Economy
15 Greycoat Place
London
SW1P 1SB
Profile: We have been unable to contact this organisation. The details given are unconfirmed.

Commonwealth Forestry Association
Oxford Forestry Institute
South Parks Road
Oxford
OX1 3RB
Tel: 01865 275072
Contact: Mrs R Mannion Daniels, Editorial Assistant
Founded: 1921
Membership: 1,592
Publications: Commonwealth Forestry Review; Commonwealth Forestry Handbook; The World's Forests – International Initiatives since Rio
Previous names: Empire Forestry Association until 1962
Profile: The objectives of the CFA are to bring together all those who are concerned with the conservation, development, management and utilisation of forests especially, but not only, in the developing world and in the tropics and sub-tropics.

Compassion in World Farming
Charles House
5a Charles Street
Petersfield
Hampshire
GU32 3EH
Tel: 01730 268863
Fax: 01730 260791
Email: tmobrien@ciwf.win-uk.net
Contact: Joyce D'Silva, Director
Founded: 1967
Membership: 14,000
Publications: Agscene (journal)
Profile: CIWF is Britain's leading farm animal welfare organisation campaigning specifically for an end to the factory farming of animals. CIWF has been campaigning against cruel farming practices since its formation in 1967. Campaign successes include an end to narrow veal crates in the UK and the phasing out of sow stalls in the UK.

Compassion in World Farming Trust
Compassion in World Farming
Charles House
5a Charles Street
Petersfield
Hampshire
GU32 3EH
Tel: 01730 268070
Fax: 01730 260791
Email: tmobrien@ciwf.win-uk.net
Contact: John Callaghan, Education Director
Founded: 1986
Publications: Range of educational resources
Previous names: Athene Trust until 1993
Profile: An educational charity promoting concern for the welfare of farm animals. The educational wing of Britain's leading farm animal welfare organisation Compassion in World Farming which has been campaigning for improvements in the welfare of farm animals since 1967. The CIWF Trust works at all levels of the education system to raise awareness of farm animal welfare and to promote serious debate of the issues.

Confederation of European Agriculture
Rue de la Science 23–25
B1040 Brussels
Belgium
Tel: 010 322 230 43 80
Fax: 010 322 230 46 77
Contact: Christophe Hemard, Secretary General
Founded: 1899
Membership: 300
Publications: CEA Dialog; CEA Reports of the Congress
Profile: The European Confederation of Agriculture is an international, non-government organisation having nearly 300 member organisations in over 30 countries. Its mission is to promote contact and exchanges between agricultural professional organisations and to represent the interests of agriculture at international level. The CEA has observer status in many international organisations like the United Nations, the OECD, the Council of Europe, and the Food and Agricultural Organisations. Thus it can appoint experts to ensure that the interests of European agricultural society are heard throughout the international bodies.

Connemara Pony Breeders Society
Hospital Road
Clifden

Co Galway
Republic of Ireland
Tel: 095 21863
Fax: 095 21005
Email: CPBS@iol.ie
Contact: Ms Marian Turley, Secretary
Founded: 1923
Membership: 650
Publications: Members newsletter
Profile: To maintain and publish the stud book of the Connemara pony. To inspect every pony before entry into the stud book. To harmonise and organise international societies worldwide as the parent society. To promote the Connemara pony breed.

Conservation and Woodland Policy Division
Ministry of Agriculture, Fisheries and Food
3 Whitehall Place
London
SW1A 2HH
Tel: 0645 335577
Email: helpline@inf.maff.gov.uk
Profile: The Conservation Policy Division deals with environmentally sensitive areas, straw and stubble burning, countryside access and amenity, wildlife and landscape conservation.

Conservation Bureau
Scottish Development Agency
Rosbery House
Haymarket Terrace
Edinburgh
EH12 5EZ
Profile: We have been unable to contact this organisation. The details given are unconfirmed.

Conservation Foundation
1 Kensington Gore
London
SW7 2AR
Tel: 0171 823 8842
Fax: 0171 823 8791
Email: conservef@gn.apc.org
Contact: David Shreeve, Director
Founded: 1982
Publications: Network 21
Profile: The Conservation Foundation creates and manages a wide range of projects and programmes covering all environmental interests often supported by commercial organisations. In addition to organising award schemes in the UK and Europe the foundation also helps fund ethno-medical research in rain forests and is helping Russian NGO's to tackle some of their country's environmental problems. The foundation also runs a regular news service to

UK environmental journalists and programme makers.

Conservative Anti-Hunt Council
PO Box 193
Welwyn
Hertfordshire
AL6 9HG
Tel: 01823 286398
Fax: 01823 286398
Contact: Mrs Diana Wilson, Chairman
Founded: 1983
Publications: Quarterly members newsletter
Profile: The council was formed to reflect the views of those supporters of the Conservative Party who are opposed to hunting with hounds. It campaigns reasonably, and by legal means, to bring about legislation in parliament to ban hunting.

Consortium of Rural TECs
CORT
12 York Road
Leicester
LE1 5TS
Tel: 0116 254 4166
Fax: 0116 254 4177
Contact: Theresa Essex, Manager
Founded: 1991
Membership: 24
Profile: The Consortium of Rural TECs is a not for profit company established in 1991 by 16 member Training and Enterprise Councils (TECs) which had a key interest in rural issues. By 1996 membership had risen to 24 TECs in addition, national organisations with an interest in rural affairs are associate members of CORT. CORT is supported by flat rate subscriptions from the member TECs.

Construction Industry Research and Information Association
6 Storeys Gate
Westminster
London
SW1P 3AU
Tel: 0171 222 8891
Email: cb@ciria.org.uk
Internet: http://www.ciria.org.uk

Consultative Panel on Badgers and Tuberculosis
Ministry of Agriculture, Fisheries and Food: Welsh Office
c/o MAFF, Block B
Hook Rise South
Tolworth
Surbiton

Surrey
KT6 7NF
Tel: 0181 330 8019
Fax: 0181 337 3640
Email: j.howell@AHDC.Maff.gov.uk
Contact: Mr J Howell, Secretary
Founded: 1975
Profile: The remit of the panel is: to keep under review the evidence relating to bovine tuberculosis in badgers, including its distribution, its prevalence and its relationship to bovine tuberculosis in cattle; to advise on operations being undertaken by the ministry in order to limit the transmission of tuberculosis from badgers to cattle; and finally, to recommend research appropriate to the problem of badgers and bovine tuberculosis.

Consumers' Association
2 Marylebone Road
London
NW1 4DF
Tel: 0171 830 6090
Fax: 0171 830 6220
Email: editor@which.co.uk
Contact: Louise Haughney, Assistant Manager Consumer Affairs
Founded: 1957
Membership: 761,000
Publications: Publications list available
Previous names: Association of Consumer Research until 1995
Profile: Consumers' Association represents the consumer interest and campaigns for improvement in goods and services, both in the public and private sector. The Consumers' Association is a registered charity which undertakes research and comparative testing of goods and services. Its trading subsidiary publishes the results of their research in it's publications.

Continuous Cover Forestry Group
Y Winllan
Brechfa
Carmarthen
SA32 7QZ
Tel: 01267 202233
Fax: 01267 202407
Contact: RH Denman, Secretary
Founded: 1991
Membership: 250
Publications: CCFG Newsletter
Profile: CCFG aims to encourage structural and biological diversity of forests and woods by the use of uneven aged silvicultural systems. CCFG organises the exchange of experience, especially through practical examples of uneven aged

forestry; attempts to persuade forestry research and training bodies to include uneven aged forestry in their programmes and to maintain contact with other groups and organisations concerned with British forests and woodlands. CCFG is affiliated to the pan-European continuous cover group, Pro Silva.

Coppice Association
Eastern Cottage
Main Road
Toft
Bourne
Lincolnshire
PE10 0JT
Profile: We have been unable to contact this organisation. The details given are unconfirmed.

Cordwainers College
182 Mare Street
London
E8 3RE
Tel: 0181 985 0273
Fax: 0181 985 9340

Cotentin Sheep Society
41 Bank Street
Carlisle
Cumbria
CA3 8HJ
Tel: 01228 34423
Fax: 01228 818022
Contact: FC Culley, Secretary
Founded: 1988

Cotswold Sheep Society
Holy Brook Cottage
Far Oakridge
Stroud
Gloucestershire
GL6 7PG
Tel: 01285 760455
Contact: Mrs Lyn Gibbings, Secretary
Founded: 1892
Membership: 180
Publications: Cotswold Sheep Society Flock Book; Cotswold Sheep Society Newsletter; The Cotswold Sheep: Breed History
Profile: The Cotswold Sheep Society is a registered charity working for the conservation and promotion of the Cotswold sheep, now a rare breed of British farm livestock. The society offers pedigree registration and transfer services, breeder workshops and training courses. An annual show is held in June and an official breed sale in September. The society publishes a quarterly newsletter and an annual flock book

and has members throughout the UK plus some in Europe and the USA. The society works closely with other organisations to develop promotional opportunities and support research projects.

Cottage and Rural Enterprises Ltd
CARE Central Office
9 Weir Road
Kibworth
Leicestershire
LE8 0LQ
Tel: 0116 279 3225
Fax: 0116 279 6384
Contact: John Higgins, Development Director
Founded: 1966
Publications: CARE News
Profile: CARE is a registered charity providing residential accommodation and workshop opportunities for people who have a learning disability. Accommodation is provided in small communities, which in turn support a range of satellite homes in the nearby community. There is an emphasis on productive and satisfying work activities leading to the provision of a service or finished product for sale. Anyone interested should write to the Regional Director at the Central Office in Kibworth, Leicestershire.

Council for Awards of Royal Agricultural Societies
Little Folly
Edneys Hill
Wokingham
Berkshire
RG41 4DR
Tel: 0118 781214
Fax: 0118 781214
Contact: JAC Gibb, Secretary to the Council
Founded: 1969
Membership: 614
Publications: Members newsletter; occasional conference reports
Previous names: Council of Fellows of Royal Agricultural Societies until 1984
Profile: The Council for Awards of Royal Agricultural Societies, assisted by national panels in England, Wales, Scotland and Northern Ireland, recognises meritorious contributions by individuals to the benefit of agriculture and the land-based industries in the UK. Associateship of the council (ARAgS) may be awarded to applicants who can demonstrate such a contribution to two assessors appointed by the council, through innovation, excellence in technical performance, leadership in agricultural

organisations or other service to the community. Fellowship (FRAgS) may be awarded to associates whose continued service to the industry is judged by the council to be of high merit.

Council for Country Sports
Welbeck House
High Street
Guildford
Surrey
GU1 3JF
Tel: 01483 83448
Profile: We have been unable to contact this organisation. The details given are unconfirmed.

Council for Environmental Education
University of Reading
London Road
Reading
RG1 5AQ
Tel: 01734 756061
Fax: 01734 756264
Contact: Christine Midgley, Head of Information
Founded: 1968
Publications: Publications list available
Profile: CEE is the national body for the co-ordination and promotion of environmental education, acting as a forum for the exchange of ideas and information and encouraging its development through various projects. CEE's main functions are: co-ordination; information and research; promotion and representation.

Council for National Parks
246 Lavender Hill
London
SW11 1LJ
Tel: 0171 924 4077
Fax: 0171 924 5761
Contact: Ms Ruth Chambers, Policy Officer
Founded: 1936
Membership: 3,600
Previous names: The Standing Committee on National Parks until 1977
Profile: CNP is the national charity which works to protect the National Parks of England and Wales and to promote their quiet enjoyment by everyone.

Council for Nature Conservation and the Countryside
Department of the Environment (NI)
Room 303
Historic Monuments and Buildings
5–33 Hill Street
Belfast
BT1 2LA

Tel: 01232 543050
Fax: 01232 543111
Contact: Carol Gilmore, Secretariat
Founded: 1989
Publications: Publications list available
Profile: CNCC is the Northern Ireland's government's advisory body on all aspects of the conservation of nature and landscape. The council comments on selected planning applications and environmental statements and on such topics as waste management, watercourse management, energy policy and transportation. The council publishes its report, usually every eighteen months.

Council for Scottish Archaeology

c/o National Museums of Scotland
York Buildings
1 Queen Street
Edinburgh
EH2 1JD
Tel: 0131 225 7534
Fax: 0131 557 9498
Email: CSA@dial.pipex.com
Contact: Patrick Begg, Director
Founded: 1944
Membership: 800
Publications: Publications list available
Previous names: Council for British Archaeology (Scotland) until 1988
Profile: The CSA is an independent voluntary body dedicated to the preservation, study and enjoyment of Scotland's archaeological heritage. It speaks for the archaeological community, amateur and professional, and has the overriding aim of securing Scotland's past for the future. CSA aims to advance the education of the public; encourage better identification and conservation of resources; press for improved policies relating to Scotland's archaeology; and facilitate liaison between all sectors of the archaeological community.

Council for the Protection of Rural England

Warwick House
25 Buckingham Palace Road
London
SW1W 0PP
Tel: 0171 976 6433
Fax: 0171 976 6373
Contact: David Conder, Deputy Director
Founded: 1926
Membership: 45,000
Publications: Publications catalogue available
Profile: The CPRE is a national charity which helps people protect their local countryside where there is threat, to enhance it where there is opportunity, and to keep it beautiful, productive and enjoyable for everyone. They work for a beautiful and living countryside on behalf of present and future generations, and for the more sustainable use of land and other resources in town and country. With 43 county branches and 200 local groups backed by an influential national office in Westminster, CPRE is a powerful combination of effective local action and strong national campaigning.

Council of Justice to Animals and Humane Slaughter Association

34 Blanche Lane
South Mimms
Potters Bar
Hertfordshire
EN6 3PA
Tel: 01707 659040
Fax: 01707 649279
Contact: Sir Michael Simmons, Secretary
Founded: 1911
Membership: 650
Publications: Annual Report; newsletter; numerous pamphlets; instructional books/videos
Profile: The HSA is an animal welfare charity. Its objectives are promotion of humane methods of slaughter of food animals; introduction of reforms in livestock markets; and improvements to livestock transport facilities. The HSA works with industry seeking improvements to animal welfare through a pragmatic co-operative relationship. To this end, staff give lectures and instruction to those working in the meat industry and produce instructional material in the form of books, pamphlets and videos.

Council of National Beekeeping Associations of the United Kingdom

Little Greengarth
60 Deben Avenue
Martlesham Heath
Ipswich
Suffolk
IP5 7QP
Profile: We have been unable to contact this organisation. The details given are unconfirmed.

Council of the National Golf Unions

Formby Golf Club
19 Birch Green
Formby
Liverpool
L37 1LG
Tel: 01704 831800
Fax: 01704 831800
Contact: Alan Thirlwell, Honorary Secretary

Publications: The Standard Scratch Score and Handicapping Scheme
Previous names: The British Golf Unions' Joint Advisory Committee
Profile: To consider and advise the national golf unions on all matters connected with the game of golf; to undertake such further duties and to exercise such further functions as shall be allotted to it from time to time by the four national unions; to act as the consultative committee between the national unions and the Royal and Ancient Golf Club of St Andrews.

Country Gentleman's Association Ltd
CGA House
Avenue 1
The Business Park
Letchworth
Hertfordshire
SG6 2HE
Tel: 01462 480011

Country Houses Association
41 Kingsway
London
WC2B 6UB
Tel: 0171 836 1624
Fax: 0171 240 1676
Contact: Mr Roy D Bratby, Chief Executive
Founded: 1955
Membership: 2,000
Previous names: Mutual Households Association Ltd

Country Landowners Association
16 Belgrave Square
London
SW1X 8PQ
Tel: 0171 235 0511
Fax: 0171 235 4696
Contact: JA Anderson, Chief Executive
Membership: 49,000
Publications: Country Landowner

Country Park Conservers
128 High Street
West Malling
Kent
ME14 2LL
Profile: We have been unable to contact this organisation. The details given are unconfirmed.

Country Trust, The
Stratford Grange
Stratford St Andrew
Saxmundham
Suffolk
IP17 1LF
Tel: 01728 604818
Fax: 01728 602233
Contact: Mrs Louisa Thorp, Office Manager
Founded: 1978
Publications: A Short Introduction to Farming in Britain
Profile: The Country Trust is a national educational charity that organises and conducts day-long and week-long educational expeditions for children from inner city areas, to see the countryside and learn first hand how it is managed and maintained from those who live and work there. The visitors are taken to farms, forests, lakes and rivers, estates and all manner of rural businesses, not normally open to the public. Many of the children have never been into the country before. No charge is made for arranging the visits; the trust exists solely on donations, but often has to subsidise the children's transport.

Countryside Commission
John Dower House
Crescent Place
Cheltenham
Gloucestershire
GL50 3RA
Tel: 01242 521381
Fax: 01242 584270
Contact: Terry Grant, Press Officer
Founded: 1949
Publications: Publications list available
Previous names: National Parks Commission (1949–1968); Countryside Commission for England and Wales (1968–1991)
Profile: To care for the natural beauty of the countryside of England and to help people to enjoy it. The Countryside Commission advises government on countryside matters; designates National Parks and Areas of Outstanding Natural Beauty, defines Heritage Coasts and establishes National Trails; provides grants and advice for landscape conservation and projects which improve public access and collaborates with local authorities, public agencies, voluntary bodies, farmers, landowners and individuals.

Countryside Council for Wales
Plas Penrhos
Penrhos Ffordd
Bangor
Gwynedd
LL57 2LQ
Tel: 01248 385500
Fax: 01248 355782

Contact: Mr Colin Brown, Central Office Team Leader
Founded: 1991
Profile: The CCW was formed by the amalgamation of the Nature Conservancy Council and the Countryside Commission for Wales. It is the government's statutory adviser on wildlife, countryside and maritime conservation matters in Wales. It is the executive authority for the conservation of habitats and wildlife. It enables local authorities, voluntary organisations and interested parties to pursue countryside management projects through grant aid. The Countryside Council is accountable to the Secretary of State for Wales who appoints it and provides its annual grant in aid.

Countryside Database
Online Leisure Information Co
35 Rose Street
Covent Garden
London
WC2E 9EW
Tel: 0171 222 4640
Fax: 0171 379 0898
Email: ann@online-leisure.com
Contact: Ann Vernon Griffiths, Managing Director
Founded: 1990
Publications: Great Escapes to the Countryside
Profile: The Countryside Database is one of the family of leisure databases created and managed by the specialist information company, Online Leisure. The databases are available to professional subscribers online via videotext and multimedia formats and are also used to produce a range of publications.

Countryside Division
Ministry of Agriculture, Fisheries and Food
Nobel House
17 Smith Square
London
SW1P 3JR
Tel: 0171 238 5637
Fax: 0171 238 6308
Profile: The Countryside Division is responsible for structural policy and rural development, grants for capital investment on farms, the Hill Farming Advisory Committee, heather and grass burning, the Vertebrate Pest Control Unit and designation of Less Favoured Areas.

Countryside Education Trust
Out of Town Centre
Palace Lane
Beaulieu
Brockenhurst

Hampshire
SO42 7YG
Tel: 01590 612401
Fax: 01590 612624
Contact: Graham Carter, Director
Founded: 1975
Profile: The Countryside Education Trust is an educational charity based at Beaulieu in the New Forest. It provides day visit and residential courses for all age groups, programmes led by graduate staff which meet requirements of the National Curriculum.

Countryside Foundation
Dean Clough
Halifax
West Yorkshire
HX3 5AX
Tel: 01422 344555
Fax: 01422 353347
Contact: Mandy Marsden, Administrator
Founded: 1986
Publications: The Lychford File (multi-media education pack)
Profile: The Countryside Foundation is an independent educational charity. Their aim is to promote an understanding of the countryside as a living, working environment, and of the issues facing those responsible for its management. This involves education in its widest sense of the effects of these activities upon the ecology, the rural environment, wildlife, agriculture, the way of life and economy of rural communities, industries, businesses connected therewith, and employment in them.

Countryside In and Around Towns Network
Scottish Natural Heritage
Caspian House
Clydebank Business Park
Clydebank
Glasgow
G81 2NR
Tel: 0141 951 4488
Fax: 0141 951 4510
Contact: Helen L Robertson, Officer
Founded: 194
Publications: Information leaflet; bi-monthly news sheet
Profile: CAT Network aims to provide promotional and communication support to the range of environmental projects throughout Scotland which work with local communities to enhance and sustain the countryside environment in their areas. Project work includes access and recreation, environmental education, wildlife and conservation, landscape

improvement and community participation. The CAT Network organises regular meetings for projects and other interested organisations to discuss matters of common interest and exchange ideas and information.

Countryside Management Association

c/o Centre for Environmental Interpretation
Manchester Metropolitan University
St Augustines
Lower Chatham Street
Manchester
M15 6BY
Tel: 0161 247 1067
Founded: 1966
Membership: 1,200
Publications: Ranger Magazine; Law in Countryside (Parkes)
Previous names: Association of Countryside Rangers until 1994
Profile: The Countryside Management Association aims to advance sustainable management of the countryside for its conservation and enjoyment by the public, to establish and promote professional standards of practice for those engaged in management of the countryside and to represent their views at national and local level. Activities of the association which further its aims include: provision of conferences, training courses and continuing professional development; operation of a national and regional network for the exchange of information and experience; operation of careers advice and jobs information services; publication of relevant literature; and collaboration with other organisations at local, national and international level to advance mutual aims.

Countryside Management Division

Department of Agriculture for Northern Ireland
Annex A
Dundonald House
Upper Newtownards Road
Belfast
BT4 3SB
Tel: 01232 524713
Fax: 01232 524152
Contact: Dr Harry Gracey, Head of Countryside Management Division
Founded: 1996
Publications: Publications list available
Profile: The Countryside Management Division aims to promote economic growth and development of the countryside of Northern Ireland.

Countryside Movement, The

Freepost
Room CT1
Bristol
BS38 7HL
Contact: Information Officer
Founded: 1996
Profile: To promote awareness of the British Countryside, demonstrating the caring, knowledge and experience which country people apply to their work and recreation, especially in their relationships with animals and with the natural world. Aim to protect country life from its detractors and promote good practice, building and welcoming an honest and informed relationship between town and countryside. Their goal is to ensure that the countryside can look forward to a healthy future, confident that its contribution to the British way of life is properly valued.

Countryside Recreation and Environmental Management Research Group

Sheffield Hallam University
School of Leisure and Food Management
Totley Campus
Totley Hall Lane
Sheffield
S17 4AB
Tel: 0114 272 0911
Fax: 0114 253 2881
Email: M.Jones@shu.ac.uk
Contact: Mr M Jones, Head of Academic Resources
Profile: The Countryside Recreation and Environmental Management Research Group is involved with the delivery of undergraduate and postgraduate courses as well as consultancy and research. Their research and consultancy expertise encompasses the sustainable use of the countryside, countryside recreation policies and planning, management planning for countryside sites and facilities, ecological surveying and analysis, habitat creation and conservation, visitor management, urban greenspace management, access issues, countryside interpretation and environmental education.

Countryside Recreation Network

Department of City and Regional Planning
University of Wales College Cardiff
PO Box 906
Cardiff
CF1 3YN
Tel: 01222 874970
Fax: 01222 874970
Email: stoce@cardiff.ac.uk

Contact: Catherine Etchell, Manager
Founded: 1992
Membership: 2,000
Publications: Publications list available
Previous names: Countryside Recreation Research Advisory Group until 1992
Profile: CRN is a UK wide network which gives easy access to information and people concerned with countryside and related recreation matters. It also acts as a UK wide network of the principal agencies involved in countryside and related recreation matters.

Countryside Resources
Ashcroft
Rectory Lane
Scrivelsby
Horncastle
Lincolnshire
LN9 6JB
Profile: We have been unable to contact this organisation. The details given are unconfirmed.

Countryside Restoration Trust
Barton
Cambridgeshire
CB3 7AG
Tel: 01223 843322
Contact: The Director
Founded: 1993
Membership: 3,500
Publications: The Lark (bi-annual newsletter)
Profile: The aims of the trust are to show that profitable farming, attractive landscape and abundant wildlife can co-exist. The trust demonstrates this by purchasing over-intensively farmed land and rehabilitating it.

Countryside Society
140 Cholmeley Road
Reading
RG1 3LR
Tel: 01734 665174
Profile: We have been unable to contact this organisation. The details given are unconfirmed.

Countryside Trust
John Dower House
Crescent Place
Cheltenham
Gloucestershire
GL50 3RA
Tel: 01242 521381
Fax: 01242 584270
Contact: Alison Lammas, Secretary
Founded: 1990
Publications: Countryside Trust Leaflet

Profile: The trust is a registered charity and was set up in 1990 with the proceeds of a generous legacy to the Countryside Commission from Miss Marjorie Broadbent of Hebden Bridge, Yorkshire. Since then other legacies and donations have been received. The trust works to conserve, preserve and restore the natural beauty of the countryside of England for public benefit. To this end it offers grants towards the cost of fundraising projects where the money raised is to be used for practical conservation in the countryside, but not in towns.

Countryside Venture Ltd
Tigbourne Farm
Wormley
Surrey
GU8 5TT
Tel: 01428 682658
Contact: Edward Thorneycroft, Chairman
Founded: 1989
Profile: A registered charity raising funds to foster and promote countryside conservation training. Countryside Venture funds establishments offering rural skills training and provides scholarships and bursaries to young people wishing to gain rural skills. They believe that rural skills are essential to maintain a vibrant, cared for countryside and retain regional and local characteristics.

County Antrim Agricultural Association (Ballymena Show)
Showgrounds
Warden Street
Ballymena
County Antrim
BT43 7DR
Tel: 01266 652666
Fax: 01266 652666
Contact: Mrs M Watterson, Secretary
Founded: 1890
Membership: 430
Publications: Annual Report; show schedule; show catalogue
Profile: Organises the Ballymena Show which is the largest two-day show in Ireland, drawing the farming community and the townspeople together over the two days. The show can proudly boast the largest numbers of overall entries of any show in the province and these increase every year. Like any other industry/business at present there are many other changes taking place and an agricultural show is no different. Ballymena Show, with a forward thinking chairman, are also having to change to meet the needs of the farmer and the

general public. The most recent introduction is an Agri-food marquee and further changes are being planned.

County Planning Officers Society
Environment Department
Hertfordshire County Council
County Hall
Peggs Lane
Hertford
SG13 8DN
Tel: 01992 555200
Fax: 01992 555202
Email: charlie_watson@hertscc.gov.uk
Contact: MC Watson, Director of Environment
Founded: 1947
Membership: 120
Profile: The objects of the society are to promote the study and practice and exchange of knowledge in town and country planning, to maintain contacts, to advise the Association of County Councils, local authority associations, government departments and other relevant bodies, and to take such actions relating to the objects as may be thought desirable.

County Surveyors Society
Department of Environment
Gloucestershire County Council
Shire Hall
Bearland
Gloucester
GL1 2TH
Tel: 01452 425523
Fax: 01452 426363
Contact: Richard Wigginton, Hon Secretary
Founded: 1885
Membership: 300
Publications: Publications list available
Profile: To promote the acquisition and exchange of knowledge and experience in the fields of transportation, highways and civil engineering. To maintain contact with appropriate government departments and to serve and advise local authorities concerned with these matters.

Crafts Council
44a Pentonville Road
London
N1 9BY
Tel: 0171 278 7700
Fax: 0171 837 6891

Croad Langshan Club
Heather Cottage
Dead Mans Lane
Goring Heath

Berkshire
RG8 7RX
Tel: 01491 680634
Contact: Caroline M Hadley, Secretary
Founded: 1904
Membership: 80
Publications: Breed Book
Profile: The Croad Langshan Club exists to promote the ancient breed which was imported from China in 1872. A dual purpose utility fowl – the Croad Langshan is of value both to those who want to keep a pure breed for eggs and to those who want a smart exhibition breed.

Crofters Commission
Scottish Office
4–6 Castle Wynd
Inverness
IV2 3EQ
Tel: 01463 663450
Fax: 01463 711820
Email: crofters_commission@cali.co.uk
Contact: Shirley Hammond, Information Officer
Founded: 1955
Publications: Annual report; numerous leaflets; information on projects in crofting communities
Profile: The commission was set up in 1955 to regulate, promote and develop crofting. Its main aim is to promote a thriving crofting community by regulating effectively, promoting best use of croft land and encouraging sustainable development in crofting areas. The commission works with local assessors and grazing clerks to ensure good consultation which informs its regulatory policies and supports development of appropriate initiatives.

Cross Country Commission
British Athletic Federation
Crossways
Caunton Lane
Caunton
Newark
Nottinghamshire
NG23 6BB
Tel: 01636 636482
Contact: Ken Rickhuss, Chair

Crown Estate, The
Crown Estate Office
16 Carlton House Terrace
London
SW1Y 5AH
Tel: 0171 210 4377
Fax: 0171 930 8259
Contact: Miss M Watson, Central Records
Founded: 1760
Publications: Annual Report

Profile: The Crown Estate Commissioners administer the hereditary land revenues of the Crown. The estate includes properties in England, Wales and Scotland, Windsor Great Park and foreshore and seabed around the coast of the UK.

Cymdeithas Edward Llwyd
c/o Maes Meheli
Sawmills
Ceri
Drenewydd
Powys
SY16 4LJ
Tel: 01686 670219
Contact: Elinor Gwynn, Secretary
Founded: 1978
Membership: 750
Publications: Y Naturiaethwr; Cylchlythyr Cymdeithas Edward Llwyd
Profile: Cymdeithas Edward Llwyd is a national society for Welsh naturalists. It aims to promote the study of the life and work of Edward Llwyd, the study of Wales' flora and fauna and geology and their interrelationships, the study of the environment in the spirit of Edward Llwyd and to promote the awareness of Wales' natural environment and heritage and campaign for their protection.

Cymdeithas Gwaith Maes
Adran yr Amgylchedd
Y Coleg Normal
Bangor
Gwynedd
LL57 2PX
Tel: 01248 370171
Fax: 01248 370461
Contact: Geraint George, Secretary
Founded: 1993
Membership: 1,000
Publications: Members newsletter; Gwaith Maes
Profile: The aim of the organisation is to promote environmental education through the medium of Welsh. Local branches exist throughout Wales. Membership is open to individuals, schools, colleges and any other organisations interested in supporting Welsh medium environmental education.

Dairy Industry Federation Ltd
19 Cornwall Terrace
London
NW1 4QP
Tel: 0171 486 7244
Fax: 0171 487 4734
Contact: REK McKeith, Company Secretary
Previous names: Dairy Trade Federation

Dales Pony Society
196 Springvale Road
Walkley
Sheffield
S6 3NU
Profile: We have been unable to contact this organisation. The details given are unconfirmed.

Dalesbred Sheep Breeders Association
1 Gib Hey Lane
Chipping
Preston
Lancashire
PR3 2WW
Tel: 01995 61570
Contact: J Whitaker
Profile: We have been unable to contact this organisation. The details given are unconfirmed.

Dartmoor National Park Authority
Parke
Haytor Road
Bovey Tracey
Newton Abbot
Devon
TQ13 9JQ
Tel: 01626 832093

Dartmoor Pony Society
57 Pykes Down
Ivybridge
Devon
PL21 0BY
Contact: Mrs Lisa Setter, Honorary Secretary
Founded: 1924
Membership: 500
Publications: The Dartmoor Pony: a history of the breed by Joseph Palmer
Profile: The Dartmoor Pony Society is run by breeders and owners and other enthusiasts to promote the breed in every sphere. The society is very active, giving encouragement, advice and help where needed. It runs an annual show in Devon, catering for all aspects of production including driving. The society also administers newtakes on Dartmoor in co-operation with the Dartmoor National Park and the Duchy of Cornwall aiming to upgrade the wild pony herds by the use of selected stallions. Approved ponies are then entered into an appendix of the society's Stud Book which contains details of fully registered ponies.

De Montfort University Lincoln
School of Agriculture and Horticulture
Caythorpe Court
Caythorpe

Grantham
Lincolnshire
NG32 3EP
Tel: 01400 272521
Fax: 01400 272722
Contact: Professor Mike Wilkinson, Head of
School
Founded: 1947
Publications: Prospectus
Previous names: Lincolnshire College of
Agriculture and Horticulture until 1994
Profile: Caythorpe Court and Riseholme Hall
have been recognised as centres of excellence in
land-based industries since their inception as
farm institutes some 50 years ago. Now part of
De Montfort University, the school offers a
unique range of opportunities in education and
training for people from all backgrounds from
BTEC First Diplomas and GNVQ Intermediate
through National Diplomas to Degrees and
research.

Defence Animal Centre
Welby Lane Camp
Melton Mowbray
Leicestershire
LE13 0SL
Tel: 01664 411811
Fax: 01664 410694
Contact: Major (Ret'd) PJN Downing, Adjutant
Founded: 1991
Membership: 180
Previous names: Army Veterinary and Remount
Depot (founded 1905); Royal Army Veterinary
Corps (founded 1946)
Profile: The Defence Animal Centre (DAC) was
formed on 1st April 1991. It is a joint service unit
under army command and embraces the former
Royal Army Veterinary Corps Centre located at
Melton Mowbray, Leicestershire and the Dog
Training Flight of the Royal Air Force Police
Training School at Newton, Nottinghamshire. The
aim of the Defence Animal Centre is to provide
the Ministry of Defence and other agencies with
horses, trained dogs and the trained personnel to
operate and support them in peace and war,
efficiently and to the required standard.

Denbighshire and Flintshire Agricultural Society
Midland Bank Chambers
Holywell
Clwyd
CH8 7SU
Tel: 01352 712131
Fax: 01352 712098
Contact: Mrs M Owen, Show Administrator

Founded: 1839
Membership: 1,200
Publications: Show schedule; show catalogue
Profile: To promote, improve and encourage
agriculture and horticulture by means of
education, scientific research, experimental work
and the holding of shows.

Department of Agriculture
University of Aberdeen
MacRobert Building
581 King Street
Aberdeen
AB24 5UA
Tel: 01224 274022
Fax: 01224 273731
Email: Agrisec@abdn.ac.uk
Contact: The Secretary
Publications: Prospectus of Undergraduate
Courses; Prospectus of Postgraduate Courses
Profile: Provides teaching at BSc and MSc level.
Runs six taught MSc courses in agricultural
development, agricultural economics, animal
nutrition, animal production, pig production and
reproductive biology. Undertakes research to
MPhil and PhD with contract research across the
disciplines of crop science, microbiology, animal
science and rural economics.

Department of Agriculture Fisheries and Food – Isle of Man
Isle of Man Government
Murray House
Mount Havelock
Douglas
Isle of Man
Tel: 01624 842495
Fax: 01624 844374
Contact: DN Peck, Chief Agricultural Adviser
Profile: Responsible for: the provision of
legislation with regard to agriculture and fisheries
and formulation of policy for support; provision of
statutory animal health controls; provision of
education (NVQ levels 1 and 2) and advice to
agriculture; administration of grant support
schemes to agriculture, horticulture and
fisheries.

Department of Agriculture for Northern Ireland
Ministry of Agriculture, Fisheries and Food
Dundonald House
Upper Newtownards Road
Belfast
BT4 3SB
Tel: 01232 520100
Fax: 01232 525015
Contact: John Magee, Press Officer

Publications: An Overview of the Northern Ireland Agri-Food Industry
Profile: Responsible for the development of agri-food, forestry and fisheries industries in Northern Ireland; veterinary, scientific and development services; food and farming policy; agri-environmental policy and rural development.

Department of Agriculture for Northern Ireland Veterinary Sciences Division
Stoney Road
Stormont
Belfast
BT4 3SD
Tel: 01232 520011
Fax: 01232 525775
Contact: M Stewart McNulty, Professor
Founded: 1925
Profile: A laboratory based multidisciplinary organisation of about 250 staff providing a diagnostic service for diseases of farm animals, poultry and fish and carrying our analytical testing and research work in support for the aims of the Department of Agriculture for Northern Ireland.

Department of Clinical Veterinary Science
University of Bristol
Langford House
Langford
Bristol
BS18 7DU
Tel: 0117 928 9280
Fax: 01934 853400
Email: Peter.Read@bris.ac.uk
Contact: Peter Read, Senior Site Administrator
Founded: 1947
Publications: Various research papers
Profile: Involved in teaching veterinary undergraduates and carrying out research in animal welfare and husbandry. They have a small animal hospital, equine diagnostic centre, small animal veterinary practice, large animal veterinary practice and a dairy/beef and sheep farm.

Department of Economics (Agricultural Economics Research Group)
University of Nottingham
University Park
Nottingham
NG7 2RD
Tel: 0115 951 5623
Fax: 0115 951 4159
Contact: Dr CW Morgan, Lecturer
Profile: This informal grouping within the economics department acts as a focus for research into a broad range of economic topics with an emphasis on the evaluation of policy. The research programme has various strands which

include: agricultural trade policy reform; futures markets; commodity market models; and farm level analysis.

Department of National Heritage
2–4 Cockspur Street
London
SW1Y 5DH
Tel: 0171 270 3000

Department of the Environment
2 Marsham Street
London
SW1P 3EB
Tel: 0171 276 3000
Fax: 0171 276 0790
Profile: The government department responsible for environmental affairs in the UK.

Department of the Environment for Northern Ireland
Clarence Court
10–18 Adelaide Street
Belfast
BT2 8GB
Tel: 01232 540843
Fax: 01232 540026
Contact: Eddie Hayes, Director of Regional Development
Profile: The Department of the Environment (DOE) NI is one of six Northern Ireland government departments staffed by the Northern Ireland civil service. Together with the Northern Ireland Office, the Northern Ireland departments are accountable to the Secretary of State for Northern Ireland. He has delegated responsibility for the conduct of matters coming within the remit of the department to a parliamentary under secretary at the Northern Ireland Office.

Department of the Environment Wildlife and Countryside Directorate
2 Marsham Street
London
SW1P 3EB
Tel: 0171 276 4583
Fax: 0171 276 3349

Department of Trade and Industry
1 Victoria Street
London
SW1H 0ET
Tel: 0171 215 5000
Fax: 0171 222 2629
Contact: MJ Phillips, Directories Section/SMD 3a

Department of Transport
Great Minster House
76 Marsham Street
London
SW1P 4DR
Tel: 0171 271 5000
Fax: 0171 271 5972
Internet: http://www.coi.gov.uk/
coi/depts/gdt/gdt.html

Derbyshire Agricultural and Horticultural Society Inc
16, Hollingworth
Sandiacre
Nottingham
NG10 5LT
Tel: 0115 946 4544
Contact: John Fayle, Gen Secretary
Profile: We have been unable to contact this organisation. The details given are unconfirmed.

Derbyshire Gritstone Sheepbreeders Society
Dyneley Farm
Cliviger
Burnley
Lancashire
BB11 3RE
Tel: 01246 206071
Contact: R Shorrock, Secretary
Founded: 1900
Membership: 170
Publications: Members newsletters
Profile: To maintain the pure breeding of Derbyshire Gritstone sheep. Also to allow members to sell registered sheep at the annual show and sale.

Derbyshire Redcap Club
Lythwon
Chelmorton Ditch
Buxton
Derbyshire
SK17 9SQ
Tel: 01298 854590
Contact: Mrs A Dawson, Secretary
Profile: A society to promote the Derbyshire Redcap breed of poultry.

Derry and Limavady Agricultural Societies
Straidarran
38 Bells Hill
Limavady
BT49 0DQ
Profile: We have been unable to contact this organisation. The details given are unconfirmed.

Development Board for Rural Wales
Ladywell House
Newtown
Powys
SY16 1JB
Tel: 01686 626965
Fax: 01686 627889
Email: rbebb@dbrw.win-uk.net
Contact: Kay Browning, Projects Assistant
Founded: 1976
Publications: Annual Report

Devon and Cornwall Longwool Flockbook Association
Cherbourne
West Lane
Dolton
Winkleigh
Devon
EX19 8QV
Tel: 01805 804449
Contact: AV Phillips, Secretary
Founded: 1976
Membership: 80
Previous names: Formed from an amalgamation of the Devon Longwool and the South Devon Flock, both founded in 1900
Profile: The breeding and maintenance and characteristics of the breed of Devon and Cornwall Longwool sheep at home and abroad to maintain the purity of the breed.

Devon Cattle Breeders' Society
Barn Lane Farm
Stoke Rivers
Barnstaple
Devon
EX32 7LD
Tel: 01598 710836
Fax: 01598 710836
Contact: Albert Beer, Breed Secretary
Founded: 1884
Membership: 270
Publications: Annual herd book
Profile: A registered charity and company registered at Companies House. Objective is to maintain the purity and viability of the Devon breed of cattle. Pedigree register lists are maintained and two shows and sales are held during the year, as well as many other commercial and academic events.

Devon Closewool Sheepbreeders Association
Barn Lane Farm
Stoke Rivers
Barnstaple
Devon
EX32 7LD

Tel: 01598 710495
Fax: 01598 710836
Contact: Albert Beer, Breed Secretary
Founded: 1923
Membership: 70
Publications: Annual flock book
Profile: A sheep breed society with the objective of maintaining the viability of the Devon Closewool sheep.

Devon County Agricultural Association
Westpoint
Exeter
EX5 1DJ
Tel: 01392 444777
Fax: 01392 444808
Contact: John Sandford, Secretary

Dexter Cattle Society
Glen Fern
Waddicombe
Dulverton
Somerset
TA22 9RY
Tel: 01398 341490
Fax: 01398 341490
Contact: Mrs S Mansell, Secretary

District Planning Officers' Society
c/o Torridge District Council
Riverbank House
Bideford
Devon
EX39 2QG
Tel: 01237 476711
Fax: 01237 478849
Contact: David Pinney, Honorary Secretary
Membership: 350
Profile: The society's membership is comprised of officers from 288 District or Borough Councils in England. Its council meets approx. four times a year, with presidential advisory group meetings approx. three times a year. The Society is divided into 16 topic groups of between 2 and 17 members dealing with issues such as conservation, development and building control, leisure, housing and transport. The society meets with other organisations such as the DoE, CBI, House Builders Federation, NFU, CPRE and the County and Metropolitan Planning Officer Societies throughout the year to discuss planning and other relevant issues.

District Surveyors Association
Greenholt
Springfield Road
Verwood
Dorset

BH31 6HY
Tel: 01202 633212
Contact: WL Stamp

Domestic Fowl Trust
Honeybourne Pastures
Honeybourne
Evesham
Hereford and Worcester
WR11 5QJ
Tel: 01386 833083
Fax: 01386 833364
Contact: Michael D Ll Roberts, Director
Founded: 1975
Publications: Gold Cockerel series of books (catalogue available)
Profile: The conservation farm for rare and minority breeds of domestic fowl including ducks, geese, hens, bantams and turkeys. Fourteen acres of grass paddocks which hold over 160 breeds. The trust supplies housing, equipment, books, incubators, foodstuffs, and sells birds from its own rearing programme.

Donkey Breed Society
The Hermitage
Pootings
Edenbridge
Kent
TN8 6SD
Tel: 01732 864414
Fax: 01732 864414
Contact: Mrs Carol Morse, Secretary
Founded: 1967
Membership: 1,250
Publications: The Donkey; Bray Talk
Profile: The charity working for all donkeys and helping to bring the donkey into the public eye. Healthy, happy and well cared for, most donkeys revel in their lives as pets, working members of the family or indeed show animals. The DBS focuses its efforts on education, experience and publicity to encourage the proper care and management of donkeys. The society has sections for donkey driving, activities (trekking, dressage, light draught work and parades), juniors, education and welfare including a rehoming scheme, and maintains a Stud Book to help in the development of quality breeding stock.

Donkey Sanctuary, The
Sidmouth
Devon
EX10 0NU
Tel: 01395 578222
Fax: 01395 579266

Email: 100731.3407@compuserve.com
Internet: http://www.vet.gla.ac.uk/inform/donkey/
Contact: Mrs Marilyn Squance, Deputy
Administrator
Founded: 1969
Publications: Newsletters; Professional
Handbook of the Donkey
Profile: The Donkey Sanctuary was founded in
1969 by Dr Elisabeth Svendsen, MBE. It is now
the largest donkey and mule charity in the UK
and comprises 1,400 acres spread over nine
farms where 6,900 donkeys and mules have
found peace, safety and expert medical care for
life. No donkey is ever sold and no donkey is put
down, unless it in their very best interest. Over
60 voluntary welfare officers investigate cases of
neglect and cruelty. The sanctuary provides
training courses on donkey care and has an
excellent veterinary hospital designed specifically
for treating donkeys.

Dorking Club
Heather Bank
Hillings Lane
Menston
Ilkley
West Yorkshire
LS29 6AU
Tel: 01943 872660
Contact: Mrs V Roberts, Secretary
Profile: A society to promote the Dorking breed
of poultry.

Dorset Down Sheep Breeders' Association
Greenway Farm
Bishops Lydeard
Taunton
Somerset
TA4 3DD
Tel: 01823 432301
Fax: 01823 432301
Contact: Mrs June Pither, Breed Secretary
Founded: 1906
Membership: 50
Publications: Annual flock book
Profile: An association set up expressly to
encourage the breeding of Dorset Down sheep
at home and abroad and the maintenance of
purity of the breed. To establish and publish an
annual flock book noting sires used or ewes
which have been bred from. Also to publish a
statement of transactions undertaken on behalf
of the breed or of general interest to
flockowners. To investigate doubtful pedigrees
and arbitrate thereon. To consider all question
affecting the interest of flockowners and act as
best fits.

**Dorset Horn and Poll Dorset Sheep Breeders'
Association**
Agriculture House
Acland Road
Dorchester
Dorset
DT1 1EF
Tel: 01305 262126
Fax: 01305 262126
Contact: Liz Johnson, Secretary
Founded: 1892
Membership: 350
Publications: Annual flock book
Profile: Breed association for the promotion and
preservation of the Dorset Horn and Poll Dorset
sheep breeds.

Drainage Council for Northern Ireland
c/o Department of Agriculture for Northern
Ireland
Watercourse Management
4 Hospital Road
Belfast
BT8 8JP
Tel: 01232 253380
Fax: 01232 253455
Contact: Hazel Campbell, Secretary of Drainage
Council
Founded: 1947
Profile: The Drainage Council has a general
scrutiny role in relation to the Department of
Agriculture's drainage programme to ensure
uniform treatment of drainage throughout
Northern Ireland. Specifically, the council
considers the recommendations of the
Department of Agriculture or of any person in
relation to the designation of watercourses and
sea defences for maintenance at public expense.
The council also examines the environmental
aspects of any drainage work.

**Drinking Fountain Association – The
Metropolitan Drinking Fountain and Cattle
Trough Association**
Oaklands
5 Queensborough Gardens
Chislehurst
Kent
BR7 6NP
Tel: 0181 467 1261
Fax: 0181 467 1261

Dry Stone Walling Association of Great Britain
c/o YFC Centre
National Agricultural Centre
Stoneleigh Park
Warwickshire
CV8 2LG

Tel: 0121 378 0493
Fax: 0121 378 0493
Contact: Jacqui Simkins, National Secretary
Founded: 1968
Membership: 1,200
Publications: Publications list available
Profile: The Dry Stone Walling Association was founded in 1968. It is an expanding charitable organisation which seeks to ensure the best craftsmanship of the past is preserved and the craft has a thriving future. The DSWA relies on subscriptions for much of its income.

Duchy College
Cornwall College
Stoke Climsland
Callington
Cornwall
PL17 8PD
Tel: 01579 370769
Fax: 01579 370920
Contact: Mr AS Counsell, Vice Principal
Founded: 1986
Profile: Duchy College is a small specialist college which operates county-wide, and offers education and training to the broad spectrum of land-based and agricultural industries. Students range in age from 16 to 60; courses range from one day legislative training through to HND and National Diploma provision of up to 3 years full-time study. The college is situated on three sites – Stoke Climsland, Wadebridge and Rosewarne.

Duck Producers Association Ltd
Imperial House
15–19 Kingsway
London
WC2B 6UA
Tel: 0171 240 9889
Fax: 0171 240 7757
Contact: Miss YP Sired, Secretary

Dun Horse and Pony Society
14 Queen Street
Chipperfield
King's Langley
Hertfordshire
WD4 9BT
Profile: We have been unable to contact this organisation. The details given are unconfirmed.

Dundee College
Old Glamis Road
Dundee
DD3 8LE
Tel: 01382 834834
Fax: 01382 858117

Contact: Dudley Collison, Marketing Officer
Founded: 1943
Publications: Annual Report, course directories, career area leaflets, course information
Previous names: A merger of Dundee College of Commerce and Kingsway Technical College in 1985
Profile: One of Scotland's largest and best equipped centres of further education, Dundee College offers a comprehensive portfolio of full-time, part-time, open and flexible learning opportunities. Committed to quality in every aspect of its operation, the college has achieved Investors in People status, the Scottish Quality Management System (SQMS) standard and is an approved SCOTVEC centre.

Durham County Agricultural Society
18 Church Chare
Chester le Street
County Durham
DH3 3PZ
Tel: 0191 388 5459
Contact: Mrs Duke, Secretary
Profile: We have been unable to contact this organisation. The details given are unconfirmed.

Durrell Institute of Conservation and Ecology
Department of Biosciences
University of Kent at Canterbury
Canterbury
Kent
CT2 7NJ
Tel: 01227 827282
Fax: 01227 827839
Contact: Dr M Walkey, Executive Director
Founded: 1989
Publications: Both scientific/academic peer reviewed publications and consultancy and privately commissioned reports
Profile: A postgraduate training and research department at the University of Kent, specialising in biodiversity management worldwide and particularly in 'high biodiversity' countries.

Dutch Bantam Club
Ty Gwyn
Coole Lane
Audlem
Cheshire
CW3 0ER
Tel: 01270 811073
Contact: Mr MJ Banks, Secretary
Profile: A society to promote the Dutch Bantam breed of poultry.

Dwr Cymru / Welsh Water
Plas y Ffynnon
Cambrian Way
Brecon
Powys
LD3 7HP
Tel: 01874 623181
Fax: 01874 624167

EarthKind
Avenue Lodge
Bounds Green Road
London
N22 4EU
Tel: 0181 889 1595
Fax: 0181 881 7662
Contact: Secretary
Founded: 1955
Publications: Publications list available
Previous names: Crusade Against All Cruelty to Animals until 1990
Profile: EarthKind is working to protect animals and the environment. They also run Britain's first wildlife rescue ship, Ocean Defender.

Earthward Institute, The
Tweed Horizons
Newtown St Boswells
Roxburghshire
TD6 0SG
Tel: 01835 822122
Fax: 01835 822199
Email: earthward@scotborders.co.uk
Contact: Derek MacKenzie-Hook, Manager
Founded: 1993
Publications: Permaculture News; The Permaculture Way; The Permaculture Garden
Profile: The institute is involved in research and development of land-use diversification with an emphasis on added value product. The underlying motive is to increase environmentally conscious land management with improved rural money supply combating rural depopulation. These objectives are addressed through demonstration sites, R&D, publications and courses.

East of England Agricultural Society
East of England Agricultural Showground
Peterborough
PE2 0XE
Tel: 01733 234451
Fax: 01733 370038
Contact: T Gibson, OBE, Chief Executive
Founded: 1970
Membership: 6,500

Publications: East of England Journal; East of England Show Catalogue and Show Programme
Previous names: Merger of Agricultural Societies for Cambridgeshire and Isle of Ely, Huntingdonshire, Peterborough and Bedfordshire
Profile: The society is a registered agricultural charity the aims and objectives of which include the promotion of British agriculture in particular and industry in general. The society annually organises a summer agricultural show with classes for all types of farm livestock, for horses and for farm machinery. Through its trading subsidiary, East of England Showground Services Ltd, the society also hires out its showground and buildings for a multiplicity of events and functions ranging from horse and pony events and dog shows to a major trucking event and a nationally acclaimed rally for motorcyclists.

Easton College
Easton
Norwich
Norfolk
NR9 5DX
Tel: 01603 742106
Fax: 01603 741438

Eco Environmental Information Trust
10–12 Picton Street
Montpelier
Bristol
BS6 5QA
Tel: 0117 942 0162
Fax: 0117 942 0164
Email: ecotrust@gn.apc.org
Contact: Monica Barlow, Projects Manager
Founded: 1989
Publications: Publications list available
Previous names: Eco Environmental Education Trust until 1992
Profile: Eco Trust is a national charity working to improve public environmental information. They are small, flexible and project based; researching people's needs and developing solutions to meet those needs.

Economics and Statistics Division
Department of Agriculture for Northern Ireland
Dundonald House
Upper Newtownards Road
Belfast
BT4 3SB
Tel: 01232 524785
Fax: 01232 525015
Contact: Stanley McBurney, Deputy Chief Agricultural Economist
Publications: Statistical Review of Northern Ireland Agriculture; Farm Incomes in Northern

Ireland; Size and Performance of the Northern Ireland Food and Drinks Processing Sector; Farm Business Data

Profile: The division is responsible for collection and compilation of statistics on Northern Ireland agriculture and provision of economic advice.

Education and Training Administration
Department of Agriculture for Northern Ireland
Room 555
Dundonald House
Upper Newtownards Road
Belfast
BT4 3SB
Tel: 01232 524432
Fax: 01232 524055

Elmwood College
Carslogie Road
Cupar
Fife
KY15 4JB
Tel: 01334 652781
Fax: 01334 656795
Contact: Rick Bond, Liaison Co-ordinator
Founded: 1956
Previous names: Elmwood Agricultural and Technical College until 1989
Profile: Elmwood College is a college of further education with a long-standing tradition of offering training in the land-based industries. Courses are available from craft to management level in agriculture; animal care; rural business administration; kennel, cattery and animal centre management; rural land use; horticulture; arboriculture; gamekeeping and wildlife conservation; and access to BSc (Hons) in Environmental Science/Environmental Technology. Tailor-made short courses are offered by Elmwood Business Training, the college's short course unit.

Emerson College
School of Biodynamic Farming and Gardening
Emerson College
Pixton
Forest Row
East Sussex
RH18 5JX
Tel: 0134282 2238
Fax: 0134282 6055
Contact: Registration Secretary
Founded: 1962
Profile: The School of Biodynamic Farming and Gardening offers short courses at Emerson College.

Endurance Horse and Pony Society of Great Britain
22 Thornhill
Wootton Bassett
Wiltshire
SN4 7RX
Tel: 01793 731212
Fax: 01793
Contact: Miss P Payne, Secretary
Founded: 1973
Membership: 1,730
Publications: Handbook

Energy Research Unit
Rutherford Appleton Laboratory
Chilton
Didcot
Oxfordshire
OX11 0QX
Tel: 01235 445559
Fax: 01235 446863
Email: j.halliday@rl.ac.uk
Contact: Dr Jim Halliday, Head, Energy Research Unit
Founded: 1978
Publications: Publications list available
Profile: The Rutherford Appleton Laboratory, which forms part of the Central Laboratory of the Research Councils, is one of the UK's major research establishments. It provides support for the academic community and undertakes in-house research in collaboration with universities and industry. The Energy Research Unit (ERU) was founded in 1978 to provide support to the UK academic community in the field of energy and, in particular, wind energy. Since that time, ERU has widened its mandate, undertaking its own research in collaboration with academia and industry both in the UK and abroad.

Engineering Council
10 Maltravers Street
London
WC2R 3ER
Tel: 0171 240 7891
Fax: 0171 240 7517
Contact: Ron Kirby, Director of Public Affairs
Founded: 1981
Membership: 290,000
Publications: Publications list available
Profile: The Engineering Council sets the standards for the education and training of engineers and technicians leading to the award of its titles: Chartered Engineer, Incorporated Engineer, and Engineering Technician.

English Apples and Pears Association
Brogdale Farm
Brogdale Road
Faversham
Kent
ME13 8XZ
Tel: 01795 530666
Fax: 01795 590177
Contact: Frazer Spence, Chief Executive

English Association of Farm Rides
East Anglian Farm Rides
Bentley Manor
Little Bentley
Colchester
Essex
CO7 8SE
Tel: 01206 251790
Fax: 01206 251820
Contact: Mr Nigel G Dyson
Founded: 1989
Membership: 200
Profile: EAFR was founded in 1989 and has
enabled horse riders to get off the increasingly
busy roads onto farm tracks which join up into
interesting riding routes where possible with
existing public bridleways. There are over
200 miles of routes of off road tracks and
headlands in Essex, with further rides in Kent,
Surrey and Bristol.

English Connemara Pony Society
2 The Leys
Salford
Chipping Norton
Oxfordshire
OX7 5FD
Profile: We have been unable to contact this
organisation. The details given are unconfirmed.

English Goat Breeder's Association
Heathgate Farm
Gill's Lane
Rooksbridge
Axbridge
Somerset
BS26 2TZ
Tel: 01934 750602
Contact: Mrs Judith A Parry, Honorary Secretary
Founded: 1978
Membership: 125
Publications: JEM (members newsletter)
Profile: The association aims to preserve and
improve the standard of English goats by
breeding; to encourage the use, appreciation,
well being and protection of the English goat and
to publish and maintain a herd book.

English Guernsey Cattle Society
The Gold Top Centre
Pednor Road
Chesham
Buckinghamshire
HP5 2LA
Tel: 01494 774114
Fax: 01494 791700
Contact: RL Dolbear, Breed Secretary
Profile: We have been unable to contact this
organisation. The details given are unconfirmed.

English Heritage
Fortress House
23 Savile Row
London
W1X 2HE
Tel: 0171 973 3000
Fax: 0171 973 3001

English Hops Limited
Hop Pocket Lane
Paddock Wood
Tonbridge
Kent
TN12 6BY
Tel: 01892 833415
Fax: 01892 836905
Contact: D V M Kean, Chairman
Founded: 1982
Previous names: Hops Marketing Board
Profile: English Hops Ltd is the largest hop
grower co-operative in the UK, accounting for
about 50% of the volume of hops grown. EGL
also owns 50% of English Hops Products Ltd, a
hop marketing and processing company which in
turn owns 100% of H G Hesselbeger, a hop
merchant.

English Nature
Northminster House
Peterborough
Cambridgeshire
PE1 1UA
Tel: 01733 340345
Fax: 01733 68834
Contact: Enquiry Service
Founded: 1991
Publications: Publications list available
Previous names: Nature Conservancy Council
Profile: English Nature was established by Act of
Parliament and is responsible for advising
government on nature conservation in England. It
promotes, directly and through others, the
conservation of England's wildlife and natural
features; selects, establishes and manages
National Nature Reserves and identifies and
notifies Sites of Special Scientific Interest;

provides advice and information about nature conservation and supports and conducts research relevant to these functions. Through the Joint Nature Conservation Committee it works with sister organisations in Scotland and Wales on UK and international nature conservation issues.

English Place Name Society
Department of English Studies
The University of Nottingham
Nottingham
NG7 2RD
Tel: 0115 951 5919
Fax: 0115 951 5924
Contact: Mrs JC Rudkin, Publications Officer
Founded: 1923
Membership: 670
Publications: The Survey of English Place-Names; The English Place-Name Society Journal)
Profile: The society publishes the results of the survey county by county in a series of volumes containing explanations of the origin, history and significance of the place-names in the area concerned. The society's volumes enjoy a world-wide reputation for sound scholarship and have become necessary equipment for the professional and the amateur historian, geographer, archaeologist and philologist.

English Quality Plum Grower's Association
Cotswold Orchards
Mount Pleasant
Broadway
Worcestershire
WR12 7JA
Tel: 01386 443142
Profile: We have been unable to contact this organisation. The details given are unconfirmed.

English Tourist Board
Thames Tower
Blacks Road
London
W6 9EL
Tel: 0181 846 9000
Fax: 0181 563 0302
Contact: Michael Kennedy, Product Development Manager
Founded: 1969
Publications: Advisory guides and promotional publications
Profile: Government agency responsible for the development of tourism in England.

English Vineyards Association Ltd
Church Road
Bruisyard
Saxmundham
Suffolk
IP17 2EF
Tel: 01728 638080
Fax: 01728 638442
Contact: Ian Berwick, Chairman
Founded: 1967
Membership: 600
Publications: The Grape Press

English Woodlands Ltd
Frilsham Nursery
Yattendon
Thatcham
Berkshire
RG16 0XX
Tel: 01635 200410
Fax: 01635 202050
Contact: Simon Stephens, Director
Profile: An organisation made up of woodland managers, contractors, nurserymen, landscapers, tree surgeons and grounds maintenance contractors.

Enniskillen College of Agriculture
Department of Agriculture for Northern Ireland
Levaghy
Enniskillen
County Fermanagh
BT74 4GF
Tel: 01365 323101
Fax: 01365 324722
Contact: Mr S B Morrow, Principal
Founded: 1967
Membership: 266
Publications: College newsletter; prospectus
Profile: One of the three Northern Ireland colleges of agriculture. Courses are offered in agriculture, food, horticulture, equine studies and communication, at further education level and at BSc level in association with The Queen's University of Belfast.

Environment Agency for England and Wales, The
Waterside Drive
Aztec West
Almondsbury
Bristol
BS12 4VD
Tel: 01454 624400
Fax: 01454 624409
Email: enquiries@environment-agency.gov.uk
Contact: Tim Mahoney, PR Policy Co-ordinator

Founded: 1996
Membership: 9,000
Publications: Publications list available
Profile: The Environment Agency for England
and Wales is a non-departmental public body
which became operational on 1st April 1996. It
brought together the National Rivers Authority,
Her Majesty's Inspectorate of Pollution and 83
local Waste Regulation Authorities, together with
some smaller units from the Department of the
Environment. The agency has major
responsibilities for the control of industrial
pollution and wastes and for the regulation and
enhancement of the environment.

Environment Agency: National Laboratory Service

The Environment Agency
Wheatcroft Business Park
Landmere Lane
Edwalton
Nottingham
NG12 4DG
Tel: 0115 9213705
Fax: 0115 9213760
Contact: Paul B Smith, Business Manager
Founded: 1993
Previous names: National Rivers Authority
(National Laboratory Service) until 1996
Profile: The group provide a
chemical/microbiological analytical service. It has
six sites in England and Wales equipped with the
latest analytical systems, highly qualified staff
with all sites NAMAS accredited.

Environment and Heritage Service

Department of the Environment for Northern
  Ireland
Commonwealth House
35 Castle Place
Belfast
BT1 1GU
Tel: 01232 251477
Fax: 01232 546660
Email: ehs@nics.gov.uk
Contact: Information Officer
Founded: 1996
Publications: Publications list available
Previous names: Environment Protection until
1991; Conservation Branch until 1991;
Environment Service until 1996
Profile: The role of the Environment and
Heritage Service is to protect the environment of
Northern Ireland for present and future
generations by controlling the pollution of air,
water and land, and by the conservation of our
natural environment and built heritage.

Environment and Heritage Service, Historic Monuments and Buildings

Department of the Environment for Northern
  Ireland
5–33 Hill Street
Belfast
BT1 2LA
Tel: 01232 235000
Fax: 01232 543111
Contact: Claire Foley, Senior Inspector – Rural
Protection
Founded: 1950
Publications: Publications list available
Previous names: Archaeological Survey of
Northern Ireland 1950–1990; Environment
Service (DOENI) 1990–1996
Profile: EHS is an integrated environmental
conservation organisation embracing the built
and natural heritage and the protection of air,
water and land from general pollution. The aim is
to protect and conserve the natural and
man-made environment and to promote its
appreciation for the benefit of present and future
generations.

Environment Council, The

21 Elizabeth Street
London
SW1W 9RP
Tel: 0171 824 8411
Fax: 0171 730 9941
Internet:
  http://www.environment.com/tec/index.htm
Founded: 1969
Publications: Habitat – digest of environmental
news, news – environment council newsletter,
Who's Who in the Environment Directories.
Publications list available
Previous names: Council for Environmental
Conservation until 1988
Profile: The Environment Council is an
independent charity dedicated to conserving the
environment through building awareness,
dialogue, understanding and effective action. Its
activities include – environmental resolve,
business programmes and conservers at work. It
produces and distributes environmental
information through a range of publications.

Environment Foundation

Sustainability Ltd
49–53 Kensington High Street
London
W8 5ED
Tel: 0171 937 9996
Fax: 0171 937 7447
Contact: John Elkington, Chair

Environment Wales

Welsh Office
c/o The Prince's Trust – BRO
4th Floor, Empire House
Mount Stuart Square
Cardiff
CF1 6DN
Tel: 01222 471121
Fax: 01222 482086
Email: env-wales@bro.cymru.net
Contact: Alan Underwood, Development Officer
Founded: 1992
Profile: Environment Wales is a Welsh Office initiative to support voluntary action which contributes to sustainable development by helping to protect the environment of Wales. Grant aid is made available to voluntary organisations undertaking project work in Wales.

Environmental Auditors Registration Association

Institute of Environmental Assessment
Welton House
Limekiln Way
Lincoln
LN2 4US
Tel: 01522 540069
Fax: 01522 540096
Contact: Emma Owen, EARA Technical Officer
Founded: 1992
Membership: 1,600
Publications: The EARA Register
Profile: An independent, non-profit making organisation dedicated to raising standards of professional competence in the environmental auditing field. EARA provides individuals with a structured route of entry to this profession and assesses and independently verifies the training, qualifications and experience of environmental auditors. Registered individuals are promoted through the referral service and training course approvals are carried out to promote good standards in EA and EMS.

Environmental Awareness Trust

66 Lincolns Inn Field
London
WC2
Profile: We have been unable to contact this organisation. The details given are unconfirmed.

Environmental Communicators' Organisation

8 Hooks Cross
Watton at Stone
Hertford
Hertfordshire
SG14 3RY
Tel: 01920 830527
Fax: 01920 830538
Contact: Alan Massam, Chairman
Founded: 1972
Publications: Occasional newsletters
Profile: Attempts to inform professional journalists and broadcasters on radical green issues; supports some groups with PR; attempts to publicise selected items to boost radical thinking.

Environmental Consortium

31 Clerkenwell Close
London
EC1R 0AT
Tel: 0171 251 4818
Fax: 0171 490 0063
Profile: We have been unable to contact this organisation. The details given are unconfirmed.

Environmental Education Advisers Association

Magic Hills Lodge
Rice Lane
Gorran Haven
St Austell
Cornwall
PL26 6JF
Tel: 01726 843101
Contact: Richard S Moseley, Secretary
Founded: 1977

Environmental Information Centre

Natural Environment Research Council
Institute of Terrestrial Ecology
Monks Wood
Abbots Ripton
Huntingdon
Cambridgeshire
PE17 2LS
Tel: 01487 773381
Fax: 01487 773467
Email: eic@ite.ac.uk
Contact: Sue Wallis, Information and Data Supply
Founded: 1989
Publications: Contract reports, papers in scientific journals
Profile: The centre is located at ITE Monks Wood, with a staff complement of approximately 30. EIC is one of seven data centres, charged by the Natural Environment Research Council with responsibility for its corporate data holdings. EIC is the hub of a network of data managers throughout each of the six ITE research stations. The centre has three principal roles: management, custodianship and dissemination of the institute's extensive terrestrial

environmental data holdings; enhancements of their value to the scientific and user communities by seeking innovative ways of using and interpreting them; undertaking ecological research which exploits the availability of these long-term or geographically extensive datasets.

Environmental Information Service
PO Box 197
Cawston
Norwich
Norfolk
NR10 4BH
Tel: 01603 871048
Fax: 01603 871048
Contact: Alan Phillips, Founder
Founded: 1988
Publications: Publications list available
Profile: A first point of contact centre for disseminating the activities of the UK environmental organisations. Information is freely provided by telephone as well as postal service (SAE required). Operates the environmental employment register.

Environmental Law Foundation
Lincolns Inn House
42 Kingsway
London
WC2B 6EX
Tel: 0171 404 1030
Fax: 0171 404 1032
Contact: Katherine Davis, Director
Founded: 1992
Membership: 250
Publications: ELFline; Annual Report; ELF Handbook; litigation manuals
Profile: The Environmental Law Foundation puts communities in touch with environmental and legal expertise to resolve environmental problems and help prevent further damage to the environment. ELF brings together lawyers and technical experts who assist communities and individuals and are keen to make the law more accessible to the public. ELF is a charity and non-profit making company.

Environmental Policy Division
Department of Agriculture for Northern Ireland
Room 650B
Dundonald House
Upper Newtownards Road
Belfast
BT4 3SB
Tel: 01232 524512
Fax: 01232 525015
Contact: Mr Brian Murphy, Head of Division

Previous names: Conservation and Lands Division
Profile: The Environmental Policy Division of the Department of Agriculture for Northern Ireland is responsible for the development and implementation of agri-environmental schemes (ESAs, Moorlands Scheme, Habitat Scheme, Countryside Access); measures to reduce farm pollution (including peace initiative cross-border anti-pollution scheme); land use and planning, liaison with environment service; pesticides, seeds, fertilisers and feeding-stuffs; and organic food, and fallen animals.

Environmental Protection Division
Ministry of Agriculture, Fisheries and Food
Nobel House
17 Smith Square
London
SW1P 3JR
Tel: 0171 238 5664
Profile: The Environmental Protection Division is responsible for environmental protection and pollution from agriculture.

Environmental Safety Centre
Building 7.12
Harwell Laboratory
Didcot
Oxfordshire
OX11 0RA
Tel: 01235 821000
Profile: We have been unable to contact this organisation. The details given are unconfirmed.

Environmental Training Organisation
Department for Education and Employment
PO Box 101
Gloucester
GL19 3YA
Tel: 01452 840825
Fax: 01452 840824
Email: greentrain@dial.pipex.com
Contact: Keith Turner, Secretary
Profile: ETO is an industry training organisation created solely for the environment sector. It exists to support all who are concerned with the well-being of the environment, whether as employers, full-time staff, volunteers, or training and education providers. ETO was formed on 1st April 1996.

Environmental Transport Association
10 Church Street
Weybridge
Surrey
KT13 8RS
Tel: 01932 828882

Fax: 01932 829015
Internet: http://www.eta.co.uk
Contact: Louise Enticknap, Public relations
Founded: 1990
Membership: 14,000
Publications: Publications list available
Profile: Britain's only provider of breakdown and recovery services which campaigns for environmentally sound transport. Includes recovery for cyclists.

Equine Behaviour Study Circle
Grove Cottage
Brinkley
Newmarket
Suffolk
CB8 0SE
Tel: 01638 507502
Contact: Olwen Way
Publications: Newsletter

Eriskay Pony Society
Houston Mill
East Linton
East Lothian
EH40 3DG
Tel: 01620 860307
Fax: 01620 860158
Contact: Mrs Anne Bell, Secretary
Founded: 1986
Membership: 60
Publications: Publicity leaflets
Previous names: Eriskay Pony Breed Society until 1995
Profile: A society to breed and promote interest in and awareness of the rare Eriskay Pony, which survived on the Island of Eriskay as the last Celtic horse.

Essex Agricultural Society
Fishers
Castle Hedingham
Halstead
Essex
CO9 3EW
Tel: 01787 460382
Fax: 01787 460382
Contact: John Hutchings, Secretary
Founded: 1858
Membership: 1,000
Publications: Members newsletter
Profile: Principal role is to stage the Essex County Show, a three-day event in June. The society also runs the Essex County Championship Ploughing Match and Cereal Show; arranges the County Harvest Festival Service; and provides administration for the Essex County Farms Competition.

Est a Laine Merino Sheep Society
The Merino Centre
Youngman's Road
Wymondham
Norfolk
NR18 0RR
Tel: 01953 607860
Fax: 01953 607626
Contact: Mr Jonathon Barber

ETSU
AEA Technology plc
Harwell
Didcot
Oxfordshire
OX11 0RA
Tel: 01235 432450
Fax: 01235 432923
Contact: New and Renewable Enquiries Bureau
Founded: 1974
Publications: Publications list available
Previous names: Energy Technology Support Unit
Profile: ETSU manages UK Government programmes on new and renewable energy, energy efficiency, clean coal technology and, in conjunction with the National Environmental Technology Centre, environmental technology. It also undertakes work for the European Commission, the International Energy Agency and other customers worldwide in a range of spheres.

European Adjuvant Association
C.E.F.I.C. (European Chemical Industry Council)
2 Ducketts Wharf
South Street
Bishops Stortford
Hertfordshire
CM23 3AR
Tel: 01279 501995
Fax: 01279 501996
Contact: RH Newman, Chairman
Founded: 1992
Membership: 17
Publications: Leaflet
Profile: The European Adjuvant Association was formed in November 1992 in response to impending legislation in the UK and the EC regarding agrochemical adjuvants. One major aim of the E.A.A. is to raise the profile, credibility and understanding of the role that adjuvants can play in the effective use of agrochemicals.

European Commission Representation in the United Kingdom
European Commission

8 Storey's Gate
London
SW1P 3AT
Tel: 0171 973 1992
Fax: 0171 973 1900
Contact: Information Network Unit

European Federation of Dairy Retailers
19 Cornwall Terrace
London
NW1 4QP
Tel: 0171 486 7244
Fax: 0171 487 4734
Contact: SC Bates, Secretary General

European Food Law Association
Chartered Institute of Environmental Health
Chadwick Court
15 Hatfields
London
SE1 8DJ
Tel: 0171 928 6006
Fax: 0171 928 6953
Contact: Anne Goodwin, Assistant Secretary

Evesham College
Cheltenham Road
Evesham
Worcestershire
WR11 6LP
Tel: 01386 41091
Fax: 01386 442041
Contact: LA Flagg, Lecturer in Engineering
Founded: 1970
Previous names: Evesham College of Further
Education
Profile: Further education establishment offering
courses in horticultural engineering, agricultural
engineering to NVQ level 2 and 3. National
Diploma in agricultural engineering and small
animal care qualifications.

Exmoor Horn Sheep Breeders' Society
Selworthy Farm
Selworthy
Minehead
Somerset
TA24 8TL
Tel: 01643 862577
Contact: Hazel Leeves, Secretary
Founded: 1906
Membership: 145
Publications: Annual flock book
Profile: The society's objectives are: the
encouragement of the breeding and
maintenance of the characteristics of the Exmoor

Horn sheep, and to maintain the purity of the
breed.

Exmoor National Park Authority
Exmoor House
Dulverton
Somerset
TA22 9HL
Tel: 01398 323665
Fax: 01398 323150
Email: 100125.451@compuserve.com
Contact: Brian Pearce, Interpretation Officer
Founded: 1954
Publications: Publications list available
Profile: The duties of the authority are: to
conserve and enhance the natural beauty, wildlife
and cultural heritage of Exmoor; to promote
opportunities for the understanding and
enjoyment of the special qualities of Exmoor by
the public. In doing this it must seek to foster the
economic and social well-being of communities
within the National Park. The authority has a wide
range of functions including development
control, local plans, community assistance,
information, education, public access, land
management, conservation, farm liaison,
recreation management and visitor facilities. In
1997 it will become a free standing authority
within local government.

Exmoor Pony Society
Glen Fern
Waddicombe
Dulverton
Somerset
TA22 9RY
Tel: 01398 341490
Fax: 01398 341490
Contact: Mr D Mansell, Breed Secretary

Falconaide
Slackwood Farmhouse
Silverdale
Carnforth
Lancashire
LA5 0UF
Tel: 01524 701353
Contact: Mr and Mrs CA Oswald, Chairman
Founded: 1980
Membership: 100
Publications: Annual Report
Profile: The collection and care of sick and
injured birds of prey and eventually their release
back into the wild. Talks are given to clubs and
schools.

Falkirk College of Further and Higher Education
Grangemouth Road
Falkirk
Stirlingshire
FK2 9AD
Tel: 01324 624981
Fax: 01324 632086
Contact: Adrian Kitchen, Head of Environmental Studies
Founded: 1960
Publications: Publications list available
Previous names: Falkirk College of Technology until 1996
Profile: A College of further and higher education offering courses to HND and Advanced Diploma level in environmental management and land management, as well as a wide range of other courses at all levels to BSc. Land-based/environmental courses include (HND) managing urban environments; environmental management; applied ecology; environmental studies; estate maintenance; horticulture; (GSVQ or SVQ level III).

Family Farmers Association
101 Church Street
Stoke Newington
London
N16 OUD
Tel: 0171 249 4790
Fax: 0171 249 4790
Profile: We have been unable to contact this organisation. The details given are unconfirmed.

Farm and Food Society
4 Willifield Way
London
NW11 7XT
Tel: 0181 455 0634
Contact: Joanne Bower, Honorary Secretary
Founded: 1996
Publications: Farm and Food News; Annual Report; publications list available
Profile: The Farm and Food Society is affiliated to the International Federation of Organic Agricultural Movements, working constructively towards humane, wholesome and fair farming. It is regularly consulted by government on proposals connected with its work and maintains contacts with the European Commission.

Farm Animal Care Trust
34 Holland Park Road
Kensington
London
W14 8LZ
Tel: 0171 602 3164

Profile: We have been unable to contact this organisation. The details given are unconfirmed.

Farm Animal Welfare Co-ordinating Executive
Springhill House
280 London Road
Cheltenham
Gloucestershire
GL52 6HS
Tel: 01242 524725
Profile: We have been unable to contact this organisation. The details given are unconfirmed.

Farm Animal Welfare Council
Room D26, Government Buildings
Hook Rise South
Tolworth
Surbiton
Surrey
KT6 7NF
Tel: 0181 330 8031
Fax: 0181 355 4274
Contact: Mr R Holdsworth, Secretary
Founded: 1967
Publications: Annual newsletter; publications list available
Previous names: Farm Animal Welfare Advisory Committee until 1979
Profile: The council is an independent advisory body on farm animal welfare, established by the government in 1979. Its terms of reference are 'To keep under review the welfare of farm animals on agricultural land, at markets, in transit and at the place of slaughter and to advise the Minister of Agriculture, Fisheries and Food and the Secretaries of State for Scotland and Wales of any legislative or other changes that may be necessary.' The council is free to investigate any topic within its remit, communicate freely with outside bodies, including outside the UK, and publish its advice.

Farm Animal Welfare Network
PO Box 2
Holmfirth
Huddersfield
West Yorkshire
HD7 1QT
Tel: 01484 688650

Farm Assured British Beef and Lamb
165 Winterhill House
Milton Keynes
Buckinghamshire
MK6 1PB
Tel: 01908 231642
Fax: 01908 609825

Contact: Tim Green, Development Manager
Founded: 1996
Membership: 4,000
Publications: The Standard
Profile: A nationwide farm assurance scheme which covers origin of stock, traceability, husbandry and welfare, feeds, medicines, housing and transport – all the aspects of production that consumers need to be reassured of.

Farm Energy Centre
EA Technology Ltd
National Agricultural Centre
Stoneleigh Park
Warwickshire
CV8 2LS
Tel: 01203 696512
Fax: 01203 696360
Contact: Dr CD Mitchell, Manager
Founded: 1967
Publications: Publications list available
Previous names: Farm Electric Centre
Profile: The Farm Energy Centre is the base for the electricity industry's advisory services to agriculture and horticulture. Working on behalf of the regional electricity companies, the aim is to help farmers be efficient, making the most of their electric power and other fuels. It has an extensive database of electrical equipment for use on farms. The FEC undertakes a programme of research and development projects into supplying, using and saving energy on farms. Subjects include livestock housing, dairying, crop storage and waste handling.

Farm Films Group
Lundholm Road
Ardeer
Stevenston
Ayrshire
KA20 3NQ
Tel: 0800 833749
Fax: 01294 842062
Contact: Andrew Hetherington, Operations Manager
Founded: 1994
Previous names: Second Life Plastics
Profile: An agricultural collection scheme for farm plastic films (i.e. silage films).

Farm Holiday Bureau (UK) Ltd
National Agricultural Centre
Stoneleigh Park
Warwickshire
CV8 2LZ
Tel: 01203 696909

Fax: 01203 696930
Email: admin@fhbaccom.demon.co.uk
Contact: Berni Thompson, Chief Executive
Founded: 1983
Membership: 1,012
Publications: Stay on a Farm – annual guide book
Profile: Agricultural co-operative with the role of promoting farm accommodation. Quality is ensured by annual tourist board inspections and membership of 92 local farm holiday groups.

Farm Livestock Trust Ltd
41 Mercator Road
Lewisham
London
SE13 5EH
Profile: We have been unable to contact this organisation. The details given are unconfirmed.

Farm Retail Association
164 Shaftesbury Avenue
London
WC2H 8HL
Tel: 0171 331 7281
Fax: 0171 331 7410
Contact: Rachel Moseley, Associations Adviser
Publications: Retail Farmer; Where to Go Guide
Previous names: Farm Shop and Pick Your Own Association until 1994
Profile: The Farm Retail Association was founded in 1994 growing out the Farm Shop and Pick Your Own Association to reflect the increasing diversity of retailing and leisure activities offered from farms and smallholdings. The FRA's aim is to represent farmers' and growers' retailing interests to government, the EU and the media and to help raise standards in the industry.

Farm Support and Rural Enterprises Division
Department of Agriculture for Northern Ireland
Dundonald House
Upper Newtownards Road
Belfast
BT4 3SB
Tel: 01232 524406
Fax: 01232 524960
Contact: Brian Morrison, Head of Division
Founded: 1996
Profile: To promote economic growth and the development of the countryside by improving the competitive position of those people operating businesses where the farm alone is not a viable entity. In fulfilling this aim the staff endeavour, primarily through group methods, to develop managers of small and very small family farm businesses by encouraging them to develop their

business and technical competences and in participation in farm based rural development and diversification projects.

Farmers Club
3 Whitehall Court
London
SW1A 2EL
Tel: 0171 930 3751
Fax: 0171 839 7864
Contact: Group Captain GP Carson, Secretary
Founded: 1842
Membership: 6,000
Publications: The Farmers Club Journal
Profile: The Farmers Club is wholly owned and run by its members. Two thirds are farmers and the remainder are people who have direct involvement with the agricultural industry. The club is fully equipped with conference and committee rooms, a restaurant, bar and 42 bedrooms.

Farmers Quota Bank
Steanbow Farm
Pilton
Shepton Mallet
Somerset
BA5 4EH
Tel: 01749 890263
Fax: 01749 890008
Contact: Finn Christensen, Secretary
Founded: 1995
Membership: 1,000
Publications: Members newsletter
Profile: An independent organisation set up by four farmers in order to collect accurate information regarding milk quota and pass it on to industry. Also involved in lobbying MPs and MEPs for a fair system.

Farmers Union of Wales
Llys Amaeth
Queens Square
Aberystwyth
Ceredigion
SY23 2EA
Tel: 01970 612755
Fax: 01970 624369
Contact: Mr GL Thomas, Director of Public Relations
Founded: 1955
Publications: Welsh Farmer; Link (annual agricultural handbook)
Profile: Farmers Union of Wales operates from a head office in Aberystwyth and 11 county branches and offices. The FUW aims to safeguard and further the interests of farmers and landowners in Wales and promote a sympathetic understanding of their problems. Seeks to represent Welsh farmers at all levels on any issue affecting the farming industry. Nine standing committees which meet regularly include: milk and dairy produce, livestock, hill farming, land use, tenants, common land, agricultural education and farm tourism.

Farmers' Link
38–40 Exchange Street
Norwich
Norfolk
NR2 1AX
Tel: 01603 765670
Fax: 01603 761645
Email: flink@gn.apc.org
Contact: Ms Angie Stratton
Founded: 1992
Publications: Publications list available
Profile: Farmers' Link aims to promote awareness of agriculture and rural development issues; to increase understanding about the links between rural development and agriculture at home and in other parts of the world; to stimulate debate on the social and environmental implications of food production and distribution; and to examine the changes needed in agricultural policies and practices to reflect the common interests of farmers and rural communities in East Anglia and worldwide.

Farmers' World Network
Arthur Rank Centre
National Agricultural Centre
Stoneleigh Park
Warwickshire
CV8 2LZ
Tel: 01203 696969
Fax: 01203 696900
Contact: Mr Adrian Friggens, Co-ordinator
Founded: 1984
Membership: 800
Publications: Landmark; What variety?; Agri-repere
Profile: The FWN aims to promote awareness in the UK farming community of the problems of developing countries and the relationships between European and Third World agriculture: and to foster links with like-minded farmers and others involved in food production and land-based industries throughout the world. It is the only national forum in the UK that is dedicated to bringing together the different factions involved in world agriculture to debate the issues surrounding the sustainability of world food production, together with the associated questions of poverty and hunger.

Farmhouse Cheese Bureau

Farmhouse Cheesemakers Ltd
Royal Bath and West Showground
Shepton Mallet
Somerset
BA4 6QN
Tel: 01749 345055
Fax: 01749 345155
Contact: David Johnson, Chief
Executive/Secretary
Founded: 1982
Membership: 23
Publications: The Story of Farmhouse Cheese
Previous names: The Cheddar and Caerphilly
Farmhouse Cheesemakers Federation; The
Cheshire and Lancashire Farmhouse
Cheesemakers Federation
Profile: A co-operative of farm cheesemakers
formed to collectively market member makers'
cheese and help develop and perpetuate the
tradition of milk producing farms (i.e. to continue
to make cheese on these farms).

Farming and Wildlife Advisory Group

National Agricultural Centre
Stoneleigh Park
Warwickshire
CV8 2LX
Tel: 01203 696699
Fax: 01203 696760
Contact: Mr David Ball, Chief Executive
Founded: 1969
Previous names: Farming and Wildlife Trust Ltd
until 1991
Profile: The Farming and Wildlife Advisory Group
promotes wildlife and conservation within the
context of a profitable farm business. Through its
team of 67 advisers it works directly with
farmers and land managers to encourage farming
practices which have a minimal impact on the
environment.

Farriers Registration Council

Sefton House
Adam Court
Newark Road
Peterborough
PE1 5PP
Tel: 01733 319911
Fax: 01733 319910
Contact: Miss JR Bailey, Training Manager
Founded: 1975
Publications: Guide to Apprenticeships in
Farriery; How to Become a Farrier
Profile: A statutory body established by the
Farriers (Registration) Act 1975 as amended by
the Farriers (Registration)(Amendment) Act 1977
to promote the training of farriers, to prevent and
avoid suffering by and cruelty to horses arising
from the shoeing of horses and to register
persons engaged in farriery and to prohibit the
shoeing of horses by unqualified persons.

Fauna and Flora International

Great Eastern House
Tenison Road
Cambridge
CB1 2DT
Tel: 01223 461471
Fax: 01223 461481
Email: info@ffint.org.uk
Contact: Mark Rose, Director
Founded: 1903
Membership: 3,500
Publications: Oryx; Fauna and Flora News;
Mountain Gorilla Update; Soundwood; Annual
Report; various leaflets
Previous names: Society for the Preservation of
Game of the British Empire; Fauna Preservation
Society; Fauna and Flora Preservation Society
until 1995
Profile: Fauna and Flora International, founded in
1903, is the world's longest established
international wildlife conservation body. It is one
of only a few whose remit is to protect the entire
spectrum of endangered species of animals and
plants worldwide. It manages major programmes
in priority areas; carries out research on
high-priority threatened species; promotes
conservation partnerships between NGOs,
governments, businesses and local populations;
empowers local people and develops their
conservation skills; disseminates reliable
information on endangered species and their
habitats; and creates awareness of the need for
conservation among the public and decision
makers.

Faverolles Society

Park House
Codsall Wood
Wolverhampton
Staffordshire
WV8 1QR
Tel: 01902 843055
Contact: Mrs S Bruton, Secretary
Profile: A society to promote the Faverolles
breed of poultry.

Federation of Agricultural Co-operatives (UK) Ltd

Agriculture House
164 Shaftesbury Avenue
London
WC2H 8HL

Tel: 0171 331 7213
Fax: 0171 331 7372
Founded: 1970
Membership: 207
Profile: The federation represents farmer controlled businesses throughout the UK. It is the UK member of COGECA (represents EU agricultural co-operatives) and therefore has the right to appoint the UK agricultural co-operative delegates to COGECA working parties and to EU advisory committees which deal with issues affecting their agricultural business. Individual farmer controlled businesses gain access to FAC services and representation through their National Agricultural Organisation Society.

Federation of Bloodstock Agents (GB) Ltd
Green Meadows
High Street
Great Chesterford
Essex
CB10 1PL
Tel: 01799 530265
Contact: James E Marshall, Secretary
Founded: 1978
Membership: 31
Profile: To represent the majority of those trading as Bloodstock Agents and to establish and maintain a high level of conduct and trading practice amongst such agents.

Federation of British Racing Clubs
4 Bosley Crescent
Wallingford
Oxfordshire
OX10 9AS
Tel: 01491 832399
Contact: Ricki Peacock

Federation of Family Farms Organisation
Lower Brown Farm
Huish Champflower
Taunton
Somerset
TA4 2EL
Contact: John Armitage, Chair
Profile: We have been unable to contact this organisation. The details given are unconfirmed.

Federation of Fresh Meat Wholesalers
227 Central Markets
Smithfield
London
EC1A 9LH
Tel: 0171 329 0776
Fax: 0171 329 0653
Contact: Peter Scott, General Secretary

Federation of Oils, Seeds and Fats Association Ltd
20 St Dunstan's Hill
London
EC3R 8HZ
Tel: 0171 283 5511
Fax: 0171 623 1310
Contact: Stuart Logan, Chief Executive and Secretary
Founded: 1970
Membership: 500

Federation of Organic Food Distributors
9 Outlook Avenue
Peacehaven
East Sussex
BN10 8XE
Tel: 01273 585551

Federation of Women's Institutes of Northern Ireland
209–211 Upper Lisburn Road
Belfast
BT10 0LL
Contact: Mrs Irene A Sproule, General Secretary
Profile: We have been unable to contact this organisation. The details given are unconfirmed.

Feline Advisory Bureau Boarding Cattery Information Service
Feline Advisory Bureau
1 Church Close
Orcheston
Salisbury
Wiltshire
SP3 4RP
Tel: 01980 621201
Fax: 01980 621201
Contact: Miss Caryl Cruickshank, Boarding Cattery Consultant
Founded: 1958
Membership: 2,000
Publications: Members journal; Boarding Cattery Construction and Management
Profile: The FAB Boarding Cattery Information Service provides guidance on boarding cattery construction and management both through its manual, Boarding Cattery Construction and Management and through residential training courses in cattery management. Advice is freely given on all aspects of planning permission, licensing and any other queries relating to setting up and running a cattery. The service inspects boarding catteries throughout the country and maintains a list of FAB approved catteries where the buildings meet FAB standards and where the proprietor has often been FAB trained.

Fell and Hill Running Commission
British Athletic Federation
165 Penistone Road
Kirkburton
Huddersfield
West Yorkshire
HD8 0PH
Tel: 01484 602922
Contact: N Berry, Chair

Fell Pony Society
Keeper's Cottage
Guyzance
Acklington
Northumberland
NE65 9AA
Tel: 01670 761317
Fax: 01670 761317
Contact: Sally M Wood, Secretary and Treasurer
Publications: Annual Stud Book
Profile: The aims of the Fell Pony Society are to
foster and keep pure the old breed of pony which
has roamed the northern fells for centuries.

Fencing Contractors Association
304–310 St Albans Road
Watford
Hertfordshire
WD2 5PE
Tel: 01923 248895
Fax: 0181 420 4926
Contact: Alec Smith, Director
Founded: 1942
Membership: 100
Publications: List of members
Profile: The primary aim of the association is to
foster and maintain a high standard of quality and
workmanship in the erection of all types of
fencing and barriers. Every applicant for
membership is carefully vetted and must
undertake to abide by a code of conduct before
being accepted into the association. The
association is an active member of technical
committees and working parties of the British
Standards Institution for BS1722.

Fermanagh Farming Society
Agricultural Centre
Lackaboy
Tempo Road
Enniskillen
County Fermanagh
BT74 4RL
Tel: 01365 322509

Fertiliser Manufacturers Association
Greenhill House
Thorpe Road

Peterborough
Cambridgeshire
PE3 6GF
Tel: 01733 331303
Fax: 01733 333617
Contact: Mrs Jane Salter, Agricultural Support
Officer
Founded: 1875
Membership: 27
Publications: Guidance leaflets and educational
material; Fertiliser Review; Health and Safety
Legislation – A Review; Health and Safety
Handbook
Profile: The FMA is involved in: the interpretation
and advice relating to the Fertiliser Regulations
which cover the chemical analysis of all fertiliser
types; health and safety matters and advice on
the aspects of fertiliser storage handling and
transportation; technical guidance notes and
advice promoting codes of fertiliser practice and
pollution prevention; promotion of the Fertiliser
Advisers Certification and Training Scheme
(FACTS); administration of the SP scheme for the
evaluation of the physical quality of solid straight
fertiliser; publication of educational material on
nutrient management and market information
and UK statistics on fertiliser consumption. The
FMA represents the interests of the industry to
Governments in the UK and Brussels.

Fertiliser Society
Greenhill House
Thorpe Road
Peterborough
Cambridgeshire
PE3 6GF
Tel: 01733 333223
Fax: 01733 333617
Contact: GEN Lance, Secretary
Founded: 1947
Membership: 400
Publications: Proceedings of the Fertiliser Society
Profile: An international society with members in
around 40 countries throughout the world. The
objects of the society are to provide a medium for
the discussion of scientific, technical,
environmental and economic aspects of the
production, use and application of fertilisers; to
promote the interchange of views and the
dissemination of information to members
concerning the matters aforesaid. Membership is
open to persons engaged in or associated with
the production, use or application of fertilisers.

Festival of the Countryside
Frolic House
23 Frolic Street
Newtown

Powys
SY16 1AP
Tel: 01686 625384

Field Studies Council
Preston Montford
Montford Bridge
Shrewsbury
Shropshire
SY4 1HW
Tel: 01743 850674
Fax: 01743 850178
Contact: Denise Carter, Publicity Officer
Founded: 1943
Membership: 4,000
Publications: Publications list available
Profile: The Field Studies Council was formed in 1943 as an independent educational charity in order to increase environmental awareness and understanding for everyone. It is now an internationally respected organisation and provides opportunities for people of every age, ability and background to explore, learn about and understand their environment through courses run at its network of 11 specially equipped field centres in some of the finest locations in England and Wales. As well as school groups, individual adults and families, commercial and statutory organisations of every size can benefit from the FSC's unrivalled experience and expertise through its environment training services. It delivers carefully planned and researched environmental awareness auditing and management services to national and local government bodies and non-governmental agencies throughout the world. Other services include advice on conservation and general wildlife issues, EIA and NVC. Membership of the FSC is open to everyone.

Field Studies Council (Cymru)
Field Studies Council
Rhyd y Creuau
Betws-y-coed
Conwy
Gwynedd
LL24 0HB
Tel: 01690 710494
Fax: 01690 710458
Contact: Julian Ellis, Director
Founded: 1943
Publications: Publications list available
Profile: A registered charity, educational institution and research body of independent status. FSC has a network of FSC centres throughout Wales and England providing course for schools (key stage 1 to 4, GCSE and A level), universities and professionals as well as

environmentally minded adults. Prices for all inclusive course, tutored by experienced staff, from £180 per week.

Fieldfare Trust
67a The Wicker
Sheffield
S3 8HT
Tel: 0114 270 1668
Fax: 0114 276 7900
Contact: Dr I Newman, Director
Founded: 1986
Profile: The Fieldfare Trust promotes countryside access and environmental education for disabled people. It provides advisory, training and information services. At present Fieldfare is working to produce national standards and guidelines for countryside access provision.

Finewool Sheep Register
Rowdens Farmhouse
Bunny Lane
Sherfield English
Romsey
Hampshire
SO51 6FT
Tel: 01794 884480
Profile: We have been unable to contact this organisation. The details given are unconfirmed.

Fisheries Conservancy Board for Northern Ireland
1 Mahon Road
Portadown
County Armagh
BT62 3EE
Tel: 01762 334666
Fax: 01762 338912
Contact: Janette McKnight, Clerk to the Board
Founded: 1944
Publications: Annual Report and Accounts
Profile: The main function of the board is to conserve and protect the salmon and inland fisheries in Northern Ireland, excluding the Foyle area, laid out in the Fisheries Act (NI) 1966 (Reprint 1969) as amended.

Fisheries Division
Department of Agriculture for Northern Ireland
Annex 5
Castle Grounds
Stormont
Belfast
BT4 3PW
Tel: 01232 523431
Fax: 01232 523121

Fisheries Society of the British Isles
82A High Street
Sawston
Cambridge
CB2 4HJ
Tel: 01223 830665
Fax: 01223 830665
Contact: David Cole, Manager
Founded: 1967
Membership: 520
Publications: Journal of Fish Biology
Profile: The Fisheries Society of the British Isles was formed in 1967 to further the study of fish and fisheries. The study of fish has many different aspects that interest professional biologists, fishermen, anglers, naturalists and fishery officers alike. The society plans to provide a link between these various interests, establishing communication by regular meetings and by publication of a journal.

Fjord Horse Society of Great Britain
Ausdan Stud
Glynarthen
Llandysul
Tel: 01239 810433
Fax: 01239 810433
Contact: Miss LD Moran

Flax and Linen Association
1 Bank Street
Dundee
DD1 1RN
Profile: We have been unable to contact this organisation. The details given are unconfirmed.

Fleece Washers Association
423 Upper Elmers End Road
Beckenham
Kent
BR3 3DA
Profile: We have been unable to contact this organisation. The details given are unconfirmed.

Flowers and Plants Association
Covent House
New Covent Garden Market
London
SW8 5NX
Tel: 0171 738 8044
Fax: 0171 622 5307
Contact: Ms Veronica Richardson, Secretary
Founded: 1984
Membership: 140
Publications: Members newsletter; promotional/educational leaflets

Profile: The Flowers and Plants Association offers information on commercially grown cut flowers and indoor pot plants. It provides statistical material on the market, facts about individual flowers and plants, gives an insight into current and future trends and offers specialist advice on all aspects of the industry. F&PA promotes the sales of cut flowers and indoor pot plants generically to the British public.

Flying Farmers Association
Ox House
Shobdon
Leominster
Herefordshire
HR6 9LT
Tel: 01568 708511
Fax: 01568 708177
Contact: Secretary

Food Advisory Committee
Ministry of Agriculture, Fisheries and Food
Room 504a Ergon House
c/o Nobel House
17 Smith Square
London
SW1P 3JR
Tel: 0171 238 6289
Contact: Miss BJ Richards, Secretary
Founded: 1983
Publications: Annual Report
Previous names: Merger of Food Standards Committee and Food Additives and Contaminants Committee in 1983
Profile: The FAC is an independent non-statutory body appointed by ministers and has the following terms of reference: to assess the risks to humans of chemicals which are used or occur in or on food and to advise ministers on the exercise of powers in the Food Safety Act 1990 relating to the labelling, composition and chemical safety of food. In exercising its functions the FAC will take the advice and work of the Committee on Toxicity and other relevant advisory committees into account.

Food and Drink Federation
6 Catherine Street
London
WC2B 5JJ
Tel: 0171 836 2460
Fax: 0171 836 0580

Food and Drink Industry Division
Ministry of Agriculture Fisheries and Food
Room 316
Whitehall Place West Block
London

SW1A 2HH
Tel: 0171 270 8519
Fax: 0171 270 8071
Contact: A Bolger
Profile: The Food and Drink Industry Division has responsibility for contacts with Food From Britain, the government's food marketing organisation, and for residual work on discontinued co-operation grants.

Food and Energy Research Centre
Cleeve Hill Agricultural Research Trust
Evesham Road
Cleeve Prior
Evesham
Worcestershire
WR11 5JY
Tel: 01789 778570
Contact: Dr DS Warren, Trustee/Director
Founded: 1975
Publications: Theoretical and practical reports
Profile: The Food and Energy Research Centre was established to develop and demonstrate ecological ways of living: sustainable life-support systems, particularly of food supply and fuel supply, which are in harmony with the natural environment.

Food and Farming Information Service
National Agricultural Centre
Stoneleigh Park
Warwickshire
CV8 2LZ
Tel: 01203 535707
Contact: Catriona Lennox
Previous names: Association of Agriculture

Food Commission
3rd Floor
5–11 Worship Street
London
EC2A 2BH
Tel: 0171 628 7774
Fax: 0171 628 0817
Contact: Information Officer
Founded: 1985
Publications: Publications list available
Previous names: London Food Commission until 1990
Profile: The Food Commission is an independent consumer watchdog which campaigns for safer and healthier food.

Food From Britain
123 Buckingham Palace Road
London
SW1W 9SA

Tel: 0171 233 5111
Fax: 0171 233 9516

Food Policy Division
Department of Agriculture for Northern Ireland
Dundonald House
Upper Newtownards
Belfast
BT4 3SB
Tel: 01232 524193

Food Science Laboratory – Norwich
Ministry of Agriculture, Fisheries and Food
Norwich Research Park
Colney
Norwich
Norfolk
NR4 7UQ
Tel: 01603 259350
Fax: 01603 501123

Food Science Laboratory – Torry
Ministry of Agriculture, Fisheries and Food
PO Box 31
135 Abbey Road
Aberdeen
AB9 8DG
Tel: 01224 877071
Fax: 01224 874246

Food Service
Department of Agriculture for Northern Ireland
Dundonald House
Upper Newtownards Road
Belfast
BT4 3SB
Tel: 01232 524579
Fax: 01232 524055
Contact: Dr J Speers, Head of Food Service
Founded: 1996
Publications: Promotional and technical documents; co-ordinates the publication of 'Agriculture in Northern Ireland'
Profile: The Food Service has five divisions which contribute to the aims of: promoting the economic growth and development of the countryside; identifying and exploiting new market opportunities; and promoting the quality and image of the products of the industry.

Food Technology Services Division
Department of Agriculture for Northern Ireland
Loughry College: The Food Centre
Cookstown
County Tyrone
BT80 9AA
Tel: 016487 62491
Fax: 016487 61043

Forest Enterprise
Forestry Commission
Westonbirt Arboretum
Tetbury
Gloucestershire
GL8 8QS
Tel: 01666 880220
Fax: 01666 880559
Contact: Tony Russell, Manager
Founded: 1918

Forest Service
Department of Agriculture for Northern Ireland
Room 21
Dundonald House
Upper Newtownards Road
Belfast
BT4 3SB
Tel: 01232 524394
Fax: 01232 525015

Forestry and Arboriculture Safety and Training Council
231 Corstophine Road
Edinburgh
EH12 7AT
Tel: 0131 334 8083
Fax: 0131 334 3047
Contact: TE Radford, Technical Secretary
Founded: 1992
Membership: 30
Publications: Register of Approved Instructors; safety guides; careers booklets
Previous names: Forestry Training Council; Forestry Safety Council; Arboriculture Safety Council

Forestry Authority
Forestry Commission
231 Corstorphine Road
Edinburgh
EH12 7AT
Tel: 0131 334 0303
Fax: 0131 334 3047
Email: forestry.commission@dial.pipex.com
Founded: 1919
Publications: Publications list available
Profile: The Forestry Authority carries out those parts of the Forestry Commission's work which involve implementation of policy and regulatory duties.

Forestry Authority Scotland
Forestry Commission
231 Corstophine Road
Edinburgh
EH12 7AT

Tel: 0131 334 0303
Contact: Alister T Jones, Development Officer
Founded: 1919
Profile: The Forestry Authority in Scotland is that part of the Forestry Commission which is responsible for implementing the regulations affecting the development and control of forestry in Scotland. It promotes the protection, management and extension of trees, woodlands and forests by means of publicity, grant aid and control of felling in both private and state owned forests.

Forestry Authority Wales
Forestry Commission
North Road
Aberystwyth
Ceredigion
SY23 2EF
Tel: 01970 625866
Fax: 01970 626177
Contact: Miss M Lewis, Higher Executive Officer
Founded: 1919
Publications: Publications list available

Forestry Commission
231 Corstorphine Road
Edinburgh
EH12 7AT
Tel: 0131 334 0303
Fax: 0131 334 3047
Email: forestry.commission@dial.pipex.com
Founded: 1919
Publications: Publications list available

Forestry Commission Research Division
Forestry Commission
Alice Holt Lodge
Wrecclesham
Farnham
Surrey
GU10 4LH
Tel: 01420 22255
Fax: 01420 23653
Contact: Dr John Parker, Research Communications Officer
Founded: 1946
Publications: Publications list available
Profile: The aim of the Forestry Commission Research Division is to increase the sustainable benefits from trees and woodlands by providing authoritative advice based on sound research. They are Britain's premier research organisation for forestry and woodland research, with two main centres at Alice Holt in Hampshire and at the Technopole, Bush Estate near Edinburgh. A network of field stations provides a

comprehensive service in establishing, maintaining and monitoring field trials, as well as providing a local source of advice.

Forestry Contracting Association Ltd
Dalfling
Blairdaff
Inverurie
Aberdeenshire
AB51 5LA
Tel: 01467 651368
Fax: 01467 651595
Email: 100732.2132@compuserve.com
Contact: Barrie Hudson, Chief Executive
Founded: 1992
Membership: 1,450
Publications: FCA News
Profile: The aim of the association is to ensure the availability of a sufficient, effective and viable contracting resource in the forestry industry, for the benefit of those who work in the industry as well as those who depend on it.

Forestry Industry Council of Great Britain
Golden Cross House
3–8 Duncannon Street
London
WC2N 4JF
Tel: 0171 930 9422
Fax: 0171 930 9426
Contact: Mrs Clare Ward, PA to Executive Director
Founded: 1987
Membership: 25
Publications: The Forestry Industry Yearbook; Wood from British Forests; The Potential for Extending Forest Cover in the Lowlands of England and Wales; keynote documents
Previous names: Forestry Industry Committee of Great Britain until 1996
Profile: The government-recognised body which brings together all strands of the forest industry: growers, sawmillers, processors, merchants, colleges and universities, in dialogue and representation.

Forestry Trust for Conservation and Education, The
Old Estate Office
Englefield Road
Theale
Reading
Berkshire
RG7 5DZ
Tel: 01189 323523
Fax: 01189 304033
Contact: Mrs Pamela Stratford, Administrator
Founded: 1988

Membership: 1,000
Profile: To create awareness and understanding of the importance of productive forests and woodland, and their contribution to sustainability; and to demonstrate that, in both, good management enhances the landscape and conservation of wildlife.

Forests Forever Campaign
4th Floor
Clareville House
26–27 Oxenden Street
London
SW1Y 4EL
Tel: 0171 839 1891
Fax: 0171 930 0094
Contact: R Michael James, Director
Founded: 1990
Membership: 240
Publications: Directory of National Forests Policies; Timber and the Environment
Profile: Forests Forever is an initiative of the Timber Trade Federation and was established in 1990 as an independent, voluntary funded body to represent the views of all timber and wood using industries in the UK on environmental issues.

Fortune Centre for Riding Therapy
Avon Tyrrell
Bransgore
Christchurch
Dorset
BH23 8EE
Tel: 01425 673297
Fax: 01425 674320
Contact: Mrs Jennifer L Dixon-Clegg, Director
Founded: 1976
Publications: Annual Report and publicity information
Profile: The Fortune Centre of Riding Therapy offers residential further education through horsemastership to young people of 16–25 years with special needs. This is a 2 year course funded by the Further Education Funding Council.

Freedom Food Ltd
Royal Society for the Prevention of Cruelty to Animals
The Manor House
Causeway
Horsham
West Sussex
RH12 1HG
Tel: 01403 264181
Fax: 01403 211514

Contact: Mike Sharpe, General Manager
Founded: 1994
Membership: 845
Publications: Focus
Profile: Freedom Food is a farm animal welfare labelling scheme devised by the RSPCA, which identifies meat, eggs and dairy products with a unique certification trade mark. This assures consumers that the food products have been derived from animals that have, from birth through to slaughter, been reared and handled in accordance with strict but achievable welfare standards developed by the RSPCA.

Fresh Fruit and Vegetable Information Bureau
Bury House
126–128 Cromwell Road
London
SW7 4ET
Tel: 0171 373 7734
Fax: 0171 373 3926
Contact: Jonathon Choat, Chief Executive
Founded: 1976
Profile: Central source of information for the media on all matters relating to fresh fruit and vegetables on sale in the UK.

Fresh Produce Consortium
266–270 Flower Market
New Covent Garden Market
London
SW8 5NB
Tel: 0171 627 3391
Fax: 0171 498 1191
Contact: Douglas Henderson, Chief Executive

Freshwater Biological Association
The Ferry House
Far Sawrey
Ambleside
Cumbria
LA22 0LP
Tel: 015394 42498
Fax: 015394 46914
Email: JGJFBA@wpo.nerc.ac.uk
Contact: Professor J Gwynfryn Jones, Director
Founded: 1929
Membership: 1,500
Publications: Numerous publications; Freshwater Forum (members newsletter)
Profile: The association conducts research into all aspects of freshwater science and technology, provides a membership organisation and independent scientific opinion.

Freshwater Fisheries Laboratory
Faskally
Pitlochry
Perthshire
PH16 5LB
Tel: 01796 472060
Fax: 01796 473523
Email: Pittype@marlab.ac.uk
Contact: Dr RGJ Shelton, Head
Founded: 1948
Publications: Annual Review; Scottish Salmon Statistics
Previous names: Brown Trout Research Laboratory

Friends of the Earth
26–28 Underwood Street
London
N1 7JQ
Tel: 0171 490 1555
Fax: 0171 490 0881
Email: foe@gn.apc.org
Internet: http://www.foe.co.uk
Contact: Tabitha Patterson

Friends of the Ridgeway
90 South Hill Park
London
NW3 2SN
Tel: 0171 794 2105
Email: bca@isise.rl.ac.uk
Contact: Nigel Forward, Secretary
Founded: 1982
Membership: 400
Publications: Quarterly newsletter
Profile: The Ridgeway is under pressure both from the legitimate activities of farming under modern conditions and from the increasing recreational use of some sections by cars and motorcycles which many people find offensive. The friends encourage the proper use and maintenance of the Ridgeway and draw attention to any threatening development, pressing public authorities to take action where it seems necessary.

Friesian Horse Association of Great Britain and Ireland Ltd
Wingfield Castle
Diss
Norfolk
IP21 5RB
Tel: 01379 388088
Fax: 01379 384748
Contact: Mrs I Lyndon-Stanford, Secretary
Founded: 1995
Membership: 40

Profile: FHAGBI's aim is to promote the pure breeding of Friesian horses in accordance with the breeding rules and regulations of Het Friesch Paarden Stamboek ("FPS"), the Royal Society, the Friesian Horse Stud Book in the Netherlands. The FPS is the worldwide authority on the Friesian Horse. FHAGBI is the sole representative of the FPS in Great Britain and Ireland and has been recognised by MAFF in compliance with the EC Regulations (Commission Decision 92/353/EEC). Members are welcome to join the association whatever their interest in the Friesian horse – breeding, dressage, competition driving, recreational or as an admirer.

Frizzle Society
Red Lion House
1 The High Street
Nettlebed
Oxfordshire
RG9 5DA
Contact: Mrs C Freeman, Secretary
Profile: A society to promote the Frizzle breed of poultry.

Fruit Identification Service
Royal Horticultural Society
Wisley Gardens
Wisley
Woking
Surrey
GU23 6QB
Tel: 01483 224234
Fax: 01483 211750
Internet:
http://www.kudos.co.uk/rhs/rhs/rhs1.html
Contact: Jim Arbury
Profile: A branch of the Royal Horticultural Society which provides information relating to the identification of fruit.

Fungicide Resistance Action Committee
GIFAP
c/o AgrEvo UK Ltd
Chesterford Park
Saffron Walden
Essex
CB10 1XL
Tel: 01799 530123
Fax: 01799 530966
Contact: Dr PE Russell, Chairman
Founded: 1981
Membership: 100
Publications: Publications list available
Profile: The Fungicide Resistance Action Committee is a specialist group of GIFAP, the international group of national associations of agrochemical manufacturers. FRAC is an intercompany committee dedicated to prolonging the effectiveness of fungicides liable to encounter resistance problems and to limit crop damage during the emergence of resistance.

Galloway Cattle Society of Great Britain and Ireland
15 New Market Street
Castle Douglas
Dumfries and Galloway
DG7 1HY
Tel: 01556 502753
Fax: 01556 502753
Contact: AJ McDonald, Breed Secretary
Founded: 1877
Membership: 700
Publications: Galloway Journal
Profile: To maintain unimpaired the purity of the breed of cattle known as Galloways and to promote the breeding of these cattle. To collect, verify and record the pedigree of these cattle and to represent the membership within the beef industry as and when applicable and required.

Game Conservancy Trust
Burgate Manor
Fordingbridge
Hampshire
SP6 1EF
Tel: 01425 652381
Fax: 01425 655848
Email: 100537.44@compuserve.com
Contact: Charles Nodder, Director External Affairs
Founded: 1968
Membership: 25,000
Publications: Publications list available
Profile: Research is undertaken on all aspects of game and the environment with a view to the development of practical game management plans for landowners and farmers.

Game Farmers Association
Upper Broadmoor Farm
Clapton
Bourton on the Water
Gloucestershire
GL54 2LQ
Tel: 01451 822023
Fax: 01451 821673

Game Marketing Executive
PO Box 11170
London
W2 1GS
Tel: 0171 724 4300

Fax: 0171 724 4324
Contact: Louisa Ayland, PR and Marketing Executive
Founded: 1996
Profile: Game Ltd is a non-profit making British organisation which aims to promote the consumption of game meats. Its two prime targets are the urban consumer and the catering trade.

Garden Centre Association Ltd
38 Carey Street
Reading
Berkshire
RG1 7JS
Tel: 01734 393900
Fax: 01734 500686
Contact: Cecilia Slinn, Administrator
Founded: 1966
Membership: 160
Publications: Members newsletter
Profile: The Garden Centre Association represents around 200 of the top garden centres in the country. Its purpose is to assist its members to maintain the highest standards of quality and service to the public. Members are regularly inspected by an independent consumer organisation to ensure that standards are maintained and improved.

Garden Industry Manufacturers Association
225 Bristol Road
Edgbaston
Birmingham
B57 UB
Tel: 0121 446 6688
Fax: 0121 446 5215
Contact: Jonathon Swift, Managing Director

Garlic Research Bureau
PO Box 40
Bury St Edmunds
Suffolk
IP31 2SS
Tel: 01284 787399
Fax: 01284 787399
Contact: David A Roser, Director
Founded: 1989
Publications: Garlic for Health; recipe booklets and leaflets
Profile: Interested in promoting the use of garlic by the UK population as both a raw product and in medicinal dosage formats. Undertakes radio broadcasts and press articles. Assists in developing research protocols and publishing results. Liaises with universities whilst research is in progress. Collects worldwide research

findings from a wide range of sources. Limited access to horticultural research.

Gascon Cattle Society
UPRA Gasconne (France)
27 Pasturelands Drive
Billington
Clitheroe
Lancashire
BB7 9LP
Tel: 01254 823688
Fax: 01254 246986
Contact: Timothy John Allen, Breed Secretary
Founded: 1990
Membership: 6
Publications: Go Gascon! (newsletter)
Previous names: Gasconne Cattle Society until 1996
Profile: Promotion of the Gascon breed to livestock producers, particularly the dairy herds and suckler herds in the UK. 'Gascon, the hardy suckler breed with shape – bred to perform, built to last'.

Gelbvieh Cattle Society
The Rowans
Warren Lane
Bythorn
Huntingdon
Cambridgeshire
Profile: We have been unable to contact this organisation. The details given are unconfirmed.

Genetics Forum
5–11 Worship Street
London
EC2A 2BH
Tel: 0171 638 0606
Fax: 0171 628 0817
Email: geneticforum@gn.apc.org.uk
Contact: Julie Sheppard, Editor
Founded: 1989
Publications: Splice of Life (journal)
Profile: Genetics Forum is a non-profit organisation committed to the socially accountable use of genetic engineering, funded by the National Consumer Council, the Green Alliance, the RSPCA and the National Food Alliance and others. GF produces occasional publications and briefing papers on key issues in biotechnology.

Geological Society
Burlington House
Piccadilly
London
W1V 0JU
Tel: 0171 434 9944
Fax: 0171 439 8975

Contact: Mr RM Bateman, Executive Secretary
Founded: 1807
Membership: 8,500
Publications: Journal of the Geological Society; Quarterly Journal of Engineering Geology; Petroleum Geoscience; Geoscientist
Profile: The Geological Society is the UK's national geological learned society and the professional body for UK geoscientists. It has the largest geological library in the UK and its own publishing house.

Geologists' Association
Burlington House
Piccadilly
London
W1V 9AG
Tel: 0171 434 9298
Contact: Dr Eric Robinson, Librarian
Founded: 1858
Membership: 2,600
Publications: Circular; Proceedings of the Geologists Association
Profile: The GA exists to serve the interest and needs of the amateur in geology. This is done through publications, through excursions and through lectures. They support conservation in the countryside through small grants and backing RIGS groups in the counties working to maintain sites and trails for geological fieldwork. No professional qualifications required for membership.

Glasgow Agricultural Society
Tel: 01786 870308
Contact: Mr Carrick
Profile: We have been unable to contact this organisation. The details given are unconfirmed.

Glasshouse Lettuce Growers Technology Group
HRI Stockbridge House
Cawood
Near Selby
North Yorkshire
YO8 0TZ
Tel: 01757 268275
Fax: 01757 268996
Contact: R Bradley

Gloucester Cattle Society
Bemborough Farm Office
Guiting Power
Cheltenham
Gloucestershire
GL54 5UG
Tel: 01451 850307
Fax: 01451 850423

Contact: Elizabeth L Henson, Secretary
Founded: 1919
Membership: 160
Publications: Herd book and newsletters
Previous names: Lapsed after second World War, reformed 1974
Profile: Breed society for the Gloucester breed of cattle.

Gloucestershire Old Spots Pig Breeders Club
Dryft Cottage
South Cerney
Cirencester
Gloucestershire
GL7 5UB
Tel: 01285 860229
Fax: 01285 860229
Contact: Richard HL Lutwyche, Secretary
Founded: 1990
Membership: 240
Publications: Spot Press (members newsletter); leaflets
Profile: The club was established to promote and encourage interest in the breed as well as to provide a focal point for breeders. This is achieved through advertising and editorial features, through a display stand and special prizes at relevant shows, through encouragement to participate in the RBST's traditional breeds meat marketing scheme and through other initiatives.

Goat Veterinary Society
British Veterinary Association
The Limes
Chalk Street
Rettendon Common
Chelmsford
Essex
CM3 8DA
Tel: 01245 353741
Fax: 01245 348564
Contact: John Matthews, Chairman
Founded: 1979
Membership: 250
Publications: Goat Veterinary Society Journal
Profile: The objectives of the GVS is the furtherance of interest in and knowledge of goats by the veterinary profession. It is a non-territorial division of the British Veterinary Association. Meetings of the society are held twice a year followed by publication of a journal containing written summaries of the papers given.

Going for Green
Department of the Environment
Churchgate House
56 Oxford Street

Manchester
M60 7HJ
Tel: 0161 237 4158
Fax: 0161 237 4155
Contact: Janet Withington, Marketing Manager
Founded: 1995
Publications: Publications list available
Profile: Going for Green is one of the government's responses to the Rio de Janeiro Earth Summit in 1992. It is a national campaign which aims to encourage and support people who want to improve the environment by making small changes to their lifestyle in all the different roles they play as individuals. Going for Green's help and guidance is targeted directly at the public through advertising campaigns and through other environmental organisations, business and authorities. The campaign aims to give people simple, clear suggestions about what they might consider changing about their daily lives and how they might do it.

Golden Guernsey Goat Club
Brambles
Green Lane
Pamber Green
Tadley
Hampshire
RG26 3AD
Tel: 01256 850410
Contact: Mrs PA Dalton, Secretary
Founded: 1969
Membership: 250
Publications: Quarterly journal and yearly stud list
Profile: The object of the society is to promote the Golden Guernsey goat and provide communication between interested persons. It is the oldest and largest goat breed society. Area and national shows are held to encourage new owners and provide help and advice to all. The breed society has an enthusiastic and expanding nationwide following. The Golden Guernsey is a small goat with a moderate milk yield, which although less than other breeds, is comparable when the lower food intake is taken into account. It is an adaptable goat with an affectionate and docile nature and is very suitable as a house goat.

Golf Course Wildlife Trust
31 Bedford Square
London
WC1B 3SG
Contact: Mr Michael Harvey

Gooseberry Society
Lone Pine
4A Westaway Road
Colyton
Axminster
Devon
EX13 6PA
Tel: 01927 553935
Contact: Anthony de Freston, Founder
Founded: 1980
Profile: The Gooseberry Society aims to protect and promote the gooseberry and to produce new cultivars.

Grain and Feed Trade Association
GAFTA House
6 Chapel Place
Rivington Street
London
EC2A 3DQ
Tel: 0171 814 9666
Fax: 0171 814 8383
Email: postagafta@demon.co.uk
Contact: Sandra Black, PR Manager
Membership: 700
Publications: GAFTA Newsletter
Profile: GAFTA is a unique organisation promoting international trade in grain, animal feedingstuffs, pulses and rice.

Grants and Subsidies Inspection Division
Department of Agriculture for Northern Ireland
Kilpatrick House
38–54 High Street
Ballymena
County Antrim
BT43 6DP
Tel: 01266 44121
Fax: 01266 48283
Contact: W J McWhirter, Head of Division
Founded: 1996
Previous names: Agricultural Development and Statutory Unit
Profile: The unit is responsible for field inspections of all grants and subsidies claimed from the Department of Agriculture for Northern Ireland.

Green Alliance
49 Wellington Street
London
WC2E 7BN
Tel: 0171 836 0341
Fax: 0171 240 9205
Email: gralliance@gn.apc.org
Internet: http://www.gn.apc.org/gralliance
Contact: Natalia Pozo, Administrative Officer
Founded: 1978

Membership: 160
Publications: Parliamentary newsletter; publications list available
Previous names: The Ecological Studies Institute until 1986
Profile: The Green Alliance works for a better environment by seeking to ensure that the environment is a prime consideration in all decision making. Their role is to focus on the processes by which decisions are made in a broad range of institutions; to bring together relevant interest groups and individuals to debate environmental problems and explore solutions; to complement the work of other organisations by providing interpretation and analysis from a broad perspective and advance the environmental agenda into new areas.

Green Wood Trust
The Stations
Station Road
Coalbrookdale
Telford
Shropshire
Tel: 01952 432769
Fax: 01952 432769
Contact: Susan Kilvert, Site Administrator
Founded: 1984
Membership: 408
Publications: Course brochure, production brochure, members magazine – Loose Leaves
Profile: The Green Wood Trust is dedicated to encouraging the effective management of woodlands and the development of products using home produced timber. The trust has three principal aims: the sensitive management of woodland resources using traditional and modern techniques; the development and production of new products using good design and aesthetic awareness; and the recording and revival of traditional woodland crafts. Hosting a comprehensive range of traditional craft courses, the trust is a multidisciplinary organisation which brings together the interests of the ecologist, forester, craftsman, designer, artist and architect, in an effort to save and regenerate our native small woods.

Greenmount College of Agriculture and Horticulture
Department of Agriculture for Northern Ireland
22 Greenmount Road
Antrim
Northern Ireland
BT41 4PU
Tel: 01849 426700
Fax: 01849 426606
Contact: RJ McClenghan, Principal

Founded: 1912
Publications: College prospectus; technology transfer and technical business support publications.
Profile: Greenmount College's primary function is the provision of education and training to meet the needs of the agri-food industry. A wide range of full-time and part-time agricultural and horticultural courses are offered. The college also undertakes systems development work on commercial farm and horticultural businesses to help establish and demonstrate the viability and acceptability of new systems and practices.

Greyfaced Dartmoor Sheep Breeders Association
The Old Rectory
Clannaborough
Crediton
Devon
EX17 6DA
Tel: 01363 84256
Contact: Wilson Mitchell, Secretary
Founded: 1900
Membership: 240
Publications: Annual Flock Book
Profile: A society for the breeders of grey faced Dartmoor sheep.

Groundwork Foundation
85–87 Cornwall Street
Birmingham
B3 3BY
Tel: 0121 236 8565
Fax: 0121 236 7356
Contact: Tricia Stewart

Guernsey Association for Shooting and Conservation
Bevlyn
Les Osmonds Lane
Coutanchez
St Sampson
Guernsey
Channel Isles
GY2 4GG
Tel: 01481 721428
Contact: Mr Rex Trott, Secretary

Guernsey Conservation Society
Tengah
Dehus Lane
Vale
Guernsey
Channel Isles
GY3 5EP
Tel: 01481 47582

Contact: Mr Richard John Collas, Chairman
Founded: 1966
Membership: 10
Profile: To promote in Guernsey the use of recycling, to encourage co-operation between local environmentally concerned organisations and to put forward and to encourage local authorities to adopt more environmental policies.

Guernsey Growers Association
Landes du Marche
Vale
Guernsey
Channel Isles
GY6 8DE
Tel: 01481 53713
Fax: 01481 54015
Contact: Mrs V Mechem, Secretary
Founded: 1894
Membership: 350
Publications: Annual Report and yearbook
Profile: The GGA is the growers' organisation with the mandate to 'watch over and protect in every possible manner, the interests of all growers'. It aims to benefit the industry generally and to increase the collaboration and co-operation between growers and their various organisations.

Guild of Agricultural Journalists
Charmwood
47 Court Meadow
Rotherfield
East Sussex
TN6 3LQ
Tel: 01892 853187
Fax: 01892 853187
Email: d.gomery@midnet.com
Contact: Don Gomery, Secretary
Founded: 1944
Membership: 578
Publications: Annual Yearbook; quarterly bulletins
Profile: Established to promote high professional standards among journalists who specialise in agriculture, to represent their interests and to promote schemes for the education of members and new entrants.

Guild of Conservation Grade Producers (Conservation Guild)
National Agricultural Centre
Stoneleigh Park
Warwickshire
CV8 2LG
Tel: 01203 696526
Fax: 01203 696990

Contact: Mrs Carol C Smith, Secretary
Founded: 1985
Membership: 130
Publications: Farm Production Standards
Profile: Aims to produce food using traditional farming practices combined with the best of modern methods; to look after the land and crops in an environmentally friendly way; to keep farm animals in kind conditions and give them only healthy natural feeds; and ensure all aspects of production are subject to strict standards, which are audited by an independent inspectorate.

Guild of Master Craftsmen
Castle Place
166 High Street
Lewes
East Sussex
BN7 1XU
Tel: 01273 478449
Fax: 01273 478606
Contact: Information Officer
Membership: 25,000
Publications: Publications list available
Profile: Trade association for skilled crafts people and professionals. It aims to protect the public by instilling among members a greater sense of responsibility and by encouraging members always to strive for excellence. The guild runs a help line and can provide selective lists of craftsmen and professionals across the country.

Guild of Taxidermists
Glasgow Art Gallery and Museum
Kelvin Grove
Glasgow
G3 8AG
Tel: 0141 287 2671
Fax: 0141 287 2690
Contact: Duncan Ferguson, Secretary
Founded: 1976
Membership: 200
Publications: Annual Journal
Profile: The guild was formed in 1976 to raise the status and standards of taxidermy in the UK. The guild organises two one day seminars plus a two/three day conference per year and has close contact with the European Taxidermy Federation.

Gun Trade Association
PO Box 7
Evesham
Worcestershire
WR11 6AN
Tel: 01386 443304
Fax: 01386 443305

Contact: Brian Carter, Director
Founded: 1912
Membership: 350
Profile: The Gun Trade Association represents all involved in the legitimate trade in firearms, ammunition and shooting accessories in the UK, including wholesalers, manufacturers, retail gun shops and gunsmiths.

Gwartheg Hynafol Cymru/Ancient Cattle of Wales

Cefn Pennar
Machynlleth
Powys
SY20 9JS
Tel: 01654 791255
Contact: Bruce McCay, Honorary Secretary
Founded: 1981
Membership: 30
Publications: Herd book; occasional newsletters
Profile: The society's objectives are to encourage the breeding of Welsh cattle of colours other than black, the registration of such cattle and the periodic publication of a herd book. Herds are now registered from Scotland to South West England.

Gwent Tertiary College Usk Campus

The Rhadyr
Usk
Gwent
NP5 1XJ
Tel: 01291 672311
Fax: 01291 672256
Contact: Mr P Sanger, Director of Usk
Publications: College Prospectus
Previous names: Usk College of Agriculture until 1992
Profile: Campus based at Usk, mainly for use by land-based students. Courses offered include agriculture, horticulture, equine studies, countryside management and animal care.

Habitat Scotland

Hazelmount
Heron Place
Portree
Isle of Skye
IV51 9EA
Tel: 01478 612898
Fax: 01478 613254
Email: sitc@skyejet.demon.co.uk
Contact: Graeme Robertson, Director
Founded: 1977
Publications: Publications list available
Profile: An independent research charity established to promote the conservation, restoration and sustainable use of the environment in Scotland for the benefit of all.

Hackney Horse Society

Clump Cottage
Chitterne
Warminster
Wiltshire
BA12 0LL
Tel: 01985 850906
Fax: 01985 850317
Contact: Sally Oliver, Secretary
Founded: 1883
Membership: 500
Publications: Yearbook; Stud book
Profile: To improve the breed and promote the breeding of Hackneys. Compilation and publishing of stud books of such horses and ponies. Holding shows of such horses and ponies.

Hadlow College

Hadlow
Tonbridge
Kent
TN11 0AL
Tel: 01732 850551
Fax: 01732 851957
Contact: Admissions Department
Founded: 1967
Previous names: Hadlow College of Agriculture and Horticulture
Profile: Hadlow College provides training and education in the areas of agriculture, horticulture, equine, floristry and other land-based careers. The college is also a major centre for continuing professional education and training, with conference and meeting facilities.

Haflinger Society of Great Britain

25 Hilltop Park
Rugby Road
Princethorpe
Warwickshire
CV23 9PW
Tel: 01926 632516
Contact: Mrs Diane Parkinson, Honorary Secretary
Founded: 1971
Membership: 400
Publications: Quarterly newsletter
Profile: The Haflinger Society was founded in 1970 and modelled itself on the Austrian precepts regarding the Haflinger and its breeding. The society is still guided by Austria, linked through membership of the World Haflinger Federation, setting the overall standard

and breeding aims. The Haflinger Society of Great Britain keeps the stud book which includes all breeding stock, a gelding register and a part bred register. Updated sales lists are available from the secretary.

Hamburgh Club
101 Abbotsham Road
Bideford
Devon
EX39 3AH
Tel: 01237 472572
Contact: Mr P Gompertz, Secretary
Profile: A society to promote the Hamburgh breed of poultry.

Hampshire Cattle Breeders Society Ltd
Beechen Lane
Lyndhurst
Hampshire
SO43 7DD
Tel: 01703 286016
Fax: 01703 282170
Contact: Roger Thomas, Chief Executive Officer
Founded: 1940
Membership: 500

Hampshire Down Sheep Breeders Association
Rickyard Cottage
Denner Hill
Great Missenden
Buckinghamshire
HP16 0HZ
Tel: 01494 488388
Contact: Richard Davis, Secretary
Founded: 1889
Membership: 170
Publications: Annual flock book; members newsletter
Profile: To encourage the breeding of Hampshire Down sheep both at home and abroad and to maintain the integrity of the breed by keeping a flock book of pedigree stock; to promote the Hampshire Down as the premier sire for the production of early lambs showing good growth rates and excellent carcass conformation and to identify leading genetic material by central testing of ram lambs and the dissemination of these genes via AI.

Hannah Research Institute
Kirkhill
St Quivox
Ayr
Ayrshire
KA6 5HL

Tel: 01292 476013
Fax: 01292 671052

Harness Goat Society
Poplar Ridge
Cornwalls Hill
Lambley
Nottinghamshire
NG4 4PZ
Tel: 0115 931 3555
Contact: Mrs Anne Cox, Secretary
Founded: 1986
Membership: 185
Publications: Training Your Goat; Harness Goat Society Magazine
Profile: A society designed to promote and protect the working goat.

Harper Adams Agricultural College
Newport
Shropshire
TF10 8NB
Tel: 01952 820280
Fax: 01952 814783
Email: principal@haac.ac.uk
Internet: http://www.haac.ac.uk
Contact: Dr EW Jones, Principal
Founded: 1901
Publications: Prospectus; research reports; discussion papers; farm guide
Profile: Harper Adams is the leading provider of higher education courses to the land-based industries in the UK. BSc courses are offered in agriculture, agricultural marketing, agricultural engineering, rural enterprise and land management, and rural environment protection with HND courses in agriculture, agricultural marketing and agricultural engineering. There is a strong and growing research programme, particularly in the crop and animal science departments.

Hartpury College
Hartpury House
Hartpury
Gloucester
GL19 3BE
Tel: 01452 700283
Fax: 01452 700629
Email: 100655.732@compuserve.com
Contact: Malcolm Wharton, Principal
Founded: 1948
Publications: College prospectus
Profile: In the heart of Gloucestershire, Hartpury College is the leading land-based college, offering a wide range of educational and training opportunities for related industries. The extensive facilities on both the Hartpury and

Blaisdon sites, along with a highly qualified body of staff, provide students with the best resources available.

Hawk and Owl Trust
National Centre for Owl Conservation
Wolterton Park
Erpingham
Norwich
Norfolk
NR11 7HL
Tel: 01263 761718
Contact: Mrs Josephine Marston, Exhibition Administrator
Founded: 1969
Membership: 2,000
Publications: Publications list available
Previous names: Hawk Trust until 1988
Profile: The trust protects and conserves birds of prey and their wild habitats through creative conservation, practical research and imaginative education.

Head Lads Association
196 New Cheveley Road
Newmarket
Suffolk
CB8 8BZ
Tel: 01638 662683
Profile: We have been unable to contact this organisation. The details given are unconfirmed.

Health and Safety Agency for Northern Ireland
Department of Economic Development
83 Ladas Drive
Belfast
BT6 9FJ
Tel: 01232 243249
Fax: 01232 235383
Contact: Lorna Brown, Secretary
Founded: 1979
Publications: Publications list available

Health and Safety Commission
Rose Court
2 Southwark Bridge
London
SE1 9HS
Tel: 0171 717 6000
Fax: 0171 717 6717

Health and Safety Executive
Information Centre
Broad Lane
Sheffield
S3 7HQ
Tel: 0541 545500
Fax: 0114 289 2333

Health and Safety Inspectorate
Department of Agriculture for Northern Ireland
Annex D
Dundonald House
Upper Newtownards Road
Belfast
BT4 3SB
Tel: 01232 525316
Fax: 01232 525205

Heather Trust, The
The Cross
Kippen
Stirlingshire
FK8 3DS
Tel: 01786 870808
Fax: 01786 870890
Contact: John Phillips, General Manager
Founded: 1984
Membership: 350
Publications: Annual Report
Previous names: The Joseph Nickerson Reconciliation Project
Profile: The purpose of the Heather Trust is to encourage the good management of heather moorland for the benefit of domestic stock, game and other wildlife, the people who live by them and the people who enjoy them. The Heather Trust carries out research on both plants and animals, manages moorlands on its own account where demonstrations of good practice are held and offers an advisory service on all matters connected with the management of plants and animals in the uplands of the UK.

Heavy Horse Preservation Society
Old Rectory
Whitchurch
Shropshire
ST13 1LF
Profile: We have been unable to contact this organisation. The details given are unconfirmed.

Hebridean Sheep Society
Knox Mill
Knox Mill Lane
Harrogate
North Yorkshire
HG3 2AE
Tel: 01423 507741
Contact: Eric Medway, Secretary
Previous names: Hebridean Sheep Breeders Group until 1993

Profile: We have been unable to contact this organisation. The details given are unconfirmed.

Hen Packers Association
Imperial House
15–19 Kingsway
London
WC2B 6UA
Tel: 0171 240 9889
Fax: 0171 240 7757
Contact: Miss YP Sired, Secretary

Henry Doubleday Research Association
Ryton Organic Gardens
Ryton on Dunsmore
Coventry
Warwickshire
CV8 3LG
Tel: 01203 303517
Fax: 01203 639229
Email: enquiry@hdra.demon.co.uk
Contact: Jo Burton, Communications Manager
Founded: 1958
Membership: 18,500
Publications: Publications list available
Profile: The aims of the HDRA are to carry out scientific research into, collate and disseminate information about, and promote interest in organic gardening and farming and food in the UK and overseas. We have a membership of 18,500 and work to protect the environment, conserve natural habitats, maintain a rich genetic diversity, sustain the soil and produce food which is unadulterated with potentially harmful chemicals.

Herb Society
134 Buckingham Palace Road
London
SW1W 9SA
Tel: 0171 823 5583
Fax: 01284 810653
Contact: Nicola Hartopp, Secretary
Founded: 1927
Membership: 2,400
Publications: Herbs (journal); Herbarium (journal)
Previous names: The Society of Herbalists
Profile: The Herb Society brings together all those who are interested in herbs, from professional growers to amateur enthusiasts. Founded in 1927 by Hilda Leyel as the Society of Herbalists, the society sold culinary, medicinal and cosmetic herbs and products. Seminars and workshops are arranged around the country and there is a growing number of local groups. The Herb Society Garden which incorporates

Apothecaries' Paradise and Knot Gardens is part of the Henry Doubleday Research Association Gardens in Yalding, Kent.

Herb Trust, The
Lone Pine
4a Westaway Road
Colyton
Devon
EX13 6PA
Tel: 01297 553935
Contact: Antony de Freston, Founder
Profile: The trust aims to preserve and promote the use of herbs and to encourage and develop new applications of these plants. The trust will place great importance on education of young people to study the history and development of herbs. The trust will compile records of all known herbs and their uses and to have specimens of these herbs in its own herb gardens.

Herbicide Resistance Action Committee
GIFAP
Ciba Geigy Ltd
R1004.5.46
CH – 4002
Switzerland
Tel: 00 4161 697 3662
Fax: 00 4161 697 6855
Email: derek.cornes@chbs.mhs.ciba.com
Internet:
　http://ipmwww.ncsu.edu/orgs/hrac/hrac.html
Contact: Derek Cornes, Publicity Officer
Founded: 1989
Publications: Publications list available
Profile: The Herbicide Resistance Action Committee aims to facilitate the effective management of herbicide resistance by fostering understanding, co-operation and communication between industry, government and farmers. Its aims are to foster a responsible attitude to herbicide use; to support research and conferences on herbicide resistance and to communicate herbicide resistance management strategies and support their implementation.

Herdwick Sheep Breeders Association
Fell View
Mockerkin
Cockermouth
Cumbria
CA13 0ST
Tel: 01946 862382
Contact: GF Brown, Secretary
Founded: 1916
Membership: 150
Publications: Flock book

Hereford Cattle Society
Hereford House
3 Offa Street
Hereford
HR1 2LL
Tel: 01432 272057
Fax: 01432 350608
Contact: David E Prothero, Breed Secretary
Founded: 1878
Membership: 800
Publications: Annual breed journal
Previous names: Hereford Herd Book Society
until 1996
Profile: Over 200 years of selective breeding has
made the red coated, white faced Hereford the
world's most numerous beef breed, with an
estimated population of pedigree and cross-bred
cattle exceeding 100 million.

Heritage Seed Library
Henry Doubleday Research Association
   Genetic Resources Department
Ryton Gardens
Ryton on Dunsmore
Coventry
Warwickshire
CV8 3LG
Tel: 01203 303517
Fax: 01203 639229
Email: enquiry@hdra.demon.co.uk
Founded: 1991
Membership: 6,500
Publications: The Fruit and Veg Finder; Seed
News
Previous names: Heritage Seed Programme
until 1995

Hertfordshire Agricultural Society
The Showground
Dunstable Road
Redbourn
Hertfordshire
AL3 7PT
Tel: 01582 792626
Fax: 01582 794027
Contact: Mr RI Lawrenson, Secretary
Founded: 1801
Membership: 600
Publications: Annual Report and Accounts;
Hertfordshire County Show Schedule;
Hertfordshire County Show
Programme/Catalogue
Profile: A company limited by guarantee and a
registered charity. The society manages the 80
acre county showground, which is owned by the
society, and organises the county show as well
as administrating other showground events.

Highland Cattle Society
59 Drumlanrig Street
Thornhill
Dumfriesshire
DG3 5LY
Tel: 01848 330438
Fax: 01848 330880
Contact: Hamish Wilson, Secretary
Founded: 1884
Membership: 1,350
Publications: Highland Breeders Journal

Highland Pony Society
Beechwood
Elie
Fife
KY9 1DH
Tel: 01333 330696
Fax: 01333 330115
Contact: I W Brown, Secretary and Treasurer
Founded: 1923
Membership: 1,250
Publications: Stud book; newsletters
Profile: The objects of the Highland Pony Society
are: to improve the breed and promote the
breeding of Highland ponies used for riding,
driving, farm work and sporting purposes; to
promote the general interests of the breeders
and owners of registered Highland ponies; and to
encourage the registration of pure bred stallions,
mares and geldings in the Highland Pony
Society's stud book.

Highlands and Islands Enterprise
Bridge House
20 Bridge Street
Inverness
IV1 1QR
Tel: 01463 234171
Fax: 01463 244469

Highlands and Islands Forum
David White House
57 Church Street
Inverness
IV1 1DR
Tel: 0146 371 3531
Fax: 0146 371 0965
Email: HIF@cali.co.uk
Contact: Karen Scott, Co-ordinator
Founded: 1986
Membership: 60
Publications: Publications list available
Profile: HIF is a democratic, community based,
voluntary organisation which aims to provide
greater involvement by local communities in
decision making about the land and natural

resources in their area. It aims to help communities and community groups to develop their skills, knowledge and confidence by sharing experiences, and learning from each other and by gaining access to knowledge and skills that have been developed elsewhere.

Hill Farming Advisory Committee
Ministry of Agriculture, Fisheries and Food
Room 721 Nobel House
17 Smith Square
London
SW1P 3JR
Tel: 0171 238 6307
Fax: 0171 238 6288
Contact: Mr Kevin Evans, Committee Secretary
Profile: The committee advises the Minister of Agriculture, Fisheries and Food and the Secretary of State for Wales on the exercise of their powers under the Hill Farming Act 1946 and on any matter relating to farming in Less Favoured Areas that may be referred to the committee by the two ministries. This includes the operation of hill farming support measures, animal health matters and general conditions and prospects for hill farming.

Hill Farming Advisory Committee for Scotland
Scottish Office Agriculture and Fisheries Department
Pentland House
47 Robb's Loan
Edinburgh
EH14 1TW
Tel: 0131 244 6375
Fax: 0131 244 6006
Contact: Mike Lyman

Hill Radnor Flock Book Society
Bulwark Chambers
The Bulwark
Brecon
Powys
LD3 7AD
Tel: 01874 623452
Fax: 01874 625435
Contact: Mr JA Lewis, Secretary

Historic Buildings Council for Northern Ireland
Environment Service
5–33 Hill Street
Belfast
BT1 2LA
Tel: 01232 235000
Fax: 01232 543111

Contact: Mrs Primrose Wilson, Chairman
Founded: 1975
Publications: HBC reports; Conservation Area Report
Profile: The Historic Buildings Council advises the Department of the Environment (NI) on listing of buildings, designation of conservation areas and other policy matters. In 1993 HBC produced a paper for the department on vernacular buildings. HBC's concerns include historic parks, gardens and demesnes.

Historic Churches Preservation Trust
Fulham Palace
London
SW6 6EA
Tel: 0171 736 3054
Fax: 0171 736 3054
Contact: Wg Cdr MW Tippen, Secretary
Founded: 1953
Membership: 2,500
Publications: Annual Report; The Review (journal)
Profile: The trust aims to preserve and repair churches and chapels of any Christian denomination. They give assistance with grants and loans to the efforts of congregations, mostly in rural areas, with the carrying out of essential repairs to the fabric of historic churches.

Historic Farm Buildings Group
Museum of English Rural Life
University of Reading
PO Box 229
Whiteknights
Reading
RG6 6AG
Tel: 01734 318663
Fax: 01734 751264
Contact: R Brigden, Secretary
Founded: 1986
Membership: 250
Publications: Annual journal; members newsletter; occasional conference proceedings
Profile: The group provides a forum for anyone interested in the study and recording of old farm buildings.

Historic Houses Association
2 Chester Street
London
SW1X 7BB
Tel: 0171 259 5688
Fax: 0171 259 5590
Contact: Peter Sinclair, Executive Secretary
Founded: 1973
Membership: 13,400

Publications: Historic House (journal); Annual Report; advisory manuals
Profile: The HHA is an association of owners of historic houses, castles, gardens and parks whose concern is to work for a fiscal, political and economic climate in which private owners can maintain Britain's historic houses and landscapes for the benefit of the nation and for future generations. Over 300 members open their house and gardens to the public.

Historic Monuments Council
Department of the Environment (NI)
Environment and Heritage Service
5–33 Hill Street
Belfast
Northern Ireland
BT1 2LA
Tel: 01232 543076
Fax: 01232 543111
Contact: Emma Gibson, Secretariat
Founded: 1971
Previous names: Ancient Monuments Advisory Committee 1926–1937; Ancient Monuments Advisory Council 1937–1971
Profile: The Historic Monuments Council advises the Department of the Environment for Northern Ireland on the exercise of its powers under the Historic Monuments and Archaeological Objects Order (NI) 1995. It carries out certain functions specified in the order, for example in connection with scheduling historic monuments for protection. The membership spans a wide range, in geographical professional and social terms, and each council is appointed for a 3 year period.

Historic Scotland
Longmoore House
Salisbury Place
Edinburgh
EH9 1SH
Tel: 0131 668 8600
Fax: 0131 668 8669

HM Customs and Excise
New King's Beam House
22 Upper Ground
London
SE1 9PJ
Tel: 0171 620 1313
Profile: For enquiries on VAT matters please contact your regional VAT Business Advice Centre. Enquiries on all other matters should be made to regional Excise and Inland Customs Advice Centres. Contact numbers are listed in the phone book under Customs and Excise.

HM Land Registry
Room 107
Lincoln's Inn Field
London
WC2A 3PH
Tel: 0171 917 8880

Holme Lacy College
Holme Lacy
Hereford
HR2 6LL
Tel: 01432 870316
Fax: 01432 870566
Contact: Nicky Whenham, Marketing Co-ordinator
Founded: 1963
Publications: Prospectus; Short Course Programme
Previous names: Herefordshire College of Agriculture until 1996
Profile: Holme Lacy College provides quality education and practical training in the land-based, outdoor industries and is based around a 600 acre working estate in Herefordshire's Wye Valley. Various full, part-time and short programmes are available in the following disciplines – tourism and leisure, environmental management, business studies, animal care, horse management, forestry, gamekeeping, arboriculture, agriculture, horticulture and floristry.

Holstein Friesian Society of Great Britain and Ireland
Scotsbridge House
Scots Hill
Rickmansworth
Hertfordshire
WD3 3BB
Tel: 01923 494600
Fax: 01923 770003
Email: mike@hfsx.demon.co.uk
Contact: Ann Hardy, Press and Publicity Manager
Founded: 1909
Membership: 12,600
Publications: Holstein Friesian Journal; Sire Summary; Annual Report and Accounts
Previous names: British Holstein Cattle Society until 1918; British Friesian Cattle Society until 1971; British Friesian Cattle Society of Great Britain and Ireland until 1988
Profile: The Holstein Friesian Society of Great Britain and Ireland is the largest independent breed society in Europe. It registers over 260,000 cattle each year which it holds on a database of over 5 million cattle. It operates the national type evaluation scheme through which animals are

awarded phenotypic type scores and genetic indexes for type. Other services include the computerised mating service, Select-a-bull; the HFS journal, and the Sire Summary, a comprehensive guide to breeding information on Holstein Friesian Bulls.

Home Grown Timber Advisory Committee

c/o Forestry Commission
231 Corstophine Road
Edinburgh
EH12 7AT
Tel: 0131 334 0303 ext 2423
Fax: 0131 316 4891
Contact: Debbie Weston, Secretary
Founded: 1951
Publications: Annual Report
Profile: The Home Grown Timber Advisory Committee is the statutory advisory body of the Forestry Commission, and comprises a range of membership drawn from forest owners, timber trade interests, environmental interests, etc.

Home-Grown Cereals Authority

Hamlyn House
Highgate Hill
London
N19 5PR
Tel: 0171 263 3391
Fax: 0171 561 6231
Email: hgca@demon.co.uk
Contact: AJ Williams, Chief Executive
Founded: 1965
Publications: Publications list available
Profile: The HGCA remit is based on the Cereals Marketing Act 1965. Its purpose is to improve the production and marketing of cereals and oilseeds grown in the UK. Its activities comprise: providing a market information service for cereals and oilseeds; sponsoring research and development for home-grown cereals and oilseeds; taking other non-trading initiatives (promoting export through British Cereals Export and cereals-related food through Food from Britain); agency work for the Intervention Board, MAFF and other bodies.

Homoeopathic Society for Animal Welfare

Newparc
Llanrhidian
Gower
Swansea
SA3 1HA
Tel: 01792 390943
Contact: Mrs Brookie Brook, Co-ordinator
Founded: 1987

Membership: 300
Publications: Quarterly newsletter
Profile: The aims of the society are: the treatment of animals with homoeopathic remedies, which are safe, effective, gentle and have no side effects; the circulation of knowledge of successful remedies used by members; to campaign for the training of more homoeopathic veterinary surgeons; to fight for the right to use natural medicines and to promote the general welfare of all animals.

Hop Merchants Association

Nettlestead Oast
Paddock Wood
Tonbridge
Kent
TN12 6DA
Tel: 01892 835155
Fax: 01892 836003

Hop Research Unit

Horticulture Research Institute
Wye College
Wye
Ashford
Kent
TN25 5AH
Tel: 01233 812179
Fax: 01233 813126
Email: peter.darby@hri.ac.uk
Contact: Dr Peter Darby, Head of Unit
Founded: 1948
Previous names: Department of Hop Research, Wye College 1948–1987, Department of Hop Research, Institute of Horticultural Research 1987–1990
Profile: The HRI Hop Research Unit at Wye is the main centre for scientific research on hops in Britain. Work concentrates on a breeding programme to produce new hop varieties with improved agronomic and brewing characteristics, and hop analysis and quality. It is funded through the National Hop Association, brewing companies, MAFF and BBSRC.

Horse and Pony Lovers against Blood Sports

23 Levernside Crescent
Glasgow
G53 5JY
Profile: We have been unable to contact this organisation. The details given are unconfirmed.

Horse Rangers Association

Royal Mews
Hampton Court Palace
East Molesey

Surrey
KT8 9BW
Tel: 0181 979 4196
Contact: Mrs DL Gordon, Commandant General
Founded: 1954
Membership: 400
Publications: Publications list available
Profile: Children can join Horse Rangers at the age of eight. The members meet at weekends in squadrons supervised by their officers to ride and learn stable management. A self-supporting charity, there are many fund raising activities. The Horse Rangers Association was established to provide the opportunity for contact with horses for those children who otherwise would not have this experience.

Horses and Ponies Protection Association
The Stables
Burnley Wharf
Manchester Road
Burnley
Lancashire
BB11 1JZ
Tel: 01282 455992
Fax: 01282 451992
Contact: Mrs I Milton-Hall, Association Secretary
Founded: 1937
Membership: 10,000
Publications: Newsletters, annual accounts, information leaflets and posters
Profile: HAPPA was founded in 1937 to protect horses, ponies and donkeys from acts of cruelty and neglect. Over 600 complaints of ill-treatment are dealt with every year by their full-time field officers. They investigate complaints of horses being ill-treated, in most cases it is ignorance of proper horse care that results in acts of cruelty.

Horticultural and Contractors' Tools Association
Light Trades House
3 Melbourne Avenue
Sheffield
S10 2QJ
Tel: 0114 266 3084
Fax: 0114 267 0910
Contact: Mr JR Markham, Secretary
Founded: 1944
Publications: British Tools Directory
Profile: The controlling body is the Executive Council of the Federation of British Hand Tool Manufacturers (FBHTM). The H&CTA deals with matters specific to its products i.e. British and International Standards through membership of the European Tools Committee. Close contact is maintained with the DTI for technical help for

exporters and outward missions as well as international exhibitions.

Horticultural Correspondence College, The
Freepost
Notton
Chippenham
Wiltshire
SN15 2BR
Tel: 01249 730326
Fax: 01249 730326
Contact: ON Menhinick, College Office Manager
Founded: 1930
Publications: Prospectus
Previous names: Agricultural Correspondence College
Profile: A great number of people enjoy horticultural occupations as their work or their hobby and frequently as both. There is often a desire to know more about the subject and often there is a need to obtain additional skills, knowledge and qualifications. The name of the HCC is well known and the course completion certificate is of value as evidence of the commitment of time and energy devoted to study the subject, of financial investment to gain knowledge and skills of the certificate holder.

Horticultural Development Council
Bradbourne House
Stable Block
East Malling
Kent
ME19 6DZ
Tel: 01732 848383
Fax: 01732 848498

Horticultural Exhibitors Association
Meadowview
Broad Marston Road
Pebworth
Stratford-upon-Avon
Warwickshire
CV37 8XR
Tel: 01789 720360
Fax: 01789 720360
Contact: Jill Daniell, Secretary/Treasurer
Founded: 1946
Membership: 235
Publications: Members newsletter; members yearbook
Profile: The HEA was formed to protect and advance the interests of nurserymen, seedsmen, bulb growers, garden architects and horticultural sundriesmen who exhibit at horticultural and agricultural shows within the UK, and is now generally recognised as a negotiating body which

is largely responsible for the improved relationship between trade exhibitors and show organisations.

Horticultural Marketing Inspectorate
Ministry of Agriculture, Fisheries and Food
Ergon House
c/o Nobel House
17 Smith Square
London
SW1P 3JR
Tel: 0171 238 6504
Fax: 0171 238 6504
Founded: 1965
Publications: Various leaflets and booklets explaining the work of the HMI
Profile: The Horticultural Marketing Inspectorate was set up in 1965 to enforce the regulations contained in the 1964 Agriculture and Horticulture Act which were amended following the UK's entry into the EEC in 1973. They inspect regulated produce at all stages of distribution, at despatch point, at distribution depots, at wholesale point and at retail outlets and exports destined for third countries. They are also involved with checking the use of some products for processing and inspect potatoes for delivery on the Potatoes Futures Market under contract to the London Commodities Exchange. Another duty is the inspection of produce withdrawn from the market for intervention purposes. There are about 100 inspectors organised in regional offices. Full details of the regional offices may be obtained from MAFF's free publication 'At the Farmer's Service' or by phoning the MAFF Helpline on 0645 335577.

Horticultural Research Association
c/o Horticulture Research International
Wellesbourne
Warwick
CV35 9EF
Tel: 01789 470382
Fax: 01789 470552
Email: ann.beeny@hri.ac.uk
Contact: Mrs Ann Beeny, Secretary
Founded: 1994
Membership: 500
Previous names: Amalgamation of Institute of Horticultural Research Association and Wellesbourne Vegetable Research Association
Profile: The association provides members' days, subject days and workshops at which information is supplied on horticultural research or overviews of the growing of the different horticultural crops grown principally in the UK.

Horticultural Trades Association
19 High Street
Theale
Reading
Berkshire
RG7 5AH
Tel: 0118 930 3132
Fax: 0118 932 3453
Contact: David Gwyther

Horticulture Research International
Wellesbourne
Warwick
CV35 9EF
Tel: 01789 470382
Fax: 01789 470552
Email: chris.wood@hri.ac.uk
Contact: Dr Chris Wood, Head of Information Services
Founded: 1990
Profile: HRI is the leading horticultural research and development organisation in the UK. Research activities include basic strategic scientific studies on plant processes leading to practical studies whose results can be taken up directly by horticulture and related industries anywhere in the world. HRI comprises six sites: Wellesbourne, East Malling, Efford, Kirton, Stockbridge House and Wye. They are supported by MAFF and BBSRC.

Horticulture Research International – East Malling
Horticulture Research International
East Malling
West Malling
Kent
ME19 6BJ
Tel: 01732 843833
Fax: 01732 849067
Email: ross.newham@hri.ac.uk
Internet: http://www.hri.ac.uk
Contact: Ross Newham, Information Officer
Founded: 1912
Membership: 850
Publications: Annual Reports; A Review of the HRI East Malling Science Programme and Related Activities; members' day reports
Profile: The East Malling Research Association has a strong history of being at the forefront of communicating perennial crops research results to industry. Its aim is to promote research in horticulture, fruit culture, production and storage, hop growing, nursery stock and forestry by personal contact with staff at Horticulture Research International (HRI), with two-way information through members' days and other meetings and by financing specific experimental

projects. This speeds up the process by which perennial crop growers can learn and adopt the results of research.

Horticulture Research International – Efford
Horticulture Research International
Lymington
Hampshire
SO41 0LZ
Tel: 01590 673341
Fax: 01590 671553
Email: Evelyn.Bartlett@HRI.ac.uk
Contact: Dr MR Shipway, Director
Founded: 1990
Publications: Annual Report
Profile: Research and development for the horticultural industry, covering hardy nursery stock, farm woodlands, soft fruit and protected crops.

Horticulture Research International – Kirton
Willington Road
Kirton
Boston
Lincolnshire
PE20 1NN
Tel: 01205 723477
Fax: 01205 724957

Horticulture Research International – Stockbridge House
Horticulture Research International
Cawood
Selby
North Yorkshire
YO8 0TZ
Tel: 01757 268275
Fax: 01757 268996

Horticulture Research International – Wye
Horticulture Research International
Department of Hop Research
Wye College
Ashford
Kent
TN25 5AH
Tel: 01233 812179
Fax: 01233 813126
Email: Peter.Darby@hri.ac.uk
Contact: Dr Peter Darby, Head, Hop Department
Founded: 1948
Publications: Horticulture Research International Annual Report
Profile: HRI aims to meet the needs of the UK horticulture industry through effective research and development and technology transfer.

Horticulture Technology and Development Service
Department of Agriculture for Northern Ireland
Greenmount College of Agriculture and Horticulture
22 Greenmount Road
Antrim
BT41 4PU
Tel: 01849 462114
Fax: 01849 428201

Houghall College Durham
Houghall
Durham
DH1 3SG
Tel: 0191 386 1351
Fax: 0191 386 0419
Contact: Ian Webster, Deputy Principal
Founded: 1921
Publications: Propectus; course leaflets; newsletters
Previous names: School of Agriculture, Durham Agricultural College
Profile: Houghall College Durham is a specialist land-based college providing training and education from foundation courses to Higher National Diploma in agriculture, environment, equestrian, horticulture, floristry and arboriculture. The college provides Youth Credit and Modern Apprenticeship training and delivers a wide range of programmes following NVQ1–4 across the land-based vocational areas. The college is a specialist centre for arboriculture and greenkeeping training and education. The college is conveniently located in the historic cathedral city of Durham with good local access to shops, banks and leisure facilities.

House of Commons Agriculture Committee
Committee Office
House of Commons
London
SW1A 0AA
Tel: 0171 219 3262
Fax: 0171 219 6606

House of Commons Environment Committee
Committee Office
House of Commons
London
SW1A 0AA
Tel: 0171 219 5462
Fax: 0171 219 2731
Contact: Secretary to the Clerk
Founded: 1979
Publications: Reports of Inquiries

Profile: The Environment Committee is a select committee of the House of Commons, responsible for monitoring the policies, expenditure and administration of the Department of the Environment and associated public bodies. The Committee consists of 11 backbench MPs and has a permanent secretariat of five officials of the House of Commons.

Huddersfield Technical College
New North Road
Huddersfield
HD1 5NN
Tel: 01484 536521
Fax: 01484 511885
Contact: M J Naden, Section Leader, Agriculture/Horticulture and Animal Care
Publications: Prospectus
Profile: Huddersfield Technical College is a large modern college with a growing rural section providing courses in agriculture, horticulture, floristry, forestry and arboriculture, animal care and horse care.

Humane Slaughter Association
34 Blanche Lane
South Mimms
Potters Bar
Hertfordshire
EN6 3PA
Tel: 01707 659040
Fax: 01707 649279
Contact: Sir Michael Simmons, Secretary
Founded: 1911
Membership: 650
Publications: Publications list available
Profile: The aim of the HSA is to improve conditions for animals and birds in abbatoirs, markets and in transit. This is achieved by a rational, practical approach and by maintaining close relationships with all associated with the transport and slaughter of food animals. Abbatoir work involves the demonstration of humane stunning methods, developing new equipment and advising on stunning and slaughter problems. Livestock markets are visited to monitor welfare conditions and money is sometimes made available for structural improvements. The association gives technical advice to government departments and industry and sponsors necessary research projects.

Hunt Saboteurs Association
PO Box 2786
Brighton
BN2 2AX
Tel: 01273 622827

Fax: 01273 622827
Email: hsa@gn.apc.org
Internet: http://envirolink.org.adn.hsa/hsa.html
Contact: R Kinder, Research Officer
Founded: 1960
Membership: 5,000
Publications: Howl
Profile: The Hunt Saboteurs Association encourages individuals to take non-violent direct action against people engaged in legal and illegal bloodsports. It campaigns for an end to these practices.

IACR – Broom's Barn
Institute of Arable Crops Research
Higham
Bury St Edmunds
Suffolk
IP28 6NP
Tel: 01284 810363
Fax: 01284 811191
Email: gillian.last@bbsrc.ac.uk
Contact: Mrs Gillian Last, Secretary to Director
Founded: 1962
Publications: Annual Report; publications list available
Profile: IACR – Broom's Barn is Europe's largest sugar beet research centre and the main source of research and education for British sugar beet growers. The purpose-built facilities include analytical, plant physiology, molecular biology and micropropogation laboratories. Broom's Barn is part of the Institute of Arable Crops Research and is principally paid for by the sugar beet industry through a levy paid jointly and equally by the processor (British Sugar plc) and the growers.

IACR – Long Ashton Research Station
Institute of Arable Crops Research
Department of Agricultural Sciences
University of Bristol
Long Ashton
Bristol
BS18 9AF
Tel: 01275 392181
Fax: 01275 394007
Contact: HM Anderson, Scientific Liaison Officer
Founded: 1903
Membership: 250
Publications: Annual report; various information leaflets
Profile: IACR – Long Ashton Research Station studies the efficiency of arable crop production, the consequences of interaction between agricultural practice and the environment, and the exploitation of developments in biology.

IACR – Rothamsted
Institute of Arable Crops Research
Harpenden
Hertfordshire
AL5 2JQ
Tel: 01582 763133
Fax: 01582 760981
Contact: Dr Roger Atkin, Marketing and PR
Manager
Founded: 1986
Publications: Annual Report
Previous names: Rothamsted Experimental
Station, Long Ashton Research Station and
Broom's Barn Experimental Station merged in
1986 to form IACR
Profile: IACR does high quality research and
provides relevant postgraduate training across
the agricultural, environmental and plant
biotechnological sciences. The aim is to maintain
and enhance the efficiency and competitiveness
of the production of major field crops, so
improving their quality and thus marketability. To
exploit the multidisciplinary strengths of the
institute, research activities cover four main
themes – inherent plant productivity, integrated
crop protection, sustainable production systems
and environmental interactions.

Icelandic Horse Society of Great Britain
12 Clare Court
Old Abbey Road
North Berwick
East Lothian
EH39 4BZ
Tel: 01620 893391
Fax: 01620 895070
Contact: Mrs Elspeth Thorburn, Secretary
Founded: 1986
Membership: 135
Publications: Newsletter
Profile: The IHSGB was formed to maintain
purity of the breed in the UK and to promote the
Icelandic horse in this country. The society is
divided into four geographical areas offering
courses and competition for local members. A
national event is held every year with a national
championship show every 2 years. World
championships are held every second year at a
different European venue – 20 countries are
eligible to take part.

Ile de France Sheep Society
Llandruidion
Goodwick
Pembrokeshire
SA64 0JQ
Tel: 0134 85696

Profile: We have been unable to contact this
organisation. The details given are unconfirmed.

Imperial College, Department of Biology
Silwood Park
Ascot
Berkshire
SL5 7PY
Tel: 01344 294206
Fax: 01344 294339

**Incorporated Society of Valuers and
   Auctioneers**
3 Cadogan Gate
London
SW1X 0AS
Tel: 0171 235 2282
Fax: 0171 235 4390
Contact: Hamlyn Whitty, Chief Executive
Founded: 1924
Membership: 7,000
Publications: The Valuer
Profile: ISVA is the professional society which is
committed to raising the standards of valuation
services to the market in the areas of estate
agency, auctioneering and surveying.

Indian Game Club
Victors Cottage
15 Campton Road
Upper Gravenhurst
Bedfordshire
MK45 4TB
Tel: 01462 711617
Contact: Mr J Cook, Secretary
Profile: A society to promote the Indian Game
breed of poultry.

Inland Waterways Amenity Advisory Council
122 Cleveland Street
London
W1P 5DN
Profile: We have been unable to contact this
organisation. The details given are unconfirmed.

Inland Waterways Association
114 Regent's Park Road
London
NW1 8UQ
Tel: 0171 586 2510
Fax: 0171 722 7213
Contact: Neil Edwards, Office Manager
Founded: 1946
Membership: 17,000
Publications: Waterways (journal); numerous
publications

Profile: The IWA campaigns for the: protection of waterways as an essential part of Britain's heritage; restoration of derelict waterways for navigation; proper funding to improve and maintain waterways for all to enjoy; protection of other user's rights; increased use of suitable canals and rivers for freight transport and the protection of historic waterway structures.

Inland Waterways Protection Society Ltd
Brow Side Farm
Mudhurst Lane
Lyme Handley
Whaley Bridge
Cheshire
SK12 7BT
Tel: 01663 732493
Fax: 01663 615276
Contact: Ian Edgar, Chairman
Founded: 1958
Membership: 300
Publications: Onward (members newsletter)
Profile: Campaigns for the restoration of inland waterways of the UK but main interest is in the restoration of Bugsworth Basin, a scheduled ancient monument at the head of the Peak Forest Canal in Derbyshire.

Institute for Animal Health – Compton Laboratory
Compton Laboratory
Compton
Newbury
Berkshire
RG20 7NN
Tel: 01635 578411
Fax: 01635 578844
Email: compton.library@bbsrc.ac.uk
Contact: Information Officer

Institute for Animal Health – Pirbright Laboratory
Pirbright Laboratory
Ash Road
Pirbright
Woking
Surrey
GU24 0NF
Tel: 01483 232411
Fax: 01483 232448

Institute for European Environmental Policy
158 Buckingham Palace Road
London
SW1W 9TR
Tel: 0171 824 8787
Fax: 0171 824 8145

Email: ieeplondon@gn.apc.org
Contact: Karen Mitchell, Research Officer
Founded: 1980
Publications: Publications list available
Profile: IEEP London is an independent body for the analysis and advancement of environmental policies in Europe. It undertakes research and consultancy on the European dimension of environmental protection, with a major onus on the development, implementation and evaluation of the European Community's environment policy.

Institute for Grassland and Environmental Research – Aberystwyth Research Centre
Plas Gogerddan
Aberystwyth
Ceredigion
SY23 3EB
Tel: 01970 828255
Fax: 01970 828357
Contact: Tim Brigstocke, Institute Business Manager
Founded: 1919
Publications: Annual Report
Previous names: Welsh Plant Breeding Station until 1990
Profile: IGER covers both environmental and agricultural aspects of British grasslands. It seeks to increase the efficiency of livestock production while minimising its input on natural environments. IGER research farms are located in typical low and upland grassland areas of Wales and Devon, including an organic dairy farm at Trawsgoed, near Aberystwyth. The institute has extensive laboratory facilities and scientific expertise. Research ranges from molecular genetics to full scale variety field trials, covering animal nutrition, pollution control and the ecology of natural communities. IGER expertise is available to undertake short term research and consultancy for private companies, local authorities and other relevant organisations.

Institute for Grassland and Environmental Research – Bronydd Mawr Research Station
Trecastle
Brecon
Powys
LD3 8RD
Tel: 01874 636480
Fax: 01874 636542
Contact: Mr D Arthur Davis, Officer in Charge
Founded: 1983
Publications: IGER Annual Report
Profile: Aim to improve the efficiency of upland livestock farming through increased understanding of soil/plant/animal processes having due

consideration for environmental, animal welfare, landscape and socio-economic factors.

Institute of Agricultural Medicine and Rehabilitation

The Rehabilitation Trust of Great Britain
AGMED Study Centre
Crediton
Devon
EX17 4AR
Tel: 01363 866353
Fax: 01363 866353
Contact: Richard Gard, Director
Founded: 1983
Publications: Various articles and information notes
Profile: AGMED combines doctors, vets and agriculturalists to understand aspects of agriculture and human health with particular emphasis on rural occupational health. Projects involving development and research are ongoing including accidents, zoonoses, agrochemicals and rural stress.

Institute of Agricultural Secretaries and Administrators

National Agricultural Centre
Stoneleigh Park
Warwickshire
CV8 2LZ
Tel: 01203 696592
Fax: 01203 417937
Contact: Mrs C O'Kane, Secretary
Founded: 1967
Membership: 820
Publications: Journal; members bulletin
Profile: Professional body for farm administrators which aims to promote the career of the farm administrator.

Institute of Animal Technology

5 South Parade
Summertown
Oxford
OX2 7JL
Contact: Careers Officer
Membership: 1,400
Publications: Animal Technology (journal); news bulletin
Profile: The IAT is the professional body for animal technicians which aims to improve animal husbandry and disseminate knowledge of animal technology throughout the world.

Institute of Aquaculture

University of Stirling
Stirling
FK9 4LA
Tel: 01786 473171
Fax: 01786 472133
Contact: Rodney Wootten, Assistant Director
Founded: 1971
Publications: Aquaculture News; Annual Report
Previous names: Unit of Aquatic Pathbiology until 1978
Profile: The Institute of Aquaculture is dedicated to teaching and research in all aspects of sustainable aquaculture in marine and freshwater temperate and tropical environments. Research programmes involve collaborating laboratories in over 20 countries worldwide. Teaching programmes include taught courses at BSc and MSc level in Aquaculture and also at MSc level in Aquatic Veterinary Studies and Aquatic Pathbiology. There is also a large scale PhD programme. The institute has extensive commercial scale salt and freshwater facilities available for research and teaching.

Institute of Auctioneers and Appraisers in Scotland

11 Glenfinlas Street
Edinburgh
EH3 6YY
Tel: 0131 226 5541
Fax: 0131 226 2278
Contact: Biggart, Baillie and Gifford, Secretaries
Founded: 1926

Institute of Biology

20–22 Queensberry Place
London
SW7 2DZ
Tel: 0171 581 8333
Fax: 0171 823 9409
Email: info@iob.primex.co.uk
Contact: Dr RH Priestley, General Secretary
Founded: 1950
Membership: 14,600
Profile: The Institute of Biology is the professional body for UK biologists. Founded in 1950, obtained a Royal Charter in 1979 and is a registered charity. Its aim is to advance the science and practice of biology, to advance education therein and co-ordinate and encourage the study of biology and its application. To achieve this, the institute provides leadership and promotes a unified approach so that the voice of professional biologists is heard on policy issues involving biology and biological education.

Institute of Chartered Foresters

7a St Cole Street
Edinburgh
EH3 6AA

Tel: 0131 225 2705
Fax: 0131 220 6128
Contact: Margaret Dick, Executive Director
Founded: 1925
Membership: 1,450
Publications: Publications list available
Previous names: Institute of Foresters until 1982
Profile: ICF is the representative body of the forestry profession in the UK and safeguards the public interest in forestry matters, maintaining the standards regulating entry to the profession and advising government on matters of policy. The institute is regulated by its Royal Charter, bylaws and regulations and its affairs are managed by an elected council. A code of ethics to which all members must subscribe is maintained; examinations for professional qualifications are offered to members, the status of foresters and the profession are kept under continuous review and representations are made whenever necessary.

Institute of Clerks of Works of Great Britain
41 The Mall
London
W5 3TJ
Tel: 0181 579 2917
Fax: 0181 579 0554
Contact: AP McNamara, General Secretary

Institute of Ecology and Environmental Management
36 Kingfisher Court
Hambridge Road
Newbury
Berkshire
RG14 5SJ
Tel: 01635 37715
Fax: 01635 550230
Email: 100347.1526@compuserve.com
Contact: Ann Tubb, Administrator
Founded: 1991
Membership: 700
Publications: Publications list available
Profile: IEEM is now the largest professional body in the UK solely representing ecologists and environmental managers. IEEM aims to: raise the profile of ecology and environmental management; to establish, maintain and enhance professional standards; and to promote an ethic of environmental care within the profession and to clients and employers of the members.

Institute of Ecology and Resource Management
University of Edinburgh
Agriculture Building
West Mains Road

Edinburgh
EH9 3JG
Tel: 0131 667 1041
Fax: 0131 667 2061

Institute of Economic Affairs (Environment Unit)
Institute of Economic Affairs
2 Lord North Street
London
SW1P 3LB
Tel: 0171 799 3745
Fax: 0171 799 2137
Email: iea@iea.org.uk
Internet: http://www.iea.org.uk
Contact: Ms Lisa MacLellan, Environment Unit Manager
Founded: 1994
Publications: Publications list available
Profile: The IEA Environment Unit was established to explain how institutions of a free society (private property, a dynamic market economy, the rule of law) can protect and improve the quality of the environment. In doing so, the unit applies rigorous scientific analysis to current scientific issues, often presenting research that runs contrary to the dominant consensus view.

Institute of Energy
18 Devonshire Street
London
W1N 2AU
Tel: 0171 580 7124
Fax: 0171 580 4420
Contact: Mr J Leach, Secretary
Founded: 1927
Membership: 5,000
Publications: Energy World (journal); Journal of the Institute of Energy; Energy World Yearbook
Previous names: Institute of Fuel until 1979
Profile: The Institute of Energy is both a learned society geared to the advancement of knowledge of energy technology, and a professional body with a duty to serve and maintain the standards of the profession. Its aims are to promote the effective provision, conversion, transmission and utilisation of energy in all its forms, with due regard to the prudent use of resources and the protection of the environment.

Institute of Environmental Assessment
Welton House
Limekiln Way
Lincoln
LN2 4US
Tel: 01522 540069

Fax: 01522 540090
Contact: Julie Tarling, Membership and Development Manager
Founded: 1990
Membership: 560
Publications: Publications list available
Profile: The Institute of Environmental Assessment is internationally supported in its work in establishing and promoting best practice standards in environmental assessment and auditing. Non-profit making, its independence is maintained by a growing membership drawn from environmental consultancies, industry, local authorities and educational establishments. This cross-sectoral approach is essential to the impartiality of its work.

Institute of Environmental Management

58–59 Timber Bush
Edinburgh
EH6 6QH
Tel: 0131 555 5334
Fax: 0131 555 5217
Email: info@iem.org.uk
Contact: Anne-Caroline Peckham, Director
Founded: 1992
Membership: 1,500
Publications: Publications list available
Previous names: Institute of Environmental Managers until 1994
Profile: The IEM is committed to the promotion of more sustainable business practices in industry, commerce and local government and endeavours to help its members evaluate both long and short term challenges faced by their organisations. Members are encouraged to adopt the Environmental Managers' Charter.

Institute of Fisheries Management

Balmaha
Coldwells Road
Holmer
Hereford
HR1 1LH
Tel: 01432 276225
Fax: 01432 822317
Contact: Honorary Secretary
Founded: 1969
Profile: The Institute of Fisheries Management is an international organisation of persons sharing a common interest in the modern management of recreational and commercial fisheries. It is a non-profit making organisation controlled by membership and governed by an elected council. Members are drawn from professional fisheries managers, research bodies, fishing and angling organisations, water authorities, fish farms and private individuals whose interests in fisheries

are represented at many levels within government and conservation bodies.

Institute of Food Research

Earley Gate
Whiteknights Road
Reading
Berkshire
RG6 2BZ
Tel: 01189 357000
Fax: 01189 267917
Email: josianne.dunn@bbsrc.ac.uk
Contact: Mrs Josianne Dunn, Business Office Manager
Founded: 1985
Publications: Annual Report; newsletter
Profile: Research at IFR: stimulates industrial innovation; improves the safety of the food supply; helps the consumer choose a healthy diet and contributes to the quality of food and ingredients.

Institute of Food Science and Technology

5 Cambridge Court
210 Shepherds Bush Road
London
W6 7NJ
Tel: 0171 603 6316
Founded: 1964
Membership: 3,500
Publications: Food Science and Technology Today; International Journal of Food Science and Technology
Profile: The IFST is open to all who wish to be involved in their activities and in upholding the image and standards of the profession. There are over 3,000 individual members in manufacturing, retailing, research, consultancy, enforcement, government and academia, including students. The IFST holds conferences and meetings and publishes a monthly newsletter as well as technical journals and brochures.

Institute of Freshwater Ecology

Natural Environment Research Council
Windermere Laboratory
Far Sawrey
Ambleside
Cumbria
LA22 0LP
Tel: 01539 442468
Fax: 01539 446914
Email: a.pickering@ife.ac.uk
Contact: Professor AD Pickering, Director
Founded: 1989
Membership: 97
Publications: Publications list available

Profile: The Institute of Freshwater Ecology is the UK's premier research organisation in its field. Its functions are: to maintain a core strategic research capability for understanding and predicting processes in the freshwater environment; to develop scientific technologies and facilities; to collect, collate and interpret environmental data and to supply environmental information; to provide independent expert advice on regional and national scales and to contribute to international programmes; to link with the user community and promote technology transfer; to educate and train in the field of freshwater ecology; to promote the public understanding of the freshwater environment.

Institute of Freshwater Ecology – Eastern Rivers Laboratory
Natural Environment Research Council
Monks Wood
Abbots Ripton
Huntingdon
Cambridgeshire
PE17 2LS
Tel: 01487 77381
Fax: 01487 77467
Email: L.Pinder@ife.ac.uk
Contact: LCV Pinder

Institute of Freshwater Ecology – Edinburgh Laboratory
Natural Environment Research Council
Bush Estate
Penicuick
Midlothian
EH26 0QB
Tel: 0131 445 43434

Institute of Freshwater Ecology – River Laboratory
Natural Environment Research Council
East Stoke
Wareham
Dorset
BH20 6BB
Tel: 01929 462314
Fax: 01929 462180
Contact: J Hilton, Head of Station

Institute of Freshwater Ecology – Teesdale Laboratory
Natural Environment Research Council
Northumbrian Water
Lartington Treatment Works
Lartington
Barnard Castle
Co Durham
DL12 9DW
Tel: 01833 50600
Fax: 01833 50827

Institute of Grassland and Environmental Research – North Wyke Research Station
Biotechnology and Biological Sciences Research Council
Okehampton
Devon
EX20 2SB
Tel: 0183 782558
Fax: 0183 782139
Email: roker@bbsrc.ac.uk
Contact: Professor RJ Wilkins, Head of Station
Founded: 1981
Publications: Annual Report; technical reviews
Previous names: Grassland Research Institute; Animal and Grassland Research Institute; Institute for Grassland and Animal Production
Profile: The institute is a registered charity, with its own governing body and main centre at Aberystwyth. It carries out research on many aspects of the production and utilisation of grassland in relation to agricultural productivity, nature conservation and the environment. Funding is principally from the Biotechnology and Biological Sciences Research Council, and the Ministry of Agriculture, Fisheries and Food. North Wyke is the base of the institute's Soils and Agroecology Department. The research station is a Partner Organisation of the University of Plymouth and an Associated Institute of the University of Reading.

Institute of Grocery Distribution
Grange Lane
Letchmore Heath
Watford
Hertfordshire
WD2 8DQ
Tel: 01923 857141
Fax: 01923 852531
Contact: Information Unit
Founded: 1909
Membership: 350
Publications: Publications list available
Previous names: Institute of Certificated Grocers 1909–1964; The Grocers Institute 1964–1972
Profile: A research organisation providing research on all sections of the supply chain.

Institute of Groundsmanship
19–23 Church Street
The Agora
Wolverton

Milton Keynes
MK12 5LG
Tel: 01908 312511
Fax: 01908 311140
Contact: Mr P Gosset, Chief Executive
Founded: 1934
Membership: 4,000
Publications: The Groundsman
Previous names: Association of Groundsmen until 1969
Profile: The Institute of Groundmanship was founded in 1934 with the purpose being to 'improve the status of Groundsmen' and 'improve the standards of Groundmanship'. It now has over 40 branches in the UK as well as overseas membership. The institute holds its own international annual exhibition (SALTEX) and publishes the monthly journal The Groundsman. The institute also sets examinations, runs an annual training programme and offers a consultancy service worldwide.

Institute of Horticulture

14–15 Belgrave Square
London
SW1X 8PS
Tel: 0171 245 6943
Fax: 0171 245 6943
Email: ioh@horticulture.org.uk
Internet: http://www.worldscope.net/horticulture
Contact: Angela Clarke, General Secretary
Founded: 1984
Membership: 2,000
Publications: The Horticulturist (journal)
Profile: The Institute of Horticulture is the authoritative organisation representing all those professionally engaged in horticulture, bringing together all aspects of horticulture. The institute offers recognition of status in the horticultural industry and the means to meet and network with professionals in the same and other spheres of horticulture, and provides the opportunity to make a really effective contribution to the future of horticulture and its importance as a career. The institute's professional and technical meetings and other activities are arranged at both national and local level.

Institute of Hydrology

Natural Environment Research Council
Maclean Building
Cromarsh Gifford
Wallingford
Oxfordshire
OX10 8BB
Tel: 01491 838800
Fax: 01491 692424
Email: marketing@ioh.ac.uk

Contact: Mr Neil Runnalls, Marketing Manager
Founded: 1965
Publications: Annual Report; hydrological summaries; IH series of hydrological reports; various software products and manuals
Profile: The Institute of Hydrology is a research body and component part of the Natural Environment Research Council in the UK. The institute carries out fundamental and applied research into the movement, behaviour and quality of water through its cycle from rainfall to runoff and evaporation. It conducts research, consultancy services and advises government, international and public agencies and the private sector. The IH is an advisor to the UK and overseas governments in the formulation of national water policy, legislation and research strategies.

Institute of Hydrology (Plynlimon)

Natural Environment Research Council
Staylittle
Llanbrynmair
Powys
SY19 7DB
Tel: 01686 430652
Fax: 01686 430441
Email: jah@ua.npn.ac.uk
Contact: Jim Hudson, Head of Experimental Catchments Section (Wales)
Founded: 1968
Publications: Annual Report; Institute of Hydrology report series; conference proceedings
Previous names: Hydrological Research Unit until 1970; Institute of Hydrology became a component part of Centre for Ecology and Hydrology in 1994
Profile: The Plynlimon station of the Institute of Hydrology is a field research centre set up to monitor the hydrology, water chemistry and climate of the head waters of the Severn and Wye basins (and lately the Dyfi), with a view to assessing the environmental effects of land use changes (mainly afforestation) and by long term climate change as a basis for recommendations to the water, agriculture, and forestry industries as to best land use practice in the uplands for the future.

Institute of Irrigation and Development Studies

Department of Civil and Environmental Engineering
University of Southampton
Highfield
Southampton
Hampshire

SO17 1BJ
Tel: 01703 593728
Fax: 01703 677519
Email: dso@soton.ac.uk
Contact: Mrs Susan Oglesby, Administrative
Assistant
Founded: 1964
Publications: Publications list available
Previous names: Institute of Irrigation Studies
until 1996
Profile: IIDS is a multi-disciplinary postgraduate
centre. It currently accepts some 30–40 students
and researchers for higher degrees each year.
The institute specialises in rural and water
resources development, and is at the forefront of
teaching, research, consultancy and training in
these disciplines both nationally and
internationally.

Institute of Leisure and Amenity Management
ILAM House
Lower Basildon
Reading
RG8 9NE
Tel: 01491 874222
Fax: 01491 874059
Contact: Mr Alan Smith, Director
Founded: 1983
Membership: 7,000
Publications: The Leisure Manager; The Leisure
Manager Bulletin; publications list available
Previous names: Merger of four associated
Institutes in 1983
Profile: The Institute of Leisure and Amenity
management is the professional body for leisure
managers in the public, private and voluntary
sectors of the industry. ILAM's agreed purpose is
to promote the better management of all leisure
resources, and to provide better public access to
a wide range of cultural and recreational
experiences in order to enhance the quality of life
for individuals and communities.

Institute of Market Officers
21 Tarnside Road
Orrell
Wigan
Lancashire
WN5 8RN
Tel: 01695 623860
Fax: 01695 623860
Contact: John Edwards, Honorary Secretary
Founded: 1943
Membership: 300
Profile: The objects for which the institute is
established are: to provide an organisation for
market officers and to improve the administration

of markets, fairs, abattoirs and cold stores by
fostering a knowledge of the work required for
their efficient management; to encourage study;
to hold meetings; to hold examinations and grant
diplomas and to act on behalf of the members for
the furtherance of the profession.

Institute of Plant Science
Maris Lane
Trumpington
Cambridge
CB2 2JB
Profile: We have been unable to contact this
organisation. The details given are unconfirmed.

Institute of Professional Soil Scientists
The Manor House
Castle Street
Spofforth
Harrogate
North Yorkshire
HG3 1AR
Tel: 01937 590376
Fax: 01423 506183
Contact: B Wilkinson, Secretary
Founded: 1991
Membership: 200
Publications: IPSS Directory; IPSS Newsletter
Profile: The IPSS is a non-profit body organised
to enhance the status, qualifications and
standards for professional soil scientists. IPSS
represents soil scientists operating in diverse
fields of work and has the standing and authority
to foster their interests, either singly or in
association with other professional bodies,
nationally or internationally. Members understand
the importance of soils and aim to encourage the
use of land resources in an environmentally
acceptable way. Members are academically
qualified and have the requisite years of
experience in their particular scientific/technical
fields. They accept and work to the IPSS code of
conduct and accept the need for continuous
professional development.

Institute of Quarrying
7 Regent Street
Nottingham
NG1 5BS
Tel: 0115 941 1315
Fax: 0115 948 4035
Contact: Michael Arthur, Secretary

Institute of Terrestrial Ecology
Natural Environment Research Council
Monks Wood
Abbots Ripton
Huntingdon

Cambridgeshire
PE17 2LS
Tel: 01487 773381
Fax: 01487 773590
Email: M.Roberts@ite.ac.uk
Internet: http://www.nmw.ac.uk/ite
Contact: Professor TM Roberts, Director
Publications: Publications list available
Profile: The ITE Director is based at ITE Monks Wood, one of the six research stations belonging to the institute.

Institute of Terrestrial Ecology – Banchory Research Station
Natural Environment Research Council
Hill of Brathens
Banchory
Kincardineshire
AB31 4BY
Tel: 013302 3434
Fax: 013302 3303
Email: Banchory@ite.ac.uk
Internet: http://www.nmw.ac.uk/ite
Contact: Professor BW Stevens
Profile: ITE at Banchory is one of six research institutes comprising the Institute of Terrestrial Ecology.

Institute of Terrestrial Ecology – Bangor Research Unit
Natural Environment Research Council
University of Wales, Bangor
Deiniol Road
Bangor
Gwynedd
LL57 2UP
Tel: 01248 370045
Fax: 01248 355365
Email: jgo@ite.ac.uk
Internet: http://www.nmw.ac.uk/ite
Contact: Professor JEE Good
Profile: ITE at Bangor is one of six research institutes comprising the Institute of Terrestrial Ecology.

Institute of Terrestrial Ecology – Edinburgh Research Station
Natural Environment Research Council
Bush Estate
Penicuik
Midlothian
EH26 0QB
Tel: 0131 445 4343
Fax: 0131 445 3943
Email: Bush@ite.ac.uk
Internet: http://www.nmw.ac.uk/ite
Contact: Professor MGR Cannell

Profile: ITE at Edinburgh is one of six research institutes comprising the Institute of Terrestrial Ecology.

Institute of Terrestrial Ecology – Furzebrook Research Station
Natural Environment Research Council
Furzebrook Road
Wareham
Dorset
BH20 5AS
Tel: 01929 551518
Fax: 01929 551087
Email: Furzebrook@ite.ac.uk
Internet: http://www.nmw.ac.uk/ite
Contact: Dr AJ Gray
Profile: ITE at Furzebrook is one of six research institutes comprising the Institute of Terrestrial Ecology.

Institute of Terrestrial Ecology – Merlewood Research Station
Natural Environment Research Council
Grange-over-Sands
Cumbria
LA11 6JU
Tel: 015395 32264
Fax: 015395 34705
Email: Merlewood@uk.ac.ite
Internet: http://www.nmw.ac.uk/ite
Contact: Professor M Hornung
Founded: 1973
Publications: Annual Report; series of symposia proceedings; series of research publications
Profile: ITE at Merlewood is one of six research institutes comprising the Institute of Terrestrial Ecology.

Institute of Terrestrial Ecology – Monks Wood
Natural Environment Research Council
Abbots Ripton
Huntingdon
Cambridgeshire
PE17 2LS
Tel: 01487 773381
Fax: 01487 773467
Email: Monkswood@ite.ac.uk
Internet: http://www.nmw.ac.uk/ite
Contact: Dr S Dobson
Profile: ITE at Monks Wood is one of six research institutes comprising the Institute of Terrestrial Ecology.

Institute of Virology and Environmental Microbiology
Natural Environment Research Council
Mansfield Road
Oxford

OX1 3SR
Tel: 01865 512361
Fax: 01865 59962
Contact: Dr P A Nuttall, Acting Director
Founded: 1963
Publications: Researchers publish widely in refereed scientific journals
Previous names: Oxford University Unit of Insect Pathology until 1971; Oxford University Unit of Invertebrate Virology until 1980; NERC Institute of Virology until 1989
Profile: The mission of IVEM is to undertake basic and strategic research, relevant to users, aimed at generating an environment. The institute's strengths are in the areas of natural resources, and in particular in the understanding and exploitation of microbial biodiversity.

Institute of Waste Management
9 Saxon Court
St Peters Garden
Northampton
NN1 1SX
Tel: 01604 20426
Fax: 01604 21339
Contact: Mike Philpott, Chief Executive
Founded: 1898
Membership: 4,000
Publications: Wastes Management (journal); publications list available
Profile: The institute is now the leading professional body representing all sections of the industry and covering every aspect of the operation and statutory control for the collection, treatment and disposal of wastes for the protection of the environment. It is the only body in the UK to specialise in this field, providing expert training in all branches of waste disposal and instigating and conducting educational qualifications.

Institute of Water Pollution Control
Leadson House
53 London Road
Maidstone
Kent
NE16 8JH
Profile: We have been unable to contact this organisation. The details given are unconfirmed.

Institution of Agricultural Engineers
West End Road
Silsoe
Bedford
MK45 4DU
Tel: 01525 861096
Fax: 01525 861660

Contact: Mr Michael H Hurst, Secretary
Founded: 1938
Membership: 1,920
Publications: Landwards, formerly The Agricultural Engineer
Previous names: Institution of British Agricultural Engineers until 1960
Profile: Professional body for engineers, scientists, technicians and managers in agriculture and related industries. Worldwide membership with 15 branches in the UK and ten specialist groups. Organises technical conferences and seminars, and monitors members' continuing professional development. Quarterly journal free to members. Active within the European Society of Agricultural Engineers. Sponsors registration with Engineering Council as Chartered Engineer, Incorporated Engineer and Engineering Technician.

Institution of Environmental Sciences
14 Princes Gate
Hyde Park
London
SW7 1PU
Tel: 01778 394846
Fax: 01778 394846
Contact: Dr RA Fuller, Honorary Secretary
Founded: 1971
Membership: 800
Publications: The Environmental Scientist (journal); Environmental Careers Handbook
Profile: The IES is a professional body for environmental scientists. It seeks to provide balanced, scientific information on the environment to members and public alike, to present advice and views to government and to promote the development of education in environmental matters.

Institution of Water Officers
Heriot House
12 Summerhill Terrace
Newcastle upon Tyne
NE4 6EB
Tel: 0191 230 5150
Fax: 0191 230 2880
Contact: Adam Liscoe, Company Secretary
Founded: 1945
Publications: Water (journal)
Previous names: The Association of Water Officers until 1945
Profile: The Institute of Water Officers is recognised as the only professional body concerned solely with the day to day running of the water industry. A nominated body of the Engineering Council, the institution has nine areas which cover the whole of the United

Kingdom, each with its own committee drawn from local membership. Area and national committees organise meetings, seminars, technical visits and conferences, as well as social events. Areas also run weekend schools at which relevant topics are studied in greater depth, providing a shop window for the latest technological developments in the industry.

International Agricultural Exchange Association
YFC Centre
National Agricultural Centre
Warwickshire
CV8 2LG
Tel: 01203 696578
Fax: 01203 696684
Contact: Sue McNulty, Manager
Founded: 1963
Membership: 1,000
Publications: The Fantastic Challenge Brochure
Profile: An IAEA exchange is for anyone aged 18–30 with good practical experience in agriculture/horticulture or in the home. Trainees pay a set programme fee which includes all travel arrangements, visas, insurance, seminar and supervision to go and live and work with a host family in either Australia, NZ, Canada, the USA or Japan for 6.5 months to 12 months.

International Association for Veterinary Homeopathy
Chinham House
Stanford-in-the-Vale
Oxfordshire
SN7 8NQ
Profile: We have been unable to contact this organisation. The details given are unconfirmed.

International Association of Agricultural Economics
Agricultural Economics Unit
University of Exeter
Lafrowda House
St German's Road
Exeter
EX4 6TL
Contact: Professor JP McInerney, UK Membership Secretary

International Association on Water Quality
Duchess House
20 Masons Yard
Duke Street
St James's
London
SW1Y 6BU

Tel: 0171 839 8390
Fax: 0171 839 8299
Email: 100065.3664@compuserve.com
Contact: A Milburn, Executive Director
Founded: 1964
Membership: 6,500
Publications: Water Research, Water Science and Technology, Water Quality International, scientific and technical reports
Profile: The IAWQ is an international professional association for engineers, scientists, administrators, etc. It is a non-governmental, non-profit, membership organisation. Among its range of interests are: sources and effects of water pollution; wastewater treatment processes; water recycling and reuse; environmental restoration. The full range of technical and managerial issues is covered and all surface waters, groundwaters and marine waters are dealt with. The association publishes journals, books, reports and a magazine. It organises between 20 and 25 conferences, symposia and workshops every year. There are 32 technical divisions, each with its conference programme and newsletter.

International Bee Research Association
18 North Road
Cardiff
CF1 3DY
Tel: 01222 372409
Fax: 01222 665522
Email: munnpa@cardiff.ac.uk
Contact: Miss Maxine Hopkin, PA to the Director
Founded: 1949
Membership: 700
Publications: Bee World; Journal of Apicultural Research; Apicultural Abstracts
Previous names: Bee Research Association until 1976
Profile: IBRA is a charity devoted to advancing apicultural education and science worldwide. It works: to promote research on bees and beekeeping; to interpret and communicate scientific data to bee keepers; to disseminate research results among scientists; to promote beekeeping as a practical and sustainable form of agriculture for developing countries and to act as a contact point and information exchange on beekeeping for governments, international agencies, research institutes, beekeepers and rural development specialists.

International Brewers Guild
8 Ely Place
Holborn
London
EC1N 6SD

Tel: 0171 405 4565
Fax: 0171 831 4995
Contact: WDJ Carling, General Secretary
Founded: 1906
Membership: 1,500
Publications: The Brewer; The Grist; Guild Directory
Profile: The guild provides a forum for personal development for those involved in the production of beer for sale, so as to contribute to the continued improvement in product quality and operational efficiency for the benefit of the individual and the industry.

International Centre for Conservation Education
Greenfield House
Guiting Power
Cheltenham
Gloucestershire
GL54 5TZ
Tel: 01451 850777
Fax: 01451 850705
Contact: Rose Marie Robbins, Resources and Information Officer
Founded: 1984
Publications: ICCE Green Letter
Previous names: WWF Education Programme 1975–1984
Profile: ICCE's mission is to promote greater understanding of conservation, the environment and sustainable development through education and communication, placing particular emphasis on the needs of developing countries.

International Centre for Underutilized Crops
Institute of Irrigation and Development Studies
University of Southampton
Southampton
Hampshire
SO17 1BJ
Tel: 01703 594229
Fax: 01703 677510
Email: Haq@soton.ac.uk
Contact: Director
Founded: 1988
Publications: Newsletter, workshop proceedings, monographs
Previous names: Centre for Underutilized Crops
Profile: The ICUC was established following a resolution passed at an international symposium held at Southampton University in 1988. Its mandate is to promote species for food, nutrition, industry and sustainable development. The ICUC has UK charitable status and is committed to develop its activities in expanding its database on underutilised crops, in

undertaking research projects on underutilised species to increase rural income. ICUC runs both short courses and also Masters and PhD work in Southampton.

International Commission on Irrigation and Drainage (British Section)
c/o Institution of Civil Engineers
1–7 Great George Street
London
SW1P 3AA
Tel: 0171 222 7722
Fax: 0171 222 7500
Email: howard_r@ice.org.uk
Contact: Richard Howard, Secretary
Publications: News and Views (newsletter); ICID Journal; ICID Bulletin
Profile: The ICID brings together the national organisations from nearly 80 countries for the development of the science and techniques of irrigation, drainage, flood control and river training. Benefits of ICID include information on international conferences, a forum for discussion and dissemination of scientific development and knowledge and a twice yearly bulletin. The British section is an associated society of the Institution of Civil Engineers and welcomes members from all backgrounds.

International Falabella Miniature Horse Society
Holding House
Hook
Hampshire
RG27 9NW
Tel: 01256 763425
Contact: S Fitzmaurice, Registrar
Founded: 1987
Membership: 30
Publications: Fact File
Profile: The International Falabella Miniature Horse Society provides a registry for pedigree Falabellas, and reputable breeding studs in both the UK and Europe. A non-profit organisation, the society hopes in the next few years to begin the promotion of Falabellas, aimed at educating the public about this fascinating horse.

International Farm Experience Programme
National Federation of Young Farmers Clubs of England and Wales
YFC Centre
National Agricultural Centre
Warwickshire
CV8 2LG
Tel: 01203 696584
Fax: 01203 696559
Contact: Janine Jones, IFEP Organiser

Founded: 1947
Previous names: UK Sponsoring Authority
Profile: IFEP is the Young Farmers' international working exchange programme offering 3–12 month placements throughout Europe, New Zealand, Australia, Canada, the US and China in agriculture, horticulture and all related fields. Applicants must be 18–28 with satisfactory references and experience. Introductory language courses are available and the scheme is reciprocal.

International Farm Management Association

Farm Management Unit
University of Reading
Earley Gate
Reading
RG6 2AT
Profile: We have been unable to contact this organisation. The details given are unconfirmed.

International Fishmeal and Oil Manufacturers Association

2 College Yard
Lower Dagnall Street
St Albans
Hertfordshire
AL3 4PE
Tel: 01727 842844
Fax: 01727 842866
Contact: Secretary

International Food Information Service

Lane End House
Shinfield
Reading
Berkshire
RG2 9BB
Tel: 01734 883895
Fax: 01734 885065
Email: ifis@ifis.org
Internet: http://www.ifis.org
Contact: Dr John Metcalfe, Managing Editor
Founded: 1969
Publications: Food Info (newsletter); Food Science and Technology Abstracts; Directory of Research and Education in Food Science, Technology and Engineering
Profile: The International Food Information Service is a not-for-profit organisation providing information, products and services, and commissioning research and providing education in information science, for the international food science, food technology and human nutrition community. Food Science and Technology Abstracts is a comprehensive database of published information covering all areas of food science, food technology and human nutrition is

the main information product of IFIS. Their database is available in print, on CD ROM or via online hosts.

International Grains Council

One Canada Square
Canary Wharf
London
E14 5AE
Tel: 0171 513 1122
Fax: 0171 712 0071
Contact: AR Woodhams, Assistant Executive Director
Founded: 1949
Publications: Grain Market Report; World Grains Statistics; Record of Shipments (Wheat and Coarse Grains); Report for the Fiscal Year
Previous names: International Wheat Council until 1995
Profile: The IGC is an intergovernmental commodity organisation which aims to contribute to the stability of the international grains trade, to secure the freest possible flow and to enhance world food security. The aims are realised through a comprehensive information service which adds to market transparency and a meeting structure providing opportunities for formal and informal consultations and discussions involving the international grains industry.

International Institute for Environment and Development

3 Endsleigh Street
London
WC1H 0DD
Tel: 0171 388 2117
Fax: 0171 388 2826
Email: iieduk@gn.apc.org

International Institute of Biological Control

Silwood Park
Buckhurst Road
Ascot
Berkshire
SL5 7TA
Tel: 01344 872999
Fax: 01344 875007
Email: cabi-iibc-hq@cgnet.com

International Jousting Association

Post Office Cottage
Cowesby Village
Thirsk
North Yorkshire
YO7 2JJ
Tel: 01845 537431
Contact: F Alan Beattie, Chairman

Founded: 1984
Membership: 350
Profile: The International Jousting Association authorises approved events, issues competition results, issues certificates of competence in jousting skills to instructor level and advises outside bodies and authorities.

International League for the Protection of Horses

Anne Colvin House
Snetterton
Norfolk
NR16 2LR
Tel: 01953 498682
Fax: 01953 498373
Contact: Sarah Louise Turner, Press Officer
Founded: 1927
Membership: 77,000
Publications: Adult Newsletter; Junior Newsletter
Profile: The ILPH has operated as a charity since 1927, dedicated to preventing and alleviating the suffering of horses and other equines, wherever they are located and however humble their roles. Based in the UK, the ILPH has become the world's leading equine welfare charity, operating in over 20 countries. Its worldwide activities embrace rescue and rehabilitation, education and training, scientific research, and influencing political opinion and legislation.

International Meat Trade Association

217 Central Markets
Smithfield
London
EC1A 9LH
Tel: 0171 489 0005
Fax: 0171 248 4733
Contact: Mr AG Gordon, Executive Director

International Mohair Association

Mohair House
68 The Grove
Ilkley
West Yorkshire
LS29 9PA
Tel: 01943 817149
Fax: 01943 817150
Contact: Nicola Waddington, Manager
Founded: 1974
Membership: 90
Profile: Founded by the international mohair industry to promote, advance and protect the interests of members and of their manufactured mohair products. The IMA owns the international mohair mark which is registered worldwide and licensed to members for use on their mohair products.

International Mycological Institute

CAB International
Bakeham Lane
Egham
Surrey
TW20 9TY
Tel: 01784 470111
Fax: 01784 470909
Email: imi@cabi.org
Contact: Professor DL Hawksworth, Director
Founded: 1920
Publications: Index of Fungi; Bibliography of Systematic Mycology; Description Sheets of Fungi and Plant Pathogenic Bacteria
Previous names: IOM Imperial Bureau of Mycology 1920–1929; IMI Imperial Institute 1930–1947; CMI Mycological Institute 1948–1985; CMI CAB International Mycological Institute 1986–1990
Profile: As a part of CAB International, IMI is an inter governmental not-for-profit organisation. Expertise in fungi and plant pathogenic fungi is directed into three main areas: biodiversity, crop protection and industrial and environmental development. The institute offers identifications, training, strain supply, consultancies, information provision and funded project research programmes in these areas. The activities are backed by the world's largest team of systematic mycologists, extensive reference collections and a unique library.

International Otter Survival Fund

Broadford
Isle of Skye
IV49 9AQ
Tel: 01471 822487
Fax: 01471 822487
Email: iosf@gael-net.co.uk
Contact: Paul Yoxon, Director
Founded: 1993
Membership: 1,300
Publications: Publications list available
Profile: Preservation and safeguarding otters and areas of good habitat worldwide, by supporting people working in research and rehabilitation.

International Plant Propagators Society

Weggs Farm
Common Road
Dickleburgh
Diss
Norfolk
IP21 4PJ
Tel: 01379 741999

Fax: 01379 741999
Email: ipps@paston.co.uk
Contact: Mr John Adlam, Secretary
Founded: 1950
Membership: 5,000
Publications: Members newsletter; directory

International Sheep Dog Society

Chesham House
47 Bromham Road
Bedford
MK40 2AA
Tel: 01234 352672
Fax: 01234 327065

International Society for the Prevention of Water Pollution

Little Orchard
Bentworth
Alton
Hampshire
GU34 5RB
Tel: 01420 562225
Contact: Chairman
Founded: 1940
Membership: 350
Profile: The society's aims are: to prevent in every possible way the pollution of the planet's water; to investigate water pollution problems wherever they may occur; to try to ascertain the causes of such pollution; to consult with such experts and authorities as can help solve the problems and to collect and collate information concerning water associated problems.

International Sugar Organization

1 Canada Square
Canary Wharf
Docklands
London
E14 5AA
Tel: 0171 513 1144
Fax: 0171 513 1146
Contact: Dr Peter Baron, Executive Director
Founded: 1937
Publications: Publications list available
Profile: The International Sugar Organization is the only worldwide forum for the exchange of views by major producing, consuming and trading countries at an intergovernmental level. The ISO administers the International Sugar Agreement. Main objectives are: to contribute to an improved market transparency through statistical and analytical activities; to hold international seminars, workshops and conferences; to formulate and sponsor projects from developing countries seeking financing from the Common Fund for Commodities with a view to improving productivity, widening product base and diversifying vertically the sugar business.

International Tree Foundation

Sandy Lane
Crawley Down
West Sussex
RH10 4HS
Tel: 01342 712536
Fax: 01342 718282
Contact: Mrs Inez Driver, Office Secretary
Founded: 1922
Membership: 3,500
Publications: Journal and Yearbook; newsletter
Previous names: Men of the Trees until 1992
Profile: The International Tree Foundation is a charity dedicated to the planting and protection of trees at home and abroad. The ITF was founded in 1922 and was originally known as Men of the Trees. It has a network of branches in the UK and affiliated groups overseas. Membership is open to all who share the foundation's aims.

Interpret Britain

12 The Grove
Benton
Newcastle upon Tyne
NE12 9PE
Tel: 0191 266 5804
Contact: Lesley Hehir, Secretary

Intervention Board

PO Box 69
Reading
Berkshire
RG1 3YD
Tel: 0118 958 3626
Fax: 0118 959 7736
Contact: Jean Auty, Press Officer
Founded: 1972
Publications: Publications list available
Previous names: Intervention Board for Agricultural Produce until 1990
Profile: The Intervention Board is an executive agency responsible for the implementation of the common agricultural policy in the UK. It is answerable to the four agriculture ministers through the Intervention Board for Agricultural Produce which consists of the ministers' representatives, the agency's Chief Executive and independent Chair. The agency operates many of the European Community's schemes to regulate the market in agricultural products, and is responsible for funding and accounting for

these schemes and those administered by the agriculture departments.

Inverness College School of Applied Science & Computing
Inverness College
3 Longman Road
Inverness
IV1 1SA
Tel: 01463 236681
Fax: 01463 711977
Email: McDOUGALL@Inverness.fc.uhi.ac.uk
Contact: Jim McDougall, Head of School
Founded: 1991
Profile: The school has two centres: Seafield Centre which runs courses on fish and shellfish farming and fisheries management, and the main site at Seafield with courses in applied environmental science.

Irish Draught Horse Society of Great Britain
4th Street
National Agricultural Centre
Stoneleigh Park
Warwickshire
CV8 2LG
Tel: 01203 696549
Fax: 01203 696729

Irish Hackney Horse Society
23 Aghnadore Road
Broughshane
Ballymena
County Antrim
BT42 4QB
Tel: 01266 861334
Profile: We have been unable to contact this organisation. The details given are unconfirmed.

Irish Moiled Cattle Society
64 Glassdrummond Road
Ballynahinch
County Down
Tel: 01238 562530
Contact: Mr SJ Smiley, Secretary
Founded: 1980
Membership: 50
Publications: Breed leaflet
Profile: The Irish Moiled Cattle Society aims to promote the breeding and development of this rare and ancient variety of cattle. The animals are distinctive, being polled and may have a white stripe along their back. The base colour is red although white animals with red ears and muzzles occasionally appear. They are dual purpose animals and thrive on poor land, being hardy and thrifty. There are under 150 pedigree

animals and are listed as critical by the Rare Breeds Survival Trust.

Isle of Wight College, The
Medina Way
Newport
Isle of Wight
PO30 5TA
Tel: 01983 526631
Fax: 01983 521707
Email: info@wightc.ac.uk
Contact: Mary Moore, Marketing Manager
Founded: 1942
Profile: A further and higher education college providing a broad curriculum to the community. Postgraduate to community leisure courses available. The college farm is situated at Branston and provides full and part-time studies plus school visits and public open days during lambing time. An associate college to Bournemouth University.

Jacob Sheep Society
242 Ringwood Road
St Leonards
Ringwood
Hampshire
BH24 2SB
Tel: 01202 894319
Fax: 01202 894319
Contact: Joyce E Earll, Secretary
Founded: 1969
Membership: 900
Publications: Jacob Journal; flock book; Members List
Profile: The breed society for the Jacob sheep.

Japanese Bantam Club
Cockhill Cottage
Cockhill
Castle Cary
Somerset
BA7 7NZ
Tel: 01963 501990
Contact: Mr MJ Flower, Secretary
Profile: A society to promote the Japanese Bantam breed of poultry.

Jersey Agricultural Marketing Federation
Westward
Daisy Hill
Gorey
Jersey
JE3 9EE
Tel: 01534 857413
Fax: 01534 857413
Contact: Mary Devenport, Secretary
Founded: 1970

Profile: Federation of marketing groups exporting fresh Jersey produce to wholesale markets and supermarkets in the UK and occasionally elsewhere.

Jersey Cattle Society of the United Kingdom
Scotsbridge House
Scots Hill
Rickmansworth
Hertfordshire
WD3 3BB
Tel: 01923 897063
Fax: 01923 897691
Contact: Mr C Barnes, Secretary
Founded: 1883
Membership: 800
Publications: Jersey Journal
Profile: The Jersey Cattle Society of the UK maintains the Jersey Cattle herd book.

Jersey Farmers Union
22 Seale Street
St Helier
Jersey
Tel: 01534 33581
Fax: 01534 33582
Contact: Maureen Rondell, Secretary
Founded: 1919

Jersey Produce Marketing Organisation
La Route du Mont Mado
St John
Jersey
JE3 4DN
Tel: 01534 864471
Fax: 01534 864472
Email: IPMO@itl.net

Jockey Club
42 Portman Square
London
W1H 0EN
Tel: 0171 486 4921
Fax: 0171 935 8703

Jockeys Association of Great Britain Ltd
39b Kingfisher Court
Hambridge Road
Newbury
Berkshire
RG14 5SJ
Tel: 01635 44102
Fax: 01635 37932
Contact: Secretary
Founded: 1969
Membership: 550

John Innes Centre and Sainsbury Laboratory
Norwich Research Park
Colney
Norwich
Norfolk
NR4 7UH
Tel: 01603 52571
Fax: 01603 56844
Contact: Dr MD Gale, Associate Director
Founded: 1910
Publications: Annual Report; John Innes Symposium
Previous names: Formerly AFRC Institute of Plant Science Research
Profile: The John Innes Centre was originally created in April 1994, from the fusion of the John Innes Institute, the Cambridge Laboratory and the Nitrogen Fixation Laboratory, Sussex. It is a company with charitable status, limited by guarantee and grant aided by the BBSRC. Research interests include plant molecular biology and genome mapping, microbial biotechnology, plant biochemistry, physiology and cell biology, plant virology and pathology. The independent Sainsbury Laboratory has shared the John Innes site since its inauguration in 1989 and has a complementary science programme in molecular plant pathology.

John Innes Manufacturers Association
PO Box 8
Department 65
Harrogate
North Yorkshire
HG2 8XB
Tel: 01423 879208
Fax: 01423 870025
Email: 100450.2613@compuserve.com
Contact: Brian L Dunsby, Secretary and Public Relations Officer
Founded: 1977
Membership: 6
Publications: Technical data sheets series; Benefits of John Innes Loam Based Compost.
Profile: Represents the leading UK manufacturers of traditional loam based John Innes composts who all use the JIMA Seal of Approval on their packaging. The JIMA Seal of Approval is a registered trademark which can only be used by approved JIMA members who meet JIMA quality standards.

John Muir Trust
12 Wellington Place
Leith
Edinburgh
EH6 7EQ

Tel: 0131 554 0114
Fax: 0131 555 2112
Email: 100655.3502@compuserve.com
Internet: http:www.ma.hw.ac.uk/jmt
Contact: Nigel Hawkins, Director
Founded: 1983
Membership: 4,848
Publications: JMT Journal, Conserving the Wild, Sharing the Land
Profile: The trust owns and manages four areas of outstanding wild landscape totalling 35,000 acres and bringing together conservation and community interest. The trust has open membership and welcomes new members.

Joint Committee for the Conservation of British Invertebrates
Royal Entomological Society
41 Queen's Gate
London
SW7 5BD
Tel: 0171 584 8361
Fax: 0171 938 8937
Contact: Stephen J Brooks, Secretary
Founded: 1968
Previous names: Joint Committee for the Conservation of British Insects until 1990
Profile: JCCBI is dedicated to promoting better conservation of invertebrates in Britain and abroad, achieved mainly through liaison with other bodies, particularly conservation organisations, and by survey of potentially threatened species.

Joint Consultative Council for the Meat Trade
1 Belgrove
Tunbridge Wells
Kent
TN1 1YW
Tel: 01892 541415
Fax: 01892 535462
Contact: C Wickham

Joint Council for Landscape Industries
ILAM House
Lower Basildon
Reading
Berkshire
RG8 9NE
Tel: 01491 874222
Fax: 01491 874059
Profile: We have been unable to contact this organisation. The details given are unconfirmed.

Joint Council of Heavy Horse Breed Societies
Park Cottage
West Dean

Chichester
West Sussex
PO18 0RX
Tel: 01243 811364
Fax: 01243 811364
Contact: Chris Zeuner, Secretary
Founded: 1988
Profile: The council provides a discussion forum for draught horse breed societies. It considers all aspects of common interest in the breeding, working and showing of heavy draught horses in the UK.

Joint Nature Conservation Committee
Monkstone House
City Road
Peterborough
Cambridgeshire
PE1 1JY
Tel: 01733 62626
Fax: 01733 555948
Contact: Dr Nick Davidson, Head of Publications
Founded: 1991
Membership: 65
Publications: Publications catalogue available
Previous names: Nature Conservancy Council until 1991
Profile: JNCC is the body constituted by the Environmental Protection Act 1990 to be responsible for research and advice on nature conservation at both UK and international levels. It is a committee of the Countryside Council for Wales, English Nature and Scottish Natural Heritage, together with independent members and with representatives from the Countryside Commission and Northern Ireland. It is supported by specialist staff.

Keep Scotland Beautiful
Tidy Britain Group
Cathedral Square
Dunblane
Perthshire
FK15 0AQ
Tel: 01786 823202
Fax: 01786 825732
Contact: Douglas S Wright, MBE, Director
Founded: 1973
Membership: 74
Publications: Annual Review
Previous names: Keep Scotland Tidy
Profile: Particularly concerned with fly tipping on countryside around towns and cities; litter prevention; elimination of graffiti and fly posting; countryside and parkland quality measurements noting all adverse environmental quality indicators. Land adjacent to beaches also of concern relating as it does to seaside awards.

Beautiful Scotland in Bloom Committees are formed locally to improve and sympathise with natural environment.

Keep Wales Tidy Campaign
Tidy Britain Group
1b Stangate House
Stanwell Road
Penarth
Cardiff
CF64 2AA
Tel: 01222 712111
Fax: 01222 712338
Contact: RG Gilchrist, Director
Founded: 1972
Publications: Annual Report; newsletter

Kent County Agricultural Society
County Showground
Detling
Maidstone
Kent
ME14 3JF
Tel: 01622 630975
Fax: 01622 630978
Contact: Mrs Frances Day, Chief Executive
Founded: 1923
Membership: 3,000
Publications: Kent View (journal); annual show catalogue and programme
Profile: The society is concerned with the improvement of agriculture, horticulture, allied industries, rural crafts and the breeding of livestock. The holding of an annual show for the exhibition of livestock, farm produce, horticultural produce, machinery etc. The society is involved in the encouragement of agricultural education, research and experimental work by means of publications and grants.

Kent Half Bred Society
Finch's
Kingsdown
Sittingbourne
Kent
ME9 0RA
Profile: We have been unable to contact this organisation. The details given are unconfirmed.

Kerry Hill Flock Book Society
The Bramleys
Broadheath
Presteigne
Powys
LD8 2HG
Tel: 01544 267353
Fax: 01544 267353
Contact: Mrs PJ Chilman, Secretary

Founded: 1898
Membership: 110
Publications: Kerry Hill Flock Book
Profile: The Kerry Hill breed is from Powys and derives its name from the village of Kerry, near Newtown. Records date back to 1809 and the first flock book was published in 1899 with 26 members. To date there are 110 members and increasing.

Kilmarnock College
Hole House Road
Kilmarnock
Ayrshire
KA3 7AT
Tel: 01563 523501
Fax: 01563 538182
Contact: Michael Roebuck, Principal
Founded: 1955
Publications: Annual Report, development plan, prospectus
Profile: Kilmarnock College provides further and higher education to a wide range of students throughout Ayrshire. It has a gross budget of £9m and around 7,000 students per year. Courses in horticulture and arboriculture are offered from the Craig Centre which is situated in the countryside outside Kilmarnock.

King's Environmental Services
Division of Life Sciences
King's College, London
Campden Hill Road
London
W8 7AH
Tel: 0171 333 4403
Fax: 0171 333 4500
Contact: Dr Anthony Bark, Director
Founded: 1989
Publications: Many reports not in public domain; environmental statements and ecological evidence for public inquiries
Profile: KES is a multi-disciplinary, flexible response organisation within the Division of Life Sciences, King's College, London. KES projects have comprised a mixture of high level applied research and more direct consultancy and advisory services. KES has earned an exemplary reputation from the maintenance of high quality standards based on sound scientific method and the production of informative and accessible reports which reflect client requirements. KES's major fields of activity have related to environmental impact assessment and aquatic management. KES has extensive experience in the management, design and execution of aquatic/terrestrial environmental survey and

monitoring programmes. Their client base includes the NRA, Department of Transport, County Councils and private sector organisations.

Kingston Maurward College
Dorchester
Dorset
DT2 8PY
Tel: 01305 264738
Fax: 01305 250059
Contact: Mike Hancock, College Development Officer
Founded: 1947

Kirkley Hall College
Kirkley Hall
Ponteland
Northumberland
NE20 0AQ
Tel: 01661 860808
Fax: 01661 860047
Email: kirkley.ac.uk
Contact: Brian Japes, Director of Studies
Founded: 1951
Publications: College Prospectus
Previous names: Kirkley Farm Institute until 1967; Northumberland College of Agriculture until 1988
Profile: Located in a rural setting, 10 miles from Newcastle upon Tyne. A college offering a wide range of land-based courses up to HND level: agriculture, horticulture; environmental and conservation; equine studies; business studies; countryside tourism, animal care, land use and recreation, woodland management, sheep management. Kirkley Hall is the sheep industry training centre for the UK. Learning resources include a 2,000 acre estate encompassing three farms, gardens, a range of freshwater and terrestrial habitats, science labs, IT suites, careers resource centre and library.

Kirkwall College of Further Education
Kirkwall
Orkney
KW15 1LX
Tel: 01856 872839
Fax: 01856 875323

Laboratory of the Government Chemist
Queens Road
Teddington
Middlesex
TW11 0LY
Tel: 0181 943 7552
Fax: 0181 943 2767
Email: jsa@lgc.co.uk
Contact: Jean Anderson, Marketing Services Manager
Founded: 1842
Publications: Annual Report; Government Chemist Newsletter
Profile: LGC employs some 270 staff at its laboratory in Teddington, and a range of services have been built around their expertise in the three core areas of forensic investigations, environmental services and food science. LGC is cited in several Acts of Parliament as referee analyst in disputes relating to chemical composition. LGC plays an important role in law enforcement, public health, the protection of government revenue, consumer and environmental matters. The laboratory is committed to a total quality approach to all aspects of its work. This is characterised by formal quality accreditations – BS EN ISO 9001, NAMAS and Good Laboratory Practice.

Laced Wyandotte Club
The Rectory
Vale Road
Ellesmere Port
Cheshire
L65 9AY
Tel: 01513 552516
Contact: Rev DC Garnett, Secretary
Profile: A society to promote the Laced Wyandotte breed of poultry.

Lackham College
Lacock
Chippenham
Wiltshire
SN15 2NY
Tel: 01249 443111
Fax: 01249 444474
Contact: Pam Dickerson, Student Services
Founded: 1946
Publications: College Prospectus
Profile: Lackham College offers a tremendous range of opportunities in a wide variety of courses for countryside and land-based careers. The college's self-contained 500 acre estate includes mixed woodlands, freshwater ponds, as well as college farms, an equestrian centre and tourist centre and small animal care centre. The wide selection of full and part-time courses include agriculture, animal care, countryside management and conservation, engineering, equine studies, farm mechanisation, floristry, horticulture, tourism and leisure.

Ladies' Golf Union
The Scores
St Andrews

Fife
KY16 9AT
Tel: 01334 475811
Fax: 01334 472818

Lake District National Park Authority
National Park Office
Murley Moss
Oxenholme Road
Kendal
Cumbria
LA9 7RL
Tel: 01539 724555
Fax: 01539 740822
Email: ldistrict@cix.compulink.co.uk
Contact: John Toothill, National Park Officer
Founded: 1952
Membership: 26
Publications: Annual Report; National Park
Management Plan
Previous names: Lake District Special Planning
Board until 1996
Profile: The LDNPA aim to conserve and
enhance the natural beauty, wildlife and cultural
heritage of the National Park and promoting
opportunities for the understanding and
enjoyment of the Lake District's special qualities
by the public.

Land Access and Rights Association
PO Box 9
Cannock
Staffordshire
WS11 2FE
Tel: 01543 467218
Contact: Caroline Garfield

Land Authority for Wales
Custom House
Custom House Street
Cardiff
CF1 5AP
Tel: 01222 223444
Fax: 01222 223330
Contact: Hilary Evans, Land Manager
Founded: 1979
Publications: Annual Report and summary of
activities
Profile: The Land Authority for Wales is an
organisation which helps to create development
opportunities. The success of its work depends
upon the partnerships it forges with a wide range
of parties, be they private developers, house
builders, industrialists or public authorities. The
authority can bring its experience to bear to help
companies maximise their investment by
releasing land beset with complex ownerships or
by adding land of its own to a site so that it can

be developed as a coherent whole. It can act as
an advisor in assessing the development
potential of land.

Land Drainage Contractors Association
National Agricultural Centre
Stoneleigh Park
Warwickshire
CV8 2LG
Tel: 01203 696683
Fax: 01203 696963
Contact: Bruce Brockway, Secretary
Publications: Technical Specifications for
Drainage Installation

Land Heritage
Devon Office
The Pound
Whitestone
Exeter
EX4 2HP
Tel: 01647 61099
Fax: 01647 61134
Contact: Mrs Pauline Huggins, Secretary to
Trustees
Founded: 1984
Publications: Newsletter
Profile: The Trust for the Protection of Britain's
Land Heritage (Land Heritage) promotes organic
farming by the direct ownership of land.
Acquisition by the trust saves organically farmed
land from passing into non-organic ownership
when it is sold and thus prevents the loss of
natural fertility which would otherwise occur.
Trust ownership can also promote conversion to
organic husbandry through the adjustment of
rents during the restoration period.

Land Registers of Northern Ireland
Department of the Environment for Northern
    Ireland
Lincoln Building
27/45 Great Victoria Street
Belfast
BT2 7FL
Tel: 01232 251555
Fax: 01232 251550
Contact: Helen McCallan, Customer Services
Manager
Founded: 1966
Publications: Corporate and business plans;
Statement of Charter Standards
Profile: Land Registers of Northern Ireland
combines the functions of the registry of deeds,
the land registry and the statutory charges
registry. These organisations have been
operating public registers since 1708, 1892 and

1951 respectively and they take great pride in this long tradition of customer service. They aim to build on this tradition and strive to become even more receptive to customer needs. The agency provides land information and registration services to the private and public sectors. Customer views are sought through the customer forum, customer survey and meetings with local groups.

Land Tribunal for Scotland
Scottish Courts Administration
1 Grosvenor Crescent
Edinburgh
EH12 5ER
Tel: 0131 225 7996
Fax: 0131 226 4812
Contact: Clerk
Founded: 1949

Land Trusts Association
2 Cornwall Mansions
Ashburnham Road
London
SW10 0PE
Tel: 0171 352 2355
Fax: 0171 352 2355
Contact: Richard Sowler, Secretary
Founded: 1979
Membership: 55
Publications: Occasional Papers
Profile: The Land Trusts Association's prime objective is to encourage and facilitate, in appropriate cases, the dedication of estates, farmlands, woodlands, houses and buildings to the public benefit through the establishment of charitable land trusts and by this means to ensure their preservation, use and development. The association is not a professional organisation. It does not give or offer professional advice. It is a facilitator only. Membership is open to people who are concerned for the future of the countryside and who support the concept of the charitable land trust.

Land Use and Tenure Division
Ministry of Agriculture, Fisheries and Food
Nobel House
17 Smith Square
London
SW1P 3JR
Tel: 0171 238 5678
Profile: The Land Use and Tenure Division is responsible for agricultural holdings legislation, policy on smallholdings, agricultural implications of planning legislation and farm woodlands.

Landlife
The Old Police Station
Lark Lane
Liverpool
L17 8UU
Tel: 0151 728 7011
Fax: 0151 728 8413
Email: info@landlife.u-net.com
Contact: Grant Luscombe, Director
Founded: 1975
Membership: 200
Publications: Natterjack
Previous names: Rural Preservation Association until 1985
Profile: Landlife is a charity taking action for a better environment by creating new opportunities for wildlife and encouraging people to enjoy them.

Landmark Trust
Shottesbrooke
Maidenhead
Berkshire
SL6 3SW
Tel: 01628 825925
Fax: 01628 825417
Contact: Rebecca Morgan, Public Affairs
Founded: 1965
Publications: The Landmark Handbook
Profile: The Landmark Trust is an independent charity which rescues buildings of historic interest or architectural importance, and then gives them new life by making them available to stay in for holidays. All of the buildings are remarkable in some way. The trust owns chapels, lighthouses, manors, castles, forts, mines, towers and temples which can be rented by anybody at all times of the year.

Lands Improvement Company
Lands Improvement Holdings plc
1 Buckingham Place
London
SW1E 6HR
Tel: 0171 222 5331
Contact: PA Clery, Managing Director

Lands Tribunal
Lord Chancellors Department – Court Service
48/49 Chancery Lane
London
WC2A 1JR
Tel: 0171 936 7200
Fax: 0171 404 0896
Contact: Mr Peter J Fisher, Chief Clerk
Founded: 1950
Publications: Explanatory leaflet
Profile: The Lands Tribunal is an independent judicial body with several jurisdictions involving

land or the valuation of land. These include compensation for compulsory purchase, land compensation claims, lifting or modifying restrictive covenants and appeals about rateable values of commercial premises. Hearings may take place anywhere in England and Wales.

Lands Tribunal for Northern Ireland
Royal Courts of Justice
Belfast
BT1 3JJ
Tel: 01232 327703
Contact: Ronnie Ross, Registrar
Founded: 1965
Profile: The Lands Tribunal for Northern Ireland is responsible for settling disputes in connection with: the valuation of land and buildings for rating; compensation for compulsory purchase and taxation; the renewal of leases of business premises; the modification or extinguishment of impediments affecting land; questions involving land valuation and law and any matter affecting the value or use of development of land and buildings.

Landscape Conservation Forum
c/o City Museum
Weston Park
Sheffield
S10 2TP
Tel: 0114 279 5705
Fax: 0114 275 0957
Profile: We have been unable to contact this organisation. The details given are unconfirmed.

Landscape Design Trust
13a West Street
Reigate
Surrey
RH2 9BL
Tel: 01737 225374
Fax: 01737 224206
Email: idesign@worldscope.net
Contact: Ken Fieldhouse, Editor – Landscape Design
Founded: 1984
Publications: Landscape Design (journal); Landscape Design Extra; Landscape Architecture Europe; Researching a Garden's History
Profile: Landscape Design Trust was set up to stimulate an informed concern for, and understanding of, the landscape of Britain. A registered charity, it has close links with the Landscape Institute whilst remaining totally independent with an altogether different role. In pursuit of these aims, in 1986 the trust took over from the Landscape Institute the ownership and management of the journal Landscape Design.

Landscape Institute
6–7 Barnard Mews
London
SW11 1QU
Tel: 0171 738 9166
Fax: 0171 738 9134
Contact: Stuart Royston, Director General
Founded: 1929
Publications: Publications list available
Previous names: Institute of Landscape Architects until 1978
Profile: The Landscape Institute is the professional body for landscape architects, landscape managers and landscape scientists. Its main objective is to promote the highest standard of professional service in the application of arts and sciences of landscape architecture and management.

Landscape Institute Scotland
5 Coates Crescent
Edinburgh
EH3 7AL
Tel: 0131 226 3939
Fax: 0131 220 3934
Contact: S Gray, Secretary
Membership: 220
Publications: Landscape Scotland Quarterly
Profile: The Landscape Institute is organised throughout Britain in regional chapters which include the Scottish Chapter, Landscape Institute Scotland. The Scottish Chapter activities include organising lectures, social events, conferences and exhibitions, liaison with other professional bodies, government organisations and the public, and advice on landscape matters.

Landscape Research Group
Exeter Faculty of Arts and Education
University of Plymouth
Earl Richards Road North
Exeter
Devon
EX2 6AS
Tel: 01392 475016
Fax: 01392 475012
Email: l.roberts@plym.ac.uk
Contact: Lyn Roberts, Administrator
Founded: 1967
Membership: 180
Publications: Newsletter
Profile: The group fosters the development and exchange of ideas about landscape in its widest sense; encourages collaboration internationally between disciplines and between researchers and practitioners; facilitates the exchange of information and ideas between those who are

separated by distance or organisation; initiates and seeks funds for research; and organises educational and promotional activities.

Langslide College School of Horticulture
Langslide College, Glasgow
Woodburn House
Buchanan Drive
Rutherglen
Glasgow
G73 3PF
Tel: 01416 476300
Fax: 01416 475895
Contact: E Proudfoot, Head of School
Publications: Langside College Prospectus
Profile: The school of horticulture is a provider of horticultural/environmental and floristry education and training provision. Courses range from recreational to HND with SCOTVEC, City & Guilds and Scottish Skills Testing being the awarding bodies.

Large Black Pig Breeders Club
Hillcrest
St Briavel's Common
Lydney
Gloucester
GL15 6SH
Contact: Tony Osborne, Secretary
Profile: The society's objects are to: promote this hardy docile breed, to keep breeders and enthusiasts in touch and to provide and circulate information with regular newsletters and meetings. Membership is open to all.

League Against Cruel Sports Ltd
83–87 Union Street
London
SE1 1SG
Tel: 0171 403 6155
Fax: 0171 403 4532
Email: 100647.3311@compuserve.com
Contact: Mr John Bryant, Head of Press and Research
Founded: 1924
Membership: 40,000
Publications: Wildlife Guardian
Profile: LACS campaigns for the protection of animals from cruelty – particularly that involved in the hunting of wild animals with dogs. The league lobbies Parliament and local authorities for greater wildlife protection, funds scientific research into human/wildlife conflicts and owns 37 wildlife sanctuaries in the West Country on which all hunting is forbidden.

Leather Conservation Centre
34 Guildhall Road
Northampton
NN1 1EW
Tel: 01604 232723
Fax: 01604 602070
Contact: Roy Thomson, Chief Executive
Founded: 1978
Publications: Publications list available

Leatherhead Food Research Association
Randalls Road
Leatherhead
Surrey
KT22 7RY
Tel: 01372 376761
Fax: 01372 386228
Email: help@lfra.co.uk
Contact: Mr Richard Swift, Sales Manager
Founded: 1919
Membership: 800
Publications: Publications list available
Previous names: British Food Manufacturing Industries Research Association (BFMIRA)
Profile: Leatherhead serves the food and drinks industry worldwide through a membership system. Its objective is to provide its member companies with a range of services designed to allow them to compete effectively in the global market. Specifically, Leatherhead helps companies by: monitoring and researching the market; conceiving and developing new products; optimising product and ingredient formulation; improving manufacturing technology; dealing with regulatory requirements; assessing shelf-life and product safety; providing manufacturing resources and know-how; developing and installing QA and QC systems; benchmarking for best practices; providing trouble-shooting services; and, offering a 24 hour, 365 day crisis management service.

Lee Valley Regional Park Authority
Myddleton House
Bulls Cross
Enfield
Middlesex
EN2 9HG
Tel: 01992 717711
Fax: 01992 719937
Contact: Secretary
Founded: 1968
Profile: The regional park for London stretching from Ware in Hertfordshire down to the Thames following the route of the River Lea and The Lee Navigation. The park and its facilities are run for the benefit of London, Hertfordshire and Essex.

Leek Growers' Association Ltd
133 Eastgate
Louth
Lincolnshire
LN11 9QG
Tel: 01507 602427
Fax: 01507 600689
Contact: Mrs Jayne Dyas, Company Secretary
Founded: 1980
Membership: 10
Profile: Marketing information.

Leghorn Club
1 Oak Tree Cottages
Barnham Lane
Walberton
Arundel
West Sussex
BN18 0AY
Tel: 01243 543483
Contact: Mr R Turner, Secretary
Profile: A society to promote the Leghorn breed of poultry.

Leicester Agricultural Society
Dishley Grange Farm
Derby Road
Loughborough
Leicestershire
LE11 2AE
Tel: 01509 646786
Fax: 01509 646787
Contact: Annabel Currer Briggs
Founded: 1833
Membership: 500
Publications: Annual Show Programme and Catalogue
Profile: It organises and promotes the county show which educates the public to all activities in farming, horses, all types of livestock, rare breeds, dog agility classes, farrier displays and show jumping.

Leicester Longwool Sheep Breeder's Association
14 Kingsmead
Driffield
East Yorkshire
YO25 7FD
Tel: 01377 253298
Contact: Secretary

Licensed Animal Slaughterers and Salvage Association
25 Somersall Lane
Chesterfield
Derbyshire
S40 3LA

Tel: 01246 566808
Fax: 01246 566808
Contact: Chris Ashworth, Technical Adviser and Secretary
Founded: 1950
Membership: 50
Publications: Members newsletter
Profile: The organisation represents the interests of the knacker industry in the UK. The group is actively involved in the review of legislation, both UK and EU, relating to the animal by products and environmental industries.

Lincoln Longwool Sheepbreeders Association
Lincolnshire Showground
Grange-de-Lings
Lincoln
LN2 2NA
Tel: 01552 511395
Fax: 01552 520345
Contact: Mrs L Newboult, Clerk
Founded: 1891
Membership: 100
Publications: Flock book
Profile: A sheep breed society to support and promote the Lincoln Longwool breed of sheep.

Lincoln Red Cattle Society
Lincolnshire Showground
Grange-de-Lings
Lincoln
LN2 2NA
Tel: 01522 511395
Fax: 01522 520345
Contact: Mrs L Newboult, Clerk
Founded: 1896
Membership: 100
Publications: Herd book
Profile: A breed society to support and promote the Lincoln Red breed of cattle.

Lincolnshire Agricultural Society
Lincolnshire Showground
Grange-de-Lings
Lincoln
LN2 2NA
Tel: 01522 524240
Fax: 01522 520348
Contact: JP Skehel, Chief Executive and Company Secretary
Founded: 1869
Membership: 5,068
Publications: The Lincolnshire (members newsletter); Annual Show Programme and Catalogue

Linking Environment And Farming

National Agricultural Centre
Stoneleigh Park
Warwickshire
CV8 2LZ
Tel: 01203 413911
Fax: 01203 413636
Contact: Caroline Drummond, Project
Co-ordinator
Founded: 1991
Membership: 400
Publications: LEAF Environmental Audit;
Practical Guide for ICM; Guidelines for ICM
(Integrated Crop Management)
Profile: LEAF is developing and promoting
Integrated Crop Management (ICM) – common
sense farming practices which are
economically viable and environmentally
responsible. LEAF shows farmers how through
ICM they can maintain optimum yields,
produce wholesome food at reasonable cost
and take effective measures to protect the
environment whilst maintaining profit. LEAF
encourages farmers to adopt ICM through
visits to LEAF Demonstration Farms, talks and
practical workshops. It also develops technical
guidance on how farmers can work towards
ICM principles. These include the LEAF
Environmental Audit – a self-assessment
management tool for farmers to objectively
assess and improve their farming practices.

Linnean Society of London

Burlington House
Piccadilly
London
W1V 0LQ
Tel: 0171 434 4479
Fax: 0171 287 9364
Contact: Dr John Marsden, Executive
Secretary
Founded: 1788
Membership: 2,100
Profile: The society promotes all aspects of
biology, but particularly those concerning the
diversity and interrelationships of organisms.
This involves the examination and collation of
a wide range of scientific evidence from such
fields as genetics, ecology, anatomy,
physiology, biochemistry, and palaeontology
and impinges on related disciplines in
agriculture, fisheries, forestry etc.

Lipizzaner Society of Great Britain

The British Lipizzaner Breeding Centre
Underhill Farm
Ludwell

Shaftesbury
Dorset
SP7 0PW
Tel: 01747 828639
Fax: 01747 851202
Contact: Mrs Una Harley, Chairman
Founded: 1982
Membership: 150
Publications: Members newsletter
Profile: LSGB has two stud books for
registering pure and part bred Lipizzaners.
There is a stallion licensing system. All horses
registered with the society have to be blood
typed, parentage tested, all breeding animals
have to be DNA and EVA tested. Owners and
non-owners are equally welcome as members.

Livestock and Meat Commission for Northern Ireland

57 Malone Road
Belfast
BT9 6SA
Tel: 01232 381022
Fax: 01232 668113
Contact: Mr David Rutledge, Chief Executive
Founded: 1967
Publications: The Bulletin; The Meat Trader
Previous names: Livestock Marketing
Commission for Northern Ireland until 1994
Profile: The commission's main activities are
beef and sheep carcase classification; an agency
service in Northern Ireland on behalf of the
Intervention Board; operation of a farm quality
assurance scheme; home and export market
initiatives and the provision of market intelligence
to producers and processors.

Livestock Auctioneers Association

Surveyor Court
Westwood Way
Coventry
Warwickshire
CV4 8JE
Tel: 0171 334 3832
Fax: 0171 334 3800
Contact: John RF Martin, Executive Secretary
Founded: 1954
Membership: 192
Publications: Annual Report; Code of Practice;
Directory of Livestock Markets in England, Wales
and Scotland
Previous names: Livestock Auctioneers Market
Committee for England and Wales until 1992
Profile: The LAA represents all the firms running
livestock markets in England and Wales. It acts
on their behalf in negotiations with other trade
associations representing all sectors of the
livestock industry, from producer to retailer. It

also negotiates with the Ministry of Agriculture, Fisheries and Food and other official and semi-official bodies on matters affecting the livestock market sector. The LAA includes 192 firms in its membership representing 223 markets.

Livestock Traders Association of Great Britain
Guthlaxton House
North Kilworth
Lutterworth
Leicestershire
LE17 6HG
Tel: 01858 880 7146
Contact: DGW Ward, Honorary Secretary
Profile: We have been unable to contact this organisation. The details given are unconfirmed.

Living Churchyard Project
Church and Conservation Project
National Agricultural Centre
Stoneleigh Park
Warwickshire
CV8 2LZ
Tel: 01203 696969
Fax: 01203 696900
Contact: David Manning, Church and Conservation Project Leader
Founded: 1989
Publications: Publications list available
Profile: The Living Churchyard Project was launched in 1989 to encourage people to take a new look at churchyards, cemeteries and other burial grounds as sanctuaries for wildlife, enhancing their natural beauty through careful conservation management. It is being promoted through Diocesan Advisory Committees, the Council for the Care of Churches as well as conservation organisations. Originally directed at rural churchyards, the project is being extended to urban cemeteries and the educational value of all burial grounds as possible study/resource centres is being promoted through schools and universities with increasing success.

Living Earth Foundation
Warwick House
106 Harrow Road
London
W2 1XD
Tel: 0171 258 1823
Fax: 0171 258 1824
Email: livearth@gn.apc.org
Contact: Gwen Vaughan, Chief Executive
Founded: 1987
Profile: Living Earth promotes the resolution of environmental issues through programmes

which empower individuals to learn about and act upon their environmental concerns and to encourage community participation and strengthening links through mutually beneficial partnerships between local groups, schools, businesses and local authorities.

Llanwenog Sheep Society
Waunlas
Taliaris
Llandeilo
SA19 7DF
Tel: 01558 685576
Contact: Miss J King, Joint Secretary
Founded: 1956
Membership: 90
Publications: Annual flock book
Profile: A breed society with the aim of improving and promoting the Llanwenog breed of sheep.

Lleyn Sheep Society
Gwyndy
Bryncroes
Sarn
Pwllheli
Gwynedd
LL53 8ET
Tel: 01758 730366
Contact: Gwenda Roberts, Secretary
Founded: 1971
Profile: A breed society for the promotion of the Lleyn breed of sheep.

London Commodity Exchange
1 Commodity Quay
St Katharine's Dock
London
E1 9AX
Tel: 0171 481 2080
Fax: 0171 702 9923
Contact: Business Development Officer
Founded: 1986
Membership: 350
Previous names: London Fox until 1993

London Grains Futures Market
London Commodity Exchange
1 Commodity Quay
St Katharine's Dock
London
E1 9AX
Tel: 0171 481 2080
Fax: 0171 702 9923

London Potatoes Futures Market
London Commodity Exchange
1 Commodity Quay
St Katharine's Dock
London
E1 9AX
Tel: 0171 481 2080
Fax: 0171 702 9923
Email: info@lc.co.uk
Contact: Doug Thow, Product Business Manager

Long Distance Walkers' Association
21 Upcroft
Windsor
Berkshire
SL4 3NH
Tel: 01753 866685
Contact: Les Maple, Honorary Secretary
Founded: 1971
Membership: 6,905
Publications: Strider; Long Distance Walkers Handbook
Profile: The LDWA was created in order to further the interests of those who enjoy long distance walking. A long distance is considered to be one of 20 miles or more in rural areas but which might be completed as a day, multi-day or holiday walk. They publish details of long distance walks and a calendar of challenge events, i.e. a walk of a given distance to be completed within a set time. There exist 40+ local groups throughout the UK.

Longhorn Cattle Society
Peel House
14 West Street
Shipston-on-Stour
Warwickshire
CV36 4HD
Tel: 01608 662967
Fax: 01608 662967
Contact: Elizabeth L Henson, Secretary
Founded: 1878
Membership: 450
Publications: Herd book; members newsletter
Profile: Breed society for the Longhorn breed of cattle.

Lonk Sheep Breeders Association
528 Red Lees Road
Cliviger
Burnley
Lancashire
BB10 4TD
Tel: 01282 427302
Contact: E Halsall, Honorary Secretary

Founded: 1905
Membership: 77
Publications: Flock book

Loughry College – The Food Centre
Department of Agriculture for Northern Ireland
Cookstown
County Tyrone
BT80 9AA
Tel: 016487 68100
Fax: 016487 61043

Luing Cattle Society Ltd, The
Ballinton Farm
Thornhill
Stirling
FK8 3QE
Tel: 01786 850219
Fax: 01786 850219
Contact: Mrs M McGregor, Secretary
Founded: 1965
Membership: 140
Publications: Annual journal

Lundy Pony Preservation Society
33 Gregorys Tyning
Paulton
Bristol
BS18 5PW
Tel: 01761 415073
Contact: Mrs Dawn Minall, Secretary
Founded: 1984
Membership: 45
Publications: Members newsletter
Profile: The aim of the society is to promote the Lundy pony, with a view to increasing its numbers with a sound breeding policy. The society runs its own small herd of brood mares and youngstock. An adoption scheme raises money for the upkeep of the herd.

Lusitano Breed Society of Great Britain
The Small House
Green End Road
Radnage
Buckinghamshire
HP14 5BY
Tel: 01494 483683
Fax: 01494 483683
Contact: Jean Chadwick, Secretary
Founded: 1980
Membership: 200
Publications: Luso News
Profile: The society works to promote the Lusitano in this country and provide a focal point for all Lusitano owners in the UK for both pure and part-bred horses. The society produces a quarterly newsletter and runs an annual breed

show. Registered with MAFF and the BHS and affiliated to the Associacao Portuguesa de Criadores do Cavalo Pure Sangue Lusitano in Portugal.

Macaulay Land Use Research Association
Craigiebuckler
Aberdeen
AB15 8QH
Tel: 01224 318611
Fax: 01224 311556
Email: mi374@mluri.sari.ac.uk
Contact: Lorraine Robertson, Librarian
Founded: 1987
Membership: 300
Publications: MLURI Annual Report
Previous names: Macaulay Institute for Soil Science
Profile: The four major themes of the institute are: land-use assessment, evaluation and monitoring and production of relational database information systems; environmental issues; developing systems of land management related to agriculture, forestry and farm forestry; improving the efficiency of the components of production systems.

Macauley Land Use Research Institute
Craigiebuckler
Aberdeen
AB2 8QH
Tel: 01224 318611
Fax: 01224 311556
Contact: Dr SP Bird, External Affairs Officer
Founded: 1987
Publications: Annual Report; publications list available
Profile: MLURI undertakes research into finding ways of using and managing the land to create wealth and support rural development without harming the quality of the environment. The institute has major research programmes in the fields of soil pollution, land and environmental management systems; spatial data handling; vegetation dynamics and herbivore foraging. MLURI receives grant in aid from the Scottish Office Agriculture, Environment and Fisheries Department.

Machinery Ring Association of England and Wales
Agriculture House
Stanton Harcourt Road
Eynsham
Witney
Oxfordshire
OX8 1TW
Tel: 01865 882999
Fax: 01865 883239

Contact: Miss Clare A Muskett, Secretary
Founded: 1991
Profile: Association representing the interests of machinery rings in England and Wales.

Maine Anjou Cattle Society of the UK
27 The Barons
Twickenham
London
TW1 2AP
Tel: 0181 892 1936
Contact: WR Crymble, Secretary

Maize Growers Association
Priston Mill
Priston
Bath
Somerset
BA2 9EQ
Tel: 01225 337566
Fax: 01225 337560

Malt Distillers Association of Scotland, The
1 North Street
Elgin
Morayshire
IV30 1UA
Tel: 01343 544077
Fax: 01343 548523
Contact: Messrs Grigor and Young (W P Mennie), Secretaries
Founded: 1874
Membership: 90
Publications: Bulletin
Previous names: North of Scotland Malt Distillers Association until 1925; Pot Still Malt Distillers Association of Scotland until 1971.
Profile: The objects of the association are to increase the friendly interchange of ideas amongst themselves; the removal of all obstructions to properly carrying out their business, not only as regards improvements in the excise laws, but also for making of new arrangements as to the customs of sales which would put both buyer and seller on a more equitable footing and ensure a uniformity of practice. The association is currently assisting in such matters as animal feeds, environmental issues, wages negotiations as well as customs and excise.

Maltsters Association of Great Britain
31b Castlegate
Newark on Trent
Nottinghamshire
NG24 1AZ
Tel: 01636 700781

Fax: 01636 701836
Contact: IR Murrell, Secretary General
Founded: 1827
Membership: 20
Profile: The organisation aims to: look after the interests of the UK malting industry, to assist training and communications within the industry; to keep a watching brief on any matters of a legal or official nature that could impact on the industry

Mammal Conservation Trust
Kentshill Farm House
Landermere
Thorpe-le-Soken
Essex
CO16 0NN
Tel: 01255 861976
Fax: 01255 862375
Contact: Tim Dansie, Chairman
Founded: 1979
Membership: 100
Profile: Professional team engaged in the capture and transportation of deer, mainly in deer parks and enclosed woodland. The team also captures deer for radio collaring. Monies earned are re-distributed on an annual basis to scientific projects which are deemed worth supporting.

Mammal Society
15 Cloisters House
8 Battersea Park Road
London
SW8 4BG
Tel: 071 498 4358
Fax: 071 498 4459
Contact: Julia Hanmer, Information and Development Officer
Founded: 1954
Membership: 1,500
Publications: Fact sheets on British mammals; booklets on British mammals; publications list available
Profile: The Mammal Society promotes the study and conservation of British mammals by: organising surveys; publishing books; providing information and advice; running events; supporting local group; encouraging young people to find out about mammals. Membership is open to anyone with an interest in mammals.

Manorial Society of Great Britain
104 Kennington Road
London
SE11 6RE
Tel: 0171 735 6633
Fax: 0171 582 7022

Contact: Robert Smith, Chairman/Administrator
Founded: 1906
Membership: 1,600
Publications: Publications list available
Profile: Legal and historical advice on manors and feudal baronies in the British Isles. Annual conferences and ad hoc conferences held throughout the year.

Manx Loghtan Sheep Breeders Group
Dairy Barn
North Houghton
Stockbridge
Hampshire
SO20 6LF
Tel: 01264 810274
Contact: Mrs SJ Gotting, Secretary
Founded: 1988
Membership: 100
Publications: Group newsletter; The Manx Loghton Story
Profile: The group has an active programme of events and arranges breeders workshops and visits to the Isle of Man to study the Manx Loghtan in its home environment. The Group aims: to support and promote the Manx Loghtan sheep breed in close association with the Rare Breeds Survival Trust and the breed society on the Isle of Man; to encourage satisfactory registration procedures for stock; to identify correct breed characteristics and ensure that they are applied in registration, in shows and in breed promotion and to demonstrate the potential of the breed.

Manx National Farmers' Union
Old School House
Cronkbourne Village
Braddan
Douglas
Isle of Man
Tel: 01624 674191
Fax: 01624 662204
Contact: JE Corlett, General Secretary

Marans Club
Shipcote
South Hill
Somerton
Somerset
Tel: 01458 241278
Contact: Mr R Richards, Secretary
Profile: A society to promote the Marans breed of poultry.

Marchigiana Cattle Society Ltd
The Old Farm House
Brook End

Little Dunmow
Essex
Tel: 01371 856234
Profile: We have been unable to contact this organisation. The details given are unconfirmed.

Market Task Force
Ministry of Agriculture, Fisheries and Food
Room 21
Whitehall Place East
London
SW1A 2HH
Tel: 0171 270 8862
Fax: 0171 270 8942
Contact: Dan Hackett, Executive Officer
Founded: 1991
Publications: Publications list available
Profile: The Market Task Force aims to help producers, processors and others in the agricultural and food industries develop their marketing skills. They administer the Marketing Development Scheme which is a non-capital grant which aims to help create more efficient marketing structures. Support is available at 50% of the total cost up to £150,000 per project. Eligible items include feasibility studies and market research, salaries of key staff, training and the cost of outside directors. Applications under this scheme must have sufficient scale within the market concerned and the proposals must represent a significant marketing development.

Masham Sheep Breeders Association
1 The Mount
Leyburn
North Yorkshire
DL8 5JA
Tel: 01969 623432
Contact: DW Ward, Secretary
Founded: 1986
Membership: 150
Profile: A breed association for breeders of quality half bred gimmers.

Master of Draghounds Association
Stable Cottage
Wheatsheaf Road
Henfield
West Sussex
BN5 9AU
Tel: 01273 495188
Fax: 01273 495199
Contact: Brian Stern, Honorary Secretary
Founded: 1960
Membership: 23

Profile: The Master of Draghounds Association governs and represents the cross-country field sport of draghunting.

Masters of Basset Hounds Association
20 St Catherines Close
Burbage
Hinkley
Leicestershire
LE10 2QD
Tel: 01455 632237
Contact: Donald A. Peacock, Honorary Secretary
Founded: 1911
Membership: 100
Profile: The association represents the interests of masters of registered packs of basset hounds at national and international level. It is also responsible for setting down rules for individual members and adjudicating on any queries. The association organises an annual show at Peterborough for hounds belonging to member packs.

Masters of Deerhounds Association
Bilboa House
Dulverton
Somerset
TA22 9DW
Tel: 01398 23475
Contact: Dr JDW Peck, Honorary Secretary
Founded: 1957
Membership: 24
Profile: The Masters of Deerhounds Association is the governing body of those packs of hounds hunting the wild deer in Great Britain. Recognised packs are Devon and Somerset Staghounds, Quantock Staghounds, Tiverton Staghounds and New Forest Buckhounds. Membership of MDHA consists of the masters of these packs together with the Honorary Secretary and certain other hunt members.

Masters of Foxhounds Association
Parsloes Cottage
Bagendon
Cirencester
Gloucestershire
GL7 7DU
Tel: 01285 831470
Fax: 01285 831737
Contact: Secretary

Meat and Livestock Commission
PO Box 44
Winterhill House
Snowdon Drive
Milton Keynes

Buckinghamshire
MK6 1AX
Tel: 01908 677577
Fax: 01908 609221
Contact: Mr AC Smith, Head of Press and
Industry Relations
Founded: 1969
Publications: Publications list available
Profile: The Meat and Livestock Commission
was founded under the 1967 Agriculture Act to
promote efficiency in the meat and livestock
industry.

Meat Hygiene Division
Ministry of Agriculture, Fisheries and Food
Block B
Government Buildings
Hook Rise South
Tolworth
Surrey
KT6 7NF
Tel: 0181 330 8329
Profile: The Meat Hygiene Division deals with
public health matters relating to inspection and
hygiene, import and export of poultry meat, red
meat and processed meat products. The division
also deals with animal health import licensing and
export certification for meat and animal products
and welfare of farm animals at slaughter.

Meat Training Council Ltd
PO Box 141
Winterhill House
Snowdon Drive
Milton Keynes
Buckinghamshire
MK6 1YY
Tel: 01908 231062
Fax: 01908 231063
Contact: Peter Huntington, Chief Executive
Founded: 1993
Publications: Publications list available; Meat
Training
Profile: The Meat Training Council is the focus
for training and development for all sectors of the
red and white meat industry. The council is the
lead body for the UK industry and runs
examination courses and certificates NVQs at
levels 1 & 2.

Meatlinc Sheep Co Ltd
Church House
Horkstow
Barton-upon-Humber
Lincolnshire
DN18 6BG
Tel: 01652 618329

Fax: 01652 618447
Contact: Henry R Fell, Managing Director and
Chairman
Founded: 1975
Publications: Meatlinc brochure
Profile: The Meatlinc Sheep Co Ltd is the
organisation responsible for the breeding,
selection, promotion and marketing of Meatlinc
sheep. Breeders of the Meatlinc operate on a
strict franchise contract with the company. The
Meatlinc is the only new breed of terminal sire
produced this century.

Media Relations
Department of Agriculture for Northern Ireland
The Press Office
Room 627
Dundonald House
Upper Newtownards Road
Belfast
BT4 3SB
Tel: 01232 524607
Fax: 01232 525003

Medical Equestrian Association
The Medical Commission on Accident Prevention
35–43 Lincoln's Inn Fields
London
WC2A 3PN
Tel: 01249 782257
Fax: 01249 782257
Contact: Dr R Marshall, Honorary Secretary
Founded: 1985
Membership: 210
Publications: MEA Newsletter
Profile: The Medical Equestrian Centre primary
aims are: improvement of medical cover at
equestrian events; to provide training for
members in the management of equestrian
accidents; education of the equestrian world and
first aid personnel in the hazards of horse riding
and the management of equestrian injuries; the
monitoring and assessment of protective
clothing for riders and research into the statistical
analysis and prevention of horse riding accidents.

Merioneth Agricultural Society
Tiry Dail
Cader Road
Dolgellau
Gwynedd
LL40 1SG
Tel: 01341 422837
Contact: E Douglas Powell, General Secretary
Founded: 1868
Membership: 500
Publications: Annual Show Catalogue

Profile: The society promotes agriculture by holding an annual agriculture show in the county of Merioneth for the exhibition of farming stock, implements and produce with a view to improving the breeding of livestock and promoting the adoption of improved methods of farming.

Merrist Wood College

Worplesdon
Guildford
Surrey
GU3 3PE
Tel: 01483 232424
Fax: 01483 236518
Email: merristwood@pcns.co.uk
Contact: John G Riddle, Principal
Founded: 1945
Profile: A specialist centre for education and training for the land-based industries.

Met. Office, The

London Road
Bracknell
Berkshire
RG12 2SZ
Tel: 01344 420242
Fax: 01344 854412
Internet: http://www.meto.govt.uk
Founded: 1854
Publications: Outlook; various brochures and information leaflets
Profile: The Met. Office provides weather services to all aspects of British and international business including the agricultural community.

Meuse Rhine Issel Cattle Society of Great Britain and Ireland

51 Farringdon Crescent
Preston
Lancashire
PR1 5TY
Tel: 01772 796236
Profile: We have been unable to contact this organisation. The details given are unconfirmed.

Milk Development Council

5–7 John Princes Street
London
W1M 0AP
Tel: 0171 629 7262
Fax: 0171 629 4820
Contact: Peter Merson, Chief Executive
Founded: 1995
Membership: 35,000
Publications: Milk Developments
Profile: The council was formed in 1995 to continue funding near-market research and development and other priority areas, such as

enhancing the public image of milk, following the abolition of milk marketing boards in 1994. Dairy farmers supported its formation in a referendum and its funding by a statutory levy on all milk production in England, Wales and Scotland. Currently the levy is set at 0.04p/litre. Dairy farmers' interests in the use of the MDC's £5 million budget are looked after by a ruling council of 11 people, of whom 7 are active milk producers. MDC has a full-time staff of three to administer the organisation.

Milk Marketing Board for Northern Ireland (Residuary Body)

456 Antrim Road
Belfast
BT15 5GD
Tel: 01232 372237
Fax: 01232 372222
Contact: SA Agnew, Secretary
Founded: 1955
Publications: Annual Report
Profile: The Milk Marketing Board for Northern Ireland ceased trading on 28th February 1995 and the Residuary MMB exists to wind up the affairs of the Milk Marketing Board for Northern Ireland.

Milk, Pigs, Eggs and Poultry Division

Ministry of Agriculture, Fisheries and Food
Room 506
Whitehall Place East Block
London
SW1A 2HH
Tel: 0171 270 8764
Fax: 0171 270 8116
Contact: Ms S Keegan, Personal Secretary to Division Head
Publications: See MAFF publications catalogue
Previous names: Merger of the Milk and Milk Products Division and the Pigs, Eggs and Poultry Division in 1995
Profile: The provision of support and advice to the Minister of Agriculture, Fisheries and Food on markets and standards for the following sectors: milk, pigs, venison, eggs, poultry, ostriches, snails, rabbits and other small farmed livestock. The division is responsible for some sponsorship of the Meat and Livestock Commission and the application of the EC Milk and Milk Products Regulations in relation to the domestic and international markets; EC Milk Quota Regulations; EC Egg Marketing Standards and Hatcheries Regulations; and the EC Poultry Meat Marketing Standards Regulations. The Milk, Pigs, Eggs and Poultry Division is also responsible for the Regional Egg Marketing Inspectorate full details of which may be found in MAFF Publications' free

booklet 'At the Farmer's Service' or by contacting the MAFF Helpline on 0645 335577.

Milking Machine Manufacturers' Association
Solva
Monkswell Road
Monmouth
NP5 3PF
Tel: 01600 712094
Fax: 01600 712094
Contact: John A Telford, Secretary
Founded: 1944
Membership: 7
Profile: The aim of the association is to represent the interests of the manufacturers of milking machines in the United Kingdom and to act as the responsible official body particularly in the fields of technical performance and installation standards.

Millennium Forest for Scotland
PO Box 16063
Glasgow
G2 6NN
Tel: 0141 204 2001
Fax: 0141 204 2225
Email: 100774.35@compuserve.com
Internet:
    http://scotweb.co.uk/environment/millforest

Ministry of Agriculture, Fisheries and Food
Whitehall Place
London
SW1A 2HH
Tel: 0171 238 6000
Publications: Publications list available
Profile: The ministry is the government department responsible for all aspects of agriculture. Nationally it has a series of divisions which are listed separately in this directory. On a regional basis it operates through a series of Regional Service Centres, details of which are given in MAFF's free publication 'At the Farmers Service'. Full details of MAFF services and other information about agriculture, fisheries and food in Britain may be obtained by telephoning the MAFF Helpline on 0645 335577.

Ministry of Agriculture, Fisheries and Food Helpline
Whitehall Place
London
Tel: 0645 335577
Profile: The MAFF Helpline is run by the MAFF Main Library and provides information about agriculture and the ministry to all enquirers at the cost of a local telephone call.

Minorca Club
17 Ronhill Crescent
Cleobury Mortimer
Kidderminster
Worcestershire
DY14 8AT
Tel: 01299 272242
Contact: Mr R Walker, Secretary
Profile: A society to promote the Minorca breed of poultry.

Modern Game Bantam Club
28 High Street
Toddington
Dunstable
Bedfordshire
LU5 6BY
Tel: 01525 873927
Contact: Mr AH Higgs, Secretary
Profile: A society to promote the Modern Game Bantam breed of poultry.

Monmouthshire Show Society Ltd
Parclands House
Raglan
Gwent
NP5 2BX
Tel: 01291 691160
Fax: 01291 691161
Contact: Mrs K Spencer, Management Secretary
Membership: 400
Profile: Agricultural show society. Classes for cattle, sheep, goats, horses, dogs and cage birds. Also horticulture, produce and handicraft. Over 200 trade stands, food hall and craft marquee. The show provides continuous entertainment with a main ring programme and entertainment for children.

Monuments and Buildings Record
Environment and Heritage Service
5–33 Hill Street
Belfast
BT1 2LA
Tel: 01232 543004
Fax: 01232 543111
Contact: T McNamara, MBR Officer
Founded: 1992
Publications: The MBR (promotional leaflet)
Profile: The MBR provides public access to the built heritage database created by the Environment and Heritage Service archaeologists and architects for Northern Ireland.

Moorland Association
Barningham Park
Richmond
North Yorkshire

DL11 7DW
Tel: 01833 621202
Fax: 01833 621298
Contact: Sir Anthony Milbank, Chairman
Founded: 1988
Membership: 250
Profile: Aims to preserve heather moorland in England and Wales by education and promoting awareness of management requirements. Acts as a clearing house for moorland matters.

Moredun Foundation for Animal Health and Welfare

Pentlands Science Park
Bush Loan
Penicuik
Midlothian
EH26 0PZ
Tel: 0131 445 5111
Fax: 0131 445 6235
Contact: Miss Margaret Bennett, Appeals and Marketing Officer
Founded: 1920
Membership: 5,000
Publications: Annual Report; animal disease newsheets; members newsletter
Previous names: Animal Diseases Research Association until 1994
Profile: The Moredun Foundation is dedicated to the belief that the greatest benefit to animal health and welfare is the prevention and elimination of disease. Over the last 75 years they have provided a link between those who raise and tend animals and those working to enhance animal health and welfare through research, leading to new or improved medicines and husbandry techniques. Financial support of relevant research at their own Moredun Research Institute has resulted in the prevention, treatment or increased understanding of many diseases and has saved millions of lives.

Moredun Research Institute

48 Gilmerton Road
Edinburgh
EH17 7JH
Tel: 0131 664 3262
Fax: 0131 664 8001

Morgan Horse Association (UK)

Pampisford Place
Pampisford
Cambridgeshire
CB2 4HG
Tel: 01223 833186
Fax: 01223 837215
Contact: Sonia Archdale, Administrative Officer
Founded: 1993

Membership: 100
Publications: Members newsletter; members magazine
Profile: The primary aim of the MHA (UK) is the promotion and welfare of the Morgan Horse in Great Britain. Active sponsorship of all disciplines in the equine world. Membership is encouraged from the non-horse-owning Morgan enthusiast to the top breeders and showers in the country. Friendly, efficient helpline through regular newsletters and magazines. The HQ is staffed throughout the working week.

Morley Research Centre

Morley
Wymondham
Norfolk
NR18 9DB
Tel: 01953 605511
Fax: 01953 601109
Contact: RJ Cook, Director
Founded: 1908
Membership: 1,000
Publications: Morley Bulletin; Annual Report
Previous names: Norfolk Agricultural Station until 1989
Profile: An independent, farmer owned research group concentrating on application of scientific advances to arable crop production. Their aim is to increase farm profits whilst caring for the environment. Morley specialises in crop protection in arable crops and the transfer of research results into practical information for decision makers.

Morris Federation

36 Foxbury Road
Bromley
Kent
BR1 4DQ
Tel: 0181 460 0623
Contact: E Neill, Secretary
Founded: 1975
Membership: 300
Publications: Members newsletter
Previous names: Women's Morris Federation until 1980
Profile: An association of 300 teams which aims to encourage and maintain interest in the practice of morris dancing by men and women of all ages, to encourage the improvement of standards of dancing among its members and to provide a channel of communication between member sides.

Morris Ring

43 Beaufort Avenue
Cubbington

Leamington Spa
Warwickshire
CV32 7TB
Tel: 01926 330771
Contact: AF Parsons, Secretary

Motoring Organisation's Land Access and Rights Association
PO Box 9
Cannock
Staffordshire
WS11 2FE
Tel: 01543 467218
Fax: 01543 467218
Email: tim@net_shopper.co.uk
Contact: G Garfield, Honorary Secretary
Founded: 1986
Membership: 33,000
Publications: Publications list available

Moulton College
West Street
Moulton
Northampton
NN3 7 RR
Tel: 01604 491131
Fax: 01604 491127
Contact: CR Moody, Principal
Founded: 1921
Publications: Annual Prospectus
Previous names: Northants College of Agriculture until 1989
Profile: Further Education College specialising in education and training for the land-based, construction and furniture industries. The college is set on a 240 ha estate, that includes a commercial farm, garden centre and ice cream enterprise. Residential accommodation for 140 persons. Conference and seminar facilities available.

Mountain Rescue Council
18 Tarnside Fold
Simmondley
Glossop
Derbyshire
SK13 9ND
Tel: 01457 853095
Fax: 01457 853095
Contact: RJ Davies, Honorary Secretary
Founded: 1930
Membership: 2,000
Publications: MRC Handbook
Previous names: Mountain Rescue Committee until 1994

Profile: Supports and provides rescue through its regional organisations, in the mountains of England and Wales.

Mountaineering Council of Ireland
Wilmont Cottage
99 Dunmurry Lane
Belfast
BT17 9JU
Tel: 01232 622019
Fax: 01232 604455
Contact: Dawson Stelfox, Technical Officer
Founded: 1971
Membership: 5,500
Publications: Irish Mountain Log; Rock Climbing Guidebooks to Ireland
Previous names: Federation of Mountaineering Clubs of Ireland until 1985
Profile: The representative body of ramblers, hillwalkers, climbers and mountaineers in both parts of Ireland. Strong environmental involvement, working with environmental bodies, landowners, farmers and government to both improve access and protect the special nature of the countryside in 55 member clubs and about 200 individuals throughout Ireland.

Mountaineering Council of Scotland
4A St Catherine's Road
Perth
PH1 5SE
Tel: 01738 638227
Fax: 01738 442095
Contact: Kevin Howett, National Officer
Founded: 1970
Membership: 1,000
Publications: Publications list available
Profile: The national representative body for climbing and walking clubs, associates, and individual members in Scotland. Deals with safety, mountain rescue, access and conservation, climbing walls, club huts list. General enquiries for mountain walkers and climbers.

Mounted Games Association of Great Britain
Europa Trading Estates
Parsonage Road
Stratton St Margaret
Swindon
Wiltshire
SN3 4RJ
Tel: 01793 820709
Fax: 01793 820716
Contact: Mrs JM Worth, Field Officer
Founded: 1984
Membership: 1,000
Publications: Pony Express (members newsletter)

Profile: The association was founded to provide and promote mounted games competitions for members. Members are encouraged to compete in county teams which provide a main ring attraction at many county shows. The association also organises competitions for teams, pairs and individuals. The association has over 60 county teams in the UK and is affiliated to over 15 nations worldwide.

Murray Grey Cattle Society
PO Box 8
National Agricultural Centre
Stoneleigh Park
Warwickshire
CV8 2LZ
Tel: 01203 696989
Fax: 01203 696716
Contact: Caroline Hadley, Office Administrator
Membership: 80

Mushroom Growers' Association
2 St Pauls Street
Stamford
Lincolnshire
PE9 2BE
Tel: 01780 66888
Fax: 01780 66558
Contact: Miss T C U Johnston, Director
Founded: 1945
Membership: 600
Publications: The Mushroom Journal
Profile: The professional trade organisation for mushroom growers in the UK and Northern Ireland. Additionally there are members from 60 other countries. Additional membership categories include trade suppliers, scientists and academic institutions. Activities include political lobbying (UK and EU), dissemination of information to members on all matters affecting the industry, conferences, seminars, production of monthly journal. It is the central reference point for the UK mushroom industry.

Myerscough College
Myerscough Hall
Bilsborrow
Preston
Lancashire
PR3 0RY
Tel: 01995 640611
Fax: 01995 640842
Email: myersco@demon.co.uk
Contact: Stuart Davidson, Marketing Assistant
Founded: 1894
Publications: Prospectus and Course Leaflets

Previous names: Lancashire College of Agriculture and Horticulture until 1993
Profile: Myerscough College offers courses from foundation up to Higher National Diploma and degree level in agriculture, horticulture, arboriculture, landscape practice, environmental science, farriery and blacksmithing, floristry, sportsturf, ecology and conservation, leisure studies, animal care, veterinary nursing, equine studies and mechanisation.

National Association for Environmental Education
Wolverhampton University
Walsall Campus
Gorway Road
Walsall
West Midlands
WS1 3BD
Tel: 01922 31200
Fax: 01922 31200
Contact: Brian Milton, General Secretary
Founded: 1960
Membership: 1,500
Publications: Environmental Education (journal)
Previous names: National Rural Studies Association until 1971
Profile: NAEE is a teachers' organisation promoting environmental education in schools and colleges.

National Association for Outdoor Education
12 St Andrews Churchyard
Penrith
Cumbria
CA11 7YE
Tel: 01768 865113
Fax: 01768 891914
Contact: Heather Heron, Administrator
Founded: 1979
Membership: 900
Publications: Newsletter; publications list available
Profile: The NAOE aims to advance education in and through outdoor education. It is a membership organisation open to professional and voluntary leaders, teachers and trainers who seek to advance the skills, knowledge and understanding of young people through outdoor education. Through its members varied involvement in outdoor challenging experiences the NAOE promotes the development of young people. It works with all voluntary bodies, statutory education and youth services, government ministries and agencies and local government and training agencies to contribute to the continuing high standard of value and safety in the field.

National Association for the Support of Small Schools

The Cottage
Little Barningham
Norfolk
NR11 7LN
Tel: 01263 577553
Contact: Mrs Molly Stiles, National Co-ordinator
Founded: 1978
Membership: 500
Publications: Bi-annual newsletter; information sheets and booklets
Profile: They aim to provide a voice and a link for those who believe that small schools, particularly in rural areas, have educational and social roles to perform and are too precious to lose.

National Association of Agricultural Contractors

Huts Corner
Tilford Road
Hindhead
Surrey
GU26 6SF
Tel: 01428 605360
Fax: 01428 606531
Contact: SE Dickens

National Association of Breeders Services

Avoncroft Sires
Sugarbrook
Stoke Prior
Bromsgrove
Worcestershire
B60 3AS
Tel: 01527 831481
Fax: 01527 879784
Contact: Margaret Rose, Executive Secretary
Founded: 1978
Membership: 11
Previous names: National Association of Semen Suppliers until 1984
Profile: An amalgam of semen embryo and DIY companies to speak with one voice on matters of importance to the future of the industry.

National Association of British and Irish Millers

21 Arlington Street
London
SW1A 1RN
Tel: 0171 493 2521
Fax: 0171 493 6785
Contact: Alex Waugh, Trade Policy Manager
Founded: 1878
Membership: 34
Publications: Facts and Figures

Profile: Trade association for the UK flour milling industry which uses 5 million tonnes of wheat each year to produce 4 million tonnes of flour.

National Association of British Market Authorities

NABMA House
21 Tarnside Road
Orrell
Wigan
Lancashire
WN5 8RN
Tel: 01695 623860
Fax: 01695 623860
Contact: John Edwards, General Secretary
Founded: 1919
Publications: Annual Report
Profile: The object of the society is to be a medium of communication between members and between the association and departments of the government and other public bodies on matters of common interest affecting the administration of markets, fairs, abbatoirs or cold stores.

National Association of Cider Makers

6 Catherine Street
London
WC2B 5JJ
Tel: 0171 836 2460
Fax: 0171 836 0580
Contact: RD Price, Secretary
Founded: 1920

National Association of Farms for Schools

National Farmers Union
Agriculture House
164 Shaftesbury Avenue
London
WC2H 8HL
Tel: 0171 331 7304
Fax: 0171 331 7382
Contact: Keith Boltman, Secretary
Founded: 1995
Membership: 160
Publications: Members Directory
Profile: Association of NFU membership with farms open to educational visits, who have agreed to a charter of good practice.

National Association of Farriers, Blacksmiths and Agricultural Engineers

Avenue B
10th Street
National Agricultural Centre
Stoneleigh Park
Warwickshire
CV8 2LG

Tel: 01203 696595
Fax: 01203 696708
Contact: Jackie Webb, National Organiser
Founded: 1902
Membership: 1,000
Publications: Forge Trade Magazine
Profile: The National Association was formed in 1905 by bringing together the several bodies then in being. The association promotes the study, practice and knowledge of the trades it represents, and encourages education with clinics and workshops, competitions, trade shows, demonstrations and social events. The association works hard towards its aim of uniting farriers and veterinary surgeons in the common cause of horse welfare.

National Association of Field Studies Officers
Stibbington Centre for Environmental Education
Great North Road
Stibbington
Peterborough
Cambridgeshire
PE8 6LP
Tel: 01780 782386
Fax: 01780 783835
Contact: Rosie Edwards, Chairman
Founded: 1969
Membership: 250
Publications: Publications list available
Profile: The National Association of Field Studies Officers is a voluntary organisation which aims to promote and encourage field studies. Membership is available to those who are employed in or have an interest in field studies centres. Benefits of membership include a regular newsletter, and annual conference, termly training events and access to a range of member services.

National Association of Fisheries and Angling Consultatives
30 Ainsdale Way
Goldsworth Park
Woking
Surrey
GU21 3PP
Tel: 01483 769736
Fax: 01483 769736
Contact: Mark Hatcher, Director
Founded: 1986
Membership: 47
Publications: Members newsletter
Previous names: Standing Conference of Consultatives
Profile: NAFAC members are consultative organisations representing local and regional fisheries and angling interests throughout the country. NAFAC is recognised by the Environment Agency as the national body representative of local consultatives, and by the CCPR as a governing body of angling. About 370,000 anglers belong to clubs and associations represented by consultatives in membership of NAFAC. Chief concerns are the impact on fisheries of water abstraction, water quality, flood defence, navigation and fish eating birds, and of the effect on angling of the rating of fisheries, anti-angling campaigns, and increased demand for access to water space.

National Association of Free Range Egg Producers
Upton Farm Shop
Alkham
Dover
Kent
Profile: We have been unable to contact this organisation. The details given are unconfirmed.

National Association of Licensed Opencast Operators
2nd Floor
The Bigg Market
Newcastle upon Tyne
NE1 1UN
Tel: 01740 652611
Fax: 01740 652583
Contact: Mr IAC Parkin, Vice Chairman
Founded: 1978
Membership: 15
Profile: NALOO exists to represent the interests of companies working opencast coal under licence, previously from the British Coal Corporation and currently from the Coal Authority.

National Association of Local Councils
109 Great Russell Street
London
WC1B 3LD
Tel: 0171 637 1865
Fax: 0171 436 7451
Contact: Mr Paul Clayden, Director
Founded: 1947
Membership: 7,500
Previous names: National Association of Parish Councils until 1972
Profile: NALC is the representative body for town, parish and community councils in England and Wales, with about 85% of all such councils in membership. It provides a legal and general advisory service and acts to promote and protect the interests of its members.

National Association of Master Bakers

21 Baldock Street
Ware
Hertfordshire
SG12 9DH
Tel: 01920 468061
Fax: 01920 46163
Contact: David Smith, Manager
Membership: 1,800
Profile: The national trade association for the craft section of the baking industry.

National Association of Poultry Suppliers

1 Belgrove
Tunbridge Wells
Kent
TN1 1YW
Tel: 01892 541412
Fax: 01892 535462
Contact: Mr JE Fuller, Secretary
Founded: 1939
Membership: 20
Previous names: National Federation of Wholesale Poultry Merchants until 1995
Profile: Represents wholesale poultry merchants and distributors within the UK. Willing to offer spokesmen on the wholesale poultry trade, including supplies and prices.

National Association of Principal Agricultural Education Officers

The Secretary
Brooksby College, Leicestershire
Brooksby
Melton Mowbray
Leicestershire
LE14 2LJ
Tel: 01664 434291
Fax: 01664 434291
Contact: John Gusterson, Secretary
Membership: 35
Profile: Membership is made up of principals and chief executives of agricultural colleges and the objectives are to support them and their colleges in the provision of land-based programmes and to assist the long term development and viability of the rural business sector.

National Association of Public Golf Courses

35 Sinclair Grove
London
NW11 9JH
Tel: 0181 458 5433
Contact: Mr K A Witte, Honorary Secretary
Founded: 1927
Membership: 110
Publications: Reference and Yearbook

Profile: NAPGC provides national and regional competitive golf for all ages and handicaps within the rules of golf. It organises biennial international tournaments. It provides representation of golf course management at the National Union and provides help and advice to enable people to play golf.

National Association of Re-enactment Societies

507 Rochford Gardens
Slough
Berkshire
SL2 5XF
Tel: 01753 521187
Contact: Chip Guarente, Public Relations Officer
Founded: 1991
Publications: Members newsletter
Profile: An umbrella organisation encompassing most of the major historical re-enactment groups in the UK covering all periods of history from the Romans through to World War 2.

National Association of Seed Potato Merchants

31 Keats Road
Copsewood
Coventry
Warwickshire
CV2 5JZ
Tel: 01203 650005
Fax: 01203 650005
Contact: ABS Paine, Secretary
Founded: 1940
Membership: 224
Profile: Formed at a time crucial to Britain when it was recognised by Lord Woolton, Minister of Food, that an efficient means of supplying healthy seed potatoes was essential to food supplies. Seed potato merchants continue to provide a high level of service to agriculture. Almost all seed potatoes traded in the UK are handled by merchants who are members of NASPM who sell under NASPM copyright sale conditions which have long been recognised and accepted by those concerned and are registered with the Office of Fair Trading. Regular educational and social events are organised for members and their staffs, and liaison with other agricultural trade bodies and government departments is maintained on a regular basis.

National Association of Speciality Food and Drink Producers

Stoke Dry Manor
Rutland
LE15 9JA
Tel: 01572 823588

Fax: 01572 322343
Contact: RJ Salmon, Secretary

National Association of Specimen Groups
10 Cape Street
Hyson Green
Nottingham
NG7 5AB
Profile: We have been unable to contact this
organisation. The details given are unconfirmed.

National Association of Teleworking
The Island House
Midsomer Norton
Bath
BA3 2HL
Tel: 01761 413869
Fax: 01761 419348
Email: 100063.462@compuserve.com
Contact: Andrew Lamb, Secretary/Director
Founded: 1992
Membership: 1,000
Publications: Journal of Teleworking; Telework
UK (newsletter)
Profile: NAT was formed in 1992 to foster and
promote best practice in the development and
application of teleworking and associated flexible
working practices. Membership is open to
companies, organisations and interested
individuals.

**National Association of UK River Protection
   Societies**
The Old House Cottage
Carters Lane
Old Woking
Surrey
GU22 8JQ
Tel: 01483 765462
Contact: Tony Jacques

National Birds of Prey Centre
Newent
Gloucestershire
GL18 1JJ
Tel: 01531 820286
Fax: 01531 821389

National Caravan Council Ltd
Catherine House
Victoria Road
Aldershot
Hampshire
GU11 1SS
Tel: 01252 318251
Fax: 01252 22596
Contact: Paul H Surridge, Director General
Founded: 1939

Membership: 950
Publications: Caravan Business; Annual Review

National Cattle Association
60 Kenilworth Road
Leamington Spa
Warwickshire
CV32 6JY
Tel: 01926 337378
Fax: 01926 334636
Contact: Mr Rowland W Kershaw-Dalby,
Secretary
Founded: 1906
Membership: 20,000
Publications: The Cattle Farmer
Previous names: National Cattle Breeders
Association until 1995
Profile: Representing the interests of the cattle
industry.

National Caving Association
Monomark House
27 Old Gloucester Street
London
WC1N 3XX
Tel: 01639 849519
Contact: FS Baguley, Honorary Secretary
Founded: 1969
Membership: 380
Profile: The association is a federation of five
regional caving councils and four specialist
organisations – as the governing body for the
sport, one of its major responsibilities is
conservation through the work of the
conservation officer and its conservation and
access committee. Activities include the active
promotion of cave conservation, production and
distribution of information leaflets, liaison with
national government and voluntary organisations
and support for the regional caving councils
where necessary on local matters.

**National Centre for Toxic and Persistent
   Substances**
Environment Agency
Kingfisher House
Goldhay Way
Orton Goldhay
Peterborough
PE2 5ZR
Tel: 01733 371811
Fax: 01733 464685
Contact: DJ Tester, Toxic Substances Manager
Founded: 1994
Publications: Publications list available
Previous names: National Rivers Authority TAPS
Centre until 1996

Profile: The TAPS centre provides a team dedicated to national water quality issues relating to toxic and persistent substances. The centre covers four key areas; international commitments to reduce the quantities of certain hazardous substances and nutrients entering the sea; pesticides and persistent substances in the aquatic environment; environmental toxicology and eutrophication and toxic algae.

National Compost Development Association
c/o University of Leeds
Department of Civil Engineering
Leeds
LS2 9JT
Tel: 0113 233 2298
Fax: 0113 233 2308
Email: ncda@leeds.ac.uk
Contact: Stuart Brown, Honorary Secretary
Publications: Composting (newsletter)

National Consumer Council
20 Grosvenor Gardens
London
SW1W 0DH
Tel: 0171 730 3469
Fax: 0171 730 0191
Contact: Press Office
Founded: 1975

National Council of Civic Trust Societies
24 Lower Street
Harnham
Salisbury
Wiltshire
SP2 8EY
Tel: 01722 320115
Profile: We have been unable to contact this organisation. The details given are unconfirmed.

National Dairy Council
5–7 John Princes Street
London
W1M 0AP
Tel: 0171 499 7822
Fax: 0171 408 1353
Email: all@ndc.telme.com
Contact: Anita Bourne, Press Officer
Founded: 1920
Publications: Dairy Mirror; Dairy Education; numerous educational and consumer leaflets
Previous names: National Milk Publicity Council until 1960
Profile: The NDC promotes milk and dairy products, and collates industry research, on behalf of dairy farmers and the majority of dairies in the UK.

National Dairy Producers Association
Perthi Mwyar
Hayscastle
Haverfordwest
Pembrokeshire
SA62 5NY
Tel: 01348 840789
Contact: Graham Davies

National Dairymens' Association
19 Cornwall Terrace
London
NW1 4QP
Tel: 0171 935 4562
Fax: 0171 487 4734
Contact: AD Moxon, Chief Executive and Secretary
Founded: 1937
Membership: 2,800
Publications: Milk Industry International
Profile: To represent and promote the liquid milk and fresh product sectors of the dairy industry.

National Egg Marketing Association Ltd
Suite 101 Albany House
324–326 Regent Street
London
W1R 5AA
Tel: 0171 580 7172
Fax: 0171 580 7082
Profile: NEMAL represents the UK egg packing industry.

National Egg Marketing Board
Suite 101 Albany House
324–326 Regent Street
London
W1R 5AA
Tel: 0171 580 7172
Fax: 0171 580 7082

National Equine Defence League
Oak Tree Farm
Wetheral Shields
Carlisle
Cumbria
CA4 8JA
Tel: 01228 560082
Fax: 01228 560985
Contact: Frank E Tebbut, Organising Secretary
Founded: 1909
Membership: 2,000
Publications: Annual Report

National Equine Welfare Council
c/o Glenda Spooner Trust
Emmetts Hill
Whichford

Shipston-on-Stour
Warwickshire
CV36 5PG
Tel: 01608 684683
Fax: 01608 684802
Contact: Honorary Chairman
Founded: 1977
Membership: 42
Profile: The objects of the society are to identify areas of abuse to equines and to provide a forum for joint discussion between member societies on matters of national and mutual interest and importance affecting their welfare; to co-ordinate methods of dealing effectively with instances of abuse, neglect, ill-usage, cruelty or malpractice; to liaise with government, police, press, the industrial sector and other interested parties and to disseminate and collate information and educational matter concerning equine welfare.

National Farm Seed Industries
Sales Office
Sleaford
Lincolnshire
NG34 7HA
Tel: 01529 304511
Fax: 01529 303908

National Farmers' Union, The
164 Shaftesbury Avenue
London
WC2H 8HC
Tel: 0171 331 7200
Fax: 0171 331 7313
Contact: Richard Macdonald, Director General
Founded: 1908
Membership: 120,000
Publications: British Farmer, NFU regional journals, Poultry Forum, NFU Countryside
Profile: The NFU represents farmers, growers and those with an interest in the countryside in England and Wales.

National Farmers' Union of Scotland
Rural Centre
West Mains
Ingliston
Newbridge
Midlothian
EH28 8LT
Tel: 0131 335 3111
Fax: 0131 335 3800
Contact: TJ Brady, Chief Executive
Founded: 1913
Membership: 13,500
Publications: Farming Leader Update; information sheets; briefing notes

Profile: The union's role is to defend the rural economy, vigorously promote the interests of Scottish Agriculture, influence events to secure the welfare of members and to get the farming industry's positive messages across to the decision makers, consumers and school children. Seventy-five secretaries with offices across Scotland serve individual members' needs, whilst at national level headquarters staff and office bearers are in regular contact with Scottish Office officials, other UK bodies and European organisations.

National Federation of Anglers
Halliday House
Eggington Junction
Hilton
Derbyshire
DE65 6GU
Tel: 01283 734735
Fax: 01283 734799
Contact: KE Watkins, Chief Administration Officer
Founded: 1903
Membership: 500

National Federation of Badger Groups
15 Cloisters House
8 Battersea Park Road
London
SW8 4BG
Tel: 0171 498 3220
Fax: 0171 498 4459
Contact: Elaine King, Conservation Officer
Founded: 1986
Membership: 14,000
Profile: Promotes the welfare, conservation and protection of badgers, their setts and habitats; are committed to develop and support a network of voluntary groups throughout the UK; to work closely with other wildlife organisations and individuals; campaign to improve protection for badgers, their setts and habitats and to encourage education concerning badgers; to represent and support approximately 90 local badger groups; to provide professional advice and information on all badger issues. Their work includes sett surveying, recording and monitoring; rehabilitating orphaned and injured badgers, giving advice to landowners, public, statutory agencies and developers, police and others involved with badgers.

National Federation of Bus Users
18 Little Southsea Street
Southsea
Hampshire
PO5 3RS
Tel: 01705 814493
Fax: 01705 863080

Contact: Dr Caroline Cahn, Chair
Founded: 1985
Publications: Bus Stop Jottings

National Federation of City Farms
The Green House
Hereford Street
Bedminster
Bristol
BS3 4NA
Tel: 0117 923 1800
Fax: 0117 923 1900
Email: 102404.14@compuserve.com
Contact: Chris Lillington, Administrator
Founded: 1980
Publications: Handbook of Polytunnel Growing
Profile: The NFCF is a national charity and company limited by guarantee. The federation mission is to promote and support sustainable regeneration through community managed farming and gardening.

National Federation of Meat & Food Traders
1 Belgrove
Tunbridge Wells
Kent
TN1 1YW
Tel: 01892 541412
Fax: 01892 535462
Contact: Mr JE Fuller, Director
Founded: 1888
Publications: Meat Trader
Profile: The federation represents the interests of thousands of independent retail butchers throughout England and Wales plus a number of small slaughterers and manufacturers linked with retail business. It is willing to offer spokesmen to give views on matters affecting members' business interests including those of supplies and prices.

National Federation of Sub-Postmasters
Evelyn House
22 Windlesham Gardens
Shoreham-by-Sea
West Sussex
BN43 5AZ
Tel: 01273 452324
Fax: 01273 465403
Contact: Paul Heasman, Assistant General Secretary
Founded: 1897
Membership: 15,000
Publications: The Subpostmaster
Profile: The federation, founded in 1897, is the only organisation recognised by the Post Office to negotiate on behalf of sub-postmasters. With over 100 branches nationally, and holding regular meetings and social events, it provides sub-postmasters with a truly open forum to discuss issues of concern or seek support from like-minded professionals. As well as representation and companionship, membership can provide insurance, security systems and a range of business services at special rates. The federation is also pleased to offer advice and assistance to those wishing to purchase a business with a Post Office.

National Federation of Women's Institutes
104 New Kings Road
London
SW6 4LY
Tel: 0171 371 9300
Fax: 0171 736 3652
Contact: Jana Osborne, General Manager
Founded: 1915
Membership: 272,650
Publications: Home and Country
Profile: The National Federation of Women's Institutes is a non-sectarian and non-party political organisation. The organisation is unique in offering its members their own adult residential lifelong learning centre, Denman College in Oxfordshire where four of the NFWI sub-committees are based. There are a total of 8,341 individual WIs throughout England, Wales and the islands.

National Federation of Young Farmers' Clubs (England and Wales)
YFC Centre
National Agricultural Centre
Stoneleigh Park
Warwickshire
CV8 2LG
Tel: 01203 696544
Fax: 01203 696559
Contact: Marie Peck, Rural Programming Officer
Founded: 1932
Membership: 28,000
Profile: Young Farmers' Clubs seek to meet the needs of rural young people through educational, training and social programmes which encourage community involvement and concern for our environment. Through participative youthwork they enable young people to make their own decisions both within YFC and beyond on issues which affect their lives.

National Ferret Welfare Society
6 St Edmond Road
Bedford
MK40 2NQ
Tel: 01234 272769

Contact: Membership Secretary
Founded: 1986
Membership: 600
Publications: Members newsletter; basic information booklet
Profile: The NFWS is primarily about improving the care of ferrets in the UK. It covers both working and pet ferrets. It holds details of vets known to be used to dealing with ferrets and has several vets regarded as experts in the field of ferret care. It welcomes members of all ages and has a number of overseas members. Membership includes insurance which covers ferret owners whether out rabbiting or attending shows.

National Field Archery Society
67 Seaburn Road
Toton
Beeston
Nottinghamshire
NG9 6HN
Tel: 01602 724615
Contact: Mr R Bickerstaffe, Honorary Secretary
Founded: 1973
Membership: 3,300
Publications: Members newsletter
Profile: The NFAS exists to foster and promote field archery as a sport in which archers enjoy themselves by shooting at inanimate objects of suitable sizes, placed at distances unknown to them, set in natural terrain, populated by trees and shrubbery with few or no clear laned targets. The society holds annual national championships. Scottish and Welsh championships are also held annually.

National Foaling Bank
Meretown Stud
Newport
Shropshire
TF10 8BX
Tel: 01952 811234
Fax: 01952 811202
Contact: Miss Johanna E Vardon, Director
Founded: 1965
Membership: 1,172
Publications: Stallion Guide
Profile: The National Foaling Bank provides an adoption service for orphan foals by matching them with a suitable foster mare which has lost its own foal. Help and advice is available on a 24 hour a day basis.

National Food Alliance
5–11 Worship Street
London
EC2A 2BH

Tel: 0171 628 2442
Fax: 0171 628 9329
Contact: Jeanette Longfield, Co-ordinator
Founded: 1985
Membership: 66
Profile: The National Food Alliance aims to enable the people of the UK to fulfil their potential through food policies and practices that enhance public health, improve the working and living environment, and enrich society.

National Food Survey Committee
Ministry of Agriculture, Fisheries and Food
Room 513 Whitehall Place (West Block)
London
SW1A 2HH
Tel: 0171 270 8563
Fax: 0171 270 8558
Email: s.dixon@esfood.maff.gov.uk
Contact: Sheila Dixon, Secretary
Founded: 1948
Publications: National Food Survey
Profile: The National Food Survey Committee is an advisory body to the Ministry of Agriculture, Fisheries and Food. Its purpose is to keep the National Food Survey under continuous review, to recommend such changes as appear desirable in the survey and to advise on the publication of annual and other reports.

National Forest Company
Department of the Environment
Enterprise Glade
Bath Lane
Moira
Swadlincote
Derbyshire
DE12 7PS
Tel: 01283 551211
Fax: 01283 552844
Contact: Susan Bell, Chief Executive
Founded: 1995
Publications: Annual Report; Corporate Plan; Forest News; Farmers News
Previous names: National Forest Development Office until 1995
Profile: The National Forest Company is a non-departmental public body, with a board of directors appointed by the Secretary of State for the Environment. The task of the company is to implement the National Forest Strategy, i.e. to create a new 200 square mile forest covering parts of Staffordshire, Derbyshire and Leicestershire. The company is testing an innovative approach to forest creation, involving a competitive tendering scheme into which landowners and others can bid for subsidy support for tree planting.

National Game Dealers Association

38 Spring Street
London
W2 1JA
Tel: 0171 224 9069
Fax: 0171 224 9061
Contact: Keith Taylor, Director
Publications: The Code of Good Game Handling
Practice
Profile: The NGDA is a trade organisation which
works to promote the interests of game dealers
and processors within the UK. It aims to raise
standards in the industry through liaison with
government and others.

National Grid Company plc

National Grid House
Kirby Corner Road
Coventry
Warwickshire
CV4 8JY
Tel: 01203 537777

National Groundwater and Contaminated Land Centre

Environment Agency
Olton Court
10 Warwick Road
Olton
Solihull
West Midlands
B92 7HX
Tel: 0121 711 2324
Fax: 0121 711 5926
Contact: RC Harris
Founded: 1996
Profile: The Environment Agency is the premier
regulatory body for the environment in England
and Wales. The National Groundwater and
Contaminated Land Centre acts as a centre of
specialist technical advice to both internal
colleagues and external bodies on all matters
pertaining to groundwater and contaminated
land.

National Gypsy Council

Greenacres Caravan Park
Hapsford
Helsby
Warrington
WA6 0JS
Tel: 01928 723138
Fax: 01928 723138
Contact: Hughie Smith, President
Founded: 1966
Membership: 10,000
Publications: Publications list available

Profile: An all gypsy, voluntary organisation
(membership at 10,000 families) dedicated to
representing the interests of gypsies as defined
in all matters relating to caravan site provision
and management, education and social welfare.

National Hedgelaying Society

YFC Centre
National Agricultural Centre
Stoneleigh Park
Warwickshire
CV8 2LG
Tel: 01203 696544
Fax: 01203 696559
Contact: FE Shields, Secretary
Founded: 1978
Membership: 183
Publications: Hedgelaying Explained
Profile: The object of the society is to promote
the craft of hedgelaying and other agricultural
crafts associated with the maintenance of field
boundaries.

National Heritage Memorial Fund

10 St James's Street
London
SW1A 1EF
Tel: 0171 930 0963
Fax: 0171 930 0968
Contact: Lydia Davies, Research and
Communications Officer
Founded: 1980
Publications: General information and guidelines
on applying to the fund
Profile: The heritage lottery fund preserves,
restores and improves landscape, buildings,
collections and other items of special importance
to the heritage of the peoples of England,
Scotland, Wales and Northern Ireland for
enjoyment of local communities throughout the
UK.

National Horse Brass Society

2 Blue Barn Cottage
Blue Barn Lane
Weybridge
Surrey
KT13 0NH
Tel: 01932 354193
Contact: Mr JV Elworthy, Secretary
Founded: 1976
Publications: Society journal, members
newsletter
Profile: Aims and objects of the society are: to
become the accepted national authority on the
decoration of the horse harness; to keep
carefully maintained archives for use by
members; to publish annually, two issues of the

society journal and two newsletters for free issue to members and to produce annually a society horse brass for free distribution to members.

National Horse Education and Training Company Ltd

CAPITB Ltd
2nd Floor
The Burgess Building
The Green
Stafford
ST17 4BL
Tel: 01785 227399
Fax: 01785 229015
Contact: Tracy Bramley, Industry Training Co-ordinator
Founded: 1985
Publications: Newsletter; information leaflet
Previous names: Joint National Horse Education and Training Council until 1995
Profile: The NHETC is an independent company set up to represent the interests of all sectors of the horse industry. It is recognised by the government as the industry training organisation and lead body and is responsible for the following key areas: identifying what training is needed by every sector of the horse industry; establishing and maintaining the standards of training; providing feedback to government of the industry's training and development needs; acting as a definitive source for training information throughout the industry; and ensuring every sector of the industry has access to relevant quality training.

National Horse Register

PO Box 14
Brixham
Devon
TQ5 9QJ
Tel: 01803 855775
Fax: 01803 855775
Contact: Robin Hooker, Proprietor
Founded: 1993
Profile: Maintenance of a database and photographic record of UK horses and ponies to prevent theft and illegal sales, and to assist in the finding of stolen horses and ponies through full liaison with the police and HM Customs. Membership fee of £10 per annum.

National Housewives Association Ltd

12 Chestnut Drive
Pinner
Middlesex
HA5 1LY
Contact: Mary Sheley, Honorary Secretary

Profile: We have been unable to contact this organisation. The details given are unconfirmed.

National Institute of Agricultural Botany

Huntingdon Road
Cambridge
CB3 0LE
Tel: 01223 276381
Fax: 01223 277602
Contact: PT Nelson, Information Resources Manager
Founded: 1919
Membership: 4,000
Publications: Variety handbooks; Annual Report; Disease identification handbooks; journal – Plant Varieties and Seeds
Profile: NIAB works mainly in the areas of agriculture and horticulture and has the objective of providing services and information of the highest quality to governments, levy boards, fellows of the institute, farmers and business. The institute offers a full range of crop variety and seeds services, including plant variety registration, variety performance trials, seed testing, laboratory analysis, seed certification, statistical analysis, computing training, information dissemination and research in a wide range of disciplines. Consultancy is available on a confidential basis.

National Light Horse Breeding Society

96 High Street
Edenbridge
Kent
TN8 5AR
Tel: 01732 866277
Fax: 01732 867464
Contact: Mr Gerald W Evans, Chief Executive
Founded: 1884
Membership: 6,000
Previous names: The Hunter Improvement Society until 1982
Profile: Established to promote and improve the breeding of horses in this country.

National Market Traders Federation

Hampton House
Hawshaw Lane
Hoyland
Barnsley
South Yorkshire
S74 0HA
Tel: 01226 749021
Fax: 01226 740329
Contact: Mr DE Feeny, General Secretary
Founded: 1899
Membership: 27,000

Publications: Federation News
Profile: A non-profit making trade association looking after the interests of market traders.

National Mountain Centre
The Sports Council
Plas-y-Brenin
Capel Curig
Betws-y-Coed
Gwynedd
LL24 0ET
Tel: 016904 214
Fax: 016904 394
Contact: Derek Mayes, Development Officer
Founded: 1955
Publications: Brochures available
Profile: A Sports Council National Centre of Excellence. The Mountain Centre runs outdoor training courses for national governing bodies and a range of taster and expert events. Residential accommodation and function support facilities are available as well as highly qualified and experienced staff for bespoke events.

National Outdoor Events Association
7 Hamilton Way
Wallington
Surrey
SM6 9NJ
Tel: 0181 669 8121
Fax: 0181 647 1128
Contact: John W Barton, General Secretary
Founded: 1979
Membership: 173
Publications: NOEA Code of Practice for Outdoor Events; NOEA Members Yearbook
Previous names: Association of Professional Outdoor Show Organisers until 1987
Profile: NOEA has a growing membership representing buyers and suppliers of equipment and services, entertainment agencies and consultants, together with practitioners generally in the world of outdoor events.

National Poisons Information Service (Edinburgh)
The Royal Infirmary of Edinburgh
Scottish Poisons Information Bureau
Edinburgh
EH3 9YW
Tel: 0131 536 2300
Fax: 0131 536 2304
Email: 101574.424@compuserve.com
Contact: Alison M Good, Manager
Founded: 1963
Profile: The bureau provides information to medical professionals on poisoning with drugs,

agrochemicals and industrial chemicals, plants, household products and toiletries. It also maintains an on-line database of 11,000 products and substances available to NHS users. They do not give information to the public directly.

National Poisons Unit (England)
Guy's Hospital
St Thomas Street
London
SE11 1LA
Tel: 0171 955 5000
Fax: 0171 635 1053

National Poisons Unit (Northern Ireland)
Royal Victoria Hospital
Regional Drug and Poisons Info Centre
Belfast
BT12 6BH
Tel: 01232 240503
Fax: 01232 248030

National Pony Society
102 High Street
Alton
Hampshire
GU34 1CN
Tel: 01420 88333
Fax: 01420 80599
Contact: Mrs L Wilkins, Secretary
Founded: 1893
Publications: Publications list available

National Proficiency Tests Council
Avenue J
National Agricultural Centre
Stoneleigh Park
Warwickshire
CV8 2LG
Tel: 01203 696553
Fax: 01203 696128
Email: Mike@NPTC.demon.co.uk
Contact: David Owen, Technical Officer
Publications: Course and test leaflets
Profile: The council is a nationally recognised awarding body for the land-based and food industries. It provides the industries with standardised awards that provide for a variety of roles. The awards range from Category Based Proficiency Tests to Certificates of Competence and have recently come to include National Vocational Qualifications (NVQs). NPTC schemes are delivered via a wide network of County Proficiency Tests Committees (CPTCs), agents and approved assessment centres. The delivery network is quality assured through assessors and verifiers

giving the awards a constant standard across the country. NPTC became ISO 9002 approved on 22nd June 1995.

National Reining Horse Association of Great Britain
Burnt Ash
Sheep Street Lane
Etchingham
East Sussex
TN19 7AY
Tel: 01580 819208
Profile: We have been unable to contact this organisation. The details given are unconfirmed.

National Remote Sensing Centre
Delta House
Southwood Crescent
Southwood
Hampshire
Tel: 01252 541464

National Renderers Association
Swan Business Centre
Fishers Lane
London
W4 1RX
Tel: 0181 995 1331
Fax: 0181 742 1717
Contact: Mrs Julie Brace-Maclean, Director

National Rural Enterprise Centre
Royal Agricultural Society of England
National Agricultural Centre
Stoneleigh Park
Warwickshire
CV8 2RR
Tel: 01203 690691
Fax: 01203 696770
Email: NREC@midnet.com
Internet: http://www.warwickshire.org/NREC
Contact: Simon Berry, Director
Founded: 1989
Publications: Publications list available
Previous names: Rural Enterprise Unit
Profile: Through projects which put ideas into practice at local level, research and information transfer, the centre promotes a living and working countryside, finding ways to help rural communities improve and strengthen local economies. NREC projects investigate critical new issues affecting rural areas and suggest appropriate action. Recent research includes: the opportunities offered by developments in information technology and telecommunications; rural tourism; and constraints on women entering the rural labour market. The NREC runs

seminars, publishes a newsletter, guides and research reports.

National Seeds Development Organisation Ltd
Newton Hall
Newton Village
Cambridge
CB2 5PS
Profile: We have been unable to contact this organisation. The details given are unconfirmed.

National Sheep Association
The Sheep Centre
Malvern
Worcestershire
WR13 6PH
Tel: 01684 892661
Fax: 01684 892663
Contact: Mr John Thorley, Chief Executive
Founded: 1892
Membership: 11,000
Publications: British Sheep; The Sheep Farmer
Previous names: National Sheep Breeders Association until 1969
Profile: An organisation funded by members' subscriptions which involves itself in all aspects of the sheep industry in its role of representing its members' interests. This involves political lobbying activity and an involvement in practical/technical advice and monitoring.

National Small Woods Association
Hall Farm House
Preston Capes
Daventry
Northamptonshire
NN11 3TA
Tel: 01327 361387
Fax: 01327 361387
Contact: Amanda Giles, Development Director
Founded: 1989
Membership: 400
Publications: Heartwood; Annual Conference Proceedings
Profile: NSWA promotes the conservation and management of small and neglected woods through: influencing policy; market development; setting standards for training and networking and information exchange.

National Society Against Factory Farming Ltd
41 Mercator Road
Lewisham
London
SE13 5EH
Profile: We have been unable to contact this organisation. The details given are unconfirmed.

**National Society for Clean Air and
Environmental Protection**
136 North Street
Brighton
East Sussex
BN1 1RG
Tel: 01273 326313
Fax: 01273 735802
Email: cleanair@mistral.co.uk
Contact: Secretary General
Founded: 1899
Membership: 1,500
Profile: NSCA membership is largely made up of
organisations with a direct involvement in
environmental protection: industry, local
authorities, universities and colleges,
consultancies and regulatory authorities. NSCA
aims to promote clean air through the reduction
of air, water and land pollution, noise and other
contaminants, while having due regard for other
aspects of the environment. The society
examines questions of environmental policy from
an air quality perspective and aims to place them
in a broader social and economic context.

**National Society of Allotment and Leisure
Gardeners Ltd**
O'Dell House
Hunters Road
Corby
Northamptonshire
NN17 5JE
Tel: 01536 266576
Fax: 01536 264509
Contact: Mr Geoff Stokes, Secretary
Founded: 1930
Membership: 103,000
Publications: Allotment and Leisure Gardener
Profile: The society aims to ensure that facilities
are made available to all who desire to follow the
recreation of gardening and endeavours to instil a
better understanding of the fact that gardening is
a recreation for the mind and body as well as a
source of economic wealth both to the individual
and nation.

National Society of Master Thatchers
20 The Laurels
Tetsworth
Thame
Oxfordshire
OX9 7BH
Tel: 01844 281568
Contact: Mrs C Jayne Ashton-Moore, Secretary
Founded: 1967
Membership: 100
Profile: The National Society of Master

Thatchers is the only trade organisation within
the thatching industry operating on a national
basis. Formed in 1967, it has experience
spanning nearly 30 years in dealing not only with
thatching but all other matters relating to the
industry. The membership comprises master
thatchers who have proved that their work is of
the highest standard. The aims of the society
include promoting a high standard of
craftmanship and business integrity and
providing an information service for all interested
parties such as owners, builders, surveyors,
architects, etc. on all matters connected with
thatching, including choice of materials,
construction, insurance and maintenance.

National Stallion Association
School Farm
School Lane
Pickmere
Knutsford
Cheshire
WA16 6RD
Tel: 01565 733222
Contact: John Keleher

National Stone Centre
Wirksworth
Derbyshire
DE4 4FY
Tel: 01629 824833
Fax: 01629 824833
Contact: IA Thomas, Director
Founded: 1983
Publications: Treasure in the Rocks; Report of
the East Midlands Aggregates Working Party
Profile: Stone production is our oldest rural
industry. The National Stone Centre's aim is to
tell the story of stone throughout the UK
(geological background, industrial history – from
prehistoric axe factories to hi-tech processing,
end-uses from sculpture to sugar refining and
related environmental issues.) Their 50 acre site
is on the edge of the Peak National Park. The
indoor Story of Stone exhibition and visitor
facilities are complemented by trails over
330 million year old fossil reefs and lagoons, and
children's activities. Professional services include
school-quarry industry liaison, stone sourcing,
historical/statistical research, quarry viewpoint
panel design, educational audits and literature.

National Summer Fruits Association
Crundalls
Matfield
Tonbridge
Kent
TN12 7EA

Tel: 0189 272 2830
Fax: 0189 272 3900
Contact: Joan Cremer, Company Secretary
Founded: 1993
Profile: The association was founded to do the work that the UK soft fruit industry needs but which individual marketing organisations cannot achieve alone. In particular it aims to promote British soft fruit, maintain a database of statistics, to develop a grower-based network, to inform government, consumers and industry about matters relating to British soft fruit, and to promote adherence to the protocol for soft fruit production.

National Traction Engine Trust
153 Micklefield Road
High Wycombe
Buckinghamshire
HP13 7HA
Tel: 01494 521727
Fax: 01494 521727
Contact: Susan Jackson, General Secretary
Founded: 1954
Membership: 3,000
Publications: Steaming (journal); Raising Steam (journal)
Previous names: National Traction Engine Club until 1984
Profile: The trust is committed to the preservation of road going steam vehicles including safety training for new owners, producing a rally code of practice and a traction engine code of practice.

National Trainers Federation
42 Portman Square
London
W1H 0AP
Tel: 0171 935 2055
Fax: 0171 465 8784
Contact: Grant Harris, Chief Executive
Founded: 1967
Membership: 500
Profile: Represents UK licensed thoroughbred racehorse trainers.

National Trust for Jersey
The Elms
St Mary
Jersey
Channel Islands
JE3 3EN
Tel: 01534 483193
Fax: 01534 485434
Contact: Roy Dobin, Secretary/Administrator
Founded: 1936
Membership: 2,000

Publications: Annual Reports, handbook, newsletters
Profile: The trust was established in 1936 for the purposes of securing the permanent preservation for the benefit of the island of lands and tenements (including buildings) of beauty or historic interest, and as regards lands, for the preservation (so far as practicable) of their natural aspect, features, and animal and plant life.

National Trust for Places of Historic Interest or Natural Beauty
36 Queen Anne's Gate
London
SW1H 9AS
Tel: 0171 222 9251
Fax: 0171 222 5097
Contact: John Young, Agricultural Advisor
Founded: 1895
Membership: 2,300,000
Publications: Publications list available
Profile: The National Trust is a registered charity, independent of government founded in 1895 to preserve places of historic interest or natural beauty permanently for the nation to enjoy. It owns nearly 240,000 hectares of the most beautiful countryside, 550 miles of coastline, and opens to the public over 200 historic houses, 160 gardens and 25 industrial monuments. The trust has the unique statutory power to declare land inalienable.

National Trust for Scotland, The
5 Charlotte Square
Edinburgh
EH2 4DU
Tel: 0131 226 5922
Fax: 0131 243 9501
Contact: John Mayhew, Planning and Research Officer
Founded: 1931
Membership: 230,000
Publications: Guide to over 100 properties; Heritage Scotland; guidebooks, leaflets and books; Annual Report
Profile: The National Trust for Scotland is a charity supported by its membership. Its remit, set out in various Acts of Parliament, is to promote the care and conservation of the Scottish landscape and historic buildings while providing access for the public to enjoy them.

National Trust of Guernsey
26 Cornet Street
St Peter Port
Guernsey
Channel Islands
Tel: 01481 728451

Contact: Mr IO Jones, Honorary Treasurer
Founded: 1960
Membership: 1,400
Publications: Official handbook, members newsletter
Profile: The National Trust of Guernsey is an independent organisation which aims to preserve Guernsey's remaining landscape, historic and architecturally notable buildings and objects connected with the island's heritage. Several large areas of land with beautiful walks are owned and maintained for the enjoyment of all. There is a large collection of local artefacts displayed at the Folk Museum, and also a Victorian parlour and shop, a working water wheel, a costume collection and various cottages in the trust's possession.

National Vegetable Society
56 Waun y Groes Avenue
Rhiwbina
Cardiff
CF4 4SZ
Tel: 01222 627994
Contact: Ivor Garland, National Secretary
Founded: 1960
Membership: 3,000
Publications: National bulletins; national newsletters; growing leaflets
Profile: Their main aim is to encourage and give advice on the growing of better quality vegetables.

National Vintage Tractor and Engine Club
Weylode
Tetbury Road
Old Sodbury
Bristol
BS17 6RJ
Tel: 01454 321015
Fax: 01454 273054
Contact: Jim Wilkie, Public Relations Officer
Founded: 1968
Membership: 5,000
Publications: Vaporising
Previous names: Fordson Owners Club; National Vintage Tractor Club
Profile: Tractors and stationary engines transformed agriculture. Members study, restore, exhibit, and enjoy the challenge of getting the best from old machinery. Ages range from youngsters to members well into their 80s. For most members the local group (there are over 30) form their point of contact. Specialist advice or spares could come from other groups; rallies, road runs, ploughing matches, and invitations to events offer a chance to see machines in action. Most importantly all those taking part enjoy their hobby.

National Water Safety Committee
RoSPA
Edgbaston Park
353 Bristol Road
Birmingham
B5 7ST
Tel: 0121 248 2000
Fax: 0121 248 2001
Founded: 1916
Publications: Publications list available
Profile: The National Water Safety Committee advises the Royal Society for the Prevention of Accidents on all aspects of water safety.

National Wind Turbine Centre
National Engineering Laboratory
Scottish Enterprise Technology Park
East Kilbride
Glasgow
G75 0QU
Tel: 01355 272079
Fax: 01355 272333
Contact: Ray Hunter, Manager Renewable Energy
Founded: 1984
Profile: The NWTC is a leading European organisation supplying test, consultancy and R and D services in wind energy. Its customers comprise purchasers, wind farm developers, wind turbine manufacturers, local authorities, UK government and the European Commission.

Native Pony Association of Devon
Rockpark Farm
Woodland Head
Yeoford
Crediton
Devon
Tel: 01647 24398
Contact: Mrs SJ Seward, Secretary
Founded: 1985
Membership: 100
Profile: To promote mountain and moorland horses and ponies including part breds in all spheres, i.e. in hand classes and all types of ridden activities. They hold spring, summer and autumn shows plus demonstrations and talks.

Natural Environment Research Council
Office of Science and Technology
Polaris House
North Star Avenue
Swindon
Wiltshire
SN2 1EU
Tel: 01793 411500
Fax: 01793 411510
Email: sand@wpo.NERC.ac.uk

Contact: Sheila Anderson, Head of Communications
Founded: 1965
Publications: NERC News; publications list available
Profile: NERC is the UK's leading body for research, survey, monitoring and training in the environmental sciences. NERC offers an unrivalled breadth of integrated research and gathers key data into unique databases, some of which now span several decades. NERC funds research in universities and in its own centres, surveys and units.

Natural Fibres Organisation
Wrest Park
Silsoe
Bedford
MK45 4HS
Tel: 01525 862095
Fax: 01525 862095
Contact: Harry Gilbertson, Marketing Manager
Founded: 1993
Membership: 400
Publications: Members newsletter
Profile: The main objectives of the NFO are to raise the profile of natural fibres generally and to investigate,evaluate and encourage the development of markets for UK produced natural fibre crops. The NFO is funded 50% by subscription and 50% by a Group Marketing Grant from MAFF.

Natural Mineral Waters Association
British Soft Drinks Association Ltd
6 Catherine Street
London
WC2B 5UA
Tel: 0171 836 5559
Profile: We have been unable to contact this organisation. The details given are unconfirmed.

Natural Resources Institute
University of Greenwich
Central Avenue
Chatham Maritime
Chatham
Kent
ME4 4TB
Tel: 01634 880088
Fax: 01634 880066/77
Email: enquiries.libraries@nri.org
Internet: http://www.nri.org
Contact: Tim Cullen, Head of Library
Founded: 1894
Publications: Publications list available
Profile: The Natural Resources Institute (NRI) is an internationally recognised centre of expertise on the natural resources sector in developing countries. Its principal aim is to alleviate poverty and hardship in developing countries by increasing the productivity of their renewable natural resources. NRI's main fields of expertise are resource assessment and farming systems, integrated pest management, food science and crop utilisation.

Natural Slate Quarries Association
26 Store Street
London
WC1E 7BT
Tel: 0171 323 3770
Fax: 0171 323 0307
Contact: Richard Toms
Founded: 1942
Membership: 7
Publications: List of members' product ranges; slate guide planned for publication
Profile: The association exists to defend and develop the collective interests of the UK industry. As such it provides a contact point for advice and information on slate, as well as a forum in which producers can address issues affecting the industry. Aside from its substantial contribution to the development of UK and European standards, it is involved in consultation with government and senior civil servants and with similar policy making organisations including the Health and Safety Executive and in many other ways on policy issues affecting the industry.

Naturewatch
122 Bath Road
Cheltenham
Gloucestershire
GL53 7JX
Tel: 01242 252871
Fax: 01242 253569
Contact: J Ruane, Director
Founded: 1993
Membership: 20,000
Publications: Guide to Compassionate Shopping; fact files on animal welfare issues; Action Pack on Live Export and Animal Experiments
Profile: Naturewatch is a campaigning organisation against animal cruelty. Their charitable arm Naturewatch Education works in schools and colleges to promote an awareness of animal welfare issues.

Network for Alternative Technology and Technology Assessment
NATTA c/o EERU
Faculty of Technology
Open University

Walton Hall
Milton Keynes
Buckinghamshire
MK7 6AA
Tel: 01908 654638
Email: S.J.Dougan@open.ac.uk
Contact: Tam Dougan, NATTA Co-ordinator
Founded: 1976
Membership: 500
Publications: Renew

New Conservation Society
Pwllyfan
Llansadwrn
Llanwrda
Carmarthenshire
SA19 8LS
Profile: We have been unable to contact this organisation. The details given are unconfirmed.

New Forest Pony and Cattle Breeding Society
Beacon Cottage
Burley
Ringwood
Hampshire
BH24 4EW
Tel: 01425 402272
Contact: Miss D MacNair, Honorary Secretary
Founded: 189
Membership: 1,000
Publications: Annual Stud Book; Annual Report
Previous names: Burley and District NFPBTCS and the Society for Improvement of New Forest Ponies amalgamated 1938
Profile: A society for the conservation and encouragement in the use of New Forest ponies.

New Forest Pony Enthusiast Club
Alderholt Mill Farm
Sandleheath Road
Alderholt
Fordingbridge
Hampshire
SP6 3EG
Tel: 01425 655527
Fax: 01425 655889
Contact: Mrs Jill Horn, Honorary Secretary
Founded: 1986
Membership: 200
Publications: Members newsletter
Profile: The New Forest Pony Enthusiast Club is a riding club affiliated to the British Horse Society Riding Club's Movement and is open to owners, riders and supporters of registered New Forest Ponies. The club organises a wide range of activities for both mounted and unmounted members, junior and senior alike, such as

skittles, tack sales, instructional lectures and rallies, annual show, dressage competitions, horse trials and visits.

Newark and Nottinghamshire Agricultural Society
The Showground
Winthorpe
Newark
Nottinghamshire
NG24 2NY
Tel: 01636 702627
Fax: 01636 610642
Contact: The Secretary
Founded: 1799
Membership: 1,500
Publications: Prize lists, show catalogue and programme
Profile: The objectives of the society are to promote agriculture and to such end generally to improve it in all its branches and to encourage skill and industry in it and all trades, crafts and professions connected with it. To promote industry in general. To hold, in pursuance of its main objectives, an annual agricultural show.

Newry Agricultural Show Society
14 Carrickcruppen Road
Camlough
Newry
County Down
BT35 7HS
Tel: 01693 830630
Profile: We have been unable to contact this organisation. The details given are unconfirmed.

Newton Rigg College
Newton Rigg
Penrith
Cumbria
CA11 0AH
Tel: 01768 863791
Fax: 01768 867249
Email: username@newtonrigg.ac.uk
Contact: Information Unit
Founded: 1896
Publications: College prospectus; Seeds of Change (Agrarian History of Cumbria)
Profile: A specialist college serving the agricultural, forestry, environmental management, game keeping, business, small animal and equine industries.

NFU Countryside
4 St Marys Hill
Stamford
Lincolnshire
PE9 2DP

Tel: 01780 65668
Fax: 01780 51519
Contact: Mrs Tina Murphy, Project Assistant
Founded: 1992
Membership: 33,000
Publications: Members newsletter
Profile: NFU Countryside is for people with more than a garden but less than a farm. Membership brings savings, information, advice and contacts.

NOAH
3 Crossfield Chambers
Gladbeck Way
Enfield
Middlesex
EN2 7HF
Tel: 0181 367 3131
Fax: 0181 363 1155
Contact: Roger Cook, Director
Founded: 1986
Membership: 57
Publications: Publications list available
Previous names: Part of Association of the British Pharmaceutical Industry until 1986
Profile: NOAH represents the companies that research, develop, manufacture and/or market licensed animal medicines in the UK.

Norfolk Horn
see **Rare Breeds Survival Trust**

North Antrim Agricultural Association Ltd
58 Carrowreagh Road
Armoy
Ballymoney
County Antrim
BT53 8RS
Tel: 012657 51327
Fax: 012657 51327
Contact: Mrs AV Morrison, Secretary
Founded: 1906
Profile: To promote and run the Ballymoney Agricultural Show on the first Saturday in June each year.

North Country Cheviot Sheep Society
16 St Vincent Road
Tain
Ross-Shire
IV19 1JR
Tel: 01862 894014
Fax: 01862 894014
Contact: William Morrison, Secretary
Founded: 1945
Membership: 400
Publications: Annual flock book
Profile: The organisation's main aim is to promote North Country Cheviot sheep. This is done by helping ensure breed purity by keeping records of all registered pedigree flocks, promotions and publicity shows and sales of the breed and providing information to interested parties on the different classes of stock and availability.

North of England Mule Sheep Association
Tunstall House Farm
Wolsingham
Bishop Auckland
County Durham
DL13 3LZ
Tel: 01388 527411
Fax: 01388 527411
Contact: Mrs DL Bell, Secretary
Founded: 1980
Membership: 2,076
Publications: Mule News; Sales Booklet; Mule Views (video)
Profile: The association was formed for the promotion of the North of England Mule as the top class commercial breeding sheep, capable of being bred from in its first year. The association promotes members' ewe lambs – with over 373,000 sold in 1995.

North of Ireland Potato Marketing Association Ltd
10 Arthur Street
Belfast
BT1 4G
Profile: We have been unable to contact this organisation. The details given are unconfirmed.

North of Scotland Grassland Society
c/o Ferguson Building
Craibstone Estate
Bucksburn
Aberdeen
AB2 9YA
Tel: 01224 480291
Fax: 01224 711293
Email: j.wilson@ab.sac.ac.uk
Contact: John F Wilson, Assistant Secretary
Founded: 1963
Membership: 350
Publications: Norgrass
Profile: A group of farmers, trade representatives, etc. who, by meetings, talks and other means aim to increase knowledge and understanding of production and utilisation of grass and forage crops for the benefit of agriculture and the public, and to advance education and research in these areas.

North Ronaldsay
see **Rare Breeds Survival Trust**

North Somerset Agricultural Society
Rocklea
East Dundry
Bristol
BS18 8NJ
Tel: 0117 964 3498
Fax: 0117 964 3298
Contact: Keith Pulman, Secretary
Founded: 1840
Membership: 1,000
Publications: Newsabout
Profile: An agricultural society promoting the North Somerset Show held in Bristol annually in May and the North Somerset Ploughing Match and Produce Show held annually in September.

North West Water Ltd
United Utilities plc
Dawson House
Liverpool Road
Great Sankey
Warrington
Cheshire
WA5 3LW
Tel: 01925 234000
Fax: 01925 233364

North York Moors National Park Authority
The Old Vicarage
Bondgate
Helmsley
North Yorkshire
Y06 5BP
Tel: 01439 770657
Fax: 01439 770691
Email: 100070.1372@compuserve.com
Contact: Information Officer
Founded: 1952
Publications: List of publications, reports and plans available
Profile: Rolling heather moorland, picturesque dales and a spectacular coastline make the North York Moors one of our most treasured landscapes. The aim of the National Park Authority is to conserve and enhance this rich heritage, working with farmers and landowners to manage the countryside. Features of historical interest are protected and development of the area is carefully monitored. The National Park Authority also helps people to enjoy and understand the North York Moors by maintaining public rights of way and producing leaflets, displays and exhibitions.

Northern Horticultural Society
Harlow Carr Botanical Gardens
Crag Lane
Harrogate
HG3 1QB
Tel: 01423 565418
Fax: 01423 530663
Contact: Mr Paul Griffiths, Trials Officer
Founded: 1946
Membership: 10,600
Publications: Northern Gardener
Profile: The chief aim of the Northern Horticultural Society is to test the suitability of plants for growing in northern conditions. Harlow Carr Botanical Gardens are the society's 68 acre headquarters. Vegetable, fruit and flower trials; rock, foliage, winter and heather gardens; alpines, herbaceous beds; streamside; woodland and arboretum. Trials are held; exhibitions; displays; guided walks and lectures.

Northern Ireland Advisory Committee on Travellers
c/o Special Programmes Branch
Clarence Court
10–18 Adelaide Street
Belfast
BT2 8GB
Tel: 01232 540540
Contact: Terry Neil
Founded: 1986
Profile: The Advisory Committee on Travellers was established in 1986 to advise the department on a range of traveller issues and in particular to promote progress in a programme of site provision by District Councils in Northern Ireland.

Northern Ireland Agricultural Producers Association
15 Molesworth Street
Cookstown
County Tyrone
Tel: 016487 65700
Fax: 016487 66900
Contact: Jim Carmichael, Development Officer
Founded: 1974
Membership: 5,500
Publications: Quarterly Bulletin
Profile: NIAPA was formed in 1974. Membership is £25 per year and brings the benefits of representation, advice on all aspects of farming, planning, housing, form filling, intermediary services in quota transactions etc. It also offers an insurance package specifically designed to suit the needs of members.

Northern Ireland Bat Group
107 Comber Road
Dundonald
Belfast
BT16 0AH
Tel: 01232 482994
Contact: Mrs Robin Moffitt, Chair
Founded: 1985
Membership: 70
Publications: The Leisler
Profile: The Bat Group promotes bat conservation and is involved in monitoring the numbers and distribution of the known species of bat within Northern Ireland. Members are also involved in educating the public and drawing attention to the plight of bats through talks to schools etc. Survey work also forms part of the activities. Details of bat roosts are kept in the Ulster Museum.

Northern Ireland Birdwatchers' Association
Larches
12 Belvoir Close
Belvoir Park
Belfast
BT8 4PL
Tel: 01232 693232
Fax: 01232 644681
Contact: Chris Murphy, Honorary Secretary
Founded: 1989
Membership: 100
Publications: Northern Ireland Bird Report
Profile: NIBA is open to all birdwatchers and is administered by a committee of seven who are elected annually. The work of the committee is essentially the assessment and compilation of records and the writing and publication of the annual bird report. In doing so, NIBA works to improve our knowledge of the population and distribution of Northern Ireland's birds.

Northern Ireland Countryside Staff Association
Lough Neagh Discovery Centre
Oxford Island National Nature Reserve
Craigavon
County Armagh
Tel: 01762 322205
Fax: 01762 347438
Contact: Maid Taylor, Secretary
Publications: NICSA News
Profile: NICSA aims to promote and enhance the development and exchange of information between staff employed in the conservation of the countryside in Northern Ireland.

Northern Ireland Dairy Association
123–137 York Street
Belfast
BT15 1AB
Tel: 01232 248385
Fax: 01232 233210
Contact: Mr John Chalmers, Executive Secretary
Previous names: Northern Ireland Dairy Trade Federation until June 1995

Northern Ireland Deer Society
9 Mount Shalgus
Randalstown
County Antrim
BT41 3LE
Tel: 01849 472626
Contact: Mrs AE McCurdy, Treasurer
Founded: 1970
Membership: 50
Previous names: Ulster Deer Society
Profile: The Northern Ireland Deer Society's aims are: the conservation of deer and their habitat; research and education; good management and control; monitoring of legal protection; liaison with kindred organisations.

Northern Ireland Driving Club
68 Edgewater
Lisburn
County Antrim
BT27 5PQ
Profile: We have been unable to contact this organisation. The details given are unconfirmed.

Northern Ireland Environment Link
47a Botanic Avenue
Belfast
BT7 1JL
Tel: 01232 314944
Contact: Dr Susan Christie, Director
Founded: 1990
Membership: 114
Publications: Our Countryside Our Concern 1990; Environmental Strategy for Northern Ireland Consultative Document July 1995; Environmental Strategy for Northern Ireland Full Document May 1996
Profile: NIEL is the forum linking and networking organisations for the voluntary environmental organisations in Northern Ireland. It facilitates the work of voluntary groups on environmental matters and acts as a conduit of information within the sector to other sectors such as government and the wider community.

Northern Ireland Forest Service
Department of Agriculture
Room 34 Dundonald House
Upper Newtownards Road
Belfast
BT4 3SB

Tel: 01232 524471
Fax: 01232 524570
Contact: RJ McCurdy, Conservation Officer
Publications: Publications list available
Profile: The role of the Forest Service of the Department of Agriculture is to promote the planting of trees and to encourage the good management of existing woodland. The Forest Service manages 60,000 ha of state forest not only to produce timber, but also providing public recreation, conservation and educational benefits.

Northern Ireland Fruit Growers Association
90 Red Lion Road
Kilmore
County Armagh
BT6 18NU
Tel: 01762 851266

Northern Ireland Goat Club
British Goat Society
35 Mullaghdrin Road
Dromara
Dromore
County Down
BT25 2AG
Tel: 01232 532685
Fax: 01232 663565
Contact: Terry Hanna, Honorary Secretary
Founded: 1965
Membership: 80
Publications: Members newsletter
Profile: The NIGC is the longest established goat keeping organisation in Ireland, formed in 1965, the club now draws its members from all walks of life and from all over Ireland. The NIGC is the main recognised goatkeeping body in the province, and promotes the interests of its members within relevant government bodies such as the Department of Agriculture for Northern Ireland. The NIGC organises three open recognised shows annually and is consulted by local agricultural societies on matters such as show classification and appointment of judges. Additionally, the NIGC organises regular winter meetings which are addressed by visiting speakers on a wide range of goat related issues.

Northern Ireland Grain Trade Association
Cooley Lodge
Coolyhill
Tandragee
County Armagh
BT62 2HT
Tel: 01762 841395
Fax: 01762 841865

Contact: Doris Robinson, Executive Secretary
Founded: 1966
Profile: The NI Grain Trade Association was founded in 1966 and comprises importers, brokers, merchants, animal feed compounders and millers who are involved in the trading, storage and transportation of grain and in the manufacture of grain into flour and animal feeds. Member companies are also involved in selling seed and fertilisers to Northern Ireland growers and in giving advice to growers and users of grain.

Northern Ireland Hackney Club
Canal Street
Newry
County Down
Profile: We have been unable to contact this organisation. The details given are unconfirmed.

Northern Ireland Horticulture and Plant Breeding Station
Department of Agriculture for Northern Ireland
Manor House
Loughgall
County Armagh
BT61 8JB
Tel: 01762 891436
Fax: 01762 891389
Contact: W Malcolm Dawson, Head of Station
Founded: 1952
Previous names: Northern Ireland Plant Breeding Station merged with The Horticultural Centre 1987 to form NIHPBS
Profile: The station seeks to underpin horticultural and agricultural enterprises in Northern Ireland as part of the co-ordinated programme of research and development carried out by the science service of the Department of Agriculture for Northern Ireland. Work focuses on several locally important industries – mushroom production, top fruit, nursery stock and protected vegetables. In addition commercially supported programmes for grass and potato breeding and investigations into the production and use of short rotation coppice as an energy crop are carried on.

Northern Ireland Hunter Pony Committee
Ballyhomra House
130 Comber Road
Hillsborough
County Down
BT26 6NA
Profile: We have been unable to contact this organisation. The details given are unconfirmed.

Northern Ireland Ploughing Association
475 Antrim Road
Belfast
BT15 3DA
Tel: 01232 370222
Fax: 01232 370739
Contact: Mrs P Adair, Secretary
Founded: 1937
Membership: 80
Publications: International Match Programme
Profile: The first international match was staged at Limavady in 1938 and since then the occasion has provided the sport of ploughing with a stage on which to demonstrate the skills involved.

Northern Ireland Quarry Owners' Association
Andras House
60 Great Victoria Street
Belfast
BT2 7ET
Tel: 01232 233152
Fax: 01232 332757
Contact: Jackson Andrews, Chartered Accountants, Secretaries
Founded: 1936
Membership: 54
Profile: The association exists to promote the interest of the quarry owners of Northern Ireland generally and members in particular in dealings with government bodies and trade unions.

Northern Ireland Shows' Association
The King's Hall
Balmoral
Belfast
BT9 6GW
Tel: 01232 665225
Fax: 01232 661264
Contact: William H Yarr, Secretary/Treasurer
Founded: 1983
Membership: 15
Profile: The Northern Ireland Shows' Association sets out to be the representative body for agricultural shows in Northern Ireland and by encouragement to further the interests and objectives of these shows.

Northern Ireland Thoroughbred Breeders Society
35 Creevytenant Road
Ballynahinch
County Antrim
Profile: We have been unable to contact this organisation. The details given are unconfirmed.

Northern Ireland Timber Trade Association
1 Rhanbuoy Court
Carrickfergus

County Antrim
BT38 8DL
Tel: 01960 360565
Contact: Robert T McCullough, Secretary
Founded: 1948
Membership: 25
Previous names: Northern Ireland Timber Importers Association
Profile: To promote the best possible use of timber and timber based materials.

Northern Ireland Tourist Board
St Anne's Court
59 North Street
Belfast
BT1 1NB
Tel: 01232 231221
Fax: 01232 240960
Contact: Mr Ian Henderson, Chief Executive
Founded: 1948
Publications: Publications list available
Profile: The main function of the Northern Ireland Tourist Board is to develop and present Northern Ireland as a quality competitive tourist destination within the international market place; to promote domestic tourism; and to maximise the tourist industry's potential to become a significant creator of wealth and jobs in Northern Ireland.

Northern Ireland Water Council
Department of the Environment (NI)
Brookmount Buildings
42 Fountain Street
Belfast
BT1 5EE
Tel: 01232 251444
Fax: 01232 251919
Contact: Mr Ray Wright, Secretary to Council
Founded: 1972
Publications: Triennial Report
Profile: The Northern Ireland Water Council is constituted under Section 4 of the Water Act (NI) 1972 and its powers were subsequently extended under Article 6 the Water and Sewerage Services (NI) Order 1973. Members of the council are jointly appointed by the ministers for the Departments of Agriculture and Environment (NI). The council consists of not more than 15 persons who represent agriculture, fisheries, industry, commerce, tourism, nature recreation, the environment, local government and trade unions . The role of the council is to advise both departments on the exercise of their functions under the above mentioned Acts.

Northern Ireland Working Hunter Association
114 Scarva Road
Banbridge

County Down
BT32 3QG
Profile: We have been unable to contact this organisation. The details given are unconfirmed.

Northern Research Station
Forestry Commission
Roslin
Midlothian
EH25 9SY
Tel: 0131 445 2176
Fax: 0131 445 5124
Contact: Dr John Parker, Research Communications Officer
Founded: 1919
Publications: Publications list available
Profile: The aim of the Forestry Commission's Research Division is to increase the sustainable benefits from trees and woodlands by providing authoritative advice based on sound research. At the Northern Research Station work is focused on coniferous silviculture, tree improvement, woodland ecology, and the control of pests and diseases. Current programmes include research into biodiversity, ecological site classification, planting stock quality and windthrow.

Northumberland National Park Committee
Eastburn
South Park
Hexham
Northumberland
NE46 1BS
Tel: 01434 605555
Fax: 01434 600522

Northumbrian Water Ltd
Abbey Road
Pity Me
Durham
DH1 5FS
Tel: 0191 383 2222
Fax: 0191 383 1209

Norton Radstock College
South Hill Park
Radstock
Bath
Somerset
BA3 3RW
Tel: 01761 433161
Fax: 01761 436173

Nuffield Farming Scholarships Trust
East Holme Farm
Maresfield
Uckfield
East Sussex

TN22 3AY
Tel: 01825 762928
Fax: 01825 768820
Email: 100523.2770@compuserve.com
Contact: Steven Bullock, Director
Founded: 1946
Membership: 800
Publications: Annual Report; Nuffield Farming Scholarship Reports
Profile: The NFST provides awards to those active in farming, growing, forestry, fish farming and countryside management, as well as those working in positions that can influence the primary 'targets'. Scholars present a study topic and if successful are funded to travel for eight weeks and upon their return report to their peers. The objective is information gathering and personal development. Scholars go on to play leading roles in industry and rural community affairs.

Oaklands College Hertfordshire
Oaklands Campus
Hatfield Road
St Albans
Hertfordshire
AL4 0JA
Tel: 01727 850651
Fax: 01727 847987
Contact: Roger Thomas, Head of School
Founded: 1921
Publications: College prospectus
Previous names: Hertfordshire College of Agriculture and Horticulture until 1989
Profile: A Further Education College offering courses in agriculture, amenity and commercial horticulture, equine studies, floristry, greenkeeping, small animal care and veterinary nursing. Ranging from NVQ level 2 to Higher National Diploma.

Oatridge Agricultural College
Ecclesmachan
Broxburn
West Lothian
EH52 6NH
Tel: 01506 854387
Fax: 01506 853373
Contact: Mr CW Nixon, Principal
Profile: Scotland's specialist land-based college providing a comprehensive range of quality education and training for all those working directly or indirectly within the land-based industries locally, nationally and internationally.

Occupational and Environmental Diseases Association
PO Box 109
Scarbrook Road

Croydon
Surrey
CR9 1QH
Profile: We have been unable to contact this organisation. The details given are unconfirmed.

Offa's Dyke Association
Offa's Dyke Centre
West Street
Knighton
Powys
LD7 1EN
Tel: 01547 528753
Contact: Mrs Rebe Brick, Correspondence Secretary
Founded: 1969
Membership: 1,000
Publications: Publications list available
Profile: The ODA was set up to provide a link between walkers, historians and conservationists and those who live and work locally. It encourages action by the official bodies responsible for maintaining and improving the path, protecting the dyke and other features of historic or natural interest, covering the natural beauty of the border area, and providing information services to the public.

Office for National Statistics
Government Offices
Great George Street
London
SW1P 3AQ
Tel: 0171 270 6081
Fax: 0171 270 6019
Contact: Public Enquiry Service
Founded: 1996
Previous names: Central Statistical Office

Office of Electricity Regulation
Hagley House
83–85 Hagley Road
Birmingham
B16 8QG
Tel: 0121 456 2100
Fax: 0121 456 4664
Contact: Bernadette Bogan, Information Officer
Founded: 1990
Publications: Publications list available
Profile: The Office of Electricity Regulation is an independent body set up by Parliament under the Electricity Act 1989 to regulate the electricity industry. It has 12 regional offices in England and Wales, one for each of the regional electricity companies. There is also an office in Glasgow which serves the interests of Scottish consumers. OFFER can help individual customers resolve complaints and other

problems. To contact your local OFFER office look for the address and telephone number on the back of your electricity bill.

Office of Gas Supply
Stockley House
130 Wilton Road
London
SW1V 1LQ
Tel: 0171 828 0898
Fax: 0171 932 1600
Contact: Consumer Affairs Directorate
Founded: 1986
Publications: Publications list available
Profile: OFGAS, created in 1986, is a non-ministerial government department headed by the Director General of Gas Supply. It has two main aims: to protect the interests of the gas consumer and to facilitate the introduction of competition in the domestic gas market (planned to take place between 1996 and 1998).

Office of Water Services
Centre City Tower
7 Hill Street
Birmingham
B5 4UA
Tel: 0121 625 1300
Fax: 0121 625 1400
Contact: Public Enquiry Unit
Founded: 1989
Publications: Publications list available
Profile: The Office of Water Services (OFWAT) is the independent economic regulator of the water and sewerage companies in England and Wales. OFWAT's main duty is to ensure that the companies can finance and carry out the functions specified in Section 2 of the Water Industry Act of 1991 and to protect the interests of water customers. OFWAT is a non-ministerial government department headed by the Director General of Water Services. Ten regional OFWAT Customer Service Committees represent customer interests and investigate customer complaints. Representation of customer interests at national level is the responsibility of the OFWAT National Customer Council.

Official Seed Testing Station for Scotland
Scottish Agricultural Science Agency
East Craigs
Edinburgh
EH12 8NJ
Tel: 0131 244 8908
Fax: 0131 244 8971
Email: Don@SASA.gov.uk
Contact: Ronald Don, Chief Officer

Founded: 1912
Publications: Publications list available
Profile: The Official Seed Testing Station for Scotland is the principle centre for seed testing and seed quality information in Scotland. The OSTS offers a wide range of laboratory tests that provide practical and reliable information for merchants and growers on the quality of seed intended for sowing. A programme of research and development aims to improve testing methods and enhance the interpretation and application of test results. The OSTS organises training courses in seed testing and sampling and is pleased to organise visits to the station for groups with interests in seed quality.

Old English Game Bantam Club
20 Beaumont Street
Hoyland Common
Barnsley
South Yorkshire
S74 0NU
Tel: 01226 749052
Contact: Mr E Trickett, Secretary
Profile: A society to promote the Old English Game Bantam breed of poultry.

Old Gloucester Cattle Society
Bemborough Farm Office
Guiting Power
Cheltenham
Gloucestershire
GL54 5UG
Tel: 01451 850307
Contact: Elizabeth L Henson, Secretary

Open Spaces Society
25a Bell Street
Henley-on-Thames
Oxfordshire
RG9 2BA
Tel: 01491 573535
Fax: 01491 573051
Contact: Kate Ashbrook, Secretary

Ordnance Survey
Romsey Road
Southampton
Hampshire
SO16 4GU
Tel: 01703 792912
Fax: 01703 792452
Email: custinfo@ordsvy.govt.uk
Contact: Keith Marsh, Customer Information Manager
Founded: 1791

Publications: Publications list available (ring 01703 792763)
Profile: OS is the official government mapping agency of Great Britain. OS surveys, manufactures and markets a wide range of mapping products and services, including large scale superplan products, digital data, conventional paper maps, and a variety of atlases and guide books.

Ordnance Survey of Northern Ireland
Department of the Environment (NI)
Colby House
Stranmillis Court
Belfast
BT9 5BJ
Tel: 01232 255755
Fax: 01232 255700
Email: 100635.2165@compuserve.com
Contact: Martin McVeigh, Manager
Founded: 1922
Publications: Publications list available
Profile: OSNI exists to provide accurate, comprehensive and up-to-date topographical information for Northern Ireland. They undertake all surveys necessary for the maintenance of the archive of trigonometrical, levelling and topographical information of Northern Ireland.

Organic Advisory Service
Elm Farm Research Centre
Hamstead Marshall
Newbury
Berkshire
RG20 0HR
Tel: 01488 658298
Fax: 01488 658503
Email: 100113.751@compuserve.com
Contact: Gillian Woodward, Administrator
Founded: 1984
Publications: Organic Farm Management Handbook
Profile: The OAS provides practical advice for both agricultural and horticultural production. It assists farmers in planning for conversion to organic agriculture using feasibility studies. Soil and compost analysis services are provided as well as consultancy in a wide number of specialist areas.

Organic Association
Barron Lodge Farm
Grub Street
Happisburgh
Norwich
NR12 0QZ
Tel: 01692 651539
Fax: 01692 651539

Organic Conversion Information Service
Ministry of Agriculture, Fisheries and Food
Whitehall Place
London
SW1A 2HH
Tel: 0171 270 8080
Fax: 0171 270 8443
Profile: Launched June 1996.

Organic Farmers and Growers Ltd
50 High Street
Soham
Ely
Cambridgeshire
CB7 5HF
Tel: 01353 722744
Fax: 01353 721571
Contact: Robert Sculthorpe, Company Secretary
Founded: 1975
Profile: Organic Farmers and Growers Ltd is run
by farmers and processors providing links with
marketing opportunities for vegetables, livestock
and cereals. Technical help is given to members.
It is a sector body that was the first to be
accredited by UKROFS. It is represented both on
the main UKROFS board and certification
committees.

Organic Food and Farming Centre
86–88 Colston Street
Bristol
BS1 5BB
Tel: 0117 929 0661
Fax: 0117 925 2504

Organic Food Federation
The Tithe House
Peaseland Green
Elsing
East Dereham
Norfolk
NR20 3DY
Tel: 01362 637314
Fax: 01362 637398
Contact: J Wade, Executive Secretary
Founded: 1986
Membership: 50
Previous names: Organic Food Manufactures
Federation until 1992
Profile: The OFF aims to: maintain the high
standards for organic food through provision of
an organic certification service for producers,
processors and importers as required by EU
legislation since January 1993; representation of
member interests at both governmental and
non-governmental level; dissemination of organic
and other relevant information to members and
to act as a focal point of contact for members.

Organic Growers Association
86 Colston Street
Bristol
BS1 5BB
Tel: 0117 929 9800

Organic Livestock Marketing Cooperative
Carpenters House
Tur Langton
Kibworth
Leicestershire
LE8 0PJ
Tel: 01858 545564
Fax: 01858 545100
Contact: Mary Weston
Founded: 1996
Profile: The OLMC is a members' co-operative
formed in 1996 by a group of organic livestock
producers. It has established a national
marketing infrastructure for all classes of
registered organic livestock.

Organic Living Association
St Mary's Villa
Hanley Swan
Worcester
WR8 0EA
Contact: Dennis C Nightingale-Smith,
Director/Secretary
Founded: 1971
Membership: 200
Publications: Members newsletter
Previous names: Malvern and District Organic
Living Group
Profile: Aims to: integrate the production and
consumption of vegetables, fruit, cereals and
dairy produce grown on healthy, naturally
fertilised soils; to promote human health; to
promote health in farm animals and food crops;
to support the Soil Association, HDRA, BDAA
and allied organisations; to increase public
awareness of the above; to promote the
establishment of ecological, self sufficient
villages; to disseminate knowledge of
alternatives to allopathic medicine and to
emphasise the spiritual component of our being.

Organisation of Horsebox and Trailer Owners
38 Newton Road
London
W2 5LT
Tel: 0171 221 2255
Fax: 0171 229 2402
Contact: Sarah Knight, Accounts Director
Founded: 1985
Membership: 3,500

Profile: A breakdown recovery organisation for people who own horseboxes and trailers. The scheme is run in conjunction with the AA Fleet Rescue and Green Flag. In the event of a breakdown members will receive roadside assistance, free recovery to any destination, tyre assistance and they also help to stable the horses if necessary and re-imburse for the privilege.

Orpington Club
4 Arthog Road
Didsbury
Greater Manchester
M20 0GH
Tel: 01614 451090
Contact: Mrs J Bridson, Secretary
Profile: A society to promote the Orpington breed of poultry.

Otley College
Otley
Ipswich
Suffolk
IP6 9EY
Tel: 01473 785543
Fax: 01473 785353
Contact: Mr AB Ferguson, Principal
Founded: 1970
Profile: Rural based college offering a wide range of programmes covering agriculture and horticultural landscape and conservation management, service engineering, leisure and tourism, business administration and management throughout Suffolk. Courses are run on a full or part-time basis and from NVQ to postgraduate.

Otter Trust
Earsham
Bungay
Suffolk
NR35 2AF
Tel: 01986 893470
Contact: Jeanne Wayre, Director
Founded: 1972
Membership: 1,500
Publications: Annual journal
Profile: The Otter Trust is the largest and oldest otter conservation organisation in Britain. The only organisation breeding British Otters regularly and re-introducing young animals into the wild every year in conjunction with English Nature.

Outdoor Writers' Guild
27 Camwood
Clayton Gardens

Bamber Bridge
Lancashire
PR5 8LA
Profile: We have been unable to contact this organisation. The details given are unconfirmed.

Outward Bound Trust
Sales and Marketing Ofice
Outward Bound Ullswater
Watermillock
Nr Penrith
Cumbria
CA11 0JL
Tel: 01990 134227
Fax: 017684 86983

Oxford Down Sheep Breeders Association
4 Brookfield
Hampsthwaite
Harrogate
North Yorkshire
HG3 2EF
Tel: 01423 770736
Contact: Mr J Stephenson, Secretary
Founded: 1889
Membership: 120
Publications: Flock book; newsletter; One Hundred Years of Breeding
Profile: To encourage the breeding of Oxford Down sheep at home and abroad; and to maintain the purity of the breed for the benefit of the community at large; the establishment and publication of a flock book of recognised pure bred rams and ewes; the arrangement of classes and the donation or augmentation of prizes and awards of certificates of merit at shows, and to promote information with reference to sheep breeding.

Oxford Farming Conference Ltd
ADAS Bridget's Research Centre
Martyr Worthy
Winchester
Hampshire
SO21 1AP
Tel: 01963 779998
Fax: 01963 779739
Contact: Dr Bridget Drew, Secretary
Founded: 1936
Publications: Annual conference papers
Profile: The Oxford Farming Conference is a charity and limited company with nine directors who voluntarily give their time to organise this leading agricultural conference, held in Oxford in the first week of January. Attracting high profile international speakers, the conference has been described as the farming industry thinking out loud.

Oxford Forestry Institute

Department of Plant Sciences
Oxford University
South Parks Road
Oxford
OX1 3RB
Tel: 01865 275000
Fax: 01865 275074
Email: Jeff.Burley@plants.ox.ac.uk
Contact: Dr Jeffrey Burley, Director
Founded: 1905
Publications: Annual Report; tropical forestry
papers; OFI occasional papers
Previous names: Department of Forestry and
Commonwealth Forestry Institute until 1983
Profile: A research and training institution within
an academic department with major activities in
education/training, research and information and
consultancy/advisory services with particular
relevance to tropical and developing countries.

Oxford Sandy and Black Pig Society

The Cottage
Stareton House
Stareton
Kenilworth
Warwickshire
CV8 2LL
Tel: 01926 429328
Fax: 01926 335213
Contact: Mrs Cathie Annetts, Honorary
Secretary
Founded: 1985
Membership: 90
Publications: Annual herd book; members
newsletter.
Profile: An independent breed society, helping
members to promote the Oxford Sandy and
Black breed.

Pagan Animal Rights

PO Box 11
Bargoed
Mid Glamorgan
CF81 8YG
Contact: Mr D Hodson, Newsletter Editor
Founded: 1986
Membership: 50
Publications: Pagan Animal Rights Newsletter;
information leaflet
Profile: PAR believes that animals possess
rights. This belief is justified by faith in the
Goddess and God. PAR's main objective is to
promote the idea of animal rights within the
pagan community. They promote
animal-exploitation-free diets, food production
methods, cultures, attitudes and lifestyles.

Painted Horse and Pony Society of Great Britain

96 Blakeland Road
Perry Barr
Birmingham
B44 8AS
Profile: We have been unable to contact this
organisation. The details given are unconfirmed.

Parnham Trust

Parnham House
Beaminster
Dorset
DT8 3NA
Tel: 01308 862204
Fax: 01308 863494
Contact: Mr John Makepeace, Chief Executive
Founded: 1977
Publications: Parnham College Prospectus;
Hooke Park Appeal Booklet
Profile: The Parnham Trust is a non-profit making
educational charity, founded in 1977. The trust
aims to encourage excellence through education
and practical training for those going into
business as designers, makers and
manufacturers of wood products. It seeks to
enhance the world for future generations by
developing renewable resources, motivated
people, management, skills, creative flair and a
market for quality products made from
indigenous timber.

Part-Bred Dartmoor Register

The Lane
Guilsfield
Welshpool
Powys
SY21 9DH
Tel: 01938 556315
Contact: Mrs GN Little, Honorary Secretary
Founded: 1965
Profile: The Part-Bred Dartmoor Register was
formed so that people could register their ponies.
Providing the pony was fully registered it could be
outcrossed to a registered thoroughbred, arab,
anglo-arab, or riding pony (NPS registered). The
pony must have not less than 25% registered
Dartmoor in its breeding and not more than 25% of
any other native breed. Two annual awards for
showing in hand and ridden ponies are run.

Parthenais Cattle Society

Housham Farm
Hives Lane
North Scarle
Lincolnshire
LN6 9HA

Tel: 01522 778359
Contact: Mrs Brenda Popplewell, Honorary
Secretary
Founded: 1988
Membership: 17
Previous names: Sectrable Ltd until 1989
Profile: The society was formed to promote the
breeding and sale of Parthenais cattle.

Partridge & Pencilled Wyandotte Club
The White Cottage
Wootton
Ashbourne
Derbyshire
DE6 2GU
Tel: 01335 324304
Contact: Mrs C Shaw, Secretary
Profile: A society to promote the Partridge and
Pencilled Wyandotte breeds of poultry.

Peak and Northern Footpaths Society
15 Parkfield Drive
Tyldesley
Manchester
M29 8NR
Tel: 0161 790 4383
Contact: Mr D Taylor, Honorary General
Secretary
Founded: 1894
Membership: 1,000
Publications: Annual Report
Previous names: Peak District and Northern
Counties Footpath Preservation Society
Profile: The preservation, maintenance and
defence of the rights of the public to the use and
enjoyment on foot of public highways, footpaths,
bridleways and other ways particularly in the
eight counties of Cheshire, Derbyshire, Greater
Manchester, Lancashire, Merseyside, South
Yorkshire, Staffordshire and West Yorkshire.

Peak Park Joint Planning Board
Aldern House
Baslow Road
Bakewell
Derbyshire
DE45 1AE
Tel: 01629 816200
Fax: 01629 816310
Contact: Mr KM Francis, Secretary
Founded: 1951
Publications: Publications list available
Previous names: In April 1997 it will become the
Peak National Park Authority
Profile: The Peak National Park Authority is the
planning authority for the 555 square mile park. It
is charged with conserving the built and natural

environment, and the provision of suitable
recreational opportunities for its 22 million annual
visitors, while safeguarding the interests of its
38,000 residents.

Peat Producers Association
213 Ashley Road
Hale
Altrincham
Cheshire
WA15 9TB
Tel: 0161 929 8747
Contact: Bernard Elliott

Pekin Bantam Club
74 New Road
Staincross
Barnsley
South Yorkshire
S75 6HS
Tel: 01226 383675
Contact: Mr TJ Heginbotham, Secretary
Profile: A society to promote the Pekin Bantam
breed of poultry.

Pembrokeshire Agricultural Society
Show Office – County Showground
Withybush
Haverfordwest
Pembrokeshire
SA62 4BP
Tel: 01437 764331
Fax: 01437 767203
Contact: Donald M Evans, Secretary

Pembrokeshire Coast National Park Authority
National Park Authority
Winch Lane
Haverfordwest
Pembrokeshire
SA61 1PY
Tel: 01437 764636
Fax: 01437 769045
Email: 1170.1366@compuserve.com
Contact: Steve Drinkwater, Information Officer
Founded: 1952
Publications: Publications list available
Previous names: National Park Department,
Pembrokeshire CC 1952–1972, National Park
Department, Dyfed CC 1972–1996
Profile: Established in 1952, Britain's only coastal
national park covers an area of 240 square miles;
this includes offshore islands, woodland,
moorland and an 186 mile coast path.
Conservation is an integral part of all the park's
work and expert advice can be sought; including
information on grants for farming, community
projects, listed buildings and archaeological

features. Advice can be given on planning, building and recreational matters. There is an information and education service providing publications, guided walks, talks, information centres and liaison with schools and colleges.

Pencoed College
Pencoed
Bridgend
Mid Glamorgan
CF35 5LG
Tel: 01656 860202
Fax: 01656 864875
Contact: Gerald Curtis, Curriculum Manager
Founded: 1922
Publications: Prospectus
Previous names: Glamorgan College of Agriculture and Horticulture until 1980
Profile: Pencoed College provides quality training for land-based industries including agriculture, horticulture, floristry, countryside management, equine, animal care, land-based engineering and outdoor leisure. Qualifications which can be gained include BTEC First, National and Higher National Diplomas, NVQs, City & Guilds, BHS.

Pennine Way Association
29 Springfield Park Avenue
Chelmsford
Essex
CM2 6EL
Tel: 01245 256772
Contact: Mr Chris Sainty, Honorary Secretary
Founded: 1970
Membership: 350
Publications: Camping and Accommodation Guide
Previous names: Pennine Way Council until 1993
Profile: To secure the protection of the Pennine Way, to provide information about the Way to the public, to educate users of the Way and its environs in a proper respect for the countryside, to assist in the organisation of voluntary effort directed at the maintenance of the Way and to provide a forum in which different interests connected with the Way and its use can discuss problems of mutual concern.

People for the Ethical Treatment of Animals
Fetter Lane
London
Profile: We have been unable to contact this organisation. The details given are unconfirmed.

People's Trust for Endangered Species
15 Cloisters House
8 Battersea Park Road

London
SW8 4BG
Tel: 0171 498 4533
Fax: 0171 498 4459
Contact: Dr Valerie Keeble, Administrator
Founded: 1977
Publications: Members newsletter
Profile: The trust was formed in 1977 with the aim of protecting creatures in the wild threatened by man-made or environmental dangers. The principal aims of the trust are to: fund scientific research; to provide emergency funds for field work to protect threatened populations from immediate danger; to commission research and to promote public awareness of and encourage education about the need to conserve wildlife in its natural habitat for future generations to enjoy.

Permaculture Association
PO Box 1
Buckfastleigh
Devon
TQ11 0LM
Tel: 01654 712188
Email: pcbritain@gn.apc.org
Contact: Rachel Banks/Sue Cameron
Founded: 1984
Membership: 1,000
Publications: Permaculture Action in Britain
Profile: The Permaculture Association promotes permaculture as a way of designing and creating sustainable communities, lives and land use. The association produces a quarterly newsletter for its members, provides contacts and course information, supports the development of permaculture projects, organises an annual convergence and develops practical ways of helping its members implement permaculture.

Permit Trainers Association
42 Portman Square
London
W1H 9FF
Tel: 01444 461235
Fax: 01444 461485
Contact: Mr F Gray, Chairman
Founded: 1973
Membership: 480
Profile: Trainers of National Hunt racehorses owned by self, wife, daughters and sons.

Pershore College of Horticulture
Avonbank
Pershore
Worcestershire
WR10 3JP
Tel: 01386 552443

Fax: 01386 556528
Contact: Mr David A Hall, Principal
Founded: 1954
Profile: Further Education Corporation which offers FE and HE programmes in horticulture and related subjects.

Perth College
Crieff Road
Perth
PH1 2NX
Tel: 01738 621171
Fax: 01738 631364
Email: Kevin-Gowdy@Perth.fc.uhi.ac.uk
Contact: Mr Kevin M Gowdy, Senior Lecturer
Founded: 1971
Publications: Flexible learning units relating to conservation/ecology
Profile: A Further/Higher Education College set within a largely rural catchment with a long association and experience of teaching/training in the rural environment. Courses offered include agriculture, horticulture, conservation/countryside recreation studies from SVQ level 1 through to Higher National Diploma in part-time, full-time and distance learning format.

Perthshire Agricultural Society
26 York Place
Perth
PH2 8EH
Tel: 01738 623780

Pesticide Exposure Group of Sufferers
4 Lloyds House
Regent Terrace
Cambridge
CB2 1AA
Tel: 01223 364707
Fax: 01223 01766 512548
Contact: Mrs Enfys Chapman, Co-ordinator
Founded: 1988
Membership: 1,000
Publications: Members newsletter
Profile: PEGS is a completely independent organisation, to which anyone suffering with the effects of pesticide use, as well as those involved with such sufferers or simply concerned about the problems, may belong. They are a support group providing advice and counselling, and collate information relating to the incidence and effects of exposure and subsequent medical reaction.

Pesticide Usage Survey Group
Ministry of Agriculture, Fisheries and Food
Central Science Laboratory
Hatching Green
Harpenden

Hertfordshire
AL5 2BD
Tel: 01582 715241
Fax: 01582 762178
Email: m.thomas@csl.gov.uk
Contact: Dr Miles R Thomas, Head, Pesticide Usage Survey Group
Founded: 1964
Publications: Publications list available
Profile: The Pesticide Usage Survey Group of the Central Science Laboratory is responsible, on behalf of the Ministry of Agriculture, Fisheries and Food and the Scottish Office Agriculture, Environment and Fisheries Department, for the Pesticide Usage Surveys. The surveys are conducted on ten major commodities: grassland and fodder crops, outdoor vegetables, top fruit, soft fruit, hops, glasshouse crops, mushrooms, hardy nursery stock and outdoor bulbs and flowers (all every four years) and arable crops (biennially). Results are raised to give national estimates of usage. Data cover usage of all pesticide groups including herbicides, insecticides, fungicides, growth regulators and molluscicides. The surveys cover Great Britain and similar data have been collected since 1965 in England and Wales, extended to cover Scotland in 1974. The surveys were combined into a single survey covering Great Britain in 1992.

Pesticides Safety Directorate
Ministry of Agriculture, Fisheries and Food
Mallard House
3 Peasholme Green
Kings Pool
York
YO1 2PX
Tel: 01904 640500
Fax: 01904 455733
Email: p.s.d.information@psd.maff.gov.uk
Contact: Information Section
Founded: 1993
Publications: Annual Report and Accounts; The Work of PSD
Previous names: MAFF Pesticides Safety Division 1987–1993
Profile: The Pesticides Safety Directorate is an Executive Agency of the Ministry of Agriculture, Fisheries and Food. Its role is to evaluate and process applications for pesticide approval to ensure that pesticides are effective and pose no unacceptable risks to people, non-target species and the wider environment. All pesticides used in agriculture, horticulture, forestry, food storage and in the home garden, are assessed by PSD for their safety and efficacy before approvals are granted. Pesticides used in other areas, such as

public hygiene, are assessed by the Health and Safety Executive. Once a pesticide is approved, strict controls are exercised over its advertisement, sale, supply, storage and use.

Pesticides Trust
Eurolink Business Centre
49 Effra Road
London
SW2 1BZ
Tel: 0171 274 8895
Fax: 0171 274 9084
Email: pestrust@gn.apc.org
Contact: David Buffin, Information Officer
Founded: 1987
Publications: Pesticides News; Current Research Monitor
Profile: An independent charity addressing the health and environmental problems of pesticides, and working for a sustainable future.

Pig Improvement Company
Dalgety plc
Fyfield Wick
Kingston Bagpuize
Abingdon
Oxfordshire
OX13 5NA
Tel: 01865 820654
Fax: 01865 820187
Contact: Information Secretary

Pig Production Development Committee
c/o Ulster Farmers' Union
475 Antrim Road
Belfast
BT15 3DA
Tel: 01232 370222
Fax: 01232 370814
Contact: Jan McDowell, Secretary
Profile: To oversee the financial management and running of the Northern Ireland Pig Testing Station.

Pig Technology and Development Service
Department of Agriculture for Northern Ireland
Greenmount College of Agriculture and
    Horticulture
22 Greenmount Road
Antrim
BT41 4PU
Tel: 01849 426666
Fax: 01849 426606
Contact: Ms Dera Brannigan, Senior Pig Technologist and Development Adviser
Founded: 1993
Publications: Occasional bulletins

Profile: The purpose of the division is to increase the competitiveness of pig production businesses by the adoption of new technology and systems and by increasing production efficiency and carcase specification.

Pig Veterinary Society
c/o British Veterinary Association
7 Mansfield Street
London
W1M 0AT
Contact: WA Nash, Honorary Secretary
Founded: 1962
Membership: 400
Publications: Pig Veterinary Journal
Profile: The aims of the society are to enhance the knowledge and understanding of disease and herd health and also of important areas of management, husbandry, economics and welfare, in order to provide a better service to the pig industry.

Pisces
PO Box 90
Bristol
BS99 1ND
Tel: 0117 955 9814
Fax: 0117 955 9814
Email: pisces@pisces.demon.co.uk
Contact: Marianne MacDonald, National Secretary
Founded: 1981
Membership: 1,900
Publications: Angling the Facts Booklet; Angling the Neglected Bloodsport (video); numerous leaflets and factsheets
Previous names: Campaign for the Abolition of Angling until 1995
Profile: Pisces exists to disseminate information concerning the cruelty of Britain's most popular bloodsport – angling – providing the scientific evidence that fish feel pain and showing the detrimental effects of angling on the environment and wildlife.

Planning Inspectorate
Department of the Environment
Tollgate House
Houlton Street
Bristol
BS2 9DJ
Tel: 0117 987 8950
Fax: 0117 987 8769
Contact: Dianne Steer, Training Officer
Founded: 1992
Membership: 590

Publications: The Planning Inspectorate Journal; annual and statistical reports
Previous names: Set up as an executive agency in 1992
Profile: The Planning Inspectorate serves the Secretaries of State for the Environment and for Wales on planning appeals and other casework: housing, environment, highways and allied legislations. Through the work of the agency the policies of the Secretaries of State are taken forward, disputes between individuals and public authorities are resolved against the background of these policies.

Planning Service, The
Department of the Environment for Northern
    Ireland
Clarence Court
10–18 Adelaide Street
Belfast
BT2 8GB
Tel: 01232 540540
Fax: 01232 540665
Contact: Mr TW Stewart, Chief Executive
Founded: 1973
Publications: Publications list available
Previous names: Town and Country Planning Service until 1996
Profile: To plan and manage development in ways which will contribute to a quality environment and seek to meet the economic and social aspirations of present and future generations.

Plant Breeding International Cambridge
Unilever
Maris Lane
Trumpington
Cambridge
CB2 2LQ
Tel: 01223 840411
Fax: 01223 845514
Internet: http://www.PBI-Camb.co.uk
Contact: Information Officer

Plant Health and Seeds Inspectorate
Ministry of Agriculture, Fisheries and Food
Foss House
1–2 Peasholme Green
Kings Pool
York
YO1 2PX
Tel: 01904 455174
Fax: 01904 455197
Contact: Kath Neild, Head of PHSI HQ Support Unit
Founded: 1964

Publications: Travellers Guide and PHSI Information Pack available on request
Previous names: Plant Health Inspectorate 1959–1963
Profile: The PHSI is part of MAFF and is responsible in England and Wales for: inspection of imported plant material and preventing the introduction and spread of serious plant pests and diseases; enforcement of the EC single market plant health regime including the issue of plant passports for the export of plants and produce; issue of phytosanitary certificates and certification of agricultural and horticultural crops including seed potatoes, cereals, other agricultural seeds and fruit plants; enforcement of seeds legislation. PHSI HQ is at York and inspectors are based at approximately 40 offices throughout England and Wales. Details are available by contacting the MAFF Helpline on 0645 335577.

Plant Health Branch
Department of Agriculture for Northern Ireland
Room 651
Dundonald House
Upper Newtownards Road
Belfast
BT4 3SB
Tel: 01232 524489
Fax: 01232 524574
Contact: Ivan Millen, Deputy Principal

Plant Health Division
Ministry of Agriculture, Fisheries and Food
Foss House
1–2 Peasholme Green
Kings Pool
York
YO1 2PX
Tel: 01904 455188
Fax: 01904 455199
Contact: Margaret Barry, Executive Officer
Profile: Safeguards and promotes plant health nationally and internationally.

Plant Variety Rights Office and Seeds Division
Ministry of Agriculture, Fisheries and Food
Whitehouse Lane
Huntingdon Road
Cambridge
CB3 0LF
Tel: 01223 342350
Fax: 01223 342386
Contact: Miss K Fox, Deputy Controller
Publications: Guide to National Listing; Guide to Plant Breeders' Rights; Guide to Seed Certification in England and Wales

Profile: A MAFF office of about 40 people in Cambridge. They exist to administer the statutory schemes for the grant of Plant Breeders' Rights and the award of National Listing of plant varieties, and to act as the certifying authority for agricultural and horticultural seeds in England and Wales. There are separate certifying authorities in Scotland and Northern Ireland. The Plant Variety Rights Office also acts as a postbox for applicants wishing to apply for Community Plant Variety rights.

Plantlife
The Natural History Museum
Cromwell Road
London
SW7 5BD
Tel: 0171 938 9111
Fax: 0171 938 9112
Contact: PR Manager
Founded: 1989
Membership: 7,000
Publications: Publications list available
Profile: Plantlife is the only charity in the UK solely devoted to saving wild plants and their habitats.

Plastics Land Drainage Manufacturers Association
7 Hill Street
Birmingham
B5 4UU
Tel: 0121 697 6000
Fax: 0121 697 6113
Contact: Sylvia Battersby, Administrator
Membership: 6
Profile: Manufacturers of plastic pipes for land drainage.

Plumpton College
Ditchling Road
Plumpton
Lewes
East Sussex
BN7 3AE
Tel: 01273 890454
Fax: 01273 890071
Contact: John Brookham, Principal
Founded: 1926
Publications: Outlook
Profile: Land-based college with residential accommodation offering courses from basic craft level to BTEC Higher National Diploma in agriculture, animal care, amenity horticulture, equine studies, forestry and arboriculture, agricultural and horticultural machinery, conservation and environmental studies and wine studies.

Plunkett Foundation
23 Hanborough Business Park
Long Hanborough
Oxfordshire
OX8 8LH
Tel: 01993 883636
Fax: 01993 883567
Email: plunkett@gn.apc.org
Contact: Mr Edgar Parnell, Director
Founded: 1919
Membership: 250
Publications: The World of Co-operative Enterprise; Directory and Statistics of Agricultural Co-operatives and other Farmer Controlled Business
Previous names: Plunkett Foundation for Co-operative Studies until 1992
Profile: A leading authority on the principles and practice of co-operative forms of business in which users are the primary stakeholders. The Plunkett Foundation was established in 1919 as an independent educational trust with charitable status. The foundation has wide ranging experience in offering advice, consultancy and training, and places particular emphasis on converting objectives into practice. In addition to a comprehensive on-site library and information service, the foundation has its own network of advisers and consultants.

Point to Point Owners Association
90A Ellis Road
Crowthorne
Berkshire
RG11 6PS
Tel: 01344 778438

Poland and Poland Bantam Club
Yew Tree Cottage
Main Road
Meriden
West Midlands
CV9 7NH
Tel: 01676 522611
Contact: Mr DW Taylor, Secretary
Profile: A society to promote the Poland breed of poultry.

Poll Charolais Cattle Society
25 Crescent Road
Windermere
Cumbria
Profile: We have been unable to contact this organisation. The details given are unconfirmed.

Poll Friesian Breeders Club
Upper Leigh Farm
East Knoyle

Salisbury
Wiltshire
SP3 6AP
Profile: We have been unable to contact this
organisation. The details given are unconfirmed.

Pollen Research Unit
Worcester College of Higher Education
Henwick Grove
Worcester
WR2 6AJ
Tel: 01905 855200
Fax: 01905 855132
Contact: Dr Jean Emberlin, Director

Pollen UK
The Pollen Research Unit
Worcester College of Higher Education
Henwick Grove
Worcester
WR2 6AJ
Tel: 01905 748677
Fax: 01905 855234
Email: J.Emberlin@worcs.ac.uk
Contact: Dr Jean Emberlin, Director, Pollen
Research Unit
Founded: 1990
Membership: 95
Publications: Airborne Pollens and Spores – A
Guide to Trapping and Counting
Profile: Pollen UK is the pollen monitoring
service of the British Aerobiology Federation. It
consists of a standardised, quality-controlled
network of sites over the UK. The sites are
mostly in hospitals, allergy clinics, universities
and environmental health offices. It includes the
National Pollen and Hayfever Bureau and the
European Aeroallergen Network which is part of
the Europe-wide system.

Polo Pony Welfare Committee
Hurlingham Polo Association
Fairview Cottage
Wicks Green
Binfield
Berkshire
RG42 5PF
Tel: 01344 860976
Fax: 01344 55413
Contact: Lord Patrick Beresford, Chairman
Founded: 1991
Publications: The Polo Advertiser
Profile: The committee was formed by the
Hurlingham Polo Association in 1991 with the
following charter: to monitor all aspects of polo
pony welfare; to liaise with other equine welfare
organisations such as the BHS and the RSPCA;

to provide an informed source for the media and
to recommend any alterations to the rules to the
Hurlingham Pony Association for the benefit of
polo ponies. Its members consist of three
leading vets, four professional players and three
amateur players.

Pond Action
Oxford Brookes University
Gipsy Lane
Headington
Oxford
OX3 0BP
Tel: 01865 483249
Fax: 01865 483282
Email: p0030049@brookes.ac.uk
Contact: Dr Jeremy Biggs, Manager
Founded: 1986
Publications: Publications list available
Profile: Pond Action is an independent non-profit
making organisation, established with the
support of the World Wide Fund for Nature, to
promote freshwater conservation. Pond Action is
a leading national centre for applied research on
pond ecology and conservation and is
responsible for the National Pond Survey. Pond
Action provides technical advice to a wide range
of organisations through its consultancy
programme.

Ponies Association (UK) Ltd
Chesham House
56 Green End Road
Sawtry
Huntingdon
Cambridgeshire
PE17 5UY
Tel: 01487 830278
Fax: 01487 832086
Contact: John Gadsby, Executive Officer
Founded: 1950
Membership: 1,800

Pony Club of Great Britain
British Equestrian Centre
National Agricultural Centre
Stoneleigh Park
Warwickshire
CV8 2LR
Tel: 01203 696697
Fax: 01203 696836
Contact: PR Lord, Development Officer
Founded: 1929
Membership: 40,000
Publications: Yearbook; numerous books,
booklets, wallcharts
Profile: An organisation for young people with an
interest in horses and riding. Aims to encourage

young people to ride and learn to enjoy all sport connected with horses and riding; to provide instruction in riding and horsemanship and instil in members the proper care of their animals; to promote the highest ideals of sportsmanship, citizenship and loyalty, thereby cultivating strength of character and self discipline.

Pony Riders Association of Great Britain
28 Hazelwood
Great Linford
Milton Keynes
Buckinghamshire
MK14 5DU
Tel: 01908 677791
Contact: Nicky Parsler, Secretary

Portland Sheep Breeders Group
Creaconbemoor Cottage
Rackenford
Tiverton
Devon
EX16 8ED
Tel: 01884 881222
Contact: Norma M Sawden, Secretary
Founded: 1996
Membership: 46
Profile: Promotion of Portland sheep.

Pot Bellied Pig Club
Low Deanery Farm
Adelaide Bank
Shildon
County Durham
DL4 1BQ
Tel: 01388 777417
Contact: Heather Powles, Founder
Founded: 1994
Membership: 350
Publications: Bimonthly newsletters
Profile: Their aim is to make the life of pet pigs a better lot by informing people of the special needs, rules, regulations, diets etc. Membership open to pig owners or pig lovers.

Potash Development Association
Brixtarw
Laugharne
Carmarthen
Dyfed
SA33 4QP
Tel: 01994 427443
Fax: 01994 427443
Contact: John Hollies, Director General
Founded: 1985
Profile: The Potash Development Association is an independent organisation providing technical information on fertilisers with particular attention

to potash. A limited amount of new research is funded but the main activity consists of reviewing technical information and disseminating this in a usable and practical form to all interested parties. Seminars, conferences and other training activities are also undertaken. The PDA also undertakes a liaison role to co-ordinate interests and activities within the industry. There is no specific membership – information is available to all.

Potato Marketing Board
Broad Field House
4 Between Towns Road
Cowley
Oxfordshire
OX4 3NA
Tel: 01865 714455
Fax: 01865 782200
Contact: SH Gerrish

Potato Processors Association
Food and Drink Federation
6 Catherine Street
London
WC2B 5JJ
Tel: 0171 836 2460
Fax: 0171 836 0580
Contact: Mr Gavin Roberts, Executive Secretary
Profile: The PPA represents the potato processing industry in the UK.

Potatoes Branch
Department of Agriculture for Northern Ireland
Room 651
Dundonald House
Upper Newtownards Road
Belfast
BT4 3SB
Tel: 01232 524489
Fax: 01232 524574
Contact: Ivan Millen, Deputy Principal

Poultry Association of Northern Ireland
6 Lisnagowan Road
Carland
Dungannon
County Tyrone,
BT70 3LH
Tel: 01232 748233
Fax: 01232 352767
Contact: Dr Alan Morrow, Secretary
Founded: 1969
Membership: 80
Previous names: Poultry Advisers Association Northern Ireland (PAANI)

Profile: Membership is drawn from individuals directly involved with poultry production within the major poultry production companies or as sole traders. In addition members are employees of ancillary companies which serve the poultry industry. The thrust of the association's activities is concerned with organising technical meetings to update members on new developments and applications in the poultry industry. The association is also active in promoting education for and careers within the poultry industry by a series of student awards.

Poultry Club of Great Britain
30 Grosvenor Road
Frampton
Boston
Lincolnshire
PE20 1DB
Tel: 01205 724081
Contact: Mike Clark, General Secretary
Founded: 1877
Membership: 2,000
Publications: Quarterly newsletters; Year Book
Profile: The aims and objectives of the Poultry Club are: the conservation of about 130 pure and rare breeds of poultry and to encourage, assist and advise domestic poultry keepers; to oversee the British Poultry Standards and the introduction of new breeds. In addition the Poultry Club administers the rules of conduct for shows and showing and the Show Awards Scheme.

Prince's Trust
18 Park Square East
London
NW1 4LH
Tel: 0171 543 1234
Fax: 0171 543 1200

Processed Vegetable Growers' Association Ltd
133 Eastgate
Louth
Lincolnshire
LN11 9QG
Tel: 01507 602427
Fax: 01507 600689
Contact: Martin Riggall, Chief Executive
Founded: 1969
Membership: 289
Profile: Working on behalf of growers to improve the strength, stability and profitability of the UK vegetable growing industry, PVGA provides commercial support and market information to its members. Activities cover both fresh and processed vegetables, as well as two wholly owned subsidiaries: Market Intelligence Services Ltd which conducts fresh produce retail price surveys; and Horticultural Export Bureau Ltd, established in 1996 to help develop export opportunities for British growers and marketing organisations.

Processors and Growers Research Organisation
The Research Station
Great North Road
Thornhaugh
Peterborough
PE8 6HJ
Tel: 01780 782585
Fax: 01780 783993
Email: pgro@dial.pipex.com
Contact: GP Gent, Director
Founded: 1944
Membership: 10,000
Publications: Pea Growing Handbook; Field Bean Handbook; Pea and Bean Progress; numerous leaflets and pamphlets
Profile: Applied research on the production and use of peas and beans for both vegetable crops and protein. R and D projects undertaken on a national scale and technical services provided, including a plant clinic for pea and bean growers. Advice provided to growers on all aspects of production.

Professional Plant Users Group
c/o Landscape Institute
6–7 Barnard Mews
London
SW11 1QU
Tel: 0171 738 9166
Contact: Tom La Dell

Progressive Farming Trust Ltd
Elm Farm Research Centre
Hampstead Marshall
Newbury
Berkshire
RG20 0HR
Tel: 01488 658298
Fax: 01488 658503
Email: 100113.751@compuserve.com
Contact: PH Walters, Finance Director
Founded: 1980
Publications: EFRC Bulletin; Organic Farm Management Handbook; publications list available
Profile: EFRC is an international research, advisory and educational organisation based in the UK. It is dedicated to the promotion of organic farming and as such it aims to evaluate and disseminate information about organic farming and its relevance to food quality, soil

fertility, human and animal welfare and the conservation of the countryside. It is a registered charity.

Pullet Hatcheries Association
Suite 101
Albany House
324–326 Regent Street
London
W1R 5AA
Tel: 0171 580 7172
Fax: 0171 580 7082

Pullet Rearers Association
Suite 101
Albany House
324–326 Regent Street
London
W1R 5AA
Tel: 0171 580 7172
Fax: 0171 580 7082

Pygmy Goat Club
106 Lower Bagthorpe
Bagthorpe
Nottingham
NG16 5HF
Tel: 01773 810401
Contact: Mrs E A Glazebrook, Secretary
Founded: 1982
Membership: 500
Publications: Pygmy Goats; Pygmy Goat Notes; herd books
Profile: The Pygmy Goat Club is a breed society formed in 1982 to protect the interests and improve the status of pygmy goats in Great Britain. Membership of the club entitles members to: register a herd name, and register qualifying goats in the herd book; attend P.G.C. meetings, shows and open paddock events; obtain and exchange information via the magazine; have a voice in the affairs of the club. The club also organises workshops and training days for judges.

Quality British Celery Association
133 Eastgate
Louth
Lincolnshire
LN11 9QG
Tel: 01507 602427
Fax: 01507 600689
Contact: Mrs Jayne Dyas, Company Secretary
Founded: 1980
Profile: Marketing information.

Quarantine Kennel Owners Association UK
Hare Lane
Blindley Heath
Lingfield
Surrey
RH7 6JB
Tel: 01342 832161
Fax: 01342 834778
Contact: Nigel Hurst, Secretary
Founded: 1990
Membership: 40
Profile: To promote understanding of Britain's anti-rabies measures and laws and to seek improvements in the care of animals in quarantine.

Quarter Horse Racing UK
Junipers
Croydon Lane
Banstead
Surrey
SM7 3AT
Profile: We have been unable to contact this organisation. The details given are unconfirmed.

RAC Motorsports Association
Motor Sports House
Riverside Park
Colnbrook
Slough
SL3 0HG
Tel: 01753 681736
Fax: 01753 682938
Contact: Information Officer

Racecourse Association Ltd
Winkfield Road
Ascot
Berkshire
SL5 7HX
Tel: 01344 873536
Fax: 01344 27233
Contact: Caroline Davies, Racecourse Liaison Executive
Founded: 1907
Membership: 59
Profile: The Racecourse Association is the trade organisation representing racecourses in Great Britain. It plays a major role in British horse racing and has two seats on the British Horse Racing Board. The RCA represents racecourses in industry discussions. It aims to advise racecourses of developments that may affect their business and provide relevant information and training to racecourses as appropriate.

Racehorse Owners Association Ltd

42 Portman Square
London
W1H 9FF
Tel: 0171 486 6977
Fax: 0171 486 5345
Contact: Mr John Paxman, Director General
Founded: 1945
Membership: 4,000
Publications: The Owner Magazine
Profile: The Race Horse Owners Association provides professional representation in negotiations and discussions with other bodies in the racing industry as well as with the government, the press and the international racing authorities.

Racehorse Transporters Association

Queensberry House
High Street
Newmarket
Suffolk
CB8 9BD
Tel: 01638 665021
Fax: 01638 660283
Contact: Mr Sean Shelley, Chairman
Founded: 1967
Membership: 50
Profile: A non-profit making organisation representing the interests of those involved in the transportation and shipment of bloodstock by air and sea.

Racing Thoroughbred Breeding and Training Board

Suite 16
Unit 8 Kings Court
Willie Snairth Road
Newmarket
Suffolk
CB8 7SG
Tel: 01638 560743
Fax: 01638 660932
Contact: LJR Nash, Director of Training
Founded: 1993
Profile: The Racing and Thoroughbred Breeding Training Board was established to provide staff training for all sectors of the racing and thoroughbred breeding industry. The RTBTB is the lead body offering NVQ/SVQs in racehorse care and management for stable and stud staff.

Radish Growers Association

133 Eastgate
Louth
Lincolnshire
LN11 9QG

Tel: 01507 602427
Fax: 01507 600689
Contact: Mrs Jayne Dyas, Company Secretary
Founded: 1980
Membership: 10
Profile: Marketing information.

Railway Ramblers

102 Salford Road
Aspley Guise
Milton Keynes
MK17 8HZ
Contact: Mr Martin Lutt, Information Officer
Founded: 1978
Membership: 500
Publications: Railway Rambling Magazine
Profile: Railway Ramblers aim to discover, explore and document disused railway lines; to encourage interest in the walking and conservation of abandoned railway lines; to bring to the attention of the appropriate authorities those disused lines most suitable for conversion into public footpaths and cycleways; to promote signposting; to create regional groups of the society throughout the UK with area organisers to organise local groups. They exist to disseminate up-to-date information through reports and newsletters and at all times to respect private property and the country code.

Ramblers' Association

1–5 Wandsworth Road
London
SW8 2XX
Tel: 0171 582 6878
Fax: 0171 587 3799
Contact: Alan Mattingly, Director
Founded: 1935
Membership: 112,000
Publications: Rambling Today; Rambler's Yearbook and Accommodation Guide
Profile: The Ramblers' Association aims to help everyone enjoy walking in the countryside, to foster care and understanding of the countryside, to protect rights of way, to secure public access on foot to open country and to defend the natural beauty of the countryside.

Raptor Foundation

490 Hern Road
Ramsey St Mary
Huntingdon
Cambridgeshire
PE17 1TJ
Tel: 01733 844266
Contact: Secretary
Profile: Involved in the care of wild disabled birds of prey, as well as raptors rescued from

breeders. Involved in promotion or research into raptor ailments. Assists the veterinary schools with placement of student vets at the centre, to obtain experience in the field of raptor treatment. A full 24 hour rescue service is on hand to respond to any call.

Rare Breeds Survival Trust
National Agricultural Centre
Stoneleigh Park
Warwickshire
CV8 2LG
Tel: 01203 696551
Fax: 01203 696706
Contact: Mr R Terry, Administration Secretary
Founded: 1973
Membership: 10,000
Publications: The Ark; leaflets and booklets
Profile: The trust looks after Britain's farm livestock heritage by identifying and monitoring rare and minority breeds, carrying out scientific evaluation and promoting and publicising them. There are currently over 40 rare breeds of cattle, sheep, pigs, horses and goats and a number of breeds of poultry. The trust also acts as the pedigree registration authority for nine breeds of sheep as well as Bagot goats.

Rare Poultry Society
Alexandra Cottage
8 St Thomas Road
Great Glen
Leicester
LE8 0EG
Tel: 01533 593730
Fax: 01533 781748
Contact: Richard J Billson, Secretary
Founded: 1969
Membership: 300
Publications: Members newsletter; breeders lists
Previous names: Rare Breeds Society until 1981

Reaseheath College
Reaseheath
Nantwich
Cheshire
CW5 6DF
Tel: 01270 625131
Fax: 01270 625665
Email: rheath1@reaseheath.ac.uk
Internet: http://www.reaseheath.ac.uk
Contact: Mr Vic Croxon, Principal
Founded: 1921
Publications: Reaseheath Farm Guide, Reaseheath Prospectus, Wildlife and Conservation Plan

Previous names: Cheshire Farm Institute, Cheshire College of Agriculture until 1993
Profile: Reaseheath College is one of Britain's leading specialist colleges offering training and education to degree level in the food, land-based and environment related industries. The college is central in Britain and easily accessible by road and rail from all directions. The college is ten minutes walking distance from the historic town of Nantwich. Reaseheath is set in over 400 acres of beautiful countryside which includes an ornamental lake, woodland, meadows and many other natural features.

Red Deer Commission
Knowsley
82 Fairfield Road
Inverness
IV3 5LH
Tel: 01463 231751
Fax: 01463 712931
Contact: Andy Rinning, Chief Executive and Secretary
Founded: 1959
Publications: Annual Report; Red Deer Management; numerous pamphlets and posters
Profile: The Red Deer Commission has the general functions of furthering the conservation and control of red deer in Scotland and of keeping under review all matters relating to deer. The commission also has the power to advise, in the interest of conservation, any landowner on the control of deer numbers. It has the statutory duty, with powers, to prevent damage to agriculture and forestry by deer and to carry out research into matters of scientific importance relating to deer. The commission employs its own team of experienced field staff which can be deployed to any location in Scotland as required.

Red Poll Cattle Society
The Market Hill
Woodbridge
Suffolk
IP12 4LU
Tel: 01394 380643
Fax: 01394 382310
Contact: P Ryder-Davies, Secretary
Founded: 1888
Membership: 187
Publications: Newsletter
Profile: The breed society of the Red Poll breed. Red Polls are a dual purpose breed of cattle with commercial herds in both the dairy and beef sectors. The breed is naturally polled, is very hardy and long lived and is producing excellent profits for both beef and milk.

Reforesting Scotland
21a Coates Crescent
Edinburgh
EH3 7AF
Tel: 0131 226 2496
Fax: 0131 226 2503
Email: reforscot@gn.apc.org
Internet:
   http://www.scotweb.co.uk/environment/reforest
Contact: Administrator
Founded: 1991
Membership: 800
Publications: Reforesting Scotland, Radical
Rowan, Norway Study Tour Report
Profile: Reforesting Scotland is dedicated to
ecological restoration and sustainable
development in a well-forested land, and regards
the regeneration of Scotland's devastated
ecology as inseparable from revitalising
communities around a thriving forest-based
economy. It aims to raise awareness of Scottish
deforestation in its local and global context, and
offer positive solutions. Its membership has a
vast amount of professional and private expertise
in ecology, forestry, community involvement,
environmental education, arts and craft skills,
design, architecture and building. Various
projects include: collecting, growing and planting
local native tree seed, encouraging forest culture,
ecological and timber building and work with
schools.

Registers of Scotland Executive Agency
Meadowbank House
153 London Road
Edinburgh
EH8 7AU
Tel: 0131 659 6111
Fax: 0131 479 3688

Remote Sensing Society
Department of Geography
University of Nottingham
Nottingham
NG7 2RD
Tel: 01602 515435
Fax: 01602 515249
Email: rss@nottingham.ac.uk
Contact: The Administrative Secretary
Founded: 1974
Membership: 800
Publications: Publications list available

Residuary Milk Marketing Board
Royal Thames House
Portsmouth Road
Thames Ditton

Surrey
KT7 0EL
Tel: 0181 910 4343
Fax: 0181 910 4302
Contact: DJ Rive, Company Secretary and
Administrator
Founded: 1933
Membership: 29,000
Previous names: Milk Marketing Board of
England and Wales until 1994
Profile: Since 1st November 1994 the Milk
Marketing Board has existed in the form of a
Residuary Body, with its functions confined to
those set out in the Milk Marketing Board
(Residuary Functions) Regulations 1994.

Respect for Animals
PO Box 500
Nottingham
NG1 3AS
Tel: 0115 952 5440
Fax: 0115 979 9159
Contact: Mark Glover, Campaigns Officer
Founded: 1993
Publications: Monthly Live Export Newsletter;
Quarterly Fur Newsletter
Profile: Respect for Animals is dedicated to
ending the fur trade, an industry that seven out
of ten people think is cruel and unnecessary.
More recently the organisation has become
involved with the campaign to end live exports
and was instrumental in persuading the ferry
companies to stop carrying live animals and is
determined to see an end to the trade. Respect
for Animals is not an anti-farming organisation
but is dedicated to ending unnecessary cruelty to
animals.

Retail Fruit Trade Federation
Office 3 Market Centre
Western International Market
Hayes Road
Southall
Middlesex
UB2 5XT
Tel: 0181 569 3090

Rhode Island Red Club
6 West Heath
Vapery Lane
Pirbright
Surrey
GU24 0QD
Tel: 01483 474888
Contact: Mr DG Love, Secretary
Profile: A society to promote the Rhode Island
Red breed of poultry.

Riding for the Disabled Association
National Agricultural Centre
Stoneleigh Park
Warwickshire
CV8 2LZ
Tel: 01203 696510
Fax: 01203 696532
Contact: WJ Davies, Director
Founded: 1969
Membership: 714
Publications: RDA News
Profile: The aim of the RDA is to provide the opportunity of riding and driving to benefit health and well-being of the disabled. 714 member groups.

Riversdale Crayfish
Riversdale Farm
Stour Provost
Gillingham
Dorset
SP8 5RZ
Tel: 01747 838495
Fax: 01747 838495
Contact: Kenneth J Richards, Partner
Founded: 1975
Publications: ABC of Crayfish Husbandry
Previous names: British Crayfish Marketing Association until 1989
Profile: Supply of information and advice on pond and stew pond construction. Supply of breeding stock, traps, etc. Supply of eating crayfish to hotels, restaurants and private parties.

Road Haulage Association Ltd
35 Monument Hill
Weybridge
Surrey
KT13 8RN
Tel: 01932 841515
Fax: 01932 852516

Rodbaston College
Rodbaston
Penkridge
Staffordshire
ST19 5PH
Tel: 01785 712209
Fax: 01785 715701

Romney Sheep Breeders' Society
2 School Road
St Mary in the Marsh
Romney Marsh
Kent
TN29 0DG
Tel: 01797 363839
Fax: 01797 363839

Contact: Mr David Roberts, Society Secretary
Founded: 1895
Membership: 150
Publications: Annual flock book; occasional hand book
Profile: Pedigree livestock society keeping bloodstock records and promoting the breed.

Rosecomb Bantam Club
1 Kielder Salmon Hatchery
Kielder
Bellingham
Hexham
Northumberland
NE48 1HX
Tel: 01434 250269
Contact: Mr P Gray, Secretary
Profile: A society to promote the Rosecomb Bantam breed of poultry.

Roslin Institute
Roslin
Midlothian
EH25 9PS
Tel: 0131 527 4200
Fax: 0131 440 0434

Rough Fell Sheep Breeders Association
Weasdale Farm
Newbiggin-on-Lune
Kirkby Stephen
Cumbria
CA17 4LY
Tel: 01539 623238
Contact: Mrs P Tyson, Secretary
Founded: 1926
Membership: 180
Publications: Annual flock book
Profile: Caters for all the needs of Rough Fell sheep breeders.

Roussin Sheep Society
Halfacre
The Park
Thornhill
Dumfriesshire
DG3 5JT
Tel: 01848 331640
Fax: 01848 331640
Contact: Allan Wright, Secretary
Founded: 1989
Membership: 52
Publications: Roussin Review
Profile: The Roussin Sheep Society is a registration society for the breed. It is also involved in breed promotion and maintaining breed standards.

Rowett Research Institute

Greenburn Road
Bucksburn
Aberdeen
AB21 9SB
Tel: 01224 712751
Fax: 01224 715349
Email: enquiries@rri.sari.ac.uk
Contact: Christine Cook, External Affairs
Manager
Founded: 1913
Publications: Annual Report
Profile: The institute is the pre-eminent
European centre for integrated research in
nutrition and biological sciences of relevance to
health, food and agriculture.

Royal Agricultural Benevolent Institution

Shaw House
27 West Way
Oxford
OX2 0QH
Tel: 01865 724931
Fax: 01865 790384
Contact: Air Commodore R Duckett CVO AFC,
Chief Executive
Founded: 1860
Publications: Annual Report
Previous names: Agricultural Benevolent
Institution until 1863
Profile: The Royal Agricultural Benevolent
Institution is the national charity for retired,
disabled and other disadvantaged farmers, farm
managers and their families and spends over
£600,000 each year in providing direct help to
well over 1,000 people. Assistance is tailored to
meet individual needs and may consist of regular
cash grants or assistance with home fees as well
as the provision of such items as telephone, TV
and licence. The institution is supported in its
work by county committees who both help find
and service the beneficiaries and raise funds.

Royal Agricultural College, The

Cirencester
Gloucestershire
GL7 6JS
Tel: 01285 652531
Fax: 01285 650219
Email: nh@racdos.demon.co.uk
Contact: Professor AS Jones, Principal
Founded: 1845
Publications: RAC Journal; prospectuses;
Annual Report
Profile: The college was founded in 1845 as the
first agricultural college in the English speaking
world. Since that time, the college has been at the
forefront of agricultural education, offering the
technical and managerial skills needed to run
successful business enterprises in the rural sector
and elsewhere. For many years, the college has
attracted students from all parts of the world, and
graduates have gone on to make significant
contributions to all areas of agriculture,
agribusiness and the rural sector throughout the
world. Cirencester graduates can now be found in
senior positions in business, government and the
agricultural advisory services across the world.

Royal Agricultural Society of England

National Agricultural Centre
Stoneleigh Park
Warwickshire
CV8 2LZ
Tel: 01203 696969
Fax: 01203 696900
Contact: Jayne Spence, Agricultural Marketing
Manager
Founded: 1838
Membership: 15,000
Publications: Journal of the Royal Agricultural
Society of England; Royal Show Guide; Royal
Show Catalogue
Previous names: English Agricultural Society
until 1840
Profile: The RASE promotes and develops the
agricultural industry. It organises the Royal Show,
Town and Country Festival and numerous other
special technical events.

Royal and Ancient Golf Club of St Andrews

St Andrews
Fife
KY16 9JD
Tel: 01334 472112
Fax: 01334 477580

Royal Association of British Dairy Farmers

Dairy House
60 Kenilworth Road
Leamington Spa
Warwickshire
CV32 6JX
Tel: 01926 887477
Fax: 01926 887585
Contact: Mr Philip M Gilbert, Chief Executive
Founded: 1876
Membership: 2,500
Publications: RABDF News

Royal Bath and West of England Society

The Showground
Shepton Mallet
Somerset
BA4 6QN

Tel: 01794 823260
Contact: Brig SDA Firth, Chief Executive
Founded: 1777
Publications: Show catalogue; show programme; catalogue of library

Royal Botanic Garden Edinburgh
Inverleith Row
Edinburgh
EH3 5LR
Tel: 0131 552 7171
Fax: 0131 552 0382

Royal Botanic Gardens
Kew
Richmond upon Thames
Surrey
TW9 3AE
Tel: 0181 940 1171
Fax: 0181 332 5197
Founded: 1759
Profile: The Royal Botanic Gardens holds the largest and most diverse collection of living plants and the most comprehensive research collection of preserved plant material in the world.

Royal Botanic Gardens – School of Horticulture
Royal Botanic Gardens
Kew
Richmond upon Thames
Surrey
TW9 3AB
Tel: 0181 332 5545
Fax: 0181 332 5574
Email: l.leese@rbgkew.org.uk
Contact: Ian Leese, Principal
Founded: 1962
Publications: Course leaflets
Profile: The Kew diploma course, offered by the School of Horticulture, since 1963 gives a broad-based training in amenity horticulture. The course aims to provide students with an opportunity to study scientific, technical and managerial subjects at first degree level, whilst gaining practical experience and responsibility working at the world's foremost botanic garden. It is now the only botanic garden in the UK to offer a three-year full-time training course.

Royal Caledonian Horticultural Society
28 SilverKnowes Southway
Edinburgh
EH4 5PX
Tel: 0131 336 5488
Fax: 0131 336 1847

Contact: John MacLennan, Secretary
Founded: 1809
Membership: 800
Publications: Caledonian Gardener
Profile: The Royal Caledonian Horticultural Society, founded in 1809, is Scotland's senior gardening society and welcomes everyone interested in gardening, professional and amateur, beginner and advanced. It is based in Edinburgh but includes members nationwide. It organises meetings, flower shows and excursions.

Royal College of Veterinary Surgeons
Belgravia House
62–64 Horseferry Road
London
SW1P 2AF
Tel: 0171 222 2001
Fax: 0171 222 2004
Contact: Andrea Samuelson, Parliamentary/External Affairs Officer
Founded: 1844
Membership: 17,000
Publications: RCVS News; RCVS Register and Directory; RCVS Directory of Practices
Profile: The Royal College of Veterinary Surgeons is a statutory body for the veterinary profession. Founded by Royal Charter in 1844, it operates under the Veterinary Surgeons Act 1966. The RCVS is responsible for the management, registration, education and training, and professional conduct of the veterinary profession in the UK. Any veterinary surgeon wishing to practice in the UK must be registered with the RCVS and is subject to the RCVS code of conduct.

Royal Commission on Ancient and Historical Monuments in Wales
Crown Building
Plas Crug
Aberystwyth
Ceredigion
SY23 1NJ
Tel: 01970 624381
Fax: 01970 627701

Royal Commission on Environmental Pollution
Church House
Great Smith Street
London
SW1P 3BZ
Tel: 0171 276 2080
Fax: 0171 276 2098
Contact: Dr David Lewis, Secretary

Founded: 1970
Publications: Nineteen reports (up to 1996), available from HMSO
Profile: The commission's terms of reference are: to advise on matters, both national and international, concerning the pollution of the environment; on the adequacy of research in this field; and the future possibilities of danger to the environment.

Royal Commission on the Ancient and Historical Monuments of Scotland

16 Bernard Terrace
Edinburgh
Midlothian
EH8 9NX
Tel: 0131 662 1456
Fax: 0131 662 1477
Contact: Mr Roger J Mercer, Secretary
Founded: 1908
Publications: Publications list available
Profile: The aims of the Royal Commission on the Ancient and Historical Monuments of Scotland are: to survey and record the man-made environment of Scotland; to compile and maintain in the National Monuments Record of Scotland a record of the archaeological and historical environment; and to promote an understanding of this information by all appropriate means.

Royal Commission on the Historic Monuments of England

National Monuments Record Centre
Kemble Drive
Swindon
Wiltshire
SN5 2GZ
Tel: 01793 414707
Fax: 01793 414707
Email: info@rchme.gov.uk
Contact: Jon Cannon, Information Officer
Founded: 1908
Membership: 260
Publications: Annual Report; newsletter; book catalogue
Profile: The national body for the survey and record of England's archaeology and architecture. Detailed surveys of archaeological sites and historic buildings throughout the country – the results are placed in the National Monuments Record, available through the headquarters in Swindon and a search room in central London.

Royal Cornwall Agricultural Association

The Royal Cornwall Showground
Wadebridge
Cornwall
PL27 7JE
Tel: 01208 812183
Fax: 01208 812713
Contact: Christopher Riddle, Secretary
Founded: 1793
Membership: 6,500
Publications: A History of the Royal Cornwall Show 1793–1993; annual show catalogues
Previous names: Cornwall Agricultural Society until 1825; Cornwall Agricultural Association until 1858
Profile: The RCAA organises the Royal Cornwall Show – a major agricultural show, regularly attracting up to 110,000 people, based on the association's permanent showground at Wadebridge.

Royal (Dick) School of Veterinary Studies

University of Edinburgh
Summerhall
Edinburgh
EH9 1QH
Tel: 0131 650 6130
Fax: 0131 650 6585
Email: Dick.vet@ed.ac.uk
Contact: JM Hackel, Senior Administration Officer

Royal Forestry Society of England, Wales and Northern Ireland

102 High Street
Tring
Hertfordshire
HP23 4AF
Tel: 01442 822028
Fax: 01442 890395
Contact: Mrs Carol Banfield, Secretary
Founded: 1882
Membership: 4,350
Publications: Quarterly Journal of Forestry
Profile: The RFS is the largest forestry society in Great Britain with more than 4,000 members. It is an independent, registered, educational charity founded in 1882. The society is a broad based organisation with open membership. It brings together all those interested in trees – woodland owners, foresters, arboriculturists, planners, scientists, woodmen, landscape architects, land managers, conservationists and the general public. The RFS promotes the conservation and expansion of tree resources through good forestry management which takes into account their wildlife, landscape, recreational and socio-economic value.

Royal Geographical Society (with the Institute of British Geographers)

1 Kensington Gore
London
SW7 2AR
Email: l.craig@rgs.org
Contact: Secretary
Founded: 1830
Membership: 13,000
Publications: Geographical Journal; Area; Transactions; Research Newsletter
Previous names: Royal Geographical Society until 1995
Profile: The RGS (with the IBG) has 19 research groups. The Rural Geography Study Group has more than 200 members drawn from academia, policy makers and others. It has a Young Rural Researchers' Forum held at the annual conference in January, in addition to a main session and a 2–3 day meeting in August/September annually. The study group has established links with counterparts in Europe and beyond.

Royal Highland and Agricultural Society of Scotland

Royal Highland Centre
Ingliston
Newbridge
EH28 8NF
Tel: 0131 333 2444
Fax: 0131 333 5236
Contact: Mr Hywel Davies, Chief Executive
Founded: 1784
Membership: 14,200
Publications: Royal Highland Review; Royal Highland Spring Newsletter
Profile: The society has been a driving force in Scottish agriculture for over 200 years. It organises the annual Royal Highland Show, the major market place for Scotland's land-based industries which generates over £80m of business. It is also a showcase which creates a wider public understanding of the management of the land and rural resources. The RHASS awards high achievers in agriculture, forestry and the food industry in Scotland.

Royal Horticultural Society

PO Box 313
80 Vincent Square
London
SW1P 2PE
Tel: 0171 834 4333
Fax: 0171 630 6060
Founded: 1804
Membership: 204,000

Publications: The Garden; The New Plantsman; The Orchid Review; books, handbooks and international registers
Profile: The RHS is one of the world's leading organisations involved in horticulture. It runs the renowned Lindley Library as well as a seed exchange scheme. A range of information services including answering enquiries and identifying plants and fruits is offered. It conducts flower shows, seminars, workshops, courses and examinations. Services are mainly free and primarily for members.

Royal Institution of Chartered Surveyors in Scotland

9 Manor Place
Edinburgh
EH3 7DN
Tel: 0131 225 7078
Fax: 0131 226 3599
Email: scot@rics.co.uk
Contact: Eileen M Masterman, Director
Founded: 1897
Membership: 6,500
Publications: Scottish Chartered Surveyor
Profile: The principal objectives of the RICS in Scotland are to: promote the knowledge and skills of Chartered Surveyors and the services they offer; maintain high standards of qualification for membership of the institution; maintain high standards of professional conduct; and ensure the continuing development of the knowledge and skill base of Chartered Surveyors.

Royal Institution of Chartered Surveyors, The

12 Great George Street
Parliament Square
London
SW1P 3AD
Tel: 0171 222 7000
Fax: 0171 222 9430
Email: infocentre@rics.co.uk
Contact: RICS Information Centre (0171 334 3842)
Founded: 1868
Membership: 92,000
Publications: List of publications available
Profile: The RICS is the world's largest source of professional advice to the property markets. Chartered Surveyors play a key role in adding value to rural property throughout the UK. The RICS regulates them in the public interest imposing rules of conduct on ethical matters such as confidentiality and conflict of interest. When advising clients they must hold professional indemnity insurance and follow strict rules on the handling of clients' money.

Continual updating of skills is compulsory for all practising members. Individual Chartered Surveyors are identified by the letters ARICS or FRICS. Titles used by firms of Chartered Surveyors working in rural property are: rural property agents/consultants; valuers/county valuers; land agents – factors (Scotland); agricultural/livestock auctioneers; estate/property managers; agricultural consultants; farm business consultants; rural consultants; and, forestry consultants.

Royal Isle of Wight Agricultural Society
169 Staplers Road
Newport
Isle of Wight
PO30 2DP
Tel: 01983 826275
Contact: AJ Wheeler, Secretary

Royal Jersey Agricultural and Horticultural Society
Springfield
St Helier
Jersey
Channel Islands
JE2 4LF
Tel: 01534 37227
Fax: 01534 246692
Contact: James W Godfrey, Chief Executive
Founded: 1833
Membership: 950
Publications: The Jersey at Home
Profile: The leading private organisation representing agriculture in Jersey. Activities include; operation of studbook facilities for Jersey cattle breeders; organisation of two agricultural shows; publication of journals; organisation of international conferences and international promotion of the Jersey breed.

Royal Lancashire Agricultural Society
5 Windmill Cottages
Preston New Road
Mellor Brook
Blackburn
BB2 7NT
Tel: 01254 813769
Fax: 01254 812522
Contact: Mrs SE Walsh, Secretary
Founded: 1767
Membership: 854
Publications: Annual Report; show programmes, schedule and catalogue
Profile: To promote the best of agriculture in Lancashire through the staging of the annual county show.

Royal Manx Agricultural Society
Kerrowmoar Farm
Kerrowkeil
Ballasalla
Isle of Man
Tel: 01624 824410
Contact: Mrs V Garrett, Secretary

Royal Meteorological Society
104 Oxford Road
Reading
Berkshire
RG1 7LL
Tel: 01734 568500
Fax: 01734 568571
Email: execsec@royal-met-soc.org.uk
Contact: Mrs A G Collins, Accounting and Administration Officer
Founded: 1850
Membership: 3,300
Publications: Publications list available

Royal Norfolk Agricultural Association
The Showground
Dereham Road
New Costessey
Norwich
NR5 0TT
Tel: 01603 748931
Fax: 01603 748729
Contact: Mr John Purling, Chief Executive
Founded: 1847
Membership: 3,500
Publications: Annual Report; Annual Show Programme and Catalogue; The Norfolk Mardler
Profile: The RNAA organises one of the largest 2 day agricultural shows in the country. The Royal Norfolk Show is in June each year. The association aims to promote improvement in the breeding of livestock and plants and the invention and improvement of agricultural machines and implements, the encouragement of skills in agriculture, horticulture and allied systems of husbandry and the encouragement of agricultural science, research and education by holding exhibitions, shows or otherwise.

Royal Scottish Agricultural Benevolent Institution
Ingliston
Newbridge
EH28 8NB
Tel: 0131 333 1023
Contact: Ian Purves-Home, Director
Founded: 1897
Publications: Annual Report; newsletter
Profile: RSABI provides financial and/or in kind help to anyone in distress or need who is or has

been in farming, forestry, aquaculture, horticulture and rural estate work in Scotland and their dependents. Help can be in the form of annual or single grants. Each case is considered on its individual circumstances.

Royal Scottish Forestry Society
62 Queen Street
Edinburgh
EH2 4NA
Tel: 0131 225 8142
Fax: 0131 225 8142
Contact: Mr Michael Osborne, Director

Royal Scottish Geographical Society
Graham Hills Building
40 George Street
Glasgow
G1 1QE
Tel: 0141 552 3330
Fax: 0141 552 3330
Contact: Maureen Thompson, Administrator
Founded: 1884
Membership: 2,200
Publications: Scottish Geographical Magazine; Geogscot
Profile: The Royal Scottish Geographical Society aims to be the foremost independent body in Scotland promoting the understanding of the inter-relationships between people, places and the environment through geographical research, education, debate, travel and exploration. RSGS has an extensive library, makes annual awards to distinguished geographers, supports exhibitions and is involved in geographical education.

Royal Smithfield Club
Brierley House
Summer Lane
Combe Down
Bath
Somerset
BA2 5LE
Tel: 01225 837904
Fax: 01225 834741
Contact: David Child, Secretary
Founded: 1798
Membership: 1,600
Publications: Publications list available
Profile: The purpose of the club is to promote improvement in the breeding of cattle, sheep, pigs, poultry and other livestock. The club's major work is the organisation and management of the world renowned livestock and carcase sections of the Royal Smithfield Show held at Earls Court Exhibition Centre, London in November.

Royal Smithfield Show
Earls Court Exhibition Centre
Warwick Road
London
SW5 9TA
Tel: 0171 370 8226
Fax: 0171 370 8230
Contact: Robin Hicks, Show Director
Founded: 1799
Profile: Organisers of the biennial Royal Smithfield Show held at London's Earls Court Exhibition Centre at the end of November in even years. The UK's premier agricultural business event with displays of agricultural machinery, supplies and services together with cattle and sheep and carcase sections.

Royal Society for the Prevention of Accidents
Edgbaston Park
353 Bristol Road
Birmingham
B5 7ST
Tel: 0121 248 2000
Fax: 0121 248 2001

Royal Society for the Prevention of Cruelty to Animals
The Causeway
Horsham
West Sussex
RH12 1HG
Tel: 01403 264181
Fax: 01403 241048
Contact: Dr Martin Potter, Head, Farm Animals Department
Founded: 1824
Membership: 26,000
Publications: Publications list available
Profile: The RSPCA, the world's leading and best known animal welfare organisation, was founded by MP Richard Martin in 1824 and received its 'Royal' seal from Queen Victoria in 1840. As a charity, the society receives no state aid and is totally dependent on the public, through donations, to achieve its objectives of promoting kindness and preventing cruelty to all animals. At headquarters, the society employs over 200 personnel including scientific and legal experts, educational officers, journalists, administrative and secretarial staff in addition to 300+ inspectors and staff at the 109 animal establishments throughout England and Wales.

Royal Society for the Protection of Birds
The Lodge
Sandy
Bedfordshire
SG19 2DL

Tel: 01767 680551
Fax: 01767 692365
Contact: Anne Harley, Head of Education
Founded: 1889
Membership: 890,000
Publications: Birds; Conservation Review;
Wingbeat; Sixth Sense; Birdlife; Fieldfare
Profile: The RSPB is the charity that takes action
for wild birds and the environment. They
research problems, campaign for solutions,
manage nature reserves, and educate and advise
others – in the UK and abroad. Farmland birds
have suffered dramatic declines in numbers in
the last 25 years and a current priority is to
research the cause of the decline and propose
solutions.

Royal Ulster Agricultural Society

The Kings Hall
Balmoral
Belfast
BT9 6GW
Tel: 01232 665225
Fax: 01232 661264
Contact: W H Yarr, Chief Executive
Founded: 1854
Membership: 3,500
Publications: Annual Report
Previous names: North East Agricultural
Association until 1903
Profile: The Royal Ulster Agricultural Society is
incorporated under the Education and
Endowments (Ireland) Act 1885 upon trust to
promote agriculture, industries, arts, sciences
and literature in Northern Ireland by holding
agricultural shows or by any other means as may
be found expedient. The Royal Ulster stages the
annual Balmoral Show, the national agricultural
show of Northern Ireland. This three day event
takes place in May each year. In addition it stages
a one day indoor dairy orientated winter fair in
December, three annual pedigree pig shows and
sales and a biennial pig and poultry fair.

Royal Veterinary College, The

Royal College Street
London
NW1 0TU
Tel: 0171 468 5000
Fax: 0171 388 2342
Email: [name]@rvc.ac.uk
Contact: Paul Probyn, Academic Registrar
Founded: 1791
Publications: Annual Report; Undergraduate
Prospectus; Postgraduate Prospectus
Profile: The Royal Veterinary College offers the
following degrees: BVetMed, leading to

membership of the RCVS; MSc degrees in food
animal health, veterinary microbiology, veterinary
pathology and wild animal health; MVetMed; and
the research degrees of MPhil, PhD and
DVetMed. Veterinary nursing courses run jointly
with the College of Animal Welfare lead to RCVS
examinations. The Unit for Veterinary Continuing
Education runs updating courses and has the
largest collection of veterinary audiovisual
material in Europe.

Royal Welsh Agricultural Society Ltd

Llanelwedd
Builth Wells
Powys
LD2 3SY
Tel: 01982 553683
Fax: 01982 553563
Contact: Mr PD Guthrie, Secretary
Founded: 1904
Membership: 12,000
Publications: The Royal Welsh Agricultural
Society Journal; Royal Welsh Show Programme;
Royal Welsh Show Catalogue
Profile: An agricultural show held annually in July
provides a prime shop window for farming, and
there are sections covering the whole of farming
and rural life in Wales. Attracts more than
230,000 visitors, 6,500 livestock entries and up
to 1,000 trade stands. Competitions and
demonstrations in forestry, horticulture, farriery,
sheep shearing, produce and hand crafts, honey
section, canine, fur and feather, pets and cavies,
tug of war, sheep dog trials, Miss Royal Welsh,
country pursuits and lots more for a truly
enjoyable four days.

Rural Action for the Environment

Rural Action National Development Team
ACRE Offices
Somerford Court
Somerford Road
Cirencester
Gloucestershire
GL7 1TW
Tel: 01285 659599
Fax: 01285 654537
Contact: G Kirkham, Development Officer
Founded: 1992
Publications: Publications list available
Profile: Rural Action for the Environment
provides advice, training and specialist help to
community groups in rural areas of England who
wish to undertake environmental projects, and
support to groups via county newsletters of
environmental and community organisations.
Project grants of up to £2,000 available to
community groups, parish and town councils,

funded by Countryside Commission, English Nature and the Rural Development Commission.

Rural and Agricultural Affairs Advisory Committee
BBC
Pebble Mill
Birmingham
B5 7QQ
Tel: 0121 414 8888
Fax: 0121 414 8634
Contact: Fiona Lynch, Secretary
Profile: To offer advice to the BBC's programme makers who operate in the subject matters of farming, food (production and distribution), the countryside and the environment.

Rural Crafts Association
Brook Road
Wormley
Surrey
GU8 5UA
Tel: 01428 682292
Fax: 01428 685969
Contact: Trevor J Sears, Director
Founded: 1970
Membership: 600
Publications: Members bulletin; annual programme of events
Profile: The association provides supervised exhibition space at the major horticultural, agricultural and equestrian events in the UK. The association organises six major 'Crafts at Christmas' shows in November/December each year. It advises on marketing, business matters, group insurance and facilitates communication between like minded people.

Rural Design and Buildings Association
Harper Adams Agricultural College
Newport
Shropshire
TF10 8NB
Tel: 01952 814555
Fax: 01952 814777
Contact: Fiona Grice, National Secretary
Founded: 1956
Membership: 420
Publications: Farm Buildings Pocketbook, Members Register, Rural Design and Buildings Journal, The Building Chronicle
Previous names: Farm Buildings Association until 1991; Farm and Rural Buildings Centre
Profile: The only UK organisation concerned with the development, research and monitoring of rural buildings. The name embraces all structures and fixed equipment either for farm buildings, rural, industrial or commercial purposes. The

membership is a mixture of college, corporate and individual members, whose professions include engineers, builders, surveyors, planners, land agents and architects.

Rural Development Commission
141 Castle Street
Salisbury
Wiltshire
SP1 3TP
Tel: 01722 336255
Fax: 01722 332769

Rural Development Council for Northern Ireland
Loughry College of Agriculture
Cookstown
County Tyrone
BT80 9AA
Tel: 01648 766980
Fax: 01648 766922
Contact: Jimmy Armstrong, Chief Executive
Founded: 1991
Publications: Publications list available
Profile: The Rural Development Council assists local communities in the disadvantaged rural areas to develop quality projects that will create sustainable employment.

Rural Development Division (DANI)
Department of Agriculture for Northern Ireland
Room 144b
Dundonald House
Upper Newtownards Road
Belfast
BT4 3SB
Tel: 01232 524880
Fax: 01232 524884
Contact: Mr GLT McWhinney, Head of Rural Development Division
Founded: 1991
Publications: Rural Development Strategy 1994–1999
Profile: To stimulate the economic and social revitalisation of the most disadvantaged rural areas of Northern Ireland through partnerships between the public, private and voluntary sectors.

Rural Development Division (DOE)
Department of the Environment
2 Marsham Street
London
SW1P 3EB
Tel: 0171 276 3000
Fax: 0171 276 0790

Profile: The RDD has responsibility for: economic and social development of rural areas; sponsorship of the Rural Development Commission; the Rural White Paper; environmental aspects of forestry policy; environmental aspects of agricultural policy; tree preservation orders, amenity trees and hedgerows.

Rural Economy and Society Study Group
c/o Department of City and Regional Planning
University of Wales, Cardiff
PO Box 906
Cardiff
CF1 3YN
Tel: 01222 87400
Contact: Dr AC Flynn

Rural Economy Group
11 Charterhouse Street
London
EC1M 6AA
Tel: 0171 253 2252
Fax: 0171 417 8033
Contact: Joe Hardwicke
Founded: 1991
Membership: 100
Publications: Submission to the 1995 Rural White Paper
Profile: The group holds regular meetings in the House of Lords under the chairmanship of Lord Wade of Chorlton. The group seeks, through the meetings, to come up with ideas and solutions about rural England.

Rural Education and Development Association
Scottish Agricultural Colleges
Oak Bank Road
Perth
PH1 1HF
Tel: 01738 636611
Fax: 01738 627860
Contact: JB Dakers, Honorary General Secretary
Founded: 1895
Membership: 140
Publications: Progress; members newsletter
Previous names: Agricultural Education Association until 1991
Profile: REDA provides a focus to enable professionals working in rural areas to develop their professional activities. It is the professional association of all those working in rural development – as advisers and consultants, whether in agricultural or in a wider rural or countryside development role; as trainers, teachers and lecturers; and as environmental or

conservation specialists. REDA provides information about rural issues such as the latest developments in agriculture, rural business management and conservation. It creates opportunities for liaison between specialists in different fields, thus promoting greater understanding between scientists, educationalists, advisers, consultants and countryside managers and helping individuals see the context in which they work. Members also gain access to sectors of the rural scene that are not routinely available.

Rural Forum
Highland House
46 St Catherine's Road
Perth
PH1 5RY
Tel: 01738 634565
Fax: 01738 638699
Email: rural@post.almac.co.uk
Contact: Dermot Grimson, Director
Founded: 1982
Membership: 800
Publications: Rural Forum; research, conference reports, case studies, grants and advice information
Profile: Rural Forum is an alliance of rural interests covering the range of rural sectors in Scotland: agriculture, social and economic issues, housing and the environment. A wide range of projects focus on two main areas: stimulating and supporting local action and addressing policy issues on an integrated basis. Rural Forum undertakes and commissions research, runs a small community grant scheme and provides practical advice and assistance to rural communities.

Rural History Centre
University of Reading
The University
Whiteknights
PO Box 229
Reading
Berkshire
RG6 6AG
Tel: 01734 318660
Fax: 01734 751264
Contact: John S Creasey, Librarian and Information Officer
Founded: 1951
Publications: Publications list available
Previous names: Museum of English Rural Life 1951–1968; Institute of Agricultural History and Museum of English Rural Life 1968–1992
Profile: A national centre for the study of the history of farming, food and the countryside, holding documents and artefactual collections,

including a library, business and society records and archives, photographs and film, the bibliographic indexes and the object collections of the museum. They provide the foundation for research into the history of agriculture, horticulture, woodlands, farm mechanisation, food production, rural trades and industries and the conservation of the rural environment. The collections of information, archives and photographs, may be viewed or consulted by appointment.

Rural Housing Trust

Head Office
Prince Consort House
27/29 Albert Embankment
London
SE1 7TJ
Contact: Moira Constable, Chief Executive
Founded: 1975
Publications: Publications list available
Previous names: The National Agricultural Centre Rural Trust until 1990
Profile: The Rural Housing Trust is the leading provider of affordable housing for local people in villages throughout England. Through the two national and 15 county based Rural Housing Associations it has established, RHT had completed 2,000 rented and shared ownership homes in over 230 villages by the end of 1996. RHT fieldworkers work closely with Parish and District Councils in identifying housing need, finding suitable sites and obtaining the finance for small clusters of houses to be built – for the young and the elderly – that help keep villages as mixed and thriving communities.

Rural Pharmacists Association, The

South Dene
Gratton Lane
Yelverton
Devon
PL20 6AW
Tel: 01822 853515
Fax: 01822 855337
Contact: Secretary
Profile: This association consists of, and provides assistance and advice to community pharmacists practising in or having an interest in rural areas. It is a professional organisation which deals with rural issues affecting pharmacists.

Rural Training Development Association

14 Meadow View
Church Lane
Cogges
Witney
Oxfordshire
OX8 6TY

Tel: 01993 778689
Fax: 01993 778689
Contact: Miss C Richmond, Honorary Secretary
Founded: 1991
Membership: 100
Publications: Members Directory
Profile: RTDA is an educational charity formed to assist instructors and organisers of training within the rural community. They aim to increase the opportunities for access to professional training; improve the quality of training offered and provide a range of services to support their members in their work. RTDA is non-political and is open to all those who are involved in rural training.

Rural Voice

The Arthur Rank Centre
National Agricultural Centre
Stoneleigh Park
Warwickshire
CV8 2LZ
Tel: 01203 696969
Fax: 01203 696900
Contact: Rosemary Keep, Secretariat
Founded: 1980
Publications: Rural Voice News; Occasional Papers
Profile: An alliance of national organisations representing rural communities. Rural Voice exists to co-ordinate groups and organisations which are based in the countryside. It lobbies and briefs government and promotes schemes and surveys which bring rural communities together to help each other.

Russian Horse Society

Priam Lodge Stables
Burgh Heath Road
Epsom
Surrey
KT17 4NN
Tel: 01372 722080
Fax: 01372 749676
Contact: Mrs Regine Lansley, Secretary
Founded: 1990
Profile: To import Russian horses with the intention of promoting the breeds in Europe.

Rutland Agricultural Society

Burley Road
Cottesmore
Oakham
Rutland
LE15 7BN
Tel: 01572 813138

Rycotewood College
Priest End
Thame
Oxfordshire
OX9 2AF
Tel: 01844 212501
Fax: 01844 218809
Contact: Evers Pearce, Marketing and Business
Development Manager
Founded: 1938
Profile: College of further education, originally
started as a college of rural crafts in 1930s.
Developed into a specialist college for
engineering, agriculture, horticulture,
construction plant design, furniture making, fine
craftsmanship and information technology.

Ryeland Flock Book Society
101 Grandstand Road
Hereford
HR4 9NE
Tel: 01432 267221
Contact: Mrs K J Bennett, Secretary
Founded: 1902
Membership: 300
Publications: Flock book, newsletters and
leaflet

Saanen Breed Society
British Goat Society
117 Lakes Lane
Newport Pagnell
Buckinghamshire
MK16 8HT
Tel: 01908 613706
Contact: Mrs J Tomlinson, Secretary
Founded: 1980
Membership: 65
Publications: Members newsletter, Annual Stud
List
Profile: A breed society for the promotion of the
Saanen dairy goat.

SAC
SAC Central Office
West Mains Road
Edinburgh
EH9 3JG
Tel: 0131 535 4000
Fax: 0131 662 1323
Contact: Ian Taylor, Head of Communications
Group
Founded: 1990
Publications: Publications list available
Previous names: East of Scotland College of
Agriculture, West of Scotland College, North of

Scotland College of Agriculture amalgamated to
form SAC in 1990
Profile: The principal activities of SAC are
advanced education and training, research and
development and technology transfer through
advice, consultancy and scientific and business
services. Its scientific expertise covers food
production, food manufacturing, land use and
environmental management alongside expertise
in economics, business management and
resource management. SAC has three Centres of
Study at Aberdeen, Ayr and Edinburgh, eight
Veterinary Centres and over 20 local Advisory
Offices in Scotland. A range of commercial
services is provided throughout the UK and
abroad through SAC's associate company
COSAR.

Sacred Trees Trust
31 Kings Avenue
Leeds
LS6 1QP
Tel: 0113 245 1309

Saddlers Company
40 Gutter Lane
London
EC2V 6BR
Tel: 0171 726 8661
Fax: 0171 600 0386
Contact: W S Brereton Martin, The Clerk
Founded: 1100
Membership: 200
Profile: A city livery company, active in support
of the craft and trade of saddlery, of
equestrianism and of education.

Saintfield and District Agricultural Society
24 Ballyminstragh Road
Killinchy
County Down
BT23 6RE
Profile: We have been unable to contact this
organisation. The details given are unconfirmed.

Salers Cattle Society
Brook House Farm
Norbury
Whitchurch
Shropshire
SY13 4HY
Tel: 01948 667223
Fax: 01948 667223
Contact: John Crowe, Secretary
Founded: 1985
Membership: 200
Publications: Salers Journal

Profile: The Salers Cattle Society was formed to run the herd book. The breed is mainly used as a suckler cow or crossed with British or continental breeds to produce cross-bred suckler cows. The breed is renowned for its ease of calving, mothering ability, milkyness, sound hooves and legs, its hardiness to adapt to both hot and cold climates and its longevity. The breed originated in the Central Massif area of France, at an altitude of 5–6,000 ft in this mountainous area based around the medieval city of Salers.

Salmon and Trout Association
Fishmongers' Hall
London Bridge
London
EC4R 9EL
Tel: 0171 283 5838
Fax: 0171 929 1389
Contact: C W Poupard, Director
Founded: 1903
Membership: 14,000
Profile: The governing body for game angling. Guardians of game angling is their motto.

Sanctuary for Donkeys
Sandhill
Wormley
Godalming
Surrey
Profile: We have been unable to contact this organisation. The details given are unconfirmed.

Sand and Gravel Association Ltd
1 Bramber Court
2 Bramber Road
London
W14 9PB
Tel: 0171 381 8778
Fax: 0171 381 8770
Contact: TA MacIntyre, Director
Founded: 1930
Membership: 90
Publications: Bulletin; Borrowed Land; Borrowing Land for a Better Britain; Association Fact Book
Previous names: Ballast Sand and Allied Trades Association until 1948
Profile: The specialist trade association for companies in England, Scotland and Wales producing sand and gravel from the land or beneath the sea. The Sand and Gravel Association represents the interests of its member companies, provides them with a range of information services and encourages them to achieve high environmental standards.

School of Agriculture, Food and Environment
Cranfield University
Silsoe
Bedford
MK45 4DT
Tel: 01525 863318
Fax: 01525 863316
Email: recruitment@silsoe.cranfield.ac.uk
Contact: Margaret Merredy, Student Recruitment Executive
Founded: 1960
Publications: Publications list available
Previous names: Merger of Silsoe College, Shuttleworth College and the Soil Survey and Land Research Centre
Profile: Silsoe College, Shuttleworth College and the Soil Survey and Land Research Centre form the School of Agriculture, Food and Environment of Cranfield University. Cranfield is one of Europe's leading universities with an international reputation for teaching and applied research in the fields of engineering and applied science and management studies. The school is a leading centre for higher education, training, research and consultancy focusing on the rural sector worldwide – the environment, food, agriculture, engineering, business management, marketing and technology.

Science Service
Department of Agriculture for Northern Ireland
Science Administration
Room 647 Dundonald House
Upper Newtownards Road
Belfast
BT4 3SB
Tel: 01232 524635
Fax: 01232 525002
Contact: Dr Cecil H McMurray, Chief Scientific Officer
Publications: Annual Report on R and D
Profile: Science and technology in agriculture, food, fisheries, forestry, horticulture, plant and animal science, agricultural economics and the environment.

Scotch Half Bred Association
Faughhill
Melrose
Roxburghshire
TD6 9HT
Tel: 01835 822226
Fax: 01835 823121
Contact: Miss Heather Thomson, Secretary
Founded: 1987
Membership: 48
Publications: Annual promotions leaflet

Profile: The association exists to promote the Scotch Half Bred sheep breed in its native area of south Scotland and Northumberland, but also further afield by attending major shows and NSA events nationwide.

Scotch Mule Association
Croftfoot
Symington
Biggar
Lanarkshire
ML12 6LW
Tel: 01899 308549
Contact: Secretary

Scotch Quality Beef and Lamb Association
Rural Centre
West Mains
Ingliston
Newbridge
Midlothian
EH28 8NZ
Tel: 0131 333 5335
Fax: 0131 333 2935
Contact: Elizabeth A Welsh, PR Manager
Founded: 1974
Profile: SQBLA's work is the promotion and marketing of Scotch beef and lamb in home and export markets, and this work ranges from delivering guarantees of approved farming practices (SQLBA farm assurance) on to meat plant guarantees of production standards and product quality (Guild of Scotch Quality Meat Suppliers, est. 1988), and confirming retailers' sourcing of Scotch beef and lamb (associate membership of guild). Both farm and plant assurances are subject to independent inspections. In addition to well established work with wholesale and retail sectors SQBLA is increasingly involved with the expanding quality catering sector.

Scots Dumpy Club
Tower Fields
Tusmore Road
Souldern
Bicester
Oxfordshire
OX6 9HY
Tel: 01869 346554
Contact: Mrs C Hamilton-Gould, Secretary
Profile: A society to promote the Scots Dumpy breed of poultry.

Scots Grey Club
21 Kerswell Avenue
Kaimend

Carnwath
Lanark
Lanarkshire
ML11 8LE
Tel: 01555 840813
Contact: Mr J Robertson, Secretary
Profile: A society to promote the Scots Grey breed of poultry.

Scott Abbott Arable Crops Station
Sacrewell Lodge
Thornhaugh
Peterborough
Cambridgeshire
PE8 6HJ
Profile: We have been unable to contact this organisation. The details given are unconfirmed.

Scottish Agricultural Arbiters Association
10 Dublin Street
Edinburgh
EH1 3PR
Tel: 0131 556 2993
Fax: 0131 557 5542
Contact: Donald G Rennie, Secretary
Founded: 1924
Membership: 250
Profile: The membership of the association consists of working farmers, surveyors, auctioneers, estate factors and others with an interest in agricultural arbitration and valuation work. The purpose of the association is to ensure consistency of approach to these matters throughout Scotland and to represent the interests of agricultural arbiters and valuers generally.

Scottish Agricultural Consultative Panel
Scottish Office Agriculture, Environment and
    Fisheries Department
Pentland House
47 Robb's Loan
Edinburgh
EH14 1TW
Tel: 0131 244 6374
Fax: 0131 244 6006
Contact: Mike Lyman

Scottish Agricultural Organisation Society Ltd
The Rural Centre
West Mains
Ingliston
Newbridge
Midlothian
EH28 8NZ
Tel: 0131 335 3777
Fax: 0131 335 3773

Contact: Mrs Eunice Mole, Resources Development Manager
Founded: 1905
Membership: 108
Publications: Newsbrief
Profile: Founded in 1905 the principal aim of the society is to strengthen the profitability of farming and other rural industries in Scotland, by supporting and developing co-operation and co-operatively organised business. SAOS promotes its members' interests to government departments, enterprise networks and within the industry itself, and is the political representative of Scottish farm and rural co-operative businesses in the UK and Europe. A team of eight permanent staff provides a business development and consultancy service, which includes feasibility studies, business planning, EC and UK grant sourcing and applications, and management recruitment. SAOS's strategic development role is supported by the Scottish Office.

Scottish Agricultural Research Institutes
Pentlansfield
Roslin
Midlothian
EH25 9RF
Profile: We have been unable to contact this organisation. The details given are unconfirmed.

Scottish Agricultural Science Agency
Scottish Office Agriculture, Environment and
    Fisheries Department
East Craigs
Edinburgh
EH12 8NJ
Tel: 0131 244 8890
Fax: 0131 244 8940
Email: library@sasa.gov.uk
Contact: Vanessa Glynn, Head of Administration
Founded: 1925
Publications: Annual Report and Accounts; Citizens Charter Standard Statement
Previous names: Official Seed Testing Station and Agricultural Science Service until 1992
Profile: The agency exists to provide government with expert scientific information and advice on agricultural crops, horticultural crops and aspects of the environment. It also performs statutory and regulatory work in relation to national, EC and other international legislation and agreements on plant health, bee health, variety registration and crop improvement, genetically manipulated organisms and the protection of crops, food and the environment. Since SASA's principal customer is SOAEFD, the agency operates mainly for

Scottish interests, but it also seeks to meet the requirements of other agriculture departments as well as various UK and international bodies, local government, academic and research institutes, and private organisations and individuals.

Scottish Agricultural Statistics Service
University of Edinburgh
James Clerk Maxwell Building
Kings Building
Mayfield Road
Edinburgh
EH9 3JZ
Profile: We have been unable to contact this organisation. The details given are unconfirmed.

Scottish Agricultural Wages Board
Room 241
Pentland House
47 Robbs Loan
Edinburgh
EH14 1TY
Tel: 0131 244 6397
Fax: 0131 244 6551
Contact: Mrs Sandra A Cranford, Board Secretary
Publications: Annual Wages Orders
Profile: The Scottish Agricultural Wages Board is sponsored by the Agricultural Wages (Scotland) Act 1949 to set minimum wage rates and other conditions of service for workers in agriculture. The board sets the wage rates or conditions and then produces a booklet called the Wages Order. The Scottish Office enforces these orders and provides secretariat services to the board.

Scottish Ancona Club
1 Leckby House
Flaxton
York
North Yorkshire
YO6 7PY
Tel: 01904 863870
Contact: Mr PE Smedley, Secretary
Profile: A society to promote the Ancona breed of poultry.

Scottish Anglers National Association
Calendonia House
South Gyle
Edinburgh
EH2 9DQ
Tel: 0131 339 8808
Contact: Jane Wright, Honorary Secretary
Founded: 1880
Publications: Sanacast; members handbook

Scottish Arboricultural Society
4 Knightsbridge Road
Dechmont
West Lothian
Profile: We have been unable to contact this organisation. The details given are unconfirmed.

Scottish Assessor's Association
Woodhill House
Westburn Road
Aberdeen
Grampian
AB9 2LU
Tel: 01224 664360
Fax: 01224 690101
Contact: David A Henry, President
Founded: 1874
Membership: 57
Profile: The object of the association is to encourage amongst its members the exchange of ideas regarding their statutory duties; to promote uniformity in the operation of valuation and council tax and to act as a consultative and advisory body; and to represent the collective interest of its members.

Scottish Association for Public Transport
5 St Vincent Place
Glasgow
G1 2HT
Tel: 0141 639 3697
Fax: 0141 639 3697
Contact: Dr John McCormick, Chairman
Founded: 1972
Membership: 150
Publications: Newsletter
Previous names: Scottish Railway Development Association
Profile: Campaigns for better public passenger transport (including innovative variants and easy interchange with cars) and shift of road freight to rail and water based modes where feasible. Supports transport and land use policies encouraging sustainable development and an improved environment.

Scottish Association of Master Bakers
Atholl House
4 Torpichen Street
Edinburgh
EH3 8JQ
Tel: 0131 229 1401
Fax: 0131 229 8239
Email: master.bakers@samb.demon.co.uk
Contact: Ian Hay, Chief Executive
Founded: 1891
Membership: 550

Publications: Annual Year Book; Scottish Baker Magazine
Profile: The association is an employers/trade association. It exists to promote and maintain the interests of the bakery trade; to deal with legislation; to negotiate wage and condition agreements; to introduce and administer schemes of benefit to members; to establish, administer and maintain education and training facilities; to publish a yearbook and other trade literature; to promote social activities; and, to administer a benevolent fund.

Scottish Association of Meat Wholesalers
Kinnaird Business and Consultancy
The Old Schoolhouse
Kinnaird
Perthshire & Kinross
PH14 9QY
Tel: 01828 686116
Fax: 01828 686377
Contact: JHA Stevenson, Executive Manager
Founded: 1970
Membership: 40
Profile: The association has been established for over 20 years to represent the views of the Scottish meat slaughtering, processing and wholesaling industries. These views are expressed in Edinburgh, London and Brussels where the association takes its place on all relevant meat committees organised by government and the meat and livestock Commission. The association, run by an executive, currently has 40 members representing all sectors of the industry, large and small. It reports to its members regularly on all relevant trade topics including legislation. It takes a keen interest in training within the industry, annually it organises a conference which is combined with its annual general meeting.

Scottish Association of Young Farmers Clubs
Young Farmers' Centre
Ingliston
Newbridge
EH28 8NE
Tel: 0131 333 2445
Fax: 0131 333 2488
Contact: Fiona Bain, National Secretary
Founded: 1938
Membership: 4,000
Publications: Members Handbook; Annual Report
Profile: A rural youth organisation in Scotland promoting education, training, personal development, friendship and fun to young people between the ages of 14 and 26 years.

Scottish Beekeepers Association
44 Dalhousie Road
Kilbarchan
Johnston
Renfrewshire
PA10 2AT
Tel: 01505 702680
Contact: David B N Blair, Publicity Convenor
Founded: 1912
Membership: 1,000
Publications: The Scottish Beekeeper
Profile: The SBA's aim is to bring together all those interested in beekeeping to the benefit of horticulture and agriculture by providing helpful facilities. It publishes a monthly magazine, maintains the Moir library in Edinburgh, conducts examinations in the art of beekeeping and provides an insurance and compensation scheme for members.

Scottish Cashmere Producers Association
Dunrowan
Armadale
Rhu
Helensburgh
Dunbartonshire
G84 8LG
Tel: 01436 820318
Fax: 01436 820318
Contact: Mr John D Barker, Secretary
Founded: 1986
Membership: 73
Publications: SCPA News and SCPA Bulletin
Profile: An association of farmers and interested bodies to promote and encourage the farming of cashmere goats. Activities include dissemination of technical and general information about cashmere farming, marketing of members' cashmere fibre, production and marketing of garments made from members' fibre.

Scottish Conservation Projects Trust
Balallan House
24 Allan Park
Stirling
FK8 2QG
Tel: 01786 479697
Fax: 01786 465359
Email: 106022.2373@compuserve.com
Contact: Katherine Johnson, Press and Publicity Officer
Founded: 1984
Membership: 1,000
Publications: Training course programme, action break programme, Curam, DIY manual
Profile: SCP is Scotland's leading charity involving people in improving the quality of the environment through practical conservation work.

Scottish Corn Trade Association
39 George Street
Edinburgh
EH2 2HZ
Tel: 0131 225 6834
Fax: 0131 225 4049
Founded: 1969
Membership: 80

Scottish Council for National Parks
15 Park Terrace
Stirling
FK8 2JT
Tel: 01786 465714
Fax: 01786 473843
Contact: Brian K Parnell, Honorary Secretary and Vice Chairman
Founded: 1991
Publications: News sheets, responses to government and recruiting material
Previous names: Originally established in 1943 inactive from 1964 to 1991
Profile: The council is a campaigning voluntary organisation which aims to secure legislation for establishing National Parks in Scotland.

Scottish Country Life Museums Trust
National Museums of Scotland
Queen Street
Edinburgh
Midlothian
EH2 1JD
Tel: 0131 333 2674
Fax: 0131 333 2674
Contact: Gavin Sprott, Secretary
Founded: 1970
Membership: 200
Publications: Annual Review
Profile: The trust aims to facilitate the foundation of a national open-air museum of country life in Scotland and to promote knowledge of the history of the Scottish countryside and country communities.

Scottish Countryside Activities Council
11 West Craigs Crescent
Edinburgh
EH12 8NB
Tel: 0131 339 7014
Contact: Dr R Aitken, Chairman

Scottish Countryside Rangers' Association
PO Box 37
Stirling
FK8 2BL

Contact: H McLeanop, Secretary
Founded: 1974
Membership: 300

Scottish Crofters Union
Old Mill
Broadford
Isle of Skye
IV49 9AQ
Tel: 01471 822529
Fax: 01471 822799
Contact: Fraser Macleod, Director
Founded: 1986
Membership: 4,000
Publications: The Crofter; Crofter Forestry
Handbook, Rural Development and the
Environment
Profile: An association of crofters (small scale
part-time tenant farmers) covering the
Highlands and Islands of Scotland. They
promote crofting, and lobby UK and EU
governments; provide advice and assistance
on crofting problems; have a competitive
insurance scheme; develop forward looking
policies for crofting; have links with similar
small farming organisations throughout the UK
and Europe and beyond.

Scottish Crop Research Institute
Invergowrie
Dundee
DD2 5DA
Tel: 01382 562731
Fax: 01382 562426
Email: mail@scri.sari.ac.uk
Contact: TD Heilbronn, Deputy Scientific Liaison
Officer
Founded: 1981
Publications: Annual Report; Bulletins of the
Scottish Society for Crop Research
Previous names: Merger of the Scottish
Horticultural Research Institute and the Scottish
Plant Breeding Station in 1981
Profile: SCRI is a major international centre for
research on agricultural, horticultural and
industrial crops important to northern Britain, to
the rest of the UK and the world, and on the
underlying processes common to all plants. It
aims to increase knowledge in the basic
biological sciences; to improve crop quality and
utilisation by the application of conventional and
molecular genetic techniques and novel
agronomic practices; and to develop
environmentally benign methods of protecting
crops from depredations by pests, pathogens
and weeds.

Scottish Dairy Association
Phoenix House
South Avenue
Clydebank
Glasgow
G81 2LG
Tel: 0141 951 1170
Fax: 0141 951 1129
Contact: K J Hunter, Company Secretary
Founded: 1989
Membership: 50
Previous names: Scottish Dairy Trade
Federation until 1995
Profile: The association represents the interests
of dairy processors and distributors active in
Scotland.

Scottish Early Potato Growers Association
Mid Dinduff Farm
Leswalt
Stranraer
Dumfriesshire
DG9 0LH
Tel: 01776 870254
Contact: WL McCrone, Chairman
Founded: 1936
Membership: 40
Profile: A group which combines early potato
growers, mostly in SW Scotland, with merchants
who handle the crop.

Scottish Egg Producer Retailers Association
11 Meadowbank
Polmont
Falkirk
FK2 0UG
Tel: 01324 715337
Fax: 01324 715337
Email: 100043.462@compuserve.com
Contact: Mr Dennis Surgenor, Secretary
Founded: 1970
Membership: 107
Publications: Weekly market report on egg
prices and market situation
Profile: The association was formed in 1970 to
counter the adverse effect of the loss of the
British Egg Marketing Board, which among many
other services, provided for the purchase of
surplus eggs from producer retailers. With the
banding together of Scottish egg producers it
was thought that an egg exchange within the
association would be possible and would enable
a base price to be established. This proved to be
most successful and continues today. The
association acts also as a contact with the
Scottish Office, government and the UK industry
through its membership of the BEIC Committee.

Scottish Egg Trade Association
98 West George Street
Glasgow
G2 1PS
Tel: 0141 333 1674
Fax: 0141 333 1675
Contact: John F Lindsay, Secretary
Founded: 1896

Scottish Endurance Riding Club
9 Elliot Road
Jedburgh
Roxburghshire
TD8 6HN
Tel: 01835 863828
Fax: 01835 864504
Contact: Lindsay Wilson, General Secretary
Founded: 1982
Membership: 600
Publications: Club newsletter; Rule and
Reference Book; Basic Skills and Training Manual
Profile: SERC is a flourishing club, administered
by volunteers, based in Scotland with nine
branches covering all regions. Over 80 rides are
held during the year ranging from 10 miles to
100 miles over two days. Special events include
Scottish Championships, Inter Branch
Competition, Gold Series, Celtic Challenge – an
exchange competition with their endurance
counterparts in Ireland.

Scottish Enterprise
120 Bothwell Street
Glasgow
G2 7JP
Tel: 0141 248 2700
Fax: 0141 221 3217
Contact: Marion Mackay-Francis, Strategic
Futures Team
Founded: 1991
Publications: Scottish Enterprise Strategy;
Annual Report; Sectoral Strategy Documents
Profile: Scottish Enterprise is a network of 13
local enterprise companies with a remit for
economic development and training across
Scotland (excluding the Highlands and Islands).
Scottish Enterprise works in urban and rural
areas, with businesses and in partnerships to
create jobs and wealth in Scotland.

Scottish Environment Protection Agency
Head Office
Erskine Court
The Castle Business Park
Stirling
FK9 4TR
Tel: 01786 457700
Fax: 01786 446885

Contact: Mr Alastair Paton, Chief Executive
Founded: 1996
Profile: The agency was established under the
Environment Act 1995. It is responsible for the
functions of Scotland's former River Purification
Boards, Her Majesty's Industrial Pollution
Inspectorate and for certain local authority
functions in respect of waste management and
air pollution. The intention of the government in
creating the agency has been to provide a
one-door approach to pollution of waters, air and
land. The agency operates through three regions,
East, West and North, and has a main board and
three regional boards.

Scottish Environmental Forum
Bonnington Mill Business Centre
72 Newhaven Road
Edinburgh
EH6 5QG
Tel: 0131 554 9977
Fax: 0131 554 8656
Email: foescotland@gn.apc.org
Contact: Phil Matthews, Co-ordinator
Founded: 1991
Publications: Publications list available
Profile: Scotland's co-ordinating body for issues
of sustainable development.

**Scottish Farm and Countryside Educational
    Trust**
Royal Highland Centre
Ingliston
Newbridge
EH28 8NF
Tel: 0131 333 3805
Fax: 0131 333 5236
Contact: Dorothy Amyes, Director
Founded: 1978
Publications: Publications list available
Previous names: Scottish Office of the
Association of Agriculture 1978–1990; Scottish
Association of Agriculture until 1994
Profile: The aim of the trust is to help the public
gain a better understanding of farming and rural
issues through the provision of an independent
information service, resource materials and other
activities relating to Scottish agriculture and the
countryside.

Scottish Farm Venison Ltd
Marketing Office
Red Lion House
Alwinton
Morpeth
Northumberland
NE65 7BQ

Tel: 01669 650286
Fax: 01669 650379
Contact: Alex Bowles, Chief Executive
Founded: 1993
Membership: 9
Publications: Poultry and Game Buyers Guide
Profile: SFV Ltd is a marketing co-op handling venison products. The company purchases stock from members and other producers and arranges slaughter and butchery, sale and distribution. The company also trades in other supplies of venison and other related products. Based in Scotland the company also purchases and trades in products from outside Scotland. The co-op is primarily a wholesaler supplying distributors and major retailers.

Scottish Federation of Egg Packers
Suite 101
Albany House
324–326 Regent Street
London
W1R 5AA
Tel: 0171 580 7172
Fax: 0171 580 7082

Scottish Federation of Meat Traders' Associations (Inc.)
8 Needless Road
Perth
PH2 0JW
Tel: 01738 637472
Fax: 01738 441059
Contact: Secretary
Founded: 1918
Membership: 600
Publications: Official Handbook, newsletter
Profile: SFMTA is a trade association representing the interests of Scotland's retail butchers. The federation has well established links with the Scottish Office, the Meat and Livestock Commission and other official bodies and works to promote the health of the retail meat trade in Scotland.

Scottish Field Studies Association
Kindrogan Field Centre
Enochdhu
Blairgowrie
Tayside
PH10 7PG
Tel: 01250 881286
Fax: 01250 881433
Contact: Alison Gimingham, Director
Founded: 1940
Membership: 200
Publications: Members newsletter

Profile: The aim of the association is to promote an understanding and appreciation of the Scottish countryside. It achieves this by running residential courses, providing facilities and tutors at its field centre in Perthshire.

Scottish Flour Millers Association
26 Newtyle Road
Ralston
Paisley
Renfrewshire
OA1 3JX
Profile: We have been unable to contact this organisation. The details given are unconfirmed.

Scottish Forestry Trust
5 Dublin Street Lane South
Edinburgh
EH1 3PX
Tel: 0131 478 7044
Fax: 0131 538 7222
Contact: Dr David Rook, Director
Founded: 1983
Publications: Annual Reports
Profile: The Scottish Forestry Trust is a charitable trust established in 1983 to promote education, training and research in forestry and silviculture. The trust's primary objective is to support private sector forestry by contributing to the scientific, technical and economic information it requires to enable it to develop its role in UK forestry. Forestry is defined as the forestry industry as a whole, including its contribution to landscape, recreation, wildlife and environment. Projects in all of the sciences which bear upon forestry are supported by the trust.

Scottish Game Club
14 Colinton Mains Loan
Edinburgh
EH13 9 AJ
Tel: 01314 414759
Contact: Mr W S Orr, Secretary
Profile: A society to promote the Game breed of poultry.

Scottish Goatkeepers Federation
Ladeside House
Gallow Hill Road
Kinross
Profile: We have been unable to contact this organisation. The details given are unconfirmed.

Scottish Inland Waterways Association
139 Old Dalkeith Road
Edinburgh
EH16 4SZ

Tel: 0131 664 1070
Contact: GA Hunter OBE, Secretary
Founded: 1960

Scottish Land Use Association
c/o Macauley Land Use Research Institute
Craigiebuckler
Aberdeen
AB9 7AT
Tel: 01224 318611
Fax: 01224 311556
Contact: Dr Peter Newbold, Secretary

Scottish Landowners' Federation
25 Maritime Street
Leith
Edinburgh
EH6 5PW
Tel: 0131 555 1031
Fax: 0131 555 1052
Contact: Brian Speed, Director
Founded: 1906
Membership: 3,700
Publications: Landowning in Scotland; Bulletin
of Activities; various booklets and leaflets
Profile: The SLF provides a unique vehicle for
landowners and rural land managers to express
their views, safeguard their interests and
exchange opinions. It is the nationally recognised
body which represents all those involved in the
ownership and management of rural land in
Scotland. The aims and objectives of the SLF are:
to promote high standards of management and
use of land; to ensure proper communication on
matters relating to the ownership of land
between its members, other organisations and
the wider public; to ensure that legislation and
government policies affecting land ownership
and use are prepared with proper consideration
for the responsibilities and rights of landowners,
in addition to the well-being of rural
communities, the environment, and the wider
public interest.

**Scottish Milk Marketing Board (Residuary
Body)**
46 Underwood Road
Paisley
Renfrewshire
PA3 1TJ
Tel: 0141 848 0404
Fax: 0141 889 8819

Scottish Milk Records Association
46 Underwood Road
Paisley
Renfrewshire
PA3 1TJ

Tel: 0141 887 1234
Fax: 0141 889 8819
Contact: Mr Jack Lawson, Director

Scottish Minorca Club
Roxburgh House
Roxburgh Street
Kelso
Roxburghshire
TD5 7DH
Tel: 01573 224210
Contact: Mr RW Murray, Secretary
Profile: A society to promote the Minorca breed
of poultry.

Scottish National Ski Council
Caledonia House
South Gyle
Edinburgh
EH12 9DQ
Tel: 0131 317 7280
Fax: 0131 339 8602
Contact: Information Officer

Scottish Natural Heritage
Battleby
Redgorton
Perth
PH1 3EW
Tel: 01738 627921
Fax: 01738 441897

**Scottish Office Agriculture, Environment and
Fisheries Department**
The Scottish Office
Pentland House
47 Robb's Loan
Edinburgh
EH14 1TY
Tel: 0131 244 6472
Fax: 0131 244 4071
Email: ranh.so.ph@gtnet.gov.uk
Contact: JN Randall, Head of Rural Affairs
Previous names: Scottish Office Environment
Department until 1995
Profile: SOAEFD is responsible for rural policy
co-ordination in Scotland.

Scottish Organic Producers Association
Milton of Cambus Farm
Doune
Perthshire
FK16 6HG
Profile: We have been unable to contact this
organisation. The details given are unconfirmed.

Scottish Ornithologists' Club

21 Regent Terrace
Edinburgh
EH7 5BT
Tel: 0131 556 6042
Contact: S Laing, Secretary
Founded: 1936
Membership: 2,500
Publications: Scottish Bird News; Scottish Birds;
Scottish Bird Report
Profile: The club has 14 branches around the
country and has the general aim of encouraging
ornithology in Scotland. Indoor meetings and
field trips are organised and there is an annual
weekend conference in the autumn with a one
day conference in the spring.

Scottish Pekin Bantam Club

94 Port Street
Dalbeattie
Kirkcudbrightshire
Dumfries and Galloway
DG5 4BG
Tel: 01556 610925
Contact: Mr T Moffat, Secretary
Profile: A society to promote the Pekin Bantam
breed of poultry.

Scottish Permaculture

c/o Earthward Institute
Tweed Horizons
Newtown St Boswell's
Roxburghshire
TD6 0SG
Tel: 01835 822122
Fax: 01835 822199
Email: earthward@scotborders.co.uk
Contact: Graham Bell, Director
Founded: 1988
Membership: 100
Publications: Publications list available
Profile: A network of those interested in a
permaculture approach to community design,
land usage and economic renewal.

Scottish Plymouth Rock

Strathmore
Beith Road
Glengarnock
Beith
Ayrshire
KA14 3BX
Tel: 01505 683251
Contact: Mr A Kirkpatrick, Secretary
Profile: A society to promote the Plymouth Rock
breed of poultry.

Scottish Potato Trade Association

25 South Methven Street
Perth
PH1 5ES
Tel: 01738 620451
Fax: 01738 631155
Contact: R David Hunter, Association Secretary
Founded: 1940
Membership: 100
Publications: Members newsletters
Previous names: Scottish Potato Trade
Executive until 1970
Profile: The Potato Trade Association exists to
promote the rights and interests of association
members and to foster, develop and protect the
Scottish potato trade in whatever manner may
be deemed expedient.

Scottish Recreational Land Association

Carhurly Farmhouse
St Andrews
Fife
KY16 8QH
Profile: We have been unable to contact this
organisation. The details given are unconfirmed.

Scottish Rhode Island Red Club

24 Biggar Road
Libberton
Carnwath
Lanark
ML11 8LX
Tel: 01555 840867
Contact: Mr J Gardiner, Secretary
Profile: A society to promote the Rhode Island
Red breed of poultry.

Scottish Rights of Way Society

John Cotton Business Centre
10 Sunnyside
Edinburgh
EH7 5RA
Tel: 0131 652 2937
Fax: 0131 652 2937
Contact: Judith Lewis, Secretary
Founded: 1845
Membership: 2,500
Publications: Publications list available
Profile: The society works to safeguard rights of
way throughout Scotland. They provide
information and assistance with disputes to
members of the public, local authorities and
others. They maintain records of rights of way
and signpost them. They liaise with government
and other organisations to ensure their policies
do not adversely affect rights of way.

Scottish Rosecomb Club
Loan Knowe Farm
Eccles
Kelso
Roxburghshire
TD5 7QT
Tel: 01573 470333
Contact: Mr A Robertson, Secretary
Profile: A society to promote the Rosecomb breed of poultry.

Scottish Salmon Board
Drummond House
Scott Street
Perth
PH1 5EJ
Tel: 01738 635973
Fax: 01738 621454
Contact: Mr Michael A Lloyd, Marketing Manager
Founded: 1988
Membership: 40
Profile: The SSB was formed in 1988 to support the market development of the SSB on behalf of its salmon farming members. Since 1991 their focus has been on a quality marketing strategy, developing members' sales of TQM salmon in the UK and Label Rouge Scottish salmon in France with a comprehensive marketing programme. Only members meeting the existing standards of the independently inspected Scottish Salmon Quality Assurance Scheme can apply the quality mark, an assurance of premium quality Scottish salmon to both trade and consumer.

Scottish Salmon Growers Association
Drummond House
Scott Street
Perth
PH1 5EJ
Tel: 01738 635420
Fax: 01738 621454
Contact: William JJ Crowe

Scottish Salmon Smokers Association
163c Cargo Terminal
Turnhouse Road
Edinburgh
EH12 0AL
Profile: We have been unable to contact this organisation. The details given are unconfirmed.

Scottish School of Forestry
Inverness College
3 Longman Road
Inverness
IV1 1SA

Tel: 01463 790431
Fax: 01463 792497
Email: John_Christian@Inverness.fc.uhi.ac.uk
Contact: DM Ward, Head of School
Founded: 1975
Profile: The school provides training and education to the forest and related industries by means of short courses, part-time and full-time courses at certificate, HNC/D and BSc levels.

Scottish Seed and Nursery Trade Association
Skateraw
Dunbar
East Lothian
EH42 1QR
Tel: 01368 840219
Fax: 01368 840677
Contact: Mrs Sandra Watson, Secretary
Founded: 1917
Membership: 21
Profile: The association exists to protect and advance the interests of those engaged in the seed trade in Scotland whether agricultural, horticultural, wholesale or retail, in the nursery trade or landscaping contractors.

Scottish Seed Potato Consultative Panel
Scottish Office Agriculture, Environment and
    Fisheries Department
47 Robb's Loan
Edinburgh
EH14 1TY
Tel: 0131 244 6343
Fax: 0131 244 6309
Contact: Mr GS Brown, Secretary
Founded: 1981
Profile: The panel's function is: to receive reports on and consider the operation of schemes for the approval of growing crops and consignments of basic seed potatoes in Scotland; in light of this consideration to advise the department of changes which should be made in the schemes and on the legislation necessary to implement them; to inform the department of the state of the seed potato industry and its organisation; to draw the attention of the department to needs which may arise in production, supply, organisation, promotion of trade, advice or research and development.

Scottish Seed Potato Development Council
4 Brewery Court
Sidegate
Haddington
Edinburgh
EH41 4DG
Tel: 01620 823488

Fax: 01620 825044
Email: 100443.2731@compuserve.com
Contact: John Bethell, Chief Executive
Founded: 1981
Membership: 18
Publications: Annual Report; Scotland – The Natural Home of Seed Potatoes
Profile: It is the purpose of SSPDC to identify successful ware potato growers throughout the world, to make them aware of the products of the Scottish Seed Potato Industry, and to encourage them to use these as their preferred planting material.

Scottish Silkie Club
Ford Farm
Plains
Airdrie
Lanarkshire
ML6 8HS
Tel: 01236 843041
Contact: Mr N Watson, Secretary
Profile: A society to promote the Silkie breed of poultry.

Scottish Skills Testing Service for Land Based Industries
Skills Testing Centre
Ingliston
Newbridge
EH28 8NE
Tel: 0131 333 2040
Fax: 0131 333 2488

Scottish Society for Crop Research
c/o Scottish Crop Research Institute
Mylnefield
Invergowrie
Dundee
DD2 5DA
Tel: 01382 562731
Fax: 01382 562426
Email: mail@scri.sari.ac.uk
Contact: Douglas Lindsay Hood, Secretary and Treasurer
Founded: 1982
Publications: Annual newsletter; biennial bulletin and proceedings of crop conference
Previous names: Scottish Society for Research in Plant Breeding and Scottish Horticultural Research Association merged in 1982
Profile: The Scottish Crop Research Institute is a major international centre for research on agricultural, horticultural and industrial crops and on the underlying biological processes common to all plants. It is the lead centre for research on potatoes, barley and soft fruit crops in the UK.

Scottish Society for the Prevention of Cruelty to Animals
Braehead Mains
603 Queensferry Road
Edinburgh
EH4 6EA
Tel: 0131 339 0222
Fax: 0131 339 4777
Contact: Maria Allen
Founded: 1839
Membership: 3,000
Publications: Annual Report; bimonthly adult membership magazine; quarterly junior membership magazine
Profile: The SSPCA has 47 inspectors who respond to calls from the public about animals at risk. They carry out rescues of birds and animals, small and large, from fledglings to whales. Fourteen animal welfare centres care for the injured animals until they are rehomed or released back into the wild. The society also works to improve legislation, both national and European. Another very important part of the society is the education department which takes the message into schools to try to prevent cruelty from an early age.

Scottish Sports Council
Caledonia House
South Gyle
Edinburgh
EH12 9DQ
Tel: 0131 317 7200
Fax: 0131 317 7202
Email: ssclis@easynet.co.uk
Contact: Mr Tony White, Information Manager
Founded: 1972
Publications: Publications list available
Profile: The council's mission is to lead the development of sport and physical recreation in Scotland, thereby increasing participation and improving standards of performance.

Scottish Standing Committee for the Calculation of Residual Values of Fertilisers and Feedingstuffs
Scottish Office Agriculture, Environment and Fisheries Department
47 Robb's Loan
Edinburgh
EH14 1TW
Tel: 0131 244 6132
Fax: 0131 244 6140
Contact: Ann Dellaquaglia, Secretary
Founded: 1948
Publications: Annual Report
Profile: An advisory committee to the Secretary of State regarding rates of compensation payable

to outgoing tenants on residual values of nutrients applied to land.

Scottish Sussex Club
Hillberry
Dunnotter
Stonehaven
Kincardineshire
AB3 2XB
Tel: 01569 766775
Contact: Mrs R Aitken, Secretary
Profile: A society to promote the Sussex breed of poultry.

Scottish Target Shooting Federation
1 Mortonhall Park Terrace
Edinburgh
EH17 8SU
Tel: 0131 664 9674
Contact: Colin R Aitken, Honorary Secretary
Founded: 1971
Previous names: Scottish Shooting Council
Profile: The representative federation for the following: Scottish Rifle Association; Scottish Clay Target Association; Scottish Smallbore Rifle Association; Scottish Pistol Association. Works with and is supported by the Scottish Sports Council.

Scottish Timber Trade Association
John Player Building
Stirling Enterprise Park
Springbank Road
Stirling
FK7 7RS
Tel: 01786 451623
Fax: 01786 474412
Contact: David Sulman, Secretary

Scottish Tourism Forum
c/o Scottish Tourist Board
23 Ravelston Terrace
Edinburgh
EH4 3EU
Tel: 0131 332 2433
Fax: 0131 332 9212
Contact: Jill Upland, Secretary
Founded: 1994
Membership: 26
Previous names: Scottish Confederation of Tourism.

Scottish Tourist Board
23 Ravelston Terrace
Edinburgh
EH4 3EU
Tel: 0131 332 2433
Fax: 0131 343 1513

Internet: www.scotourist.org.uk/stb/
Contact: Gillian Upton, Secretary
Founded: 1969
Publications: Annual Report, Strategic Plan, research data, marketing publications, etc.
Profile: The Scottish Tourist Board was established under the Development of Tourism Act to attract visitors to Scotland and encourage them to travel widely within Scotland. STB aims to promote the highest standards of service and of training. As the leading marketing agency in tourism, the board works closely with the private sector and with the various statutory agencies whose activities affect tourism. The board is financed by government through the Scottish Office, and also derives revenue from the sale of publications and the provision of specialist services.

Scottish Valuation and Rating Council, The
Scottish Office
Local Government Finance
Victoria Quay
Edinburgh
EH6 6QQ
Tel: 0131 556 8400
Fax: 0131 244 7020
Contact: Pete Hancock, Senior Executive Officer
Founded: 1996
Publications: Annual Report
Previous names: Scottish Valuation Advisory Council
Profile: The council's remit is to advise the Secretary of State for Scotland on any matter pertaining to valuation and rating, including evaluation of representations and recommendations made to him, the identification of issues requiring consideration, and advice in the preparation of legislation.

Scottish Waterfowl Club
Doon Valley Rare Breeds
Old Skares Road
Cumnock
Ayrshire
KA18 2SG
Tel: 01290 421553
Contact: Mr K Edwards, Secretary

Scottish Wild Land Group
8 Hartington Place
Edinburgh
EH3 9EZ
Tel: 0131 229 2094
Contact: Alistair Cant, Co-ordinator
Founded: 1983
Membership: 500

Publications: Wild Land News
Profile: To protect wild land in Scotland from insensitive development and to promote appropriate development of such land and associated communities.

Scottish Wildlife and Countryside Link
PO Box 64
Perth
PH2 0TF
Tel: 01738 630804
Fax: 01738 643290
Contact: Jen Anderson, Coordinator
Founded: 1987
Publications: Publications list available
Profile: Scottish Wildlife and Countryside Link is the liaison body for the voluntary organisations in Scotland concerned with the environment. It provides a forum for information exchange, discussion and, where appropriate, concerted action.

Scottish Wildlife Trust
The Wildlife Trusts
Cramond House
Kirk Cramond
Cramond Glebe Road
Edinburgh
EH4 6NS
Tel: 0131 312 7765
Fax: 0131 312 8705
Contact: Rita Crowe, Head of Marketing and Education
Founded: 1964
Membership: 16,300
Publications: Scottish Wildlife magazine; Annual Review; Wildtalk
Profile: The Scottish Wildlife Trust is the leading Scottish voluntary organisation for the conservation of all forms of wildlife and their habitats. The trust manages more than 100 reserves covering 18,500 ha of Scotland's finest countryside. SWT's work is supported by 15,000 members and 1,300 junior members, with active branches and volunteer groups throughout Scotland.

Scottish Women's Rural Institutes
42 Heriot Row
Edinburgh
EH3 6ES
Tel: 0131 225 1724
Fax: 0131 225 8129
Contact: Mrs Anne Peacock, General Secretary
Founded: 1917
Membership: 33,500
Publications: Scottish Home and Country

Profile: The organisation aims to advance the education and training of those who live and work in the country, or are interested in country life, in home skills, family welfare and citizenship; to promote the preservation of Scotland's traditions and its rural heritage; to promote the provision of facilities in the interests of social welfare for recreational and leisure time occupation so that the conditions of life of people who live and work in the country, or who are interested in country life, may be improved.

Scottish Woodland Owners Association
6 Chester Street
Edinburgh
EH3 7RD
Profile: We have been unable to contact this organisation. The details given are unconfirmed.

Scottish Wyandotte Bantam Club
Lindsayton Farm
Dalrymple
Ayr
KA6 6BA
Tel: 01292 560240
Contact: Mr R M Dale, Secretary
Profile: A society to promote the Wyandotte Bantam breed of poultry.

Scottish Youth Hostels Association
7 Glebe Crescent
Stirling
FK8 2JA
Tel: 01786 451181
Fax: 01786 450198
Contact: WB Forsyth, General Secretary
Founded: 1931
Membership: 44,000
Publications: SYHA Handbook; Scottish Hosteller Magazine; SYHA Hostels Map; information leaflets
Profile: Scottish Youth Hostels run almost 80 youth hostels throughout Scotland, enabling young people to see the best of Scotland by offering low cost, comfortable, friendly and safe accommodation.

Seale Hayne Faculty of Agriculture, Food and Land Use
University of Plymouth
Newton Abbot
Devon
TQ12 6NQ
Tel: 01626 325800
Fax: 01626 325605
Contact: Professor Fred Harper, Dean of Faculty
Founded: 1914

Publications: Research reports, annual reports, prospectuses
Previous names: Seale Hayne College until 1989; Polytechnic South West until 1992.
Profile: Seale Hayne is a major provider of teaching and research at higher education level in the land-based and food industries in the south west of England. It is a faculty of the University of Plymouth offering HND, BSc and PhD provision in agriculture, rural resource management, rural estate management, food science and technology, hospitality and tourism management. The faculty is committed to providing programmes of the highest possible quality underpinned by appropriate research. It is committed to working closely with the professions and small and medium-sized enterprises in the region and nationally.

Sealed Knot Ltd
94 Hamilton Road
West Norwood
London
SE27 9SE
Profile: We have been unable to contact this organisation. The details given are unconfirmed.

Sebright Club
Lynwood
37 Garstang Road
Bowgreave
Garstang
Lancashire
PR3 1YD
Tel: 01995 602042
Contact: Mr JK Sharpe, Secretary
Profile: A society to promote the Sebright breed of poultry.

Second Land Utilisation Survey of Britain
Kings College
Strand
London
WC2R 2LS
Tel: 0181 244 6733
Fax: 0181 244 6733
Contact: Alice Coleman, Professor
Founded: 1960
Publications: Publications list available
Profile: The survey recruited some 3,000 voluntary assistants to map some 250 categories of land use throughout England, Wales and lowland Scotland. A new area measurement method and a new technique for analysing maps were devised, and revealed serious planning problems. The data has been successfully used in many planning appeals and public enquiries.

Secretary of State's Advisory Committee on Scotland's Travelling People
Scottish Office Development Department
Housing Division
Room 1–F
Victoria Quay
Edinburgh
EH6 6QQ
Tel: 0131 244 0132
Fax: 0131 244 0153
Contact: Ms Sylvia Hamon, Acting Secretary
Founded: 1971
Publications: Publications list available
Profile: To advise the Secretary of State on issues relating to travelling people and in particular: to encourage progress towards achievement of the Secretary of State's pitch targets by the end of 1997; to monitor progress towards achievement of these targets; to advise local authorities on appropriate ways to secure adequate provision of new sites for travelling people; to advise on the upgrading of existing official traveller sites; to liaise with local authorities on the social needs of travellers and to identify any need for further guidance on any aspect relating to travelling people and to recommend how that need might best be met.

Sector of Rural and Recreational Studies
Aberdeen College
Clinterty
Kinellar
Aberdeen
AB5 0TN
Tel: 01224 640366
Fax: 01224 790326
Contact: Mr Robert Bellfield, Sector Manager
Founded: 1991
Previous names: Clinterty Agricultural College until 1991
Profile: Provides education and training for the land-based sector in agriculture, horticulture, arboriculture, agricultural engineering, leisure management, sports coaching and development and outdoor pursuits.

Seed Bank & Exchange
Lower Llanbella
Huntington
Kington
Herefordshire
HR5 3PE
Contact: Caroline Barnett, Administrator
Founded: 1979
Publications: Members newsletter; seed list
Profile: Conservation group with a facility for exchanging seeds through the administrator.

Seed Crushers and Oil Processors Association
6 Catherine Street
London
WC2B 5JJ
Tel: 0171 836 2460
Fax: 0171 836 0580
Contact: Ms A Bowden, Secretary General
Membership: 8
Publications: SCOPA Update
Profile: SCOPA is the trade association for companies engaged in oilseed extraction and oils and fats processing in the UK. It comprises three seed crushers and seven oil processors concentrated in London, Merseyside and Hull.

Selborne Society
89 Daryngton Drive
Greenford
Middlesex
UB6 8BH
Tel: 0181 578 3181
Contact: Roy J Hall, Secretary

Send A Cow
Unit 4 Priston Mill
Priston
Bath
Somerset
BA2 9EQ
Tel: 01225 447041
Fax: 01225 317627
Email: ian.clarke@netgates.co.uk
Internet: http://www.g.w.a.co.uk/sendacow/sac.htm
Contact: Georgia Clark, Manager, UK
Founded: 1988
Publications: Lifeline, Annual Report and Accounts
Profile: Send A Cow works with people in East Africa to overcome poverty and malnutrition in a sustainable manner. Work began in Uganda in 1988 and is now spreading to Kenya and Ethiopia. Poor families are trained to manage a high-yield dairy cow which is given either by direct donation from the UK, or as a result of crossbreeding using a purebred bull or artificial insemination. First-born female offspring are passed on as a gift to another needy family. Local groups, often women, are responsible for the management of projects under the guidance and supervision of Ugandan veterinary staff. Send A Cow was started by farmers motivated by Christian concern of whom many are members of the board of 12 trustees. The majority of funds are by individual and group donations, with some support from ODA and trusts.

Severn Trent plc
2297 Coventry Road
Sheldon
Birmingham
B26 3PU
Tel: 0121 722 4000
Fax: 0121 722 4800

Sheep Veterinary Society
SVS Secretariat
Moredun Research Institute
408 Gilmerton Road
Edinburgh
EH17 7JH
Tel: 0131 664 3262
Fax: 0131 664 8001

Shell Better Britain Campaign
Victoria Works
21a Graham Street
Hockley
Birmingham
B1 3JR
Tel: 0121 212 9221
Fax: 0121 212 9220
Email: 100646.3474@compuserve.com
Contact: Sarah Betteridge, Grants Manager
Founded: 1970
Publications: Interactive; newsletter
Profile: The Shell Better Britain Campaign encourages action by local people to improve the quality of life at neighbourhood level in ways that respect the Earth's resources. The campaign has an information service and provides grants for local action.

Shellfish Association of Great Britain
Fishmonger's Hall
London Bridge
London
EC4R 9EL
Tel: 0171 283 8305
Fax: 0171 929 1389
Contact: Dr Eric Edwards OBE PhD, Director
Founded: 1903
Membership: 400
Publications: Members newsletter; proceedings of the annual shellfish conference
Previous names: Oyster Merchants and Planters Association 1903–1969
Profile: The Shellfish Association provides a technical advisory service for its members. It actively promotes and represents the shellfish industry at all levels and deals with members' problems. Their trained staff also do coastal surveys and are involved with environmental issues of all types.

Shetland Cattle Herd Book Society
Hogan
Bridge of Walls
Shetland
ZE2 9NT
Tel: 01595 809375
Fax: 01595 809475
Email: evelyn_leask@wcg.org
Contact: Mrs J Evelyn Leask, Secretary
Membership: 95
Publications: Newsletter; Shetland Cattle Herd Book

Shetland Cheviot Marketing Society
Fairview
Vidlin
Shetland
ZE2 9QB
Tel: 01806 577227

Shetland Flock Book Society
Fairview
Vidlin
Shetland
ZE2 9QB
Tel: 01806 577227
Contact: James A Johnson, Secretary
Founded: 1922
Membership: 104
Profile: The Shetland Flock Book Society has done much to preserve and improve the breed – the object being to retain the traditional quality of the wool, to maintain a hardy, healthy and robust stock and to increase the mutton yield of the breed.

Shetland Pony Stud-Book Society
Pedigree House
6 King's Place
Perth
Tayside
PH2 8AD
Tel: 01738 623471
Fax: 01738 442274
Contact: Mrs E Ward, Secretary
Founded: 1891
Membership: 2,100
Publications: Annual stud-book; annual magazine; Shetland Pony Care and Management
Profile: The society's functions are registration of Shetland ponies and provision of help and advice regarding all aspects of Shetland ponies. Sales are held under the society's auspices throughout the country with an annual breed show in a different location annually. A magazine and stud book are produced annually.

Shetland Salmon Farmers' Association
Shetland Seafood Centre
Stewart Building
Lerwick
Shetland
ZE1 0LL
Tel: 01595 695579
Fax: 01595 694494
Email: ssfa@zetnet.co.uk
Contact: Mr Magnus L Flaws, Chief Executive
Founded: 1985
Membership: 51

Shetland Sheep Breeders Group
Bartiestown
Hethersgill
Carlisle
Cumbria
CA6 6JB
Tel: 01228 577374
Contact: Mrs Elizabeth Brown, General Secretary
Founded: 1985
Membership: 300
Publications: The Shetland Breed

Shire Horse Society
East of England Showground
Peterborough
Cambridgeshire
PE2 6XE
Tel: 01733 234451
Fax: 01733 370038
Contact: T Gibson, Secretary
Founded: 1878
Profile: A society committed to the promotion of the Old English breed of cart horses.

Shooters' Rights Association
PO Box 3
Cardigan
SA43 1BN
Tel: 01239 698607
Fax: 01239 698614
Contact: Richard Law, Secretary
Founded: 1984
Membership: 6,000
Publications: Shooters' Journal; occasional papers
Profile: The association insures firearm and shotgun certificate holders for public liability purposes, and deals with legal problems relating to firearms ownership. Membership is available, at modest cost, to individuals, families, groups, clubs and syndicates.

Shorthorn Society of the United Kingdom of Great Britain and Ireland
4th Street
National Agricultural Centre
Stoneleigh Park
Warwickshire
CV8 2LG
Tel: 01203 696549
Fax: 01203 696729

Showmen's Guild of Great Britain
Guild House
41 Clarence Street
Staines
Middlesex
TW18 4SY
Tel: 01784 461805
Fax: 01784 461732
Contact: Keith Miller, General Secretary
Founded: 1889
Membership: 4,500
Profile: The Showmen's Guild of Great Britain is the trade association for travelling showmen (fairground operators). The guild's objectives are to secure the combination and organisation of all its members to promote, support or oppose any petition to Parliament, and any legislative or other measures affecting the rights of its members.

Shropshire and West Midlands Agricultural Society
PO Box 62
Shrewsbury
Shropshire
SY1 1ZZ
Tel: 01743 362824
Fax: 01743 363779
Contact: Richard Smith, Chief Executive
Founded: 1875
Membership: 4,000
Publications: Members newsletter; show catalogue and competition schedules
Profile: An agricultural association formed in 1875 registered as a charity whose objectives are educational. To provide through an annual show, demonstrations of modern agricultural techniques to farmers and growers and to provide an insight into the countryside and conservation to the general public.

Shropshire Sheep Breeders Association and Flock Book Society
40 Droitwich Road
Noah's Green
Feckenham
Worcestershire

B96 6RU
Tel: 01527 821371
Contact: Mr P Cotton, Secretary
Founded: 1882
Membership: 90
Publications: Annual flock book
Profile: A breed society founded in 1882 publishing its first flock book in 1883. Involved in the promotion of the Shropshire sheep.

Side Saddle Association
19 High Street
Welford
Northampton
NN6 6HT
Tel: 01858 575300
Fax: 01858 575051
Email: 100600.1531@compuserve.com
Contact: Mrs RN James, Honorary Secretary
Founded: 1974
Membership: 1,200
Publications: Annual Rule/Handbook; newsletters; National Show Schedule
Previous names: Ladies Side Saddle Association until 1981
Profile: The Side Saddle Association was formed in 1974 with the aim of reviving the art of riding side saddle and encouraging more riders to take it up. Its objectives are: to promote and encourage the art of riding side saddle and to further the interest of side saddle riders and to support and co-operate with the commonly recognised organisations interested in the welfare and breeding of horses and ponies, especially those suitable for riding side saddle.

Silkie Club, The
Olde Barn Farm
School Lane
Stapleton
Leicestershire
LE9 8JR
Tel: 01455 845105
Fax: 01455 845105
Contact: SP Flude, Secretary
Founded: 1898
Membership: 198
Publications: Members newsletter; yearbook
Profile: The objects of the club are to promote the breeding and exhibition of Silkie fowl, to maintain the breed standards and to promote classifications for Silkies at shows. The annual club show is held at Bingley Hall, Stafford, each December.

Silsoe Research Institute
Wrest Park
Silsoe

Bedford
MK45 4HS
Tel: 01525 860000
Fax: 01525 860156
Email: sri.pr@bbsrc.ac.uk
Contact: Miss Kelly Holman, Communications Manager
Founded: 1924
Publications: Publications list available
Previous names: National Institute of Agricultural Engineering until 1986; AFRC Institute of Engineering Research until 1991
Profile: Silsoe Research Institute is the UK's premier centre of excellence for research in engineering and physical sciences for biologically-based industries and, in particular, the agricultural, horticultural and food industries. It provides scientific understanding and engineering innovation to advance the efficiency of these industries.

Silvanus Trust
Unit 4 The National School
St Thomas Road
Launceston
Cornwall
PL15 8BL
Tel: 01566 772802
Fax: 01566 776969
Contact: Mr S Humphreys, Trust Director
Founded: 1989
Publications: Annual reports; Root and Branch Review 1989–1993
Previous names: Dartington Action Research Trust until 1989
Profile: The Silvanus Trust works for the future of woods in the west country. It promotes awareness and understanding of the value of woodlands as a resource for the whole community. It also helps and encourages participation in the planting, management and recreational enjoyment of woods for the whole community. It seeks to develop awareness and increase understanding of the importance of woods and their management. It calls its approach the woodland IDEA – Information (to woodland owners, public, etc.), Demonstration (practical demonstration of management work), Education for all and Advice for all.

SJAI Northern Region
Drum-a-Hoy
78A Carsonstown Road
Saintfield
Ballynahinch
County Down
BT24 7EB
Tel: 01238 519229

Fax: 01238 519229
Contact: Myrtle Peak

Small Farmers Cooperative Society
Twin
345 Goswell Road
London
EC1V 7JT
Profile: We have been unable to contact this organisation. The details given are unconfirmed.

Small Farmers' Association
PO Box 18
Woodbridge
Suffolk
IP13 0QQ
Profile: We have been unable to contact this organisation. The details given are unconfirmed.

Smallholders Association
Tolleywood
Hillcommon
Taunton
Somerset
TA4 1BT
Profile: We have been unable to contact this organisation. The details given are unconfirmed.

Snail Centre
72 High Street
Ketton
Nr Stamford
Lincolnshire
PE9 3TE
Tel: 01780 722031
Fax: 01780 720226
Contact: Mr Martin Downes, Director
Founded: 1986
Publications: To Cook a Snail; Transcripts of Seminar
Profile: The Snail Centre is an international organisation concerned with the dissemination of information, liaison with governments and the organisation of training in snail farming. It has contacts in some 30 countries and is a member of research organisations in France, Italy and the Far East.

Snowdonia National Park Authority
Penrhyndeudraeth
Gwynedd
LL48 6LF
Tel: 01766 770274
Fax: 01766 771211
Contact: Barbara Jones, Information Officer
Founded: 1951
Publications: Annual Report, Management Plan, Eryri Local Plan and numerous leaflets

Previous names: National Park Department of Gwynnedd County Council until 1996
Profile: Free standing local authority since 1996. The two statutory purposes are to conserve and enhance the natural beauty, wildlife and cultural heritage of the park and to promote opportunities for the understanding and enjoyment of special qualities by the public.

Snowdonia National Park Society
Ty Hyll (The Ugly House)
Capel Curig
Betws y Coed
Gwynedd
LL24 0DS
Tel: 01690 720287
Fax: 01690 720247
Email: snps@gn.apc.org
Contact: Rory Francis, Director
Founded: 1967
Membership: 3,000
Publications: Eryri News
Profile: The society works to conserve the scenery, wildlife and natural and historic features of Snowdonia, to keep them unimpaired for the enjoyment of present and future generations. The society runs both proactive and reactive campaigns on planning and conservation issues; a farm award scheme; a dry stone walling competition; a litter clearing campaign and a programme of walks for members. Its headquarters, the famous Ugly House, is open to the public.

Snowdonia Wildlife Forum
c/o Snowdonia National Park
Penrhyndeudraeth
Gwynedd
LL48 6LS
Tel: 01766 770274
Fax: 01766 771211
Email: 100070.1367@compuserve.com
Contact: Dr Rod Gritten, Ecologist
Founded: 1992
Publications: First Level Directory
Profile: To provide a forum for a wide range of relevant organisations within the Snowdonia National Park to discuss conservation/wildlife issues in the context of the National Park. The Snowdonia Wildlife Forum meet twice a year at Plas-Tan-y-Bwlch, the residential study centre of the Snowdonia National Park Authority.

Soay
see **Rare Breeds Survival Trust**

Society for Applied Bacteriology
PO Box 510
Harrold
Bedfordshire
MK43 7YU
Tel: 01234 720047
Fax: 01234 720048
Contact: Dr Ann Baillie, Executive Secretary
Founded: 1931
Membership: 1,800
Publications: Journal of Applied Bacteriology; Letters in Applied Microbiology; SAB Technical Series
Previous names: Society of Agricultural Bacteriologists until 1945
Profile: Originally formed in 1931 by dairy bacteriologists, the society has evolved to cover all aspects of applied microbiology. Apart from its publications, it runs three regular meetings a year and occasional joint meetings with other societies. There are very favourable membership rates for students. The society offers its members financial assistance to attend meetings, and administers several substantial awards.

Society for Folk Life Studies
Blaise Castle House Museum
Henbury
Bristol
BS10 7QS
Tel: 0117 950 6789
Fax: 0117 959 3475
Contact: David Eveleigh, Secretary
Founded: 1961
Membership: 550
Publications: Folk Life; Journal of Ethnological Studies
Profile: The society aims to further the study of the traditional and changing ways of life of Great Britain and Ireland and to provide a common meeting point for the many people and institutions engaged with the various aspects of the subject. Each year a conference is held in various centres around these islands and a volume of Folk Life, Journal of Ethnological Studies, is published. Membership is open to all.

Society for Landscape Studies
c/o RCHME
Kemble Drive
Swindon
SN2 2GZ
Tel: 01793 414700
Fax: 01793 414707
Contact: Carenza Lewis, Secretary

Founded: 1979
Membership: 400
Publications: Landscape History; members newsletter
Profile: The society exists to promote the study of all aspects of the historic landscape. It publishes a well regarded academic journal which includes papers by archaeologists, historians, geographers and conservationists from Britain and beyond. The society also holds two conferences each year, on different aspects of landscape history, held in different locations around the country.

Society for National Park Staff
Lake District National Park
Murley Moss
Oxenholme Road
Kendal
Cumbria
Tel: 01539 724555
Fax: 01539 740822
Contact: Mr P J Winter, Secretary
Founded: 1992
Membership: 600
Publications: Quarterly newsletter
Previous names: National Park Staff Association until 1992
Profile: The society promotes and maintains links between the staff of the National Parks of England and Wales; promotes the study and understanding of National Parks; provides an input into professional and in-service training of National Park staff; seeks to develop relationships with other organisations to promote mutual understanding; and represents the views of staff on professional matters.

Society for Practising Veterinary Surgeons
Briery Hill Cottage
Stannington
Morpeth
Northumberland
NE61 6ES
Tel: 01670 789054
Fax: 01670 789359
Contact: Jean Thompson, Secretary
Founded: 1933
Membership: 1,400
Publications: Bulletin
Profile: Aims to promote the interests of veterinary surgeons in private practice. The society concentrates primarily on matters of practice management and finance, providing a source of information for both partners and assistants. The society exists to offer advice and practical guidance to the practitioner.

Society for the Protection of Ancient Buildings
37 Spital Square
London
E1 6DY
Profile: We have been unable to contact this organisation. The details given are unconfirmed.

Society for the Responsible Use of Resources in Agriculture and on the Land
12 Hillbury Road
Alderholt
Fordingbridge
Hampshire
SP6 3BQ
Tel: 01425 652035
Contact: Brig H John Hickman, Director
Founded: 1981
Publications: Rural News
Profile: RURAL exists to assist the process of positive policy development for farming, food and countryside. It does this through closed policy seminars and high quality information exchange.

Society for the Welfare of Horses and Ponies
Tregaer Mill
Nr Monmouth
Gwent
NP5 4DX
Tel: 01600 740225
Fax: 01600 740473
Contact: Mrs Jenny McGregor, Chair

Society for Veterinary Epidemiological Preventive Medicine
Department of Agriculture
University of Reading
Earley Gate
PO Box 236
Reading
Berkshire
RG6 2AT
Tel: 01734 264888
Fax: 01734 262431
Email: a.d.paterson@reading.ac.uk
Contact: Andrew Paterson, Secretary
Founded: 1982
Membership: 270
Publications: Proceedings of annual conference
Profile: The society, founded in the UK, was one of the first national organisations in the field of epidemiology in the world. Veterinary scientists drawn from all specialist areas meet with statisticians, mathematical modellers, and economists at an annual three day conference in March or April. The published Proceedings of the

Society, comprising an edited collection of papers presented at the meeting are made available to all conference delegates on registration. The society continues to enjoy a substantial growth in its annual membership. About 40% of its members are from outside the UK.

Society for Wildlife Art of the Nations

Nature in Art
Wallsworth Hall
Twigworth
Gloucester
GL2 9PA
Tel: 01452 731422
Fax: 01452 730937
Contact: Simon Trapnell, Deputy Director
Founded: 1982
Membership: 1,500
Publications: Nature in Art; video; education pack
Profile: The world's first museum dedicated exclusively to art inspired by nature from David Shepherd to Picasso to ethnic art. Work spanning 1,500 years from over 50 countries. Specially commended in National Heritage Museum of the Year awards, housed in a Georgian mansion with nature garden, ponds etc. There is a very active adult and children's education programme focusing on conservation/environment art and common ground between the two. Fully accessible to wheelchair users.

Society of Border Leicester Sheep Breeders

4 Alexander Drive
Edinburgh
EH11 2RH
Tel: 0131 313 5037
Fax: 0131 313 5037
Contact: Colin E Douglas, Secretary
Founded: 1896
Membership: 330
Publications: Flock book; Breed Journal
Profile: They exist to encourage and promote the breeding of Border Leicester Sheep. They are involved in the maintenance and registration of pedigrees through the publication of a flock book.

Society of Chemical Industry – Pesticides Group

Society of Chemical Industry
Highlands
Hackington Close
Canterbury
Kent
CT2 7BB
Tel: 01227 765066
Fax: 01227 765066
Contact: BT Grayson, Honorary Secretary
Founded: 1954
Membership: 500
Publications: Pesticide Science
Profile: The Pesticides Group is one of the subject groups of the SCI whose function is to organise scientific meetings on topics of relevance to pesticide research, development, production and use. Attendance is open to everyone (SCI members pay reduced fees) and details are to be found in the SCI Bulletin, published every month.

Society of Dairy Technology

Crossley House
72 Ermine Street
Huntingdon
Cambridgeshire
PE18 6EZ
Tel: 01480 450741
Fax: 01480 431800
Contact: Mrs RA Gale, Executive Secretary
Founded: 1943
Membership: 1,700
Publications: Publications list available

Society of Feed Technologists

85 St Peters Road
Reading
Berkshire
RG6 1PP
Tel: 01734 265130
Fax: 01734 351890
Contact: S Foye, Secretary
Founded: 1967
Membership: 400
Publications: Annual Proceedings
Profile: The Society of Feed Technologists was founded in 1967 by a group of forward thinking members of the feed industry. They saw the need to provide a regular forum for identifying advances in technology and to offer opportunity for members to discuss the importance and implications of these changes. It holds four meetings a year. Members work in both large and small feed businesses and those enterprises which are closely associated with feeds and livestock production.

Society of International Thoroughbred Auctioneers

Toomer's Wharf
Newbury
Berkshire
RG14 1DY
Tel: 01635 551515
Fax: 01635 550228
Contact: Matthew McCloy

Society of Ploughmen Ltd
Quarry Farm
Loversall
Doncaster
South Yorkshire
DN11 9DH
Tel: 01302 852469
Fax: 01302 852469
Contact: Ken Chappell, Executive Director
Founded: 1972
Membership: 1,000
Publications: Members newsletter
Profile: Organisers of the Annual British National Ploughing Championships in a different part of Great Britain each year. Includes competition ploughing (horses and tractors), trade stands, crafts, demonstrations, vintage equipment etc. Qualifying ploughmen compete in the Annual World Ploughing Contest.

Society of Surveying Technicians
RICS
Surveyor Court
Westwood Way
Coventry
CV4 8JE
Tel: 01203 694757
Contact: Joan Goodwin

Society of Sussex Downsmen
10 The Drive
Hove
East Sussex
BN3 3JA
Tel: 01273 771906
Fax: 01273 771567
Contact: Peter Harris, Secretary
Founded: 1923
Membership: 2,600
Publications: Publication list available
Profile: The Society of Sussex Downsmen make representations at all levels on planning applications which would damage the Downs; liaise with other groups involved in protecting the countryside; have an interesting programme of meetings and excursions and produce descriptive books for walkers with maps.

Soil and Water Management Association Ltd
Institution of Agricultural Engineers
West End Road
Silsoe
Bedfordshire
MK45 4DU
Contact: Secretary

Soil Association Ltd
86–88 Colston Street
Bristol
BS1 5BB
Tel: 0117 929 0661
Fax: 0117 925 2504
Email: soilassoc@gn.apc.org
Contact: Patrick Holden, Director
Founded: 1946
Membership: 5,000
Publications: Living Earth; New Farmer and Grower; Organic News; Woodmark News; publications list available
Profile: Research, education and promotion of organic agriculture and the links with health and the environment. Certification of organic farming and food processing, and sustainable forestry and timber processing. Local Food Links project to encourage direct marketing systems and producer–consumer links. There is a network of local groups for both producers and general members. There is a mail order book catalogue both of their own publications and specialist titles. A dedicated helpline (01179 227707) is available for free assistance and information for those interested in converting to organic farming.

Soil Survey and Land Research Centre
Cranfield University
Silsoe
Bedfordshire
MK45 4DT
Tel: 01525 863264
Fax: 01525 863253
Contact: Michael G Jarvis, Head of Land Resource Management
Founded: 1939
Publications: Publications list available
Previous names: Soil Survey of England and Wales until 1987
Profile: SSLRC is the national centre for information about the properties and distribution of soils in England and Wales and their consequences for land management in agriculture, recreation, water pollution, pesticide fates, and planning. SSLRC holds digital data in a large computerised information system, Land IS.

South Devon Herd Book Society
24 Courtenay Park
Newton Abbot
Devon
TQ12 2HB
Tel: 01626 331144
Fax: 01626 331035

Contact: Mrs Lesley T Lewin, Breed Secretary
Founded: 1891
Membership: 650
Publications: Annual journal; Annual Sire and Dam Summary; Organisation Centenary History
Profile: To maintain the purity and to improve the breeding of South Devons.

South of England Agricultural Society
The Show Ground
Selsfield Road
Ardingley
Haywards Heath
West Sussex
RH17 6TL
Profile: We have been unable to contact this organisation. The details given are unconfirmed.

South Wales Mountain Sheep Society
Penrhiw Farm
Trelewis
Treharris
Merthyr Tydfil
CF46 6TA
Tel: 01433 412949
Contact: John Thomas, Secretary
Membership: 38
Profile: The breed society for the South Wales Mountain sheep.

South West Water plc
Peninsula House
Rydon Lane
Exeter
Devon
EX2 7HR
Tel: 01392 446688
Fax: 01392 434966
Contact: HG Weatherley, Corporate Communications Manager
Founded: 1989
Publications: Publications list available
Profile: South West Water plc is one of the ten major water and sewerage authorities privatised by the government in 1989. The company provides water and sewerage services in Devon, Cornwall and small areas of Dorset and Somerset.

South West Way Association
1 Orchard Drive
Kingskerswell
Devon
TQ12 5DG
Tel: 01803 873061
Contact: Mrs M Macleod, Membership Secretary

Founded: 1973
Membership: 2,000
Publications: The South West Way 1996
Profile: The Association's objectives are to secure the protection and preservation of an acceptable south west long distance coast path and public access to it, in order to improve the conditions of life of the users of the path and to educate walkers along it in a proper respect for the countryside. For practical advice or information for the actual walking of the trail or planning a walking holiday please contact the Secretary – Eric Wallis, Windlestraw, Penquit, Ermington, Devon, PL21 0LU (01752 896237).

Southdown Sheep Society
Southdown Lodge
300 Cople Road
Cardington
Bedford
MK44 3SH
Tel: 01234 838807
Contact: Clive Pritchard, Secretary
Founded: 1891
Membership: 300
Publications: Flock book
Profile: A breed society for the promotion and preservation of the Southdown Sheep.

Southern Cleveland Bay Breeders Association
SGTS Mess
RM Condor
Arbroath
Angus
DD11 3SJ
Profile: We have been unable to contact this organisation. The details given are unconfirmed.

Southern Water plc
Southern House
Yeoman Road
Worthing
West Sussex
BN13 3NX
Tel: 01903 264444
Fax: 01903 262185
Profile: The water supply company for the southern region. Southern Water also runs Southern Water Services Recycling Group which is responsible for recycling wastewater bioproducts to agriculture. The group currently delivers 40,000 tonnes of dry solids to agriculture and this will rise over the next 10 years to 132,000 tonnes. The group is continually examining new treatment and application methods in order to produce the best products and service to the benefit of agriculture.

Sparsholt College Hampshire
Sparsholt
Winchester
Hampshire
SO21 2NF
Tel: 01962 776441
Fax: 01962 776587
Contact: David Alderson, Director of Marketing
Founded: 1916
Publications: Prospectus and careers leaflets
Profile: Sparsholt College, near Winchester in Hampshire, is currently the largest UK College providing further and higher training and education for careers in the land-based industries. Some 45 different full-time courses are offered in a wide range of subject areas including: agriculture, animal management, fishery studies and aquatics, horse management, mechanisation, game and wildlife management and horticulture. The academic range of the full-time courses include BTEC First Diplomas, National Certificates and Diplomas and also Higher National Diplomas and a degree. Many part-time and short course programmes are also available.

Specialist Cheesemakers' Association
PO Box 448a
Newcastle under Lyme
Staffordshire
ST5 0BF
Tel: 01782 580580
Fax: 01782 580680
Contact: Jane Maskow, Company Secretary
Founded: 1989
Publications: Newsletter; Guide to the Finest Cheeses of Britain and Ireland

Speciality Salad Producers Association
133 Eastgate
Louth
Lincolnshire
LN11 9QG
Tel: 01507 602427
Fax: 01507 600689
Contact: Mrs JA Dyas, Company Secretary
Founded: 1980
Membership: 12
Profile: Provision of marketing information.

Spongiform Encephalopathy Advisory Committee
MAFF Secretariat
Government Buildings
Hook Rise South
Tolworth
Surbiton
Surrey

KT6 7NF
Tel: 0181 330 8042
Fax: 0181 330 7862
Profile: An advisory committee advising both the Department of Health and MAFF on issues relating to spongiform encephalopathies.

Sports Council
16 Upper Woburn Place
London
WC1H 0QP
Tel: 0171 388 1277
Fax: 0171 383 5740
Contact: Information Officer
Founded: 1972
Publications: Publications list available
Profile: The Sports Council is a public sector advisory body set up in 1972 to promote participation in sport, provision of sports facilities, excellence in sport and information about sport. Following a restructuring process in 1995–96, the Sports Council will be concentrating its work on the National Junior Sports Programme, the British Academy of Sport and the Lottery Sports Fund.

Sports Council for Northern Ireland
House of Sport
Upper Malone Road
Belfast
BT9 5LA
Tel: 01232 381222
Fax: 01232 682757
Contact: Stephen Wilson, Development Officer
Founded: 1974
Publications: Fact files and fact sheets, Annual Report, policy frameworks and research
Profile: The Sports Council for Northern Ireland is responsible for promoting and developing sport in Northern Ireland. In pursuing its objectives of increasing participation levels, raising standards of performance and promoting the good reputation and efficient administration of sport, the council works in partnership with government bodies, district councils, area education and library boards and central agencies such as the Department of the Environment, the Department of Agriculture and the Northern Ireland Tourist Board.

Sports Council for Wales
Welsh Institute of Sport
Sophia Gardens
Cardiff
CF1 9SW
Tel: 01222 397571
Fax: 01222 222431

Sports Turf Research Institute, The
St Ives Estate
Bingley
West Yorkshire
BD16 1AU
Tel: 01274 565131
Fax: 01274 561891
Contact: Anne Wilson, External Affairs Manager
Founded: 1929
Membership: 2,500
Publications: International Turfgrass Bulletin (formerly Sports Turf Bulletin); The Journal of the Sports Turf Research Institute; research papers
Previous names: The Board of Greenkeeping Research until 1951
Profile: The STRI is an independent body established in 1929. It is a major international research centre and the UK's national centre for investigation of problems affecting the establishment and maintenance of turf for sports and amenities. Its work covers research, education, publishing, advice and consultancy for all turf sports. A highly trained consultancy team, including 18 turfgrass agronomists, covers the UK, Ireland and overseas. It offers advice and expertise in design, architecture, construction, drainage, ecology, conservation and turf agronomy. It is backed by extensive laboratory facilities with a team of scientists in soil physics, chemistry, pathology and ecology.

Spotted Horse and Pony Register
17 School Lane
Dronfield
Sheffield
South Yorkshire
S18 6RY
Tel: 01246 413201
Contact: Miss LR Marshall, Registrar
Founded: 1992
Publications: Annual Yearbook and Stud Book
Profile: The register was formed to provide registration facilities for spotted horses and ponies irrespective of type or breeding and with the Spotted Horse and Pony Supporters Club to promote and improve spotted equines.

St Tiggywinkles Wildlife Hospital Trust
Aston Road
Haddenham
Aylesbury
Buckinghamshire
HP17 8AF
Tel: 01844 292292
Fax: 01844 292640
Contact: Sue Stocker, Founder
Founded: 1983

Membership: 7,000
Publications: Bright Eyes; Bright Ideas; various medical publications and fact sheets
Profile: St Tiggywinkles takes in, treats and rehabilitates all sick, injured and orphaned British wild animals and birds.

Stable Lads Association
4 Dunsmore Way
Midway
Swadlincote
Derbyshire
DE11 7LA
Tel: 01283 211522
Fax: 01283 211522
Contact: Bill Adams, National Secretary
Founded: 1975
Publications: Members newsletter
Profile: Sole representative (independent trade union) of stable staff working within the British horse racing industry. Is responsible for negotiating wages and conditions and promotes a better way of living. To represent at all levels within the industry to negotiate and represent in all disputes between employee and employer. To represent stable staff on various committees within racing.

Staffordshire Agricultural Society
County Showground
Stafford
ST18 0BD
Tel: 01785 258060
Fax: 01785 246458
Contact: Mrs C Hammond, Secretary
Founded: 1799
Membership: 1,700
Publications: Staffordshire County Show Official Programme; Annual Report and Accounts
Profile: The society is a registered charity with the aim of promoting and improving agriculture and competition in agriculture in Staffordshire and a radius of 10 miles beyond the geographical boundary of the county. The society has eight self-governed District Societies and owns its own permanent showground of 110 acres at Stafford. The showground hosts the two day County Show and is rented out for other uses at other times of the year.

Standing Conference on Countryside Sports
College of Estate Management
Whiteknights
Reading
Berkshire
RG6 6AW
Tel: 01734 861101
Fax: 01734 755344

Contact: HJB Rice, Secretary
Founded: 1978
Publications: Countryside Sports: Their Economic and Conservation Significance
Profile: The Standing Conference is non-political, although many of the subjects it discusses have political undertones. Its purpose is to be a forum where senior representatives of national associations concerned with country sports, mainly hunting, shooting and fishing come together to identify and discuss major problems so that, where necessary, the attention of the government can be drawn to any action needed.

State Veterinary Service
Ministry of Agriculture, Fisheries and Food
Government Buildings
Hook Rise South
Tolworth
Surbiton
Surrey
KT6 7NF
Tel: 0181 330 4411
Fax: 0181 337 3640
Publications: Publications list available
Profile: The State Veterinary Service has a national organisational structure of five Regional Offices and 23 Divisional Offices, with headquarters in Surrey, Edinburgh and Cardiff. Full details may be obtained from the Head Office or by contacting the MAFF Helpline on 0645 335577

States of Guernsey Horticultural Advisory Service
States Committee for Horticulture
Raymond Falla House
Longue Rue
St Martin
Guernsey
Channel Isles
Tel: 01481 35741
Fax: 01481 35015
Contact: Mr ND Lewis, Chief Executive
Founded: 1932
Publications: Annual Statistical Report; promotional literature
Profile: The States Committee for Horticulture's primary objective is to maximise the net economic, social, and other benefits to the island arising from the horticultural industry. It has also been given responsibility to protect the island's plant life from plant diseases and pests which might pose an economic or environmental threat.

States of Jersey Department of Agriculture and Fisheries
PO Box 327
Howard Davis Farm

Trinity
Jersey
Channel Isles
JE4 8UF
Tel: 01534 866200
Fax: 01534 866201

Stationery Office, The
PO Box 276
London
SW8 5DT
Tel: 0171 873 9090
Email: book.orders@hmso.gov.uk
Previous names: HMSO until 1996
Profile: For orders ring: 0171 873 9090. For general enquiries ring: 0171 873 0011.

Stilton Cheese Makers' Association
PO Box 384A
Surbiton
Surrey
KT5 9YL
Tel: 0181 255 1334
Fax: 0181 255 1335
Contact: Nigel White, Secretary
Founded: 1936
Membership: 6
Publications: The History of Stilton; recipe leaflets
Profile: The Stilton Cheese Makers' Association is an unincorporated trade association representing the interests of its six members who manufacture Stilton cheese. Stilton is the only British cheese protected by a certification trade mark (CTM) which is vested in the SCMA. This provides that only cheese made in the three counties of Nottinghamshire, Derbyshire and Leicestershire, by an approved method and by a registered user of the CTM may be called Stilton. The association polices the use of the CTM, inspects manufacturer's plants, promotes the use of Stilton cheese and represents the interests of its members to the legislature.

Stone Federation of Great Britain
18 Mansfield Street
London
W1M 9FG
Tel: 0171 580 5404
Fax: 0171 636 5984
Contact: Robert Osborne, Regional Administrator
Founded: 1980
Membership: 150
Publications: Handbook and Directory of Members; data sheets

Profile: The SFGB is the trade association for the natural stone industry. Member companies include quarry operators, masonry contractors, stone cleaning and repair specialists and marble and granite contractors. The federation promotes the use of natural stone as a building material and provides information to architects and specifiers.

Stourbridge College Horticultural and Conservation Unit
Leasowes Park Nursery
Leasowes Lane
Halesowen
West Midlands
B62 8QF
Tel: 0121 550 0007

Student Campaign for Animal Rights
PO Box 155
Manchester
M60 1FT
Contact: Cath, Campaigns Officer
Profile: The campaign works to co-ordinate, support and network student animal rights groups – also to help with requests for information on animal abuse from students of all ages.

Suffolk Agricultural Association
Showground
Bucklesham Road
Ipswich
IP3 8UH
Tel: 01473 726847
Fax: 01473 721973
Contact: Christopher Bushby, Secretary
Founded: 1831
Membership: 3,500
Publications: Suffolk Scene
Profile: An agricultural charity whose main aim is to promote the advancement of and education in agriculture and also to stage an annual county agricultural show.

Suffolk Deer Management Working Group
Fiveways Farmhouse
Stanway Green
Colchester
Essex
Contact: Mr Clive Sebborn

Suffolk Horse Society
The Market Hill
Woodbridge
Suffolk
IP12 4LU

Tel: 01394 380643
Fax: 01394 382310
Contact: P Ryder-Davies, Secretary
Founded: 1888
Membership: 200
Publications: Newsletters
Profile: The breed society of the Suffolk horse breed – the oldest heavy horse breed in the world.

Suffolk Sheep Society
The Sheep Centre
Blackmore Park Road
Malvern
Worcestershire
WR13 6PH
Tel: 01684 893366
Fax: 01684 893390
Contact: Penny Lawrence, Secretary
Founded: 1886
Membership: 2,350
Publications: Flock book; Year Book; magazines and newsletters
Profile: The society has members throughout the British Isles. It uses a computerised system to verify and produce an annual flock book of Suffolks added to members' flocks. It organises shows and sales of Suffolks for members and sponsors prizes at agricultural shows and for prime lamb competitions. It promotes the breed by having a stand and information at shows and sheep events, demonstrating the benefits of using Suffolks. The year book provides reports on the activities of Suffolk breeders in shows, sales and social events at national, regional and local levels and members also receive newsletters with information from the Council of Management.

Sugar Beet Research and Education Committee
Ministry of Agriculture, Fisheries and Food
Room 406
Whitehall Place East Block
London
SW1A 2HH
Tel: 0171 270 8187
Fax: 0171 270 8188
Contact: Miss J E Alcock, Secretary
Founded: 1933
Publications: SBREC Yearbook; SBREC Research Papers
Profile: The SBREC was originally established under the Sugar Industry (Research and Education Scheme) (Approval) Order 1993 and is now non-statutory. It is appointed by the Minister of Agriculture, Fisheries and Food and the Secretary of State for Wales to administrate the

Sugar Beet Research and Education Fund, which finances an annual programme of research and education in matters affecting the growing of home-grown sugar beet. This fund is raised by an annual levy on growers and the processor (British Sugar plc) of sugar beet. The committee consists of members representing British Sugar, the NFU, the Biotechnology and Biological Sciences Research Council, MAFF and two independent members.

Sugar Bureau
Duncan House
Dolphin Square
London
SW1V 3PW
Tel: 0171 828 9465
Fax: 0171 821 5393

Sugar, Tobacco, Oilseeds and Proteins Division
Ministry of Agriculture, Fisheries and Food
Room 10 Whitehall Place
East Block
London
SW1A 2HH
Tel: 0171 270 8233
Profile: This division is responsible for UK policy for arable crops other than cereals, i.e. oilseeds, including linseed, proteins, including peas and beans, sugar, tobacco and fibre crops.

Surrey County Agricultural Society
45 Bridge Street
Godalming
Surrey
GU7 1HL
Tel: 01483 414651
Fax: 01483 425697
Contact: Juliet Lance, Secretary
Founded: 1954
Membership: 1,000
Profile: Organisers of large one day agricultural show together with farm competitions and ploughing match.

Sussex Cattle Society
Station Road
Robertsbridge
East Sussex
TN32 5DG
Tel: 01580 880105
Contact: Miss S Kennedy, Secretary

Sussex Club
Exbury
Ashford Hill Road
Headley

Newbury
Berkshire
RG15 8AB
Contact: Mr MN Raisey, Secretary
Profile: A society to promote the Sussex breed of poultry.

Sustainable Agriculture, Food and Environment Alliance
38 Ebury Street
London
SW1W 0LU
Tel: 0171 823 5660
Fax: 0171 823 5673
Email: safe@gn.apc.org
Contact: Vicki Hird, Coordinator
Founded: 1991
Membership: 33
Publications: Publications list available
Profile: The Sustainable Agriculture, Food and Environment Alliance exists to unite farmer, environmental, consumer, animal welfare and development organisations. They share a common vision of food production which is beneficial to the environment, sensitive to consumer demand and the need for global equity, and which produces safe and healthy food in a manner supportive of rural life and culture. The SAFE Alliance provides links between a wide range of public interest groups and through analysis, research, education and information they promote sustainable food production and generate pressure for change in farming policy and the food economy.

Sustrans Ltd
35 King Street
Bristol
BS1 4DZ
Tel: 01272 268893
Fax: 01272 294173
Email: sustrans@sustrans.co.uk
Contact: Tricia Glinski, Project Information Manager
Founded: 1978
Membership: 15,000
Publications: Publications list available
Profile: Sustrans (sustainable transport) designs and builds traffic-free routes for cyclists, walkers and people with disabilities. The National Cycle Network is being created by Sustrans in partnership with local authorities and many other bodies.

Sustrans Scotland
53 Cochrane Street
Glasgow
G1 1HL

Tel: 0141 552 8241
Fax: 0141 552 3599
Contact: Tony Grant, Regional Manager
Founded: 1976
Membership: 17,000
Publications: Various leaflets, maps etc.
Profile: Sustrans design, promote and build safe and attractive off-highway routes. Sustrans aims to build a national cycle network of over 6,500 miles by the year 2005. In Scotland they are agent partners in 'Forward Scotland' (formerly UK 2000 Scotland).

Swaledale Sheep Breeders Association
2 Skelton Hall
Marske
Richmond
North Yorkshire
DL11 7NE
Tel: 01748 850280
Contact: R Waggett, Secretary
Founded: 1920
Membership: 1,288
Publications: Flock book
Profile: The sheep breed society for the hardy hill breed of Swaledale sheep.

Technical Development Branch
Forestry Commission
Ae Village
Dumfries
DG1 1QB
Tel: 01387 86264
Fax: 01387 86386
Contact: Mr Michael Wall, Head of Technical Development Branch
Founded: 1960
Publications: Publication list available
Previous names: Work Study Branch
Profile: The Technical Development Branch is the part of the Forestry Commission with the responsibility to develop and evaluate safe and efficient equipment and methods of work, maintain output guidance and provide advice in connection with forestry and woodland operations. TDB is staffed by experienced, qualified foresters who are also trained work study practitioners. The branch undertakes a wide range of work for other parts of the FC and on outside contracts.

Teeswater Sheep Breeders' Association
1 The Mount
Leyburn
North Yorkshire
DL8 5JA
Tel: 01969 623432

Contact: D W Ward, Secretary
Founded: 1949
Membership: 120
Publications: Annual flock book; occasional newsletters
Profile: Members are breeders in both large and small flock sections, of the Teeswater sheep. Teeswaters are producers of high quality, lean, large lambs and the sire of the Masham half bred, whose breeders have a separate organisation.

Telework, Telecentre and Telecottage Association
National Agricultural Centre
Stoneleigh Park
Warwickshire
CV8 2RR
Tel: 01203 696986
Fax: 01203 696538
Email: 100272.3137@compuserve.com
Contact: Alan Denbigh, Executive Director
Founded: 1993
Membership: 2,200
Publications: Teleworker Magazine
Previous names: Telecottage Association until 1996
Profile: Set up to encourage the take up of teleworking, the TCA provides information and advice to people setting up to telework, teleworking schemes and telecottages.

Tenant Farmers' Association
7 Brewery Court
Theale
Reading
RG7 5AJ
Tel: 01734 306130
Fax: 01734 303424
Contact: Maureen Glenister, National Secretary
Founded: 1981
Membership: 3,500
Publications: TFA News
Profile: The TFA is the only organisation solely representing the tenanted sector.

Tennessee Walking Horse Club
Uplands
Alfriston
East Sussex
BN26 5XE
Profile: We have been unable to contact this organisation. The details given are unconfirmed.

Thames Water plc
Nugent House
Vastern Road

Reading
Berkshire
RG1 8DB

Thatching Advisory Services Ltd
Faircross Offices
Stratfield Saye
Reading
Berkshire
RG7 2BT
Tel: 01256 880828
Fax: 01256 880866
Contact: RC West, Managing Director
Founded: 1974
Publications: Complete Thatch Guide
Profile: Production of thatching materials,
thatched property insurance and thatching home
and abroad.

Thoroughbred Breeders' Association
Stanstead House
The Avenue
Newmarket
Suffolk
CB8 9AA
Tel: 01638 661321
Fax: 01638 665621
Contact: Gavin Pritchard-Gordon, Chief
Executive
Founded: 1917
Membership: 2,600
Publications: Pacemaker and Thoroughbred
Breeder
Profile: The TBA is recognised nationally and
internationally as a representative body for British
horse breeding. It is managed by a council of 17
elected, co-opted, and ex-officio members. The
TBA is a registered charity with the primary
objective of encouraging, by means of provision
of educational or research facilities or otherwise,
the science of maintaining and improving the
thoroughbred horse in Great Britain.

Three Counties Agricultural Society
The Showground
Malvern
Worcestershire
WR13 6NW
Tel: 01684 892751
Fax: 01684 568236
Contact: LM Downes, Chief Executive
Founded: 1797
Membership: 5,876
Publications: Annual Show Catalogue; Three
into One (society history) to be published 1997
Profile: Agricultural society organising an annual
show and promoting agriculture, livestock
breeding, horticulture, forestry, education,

conservation and care of the countryside. The
society organises a spring horticulture show and
an autumn countryside show.

Thurso College
Ormlie Road
Thurso
Caithness
KW14 7EE
Tel: 01847 66161
Fax: 01847 63872
Contact: James Labor, Marketing Manager
Founded: 1959
Publications: Prospectus
Profile: Thurso College is renowned for the
range of specialist courses it offers: equestrian
skills, veterinary nursing, childcare and education,
gamekeeping, hospitality, Scottish country
nanny, environmental studies, music, art and
media studies.

Tidy Britain Group
The Pier
Wigan
Lancashire
WN3 4EX
Tel: 01942 824620
Fax: 01942 824778
Contact: Professor Graham Ashworth, Director
General
Founded: 1954

Tidy Northern Ireland
Philip House
123 York Street
Belfast
BT15 1AB
Tel: 01232 328105
Fax: 01232 326645

Timber Growers Association
5 Dublin Street Lane South
Edinburgh
EH1 3PX
Tel: 0131 538 7111
Fax: 0131 538 7222
Contact: Ben Gunneberg, Regions Co-ordinator
Founded: 1983
Membership: 2,000
Publications: Timber Grower Magazine; TGA
Bulletin; TGA Regional Newsletter
Previous names: Timber Growers UK until 1993
Profile: TGA is a trade association which
represents growers at local, national and
European level, regularly lobbying government. It
provides regular marketing information and
analysis and provides owners with advice.

Current aims are: to foster an environment in which timber growers can operate effectively, responsibly and profitably and to provide effective support to the membership through a range of member services.

Timber Research and Development Association
Chiltern House
Stocking Lane
Hughenden Valley
High Wycombe
Buckinghamshire
HP14 4ND
Tel: 01494 563091
Fax: 01494 565487
Contact: Technical Advisory Section
Founded: 1934
Membership: 1,000
Publications: Wide range of timber related technical publications and books
Profile: TRADA acts as the interface between timber as a natural resource and its commercial use as a material. It promotes research and development into the end uses of timber, including the provision of timber design and the dissemination of literature.

Timber Trade Federation
Clareville House
26–27 Oxendon Street
London
SW1Y 4EL
Tel: 0171 839 1891
Fax: 0171 930 0094
Contact: R M James, PR and Hardwood Executive
Founded: 1892
Membership: 500
Publications: Leaflets
Profile: The Timber Trade Federation represents the timber importing trade, and aims to create the best conditions in the market place for its members to trade. Services to members include: representing the trade to government and overseas interests; promoting the merits of wood; assisting specifiers and purchasers; providing authoritative statistics and marketing information; standard contracts; legal advice and arbitration; industrial relations advice; training schemes; guidance on insurance and shipping matters; and leading the trade's contribution to British and European Standards.

Toggenburg Breeders Society
2 Kelloe Villas
Kelloe

County Durham
DH6 4PN
Tel: 01913 771689
Contact: Mr C Drury, Secretary
Founded: 1978
Membership: 93
Publications: Quarterly members newsletter
Profile: A breed society for the promotion of the Toggenburg Dairy goat within the British Isles. Membership is open to all breeders and supporters of the breed. Members enjoy the benefits of a newsletter, an annual general meeting, national and regional breed shows, the support of their area representative and the opportunity to contact other enthusiasts of the breed.

Tourism Concern
Southlands College
Wimbledon Parkside
London
SW19 5NN
Tel: 0181 944 0464
Fax: 0181 944 6583
Email: tourconcern@gn.apc.org
Contact: Ms P Barnett, Director
Founded: 1989
Membership: 1,000
Publications: In Focus
Profile: Tourism Concern is an educational charity whose aim is to raise awareness of the impact of tourism on people and their environment.

Town and Country Planning Association
17 Carlton House Terrace
London
SW1Y 5AS
Tel: 0171 930 8903
Fax: 0171 930 3280
Publications: Town and Country Planning Magazine

Town and Country Planning Association Scotland
Wellknowe Place
Thornton Hall
Lanarkshire
G74 5AX
Tel: 0141 644 1255

Towpath Action Group
23 Hague Bar Road
New Mills
Stockport
Cheshire
SK12 3AT
Tel: 01663 742198

Contact: Andy Screen, Secretary
Founded: 1988
Membership: 180
Publications: Newsletter; Trouble on the Towpath and Trouble on the Towpath 2
Profile: A pressure group campaigning for improved access along and on/off canal towpaths and river paths. TAG has close links with other walking groups (e.g. Ramblers) and the inland waterways sector (e.g. British Waterways, Inland Waterways Association and many individual canal societies/trusts).

Tractor Pullers Association of Great Britain
41 Sunny Hill
Sea Mills
Bristol
BS9 2NG
Tel: 0117 9877963
Contact: Mr David Trivett, Membership Secretary

Trade Policy and Tropical Foods Division
Ministry of Agriculture, Fisheries and Food
Room 409 Whitehall Place
East Block
London
SW1A 2HH
Tel: 0171 270 8171
Profile: The Trade Policy and Tropical Foods Division is responsible for all agricultural trade policy, also for coffee, cocoa, banana and other tropical food policy.

Traditional Farmfresh Turkey Association
5 Beacon Drive
Seaford
East Sussex
BN25 2JX
Tel: 01323 899802
Fax: 01323 899583
Contact: Mrs Penny Jones, Administrative Secretary
Founded: 1984
Membership: 35
Profile: The association is involved in the marketing of traditional farmfresh turkeys at Christmas and provides opportunities for members to meet and discuss problems and issues.

Trail Riders Fellowship
PO Box 196
Derby
DE1 9EY
Profile: We have been unable to contact this organisation. The details given are unconfirmed.

Trakehner Breeders Fraternity
Highwell Stud
Houghton Bank
Darlington
County Durham
DL2 2UQ
Tel: 01388 775148
Contact: Liz Horn

Transport 2000
Walkden House
10 Melton Street
Euston
London
NW1 2EJ
Tel: 0171 388 8386
Fax: 0171 388 2481
Contact: Jane Puzey, Communications Manager
Founded: 1973
Membership: 1,400
Publications: Publications catalogue available
Profile: Transport 2000 campaigns for a coherent and sustainable national transport policy which meets transport needs with least damage to the environment. Transport 2000 works for policies which will: cut road traffic; improve rail and bus services; encourage walking and cycling; make maximum use of rail and water freight and give greater priority to protecting the environment, saving lives and conserving natural resources.

Transport and General Workers Union
Transport House
Palace Street
Victoria
London
SW1E 5JD
Tel: 0171 828 7788
Fax: 0171 630 5861
Contact: Bill Morris, General Secretary
Profile: Includes the Racing and Equestrian Section and the Rural Agricultural and Allied Workers Section

Tree Advice Trust
Alice Holt Lodge
Wrecclesham
Farnham
Surrey
GU10 4LH
Tel: 01420 22022

Tree Aid
28 Hobbs Lane
Bristol
BS1 5ED
Tel: 0117 934 9442

Fax: 0117 934 9592
Contact: Sarah King, Office Manager
Founded: 1987
Membership: 2,000
Publications: Publicity leaflet, annual newsletter, publications on desertification
Profile: Tree Aid – helping people who need trees most. The charity was set up by UK foresters in response to the environmental crisis largely responsible for the famine in Africa in the mid-1980s. Because of the food crisis facing that continent projects focus on food trees, agroforestry, soil conservation and woodland income generation projects. The aim is to help villagers improve their environment towards self-sufficiency, especially in food, as well as to provide an incentive for the sustainable management of their woodland whilst at the same time ensuring that they have the purchasing power when there is food scarcity.

Tree Council
51 Catherine Place
London
SW1E 6DY
Tel: 0171 828 9928
Fax: 0171 828 9060
Contact: Robert Osborne, Director
Founded: 1974
Membership: 194
Publications: Tree News
Profile: The Tree Council was founded in 1974 with support from the Department of the Environment and in 1978 became an independent registered charity. The Tree Council's aims are: to improve the environment in town and country by promoting the planting and conservation of trees and woods throughout the UK; to disseminate knowledge about trees and their management; to act as a forum for organisations concerned with trees; to identify national problems and to provide initiatives for co-operation.

Tree Link
Rotary International
PO Box 1206
High Street
Marlow on Thames
Buckinghamshire
SL7 1WA
Tel: 01494 443870
Fax: 01494 472459
Email: campbell@efgl.demon.co.uk
Contact: John Campbell, Director
Founded: 1990
Publications: Treelink Review

Profile: Treelink's objective is to bring children around the world together through treeplanting.

Tree Register of the British Isles
2 Church Cottages
Westmeston
Hassocks
West Sussex
BN6 8RJ
Contact: VE Schilling, Registrar
Founded: 1987
Publications: Annual newsletter; biennial lectures

Tree Spirit
95 Anstey Road
Perry Barr
Birmingham
B44 8AN
Tel: 0121 356 2206
Email: shelley@tspirit.demon.co.uk
Contact: Martin Blount, Co-ordinator
Founded: 1984
Membership: 300
Publications: Members newsletter
Profile: A voluntary registered charity to protect or conserve trees and woodlands, to create new woods, promote a greater understanding of all matters related to trees, to create a deeper awareness, affection and respect for trees, the natural environment and the whole earth. Tree Spirit undertake tree planting and run a small tree nursery.

Tree Trust
Wellspring Cottage
Deerfold
Lingen
Bucknell
Shropshire
SY7 0EE
Profile: We have been unable to contact this organisation. The details given are unconfirmed.

Trees for Life
The Park
Findhorn Bay
Forres
Morayshire
IV36 0TZ
Tel: 01309 691292
Fax: 01309 691155
Email: treesforlife@gn.apc.org
Contact: Alan Watson Featherstone, Executive Director
Founded: 1987
Membership: 1,020
Publications: Newsletter

Profile: Trees for Life is a Scottish charity based at Findhorn Bay on the Moray coast in the north-east of Scotland. Their primary aim is to regenerate and restore the native Caledonian forest to a large area in the highlands, and eventually to reintroduce the missing species of wildlife which formerly lived in the old forest. In this they seek not only to counteract the centuries of deforestation which have led to the almost complete loss of Scotland's native woodlands, but also to be pioneers in the newly-emerging field of ecological restoration.

TreeSearch UK
1 Meadow Cottages
Springhill Farm
Cuddington Road
Dinton
Aylesbury
Buckinghamshire
HP18 0AD
Tel: 01296 747155
Profile: We have been unable to contact this organisation. The details given are unconfirmed.

Treewise
Larchgrove
1212 Edinburgh Road
Glasgow
G33 4EJ
Tel: 0141 774 5115
Fax: 0141 774 0566
Contact: Mr Drysdale, Manager

Trekking and Riding Society of Scotland
Boreland Farm
Fearnan
By Aberfeldy
Perth
PH15 2PG
Tel: 01887 830274
Fax: 01887 830606
Contact: Mrs Liz Menzies, Administrative Secretary
Founded: 1990
Membership: 80
Previous names: Scottish Trekking and Riding Association
Profile: TRSS specialises in looking after the interests of all those involved in leisure and holiday riding in Scotland. It provides advice and training to individuals, professional bodies and riding centres and operates an inspection scheme for its member centres. Those wishing for a riding holiday in Scotland are advised to contact the secretary for help in choosing the right holiday to suit requirements.

Tug of War Commission
British Athletic Federation
22 Annahugh Road
Loughgall
County Armagh
BT61 8PQ
Tel: 01762 891661
Contact: C McKeever, Chair

Tyrone Farming Society
The Showgrounds
Omagh
County Tyrone
Tel: 01662 242500
Contact: Robert A Pollock, Secretary
Founded: 1839
Membership: 220
Publications: Show catalogues
Profile: The society organises the annual Omagh Agricultural Show and Equestrian Events. They also promote community relations within the district. Omagh retains its position as the 'county show'.

UK Egg Producers Association
Rocklea
East Dundry
Bristol
BS18 8NJ
Tel: 0117 964 3498
Fax: 0117 964 3298
Contact: Keith Polman, Secretary
Founded: 1972
Membership: 500
Publications: UKEPRA News
Profile: A pressure group acting on behalf of all UK egg producers.

UK Forest Network
48 Bethel Street
Norwich
Norfolk
NR2 1NR
Tel: 01603 611953
Fax: 01603 666879
Email: reforest@gn.apc.org
Contact: Kath McNulty, Co-ordinator
Founded: 1992
Membership: 86
Publications: Forest Memorandum
Profile: The UK Forest Network circulates information among UK non-governmental organisations on issues connected with forests all over the world. It is also open to enquiries from the general public. It holds bimonthly meetings at which presentations are made about specific subjects.

UK Polocross Association
The Drift
Sandy Lane
Iken
Suffolk
Tel: 01728 688801
Profile: We have been unable to contact this
organisation. The details given are unconfirmed.

UK Sunflower Association
c/o ADAS Boxworth
Boxworth
Cambridgeshire
CB3 8NN
Tel: 01954 267666
Fax: 01954 267659
Contact: Dr Sarah Cook, Research Consultant
Founded: 1994
Membership: 50
Publications: Growers guide
Profile: The UK Sunflower Association has been
formed by a group of seed companies,
co-operatives, farmers and scientists with an
interest in developing the crop. It aims to
promote all aspects of UK sunflower production
and marketing, identify and publish grower
information, encourage structured development
of the crop to satisfy UK demand, to explore new
opportunities for the crop, to establish and
publish quality standards, to relate UK crop
potential to existing or future quality
requirements and to exchange and provide
independent information.

Ulster Agricultural Organisations Society Ltd
109 Church Street
Portadown
County Armagh
BT27 6YW
Tel: 01762 333144
Fax: 01762 350369
Contact: Ian C Murray, Chief Executive
Founded: 1922
Profile: The UAOS is the central body of
agricultural, rural, tourism and fisheries
co-operatives in Northern Ireland. It is entrusted
with co-operative development. It operates a
subsidiary company called Gateway Resource
Management Services Ltd which provides
consultancy, training and a personnel service to
the agri-food sector.

Ulster Curers Association
Lynwood
7 Sycamore Park
Jordanstown
Newtownabbey

County Antrim
BT37 0NR
Tel: 01232 865864
Contact: Hamilton Martin, Secretary

Ulster Farmers Union
475 Antrim Road
Belfast
BT15 3DA
Tel: 01232 370222
Fax: 01232 370739
Profile: We have been unable to contact this
organisation. The details given are unconfirmed.

Ulster Pony Society
67 Carnbane Road
Lisburn
County Antrim
BT27 5NG
Tel: 01232 781811
Profile: We have been unable to contact this
organisation. The details given are unconfirmed.

Ulster Poultry Federation
The Gardens
Dunleath Estates Lt
Ballywalter
Newtownards
County Down
Profile: We have been unable to contact this
organisation. The details given are unconfirmed.

**Ulster Society for the Preservation of the
Countryside**
Peskett Centre
2a Windsor Road
Belfast
BT9 7FQ
Tel: 01232 381304
Contact: AG Kennedy, Honorary Secretary
Founded: 1937
Membership: 400
Publications: Caring for the Countryside
Profile: A small, completely voluntary group,
funded by subscriptions, which acts as a
pressure group in local and central government in
order to preserve the beauties of the Ulster
countryside.

**Ulster Society for the Prevention of Cruelty to
Animals (Inc)**
11 Drumview Road
Lisburn
County Antrim
BT27 6YF
Tel: 01232 813178
Fax: 01232 812260

Contact: Francis Fox, Superintendent
Founded: 1836
Membership: 1,000
Publications: Annual Report and Accounts
Profile: The society is the second oldest animal welfare society in the world. Their main objective is to obtain justice for animals and to endeavour by every legitimate means to put an end to cruelty to animals and to encourage kindness and humanity in their treatment.

Ulster Tourist Development Association Ltd
Riada House
14 Charles Street
Ballymoney
County Antrim
BT53 6DZ
Tel: 012656 62280
Contact: WJ Williamson, Director
Founded: 1924
Membership: 120
Publications: 60 Years On (A history 1924–1984)
Profile: The UTDA is a voluntary tourist development association for Northern Ireland in which the tourist industry, local government and those in the community who are interested in tourism can foster the development of tourist traffic, encourage interest and involvement at local level and increase public awareness of the contribution a thriving tourist industry can make to the prosperity of Northern Ireland.

United Kingdom Agricultural Supply Trade Association Ltd
3 Whitehall Court
London
SW1A 2EQ
Tel: 0171 930 3611
Fax: 0171 930 3952
Contact: Jeremy A Smith, Company Secretary
Founded: 1977
Membership: 400
Publications: Publications list available
Profile: UKASTA represents about 400 companies and co-operatives which are either manufacturers of animal feedingstuffs or agricultural merchants who sell inputs such as feed, seed, fertilisers, agrochemicals and forage additives to farmers and or market arable crops on their behalf.

United Kingdom Association of Fish Meal Manufacturers
2 College Yard
Lower Dagnall Street
St Albans
Hertfordshire
AL3 4PA
Tel: 01727 842844

Fax: 01727 842866
Contact: Dr Ian H Pike, Secretary
Founded: 1909
Membership: 5
Publications: Statistics relating to the production and use of fish meal and fish oil in the UK; guide to the use of fish meal and fish oil for all species
Profile: The UKAFMM is a non-profit making trade association set up to advise members on the best methods of producing high quality fish meal and fish oil, and advising users on the benefits from the use of these products. Information is made available to users through technical publications, articles in scientific literature, press articles, etc.

United Kingdom Cheese Guild
Stanstead Farm
177 Stanstead Road
Caterham
Surrey
CR3 6AJ
Profile: We have been unable to contact this organisation. The details given are unconfirmed.

United Kingdom Dairy Association
5/7 John Princes Street
London
W1M 0AP
Tel: 0171 499 7822
Fax: 0171 491 0529
Email: All@NDC.Telme.com
Contact: Ian Wakeling, Secretary
Founded: 1950
Publications: UKDA newsletter
Profile: The UKDA serves as the United Kingdom National Committee of the International Dairy Federation. It represents UK dairying interests at the International Dairy Federation (IDF) and at other international bodies. Detailed consideration of technical matters is delegated to the UKDA technical committee and representatives, nominated by the technical committee, on expert groups each working on a specific topic within the six commissions that deal with the main body of the work of the IDF. The UKDA also acts as an agent for the sale of IDF publications and offers a 10% discount on the published price to members.

United Kingdom Environmental Law Association
Honeycroft House
Pangbourne Road
Upper Basildon
Berkshire
RG8 8LP

Tel: 01491 671631
Fax: 01491 671631
Contact: Dr Christina Hill, Company Secretary

United Kingdom Irrigation Association
Silsoe College
Silsoe
Bedfordshire
MK45 4DT
Tel: 01525 860428
Fax: 01525 861527
Contact: EK Weatherhead, Honorary Secretary
Founded: 1980
Membership: 300
Publications: Irrigation News
Profile: The UKIA exists to promote interest in, and a better understanding of, all aspects of irrigation in the UK; to collect and exchange information; to raise standards of knowledge and competence in irrigation design, installation and management.

United Kingdom Land and Hydrographic Survey Association
33 Catherine Place
London
SW1E 6DY
Tel: 0171 828 0933
Fax: 0171 834 5747
Contact: NW Granger, Secretary General
Founded: 1979
Membership: 52
Publications: Annual Membership Directory
Profile: The association is the representative organisation for UK private sector surveying firms. Its aim is to provide a vehicle for members to act effectively together to promote the interests of the profession to all those who determine the economic and social conditions in which the industry operates.

United Kingdom Provision Trade Federation Ltd
17 Clerkenwell Green
London
EC1R 0DP
Tel: 0171 253 2114
Fax: 0171 608 1645
Contact: Mrs Clare Cheney, Director General
Founded: 1887
Membership: 200
Profile: The UKPTF represents, protects and promotes the interests of its members by negotiating with and making or receiving representations to or from organisations or official bodies representing the EU institutions, the UK government, any local or regional

authority or other trade association. It provides an information service covering legislative and trading matters to its membership which includes manufacturers, traders, importers, exporters, distributors and retailers involved in trading in dairy products, speciality cheese, yogurt and short life dairy products, bacon and pigmeat, chilled and processed meats and canned foods sectors of the food industry.

United Kingdom Register of Organic Standards
Room 320c
Nobel House
17 Smith Square
London
SW1P 3JR
Tel: 0171 238 5915
Fax: 0171 238 6553
Contact: Peter Crofts

United Kingdom Renderers Association
PO Box 233
Redhill
Surrey
RH1 4YU
Tel: 01737 644016
Fax: 01737 644988
Contact: Alan Sadler, Secretary

United Kingdom Softwood Sawmillers' Association
John Player Building
Stirling Enterprise Park
Springbank Road
Stirling
FK7 7RS
Tel: 01786 449029
Fax: 01786 474412
Contact: David Sulman, Secretary

United Saddlebred Association (UK)
Birchwood Forge
Storridge
Malvern
Worcestershire
WR13 5EZ
Tel: 01886 884285
Contact: Mrs Ann Farman, Secretary
Founded: 1994
Membership: 50
Publications: Newsletter; Year Book; articles and handouts
Profile: Started in 1994 to promote and publicise the American Saddlebred horse, which was first imported into this country in the 1960s. The organisation aims to get shows in the country to put on classes for Saddlebreds. The parent

organisation, the American Saddle Horse Association is one of the longest running breed societies in the world. A very active membership is growing every year. Members are very keen on learning the American way of producing and showing their horses.

Universities Federation for Animal Welfare
8 Hamilton Close
South Mimms
Potters Bar
Hertfordshire
EN6 3QD
Tel: 01707 658202
Fax: 01707 649279
Email: trevor.poole@ucl.ac.uk
Contact: Sir Michael Simmons, Chief Executive
Founded: 1926
Membership: 1,000
Publications: Annual Report and Accounts; newsheet; Animal Welfare; research reports, guidance booklets and videos
Profile: UFAW is an animal welfare charity which seeks to promote a humane, caring attitude towards all animals used or influenced by man and his activities. Research to discover the needs of different species in varying environments is funded and supported. Balanced technical advice on animal welfare matters is offered to other similar groups, charities, educators, religious bodies and government departments.

University of Cambridge Agricultural Economics Unit
Department of Land Economy
19 Silver Street
Cambridge
CB3 9EP
Tel: 01223 337147
Fax: 01223 337130
Email: fsll@cus.cam.ac.uk
Contact: Ian Sturgess, Director
Founded: 1925
Publications: Farming in the Eastern Counties; occasional publications
Previous names: Farm Economics Branch until 1968
Profile: Holds the MAFF contract for the Farm Business Survey for the Eastern Counties and undertakes specific commissioned work. Staff are involved in teaching the land economy tripos. Other research mainly concerns agricultural policy and international trade.

University of Glasgow Chemistry Department
University Avenue
Glasgow
G12 8QQ

Tel: 0141 399 8855
Fax: 0141 330 4888

University of Glasgow Faculty of Veterinary Medicine
Bearsden Road
Glasgow
G61 1QH
Tel: 0141 330 5703

University of Leeds Department of Animal Physiology and Nutrition
Leeds
LS2 9JT
Tel: 0113 233 3065
Fax: 0113 233 3072
Contact: Dr CC Johnson, Head of Department
Founded: 1891
Profile: The agricultural science interests are vested in a range of departments in the faculties of science, engineering, business and economic studies, etc. Groups form as appropriate for various multidisciplinary research programmes. Teaching is based on modular programmes which also allows integration of modules from cognate areas within the core modules of animal science, plant science, etc.

University of Newcastle upon Tyne Department of Agricultural Economics and Food Marketing
Newcastle upon Tyne
NE1 7RU
Tel: 0191 222 6900
Fax: 0191 222 6720

University of Nottingham Faculty of Agricultural and Food Sciences
University of Nottingham
Sutton Bonington Campus
Loughborough
Leicestershire
LE12 5RD
Tel: 0115 951 5151
Fax: 0115 951 6350
Contact: Mr A Whiting, Faculty Secretary
Founded: 1948
Membership: 600
Publications: Triennial Report
Previous names: Variations on Midland Dairy and Agricultural College from 1895–1947
Profile: The Faculty of Agricultural and Food Sciences occupies its own campus ten miles south of Nottingham in the rural setting of Sutton Bonington village, on the borders of Nottinghamshire and Leicestershire. The Faculty has about 400 undergraduates, 135 research and

30 taught postgraduates and 50 academic staff, together with research staff and technicians.

University of Oxford Department of Plant Sciences
South Parks Road
Oxford
OX1 3RB
Tel: 01865 275000
Fax: 01865 275074

University of Reading Faculty of Agriculture and Food
No 2 Earley Gate
PO Box 239
Reading
Berkshire
RG6 6AU
Tel: 01734 318373
Fax: 01734 352063
Email: P.Moss@reading.ac.uk
Internet: http://www.rdg.ac.uk
Contact: Paul Moss, Sub-Dean
Founded: 1892
Publications: Propectuses (undergraduate and postgraduate), Annual Proceedings, Report
Profile: For over 100 years the Faculty of Agriculture and Food at Reading has been one of the largest in the UK. It has educated and trained men and women who have become farmers, research workers, teachers, advisers, administrators and managers. They work in agriculture, horticulture, food and other industries, in official services or in education, in the UK and overseas. The faculty is closely linked with these industries and services, and with research.

University of Wales Bangor School of Agriculture and Forest Sciences
Bangor
Gwynedd
LL57 2DG
Tel: 01248 351151
Fax: 01248 354997
Email: SAFS@bangor.ac.uk
Contact: Dr David Wright

University of Wolverhampton Centre for Rural Development and Training
Walsall Campus
Gorway Road
Walsall
West Midlands
WS1 3BD
Tel: 01902 323219
Fax: 01902 323212
Email: in4746@wlv.ac.uk

Contact: Professor JC Lowe, Head of Centre
Founded: 1973
Previous names: Agricultural Education and Training Unit until 1991
Profile: The CRDT, a specialist centre of the University of Wolverhampton, is the UK's foremost international centre for the training of teachers and trainers who are working in the fields of natural resources and rural development. Consultancy and training services are offered worldwide in natural resource education training; women in rural development; social forestry and agroforestry extension; communication skills; training materials and media production; project identification, preparation, management and evaluation; staff development programmes and training of trainers; management in training; gender and development; extension strategies and technology transfer; curriculum development; institutional strengthening and management.

Upkeep: The Trust for Training and Education in Building Maintenance
Apartment 39 Hampton Court Palace
East Molesey
Surrey
KT8 9BS
Tel: 0181 943 2277
Fax: 0181 943 9552
Contact: Annette McGill
Previous names: Building Conservation Trust

Valuation and Lands Agency
Queen's Court
56–66 Upper Queen Street
Belfast
BT1 6FD
Tel: 01232 250700
Fax: 01232 543750
Contact: Lorraine Snoddy, Personnel
Founded: 1993
Publications: Corporate Plan; Business Plan; Annual Report and Accounts
Previous names: Valuation and Lands Office until 1993
Profile: The maintenance of the valuation list for rating purposes in Northern Ireland, advice on all matters relating to land management and valuation to the department and ministers, and the provision of a valuation, estate management and property data service to the public sector.

Valuation Office
New Court
Carey Street
London
WC2A 2JE

Tel: 0171 324 1075
Fax: 0171 324 1073
Contact: G Barton Greenwood, Principal Valuer, Client Services
Founded: 1910
Publications: Valuation Office Market Report; Ryde's Scale
Previous names: Valuation Office until 1991
Profile: The Valuation Office agency provides property valuation services to all government departments, local authorities and other publicly funded bodies, in both the rural and urban context. The work is carried out through a network of 100 District Valuers, supported by regional and central expertise in specific matters such as building surveying, property development and minerals. In addition to acquisitions and disposal of rural property, advice is available on rent reviews, landfill, quota, set-aside, compensation claims, damage claims, access agreements and conservation agreements, under the Agriculture Act, Agricultural Holdings Acts, Land Compensation Acts, Wildlife and Countryside Act and other relevant legislation.

Vegetable Protein Association
6 Catherine Street
London
WC2B 5JJ
Tel: 0171 836 2460
Fax: 0171 836 0580
Contact: Ms L Hilsley, Executive Secretary
Founded: 1986
Membership: 5
Profile: The VPA represents the interests of UK companies engaged in the manufacture or supply of vegetable proteins. The principal products are those derived from the soybean. VPA makes representations to legislators in Westminster and their European association (EUVEPRO) acts at commission level from its base in Brussels, in order to safeguard members' interests in the face of legislative change. The association also deals with the media and consumer bodies and acts as a general source of information on soy and vegetable protein products.

Venture Scotland
Bonnington Mill
72 Newhaven Road
Edinburgh
EH6 5QG
Tel: 0131 553 5333
Fax: 0131 553 5333
Contact: Rob Bushby, Co-ordinator
Founded: 1987

Membership: 1,000
Publications: Leaflet; Annual Report; monthly newsletter
Profile: Provide outdoor development programmes, for young adults who don't usually have access to such opportunities. Courses are based at a bothy in Glen Etive. This wilderness setting is ideal for a range of outdoor and conservation activities, which are led by a team of skilled volunteers.

Veterinary Deer Society
British Veterinary Association
Moredun Research Institute
408 Gilmerton Road
Edinburgh
EH17 7JH
Tel: 0131 664 3262
Fax: 0131 664 8001
Contact: Hugh W Reid, Editor
Founded: 1980
Membership: 120
Publications: Veterinary Deer Society Publication
Profile: The VDS is involved in all aspects of deer health and management with particular reference to farmed animals. Membership is largely restricted to veterinary graduates.

Veterinary History Society
32 Belgrave Square
London
SW1X 8QP
Profile: We have been unable to contact this organisation. The details given are unconfirmed.

Veterinary Investigation Division
Veterinary Laboratories Agency
Block C Government Buildings
Hook Rise South
Tolworth
Surbiton
Surrey
KT6 7NF
Tel: 0181 330 4411
Fax: 0181 330 8623
Contact: Kevin Jackson, Librarian
Founded: 1995
Previous names: Veterinary Investigation Service until 1995
Profile: The network of Veterinary Investigation Centres throughout England and Wales provides laboratory and veterinary support to ensure that the VLA supplies the necessary services for the statutory requirements of MAFF. There is close liaison with private veterinary surgeons to ensure effective monitoring of notifiable and new and emerging diseases. They also provide a broad

range of services to pharmaceutical and other industries.

Veterinary Laboratories Agency
Ministry of Agriculture, Fisheries and Food
New Haw
Addlestone
Surrey
KT15 3NB
Tel: 01932 341111
Fax: 01932 347046
Contact: Kevin Jackson, Librarian
Founded: 1995
Publications: Annual Report; VIDA
Previous names: Central Veterinary Laboratory until 1995
Profile: The Veterinary Laboratories Agency is an executive agency of MAFF. The aim of the VLA is to provide the Ministry of Agriculture with an effective and efficient service of specialist veterinary, scientific and technical support, consultancy and surveillance in the fields of animal health, welfare, food safety and the environment. There is a network of Veterinary Investigation Centres throughout England and Wales, organised on a regional basis. Full details may be found in MAFF's free publication 'At the Farmer's Service' or by contacting the MAFF Helpline on 0645 335577.

Veterinary Medicines Directorate
Ministry of Agriculture, Fisheries and Food
Woodham Lane
New Haw
Addlestone
Surrey
KT15 3NB
Tel: 01932 336911
Fax: 01932 336618
Email: maninf@vmd.maff.gov.uk
Contact: C Bennett
Founded: 1990
Publications: Annual Report; Corporate Plan; Framework Document; MAVIS
Previous names: Animal Medicines Division, MAFF
Profile: The Veterinary Medicines Directorate is responsible to agriculture and health ministers in the UK for the licensing and other controls on the manufacture, sale and distribution of veterinary medicines; for the surveillance of residues in meat, and for monitoring suspected adverse reactions to veterinary medicines in animals and humans. In carrying out these activities the VMD is advised by the independent and expert Veterinary Products Committee. The primary aim of the VMD is to ensure the safety, quality and

efficacy of veterinary medicines in the UK, thereby safeguarding public health, animal health and the environment and promoting animal health.

Village Retail Services Association
Halstock
Yeovil
Somerset
BA22 9QY
Tel: 01935 891614
Fax: 01935 891544
Contact: Derek Smith, Director
Founded: 1991
Membership: 500
Publications: Publications list available
Profile: VIRSA helps parish councils and action groups to set up investment packages to rescue, sustain or revive village shops and post offices. VIRSA has researched and developed model financial and legal documentation for a variety of schemes which can be tailored to suit the needs and capabilities of individual villages. They actively lobby local and central government. VIRSA is a not-for-profit organisation which provides support and encouragement to all villages which wish to retain or resuscitate their village shop or post office.

Voluntary Service Overseas
317 Putney Bridge Road
London
SW15 2PN
Tel: 0181 780 2266
Fax: 0181 780 1326
Email: Enquiry@v.s.o.1.+com.co.uk
Contact: Jamie Elliott, Recruitment Officer
Founded: 1958
Publications: Orbit Magazine; Is VSO for you?
Profile: VSO enables men and women to work alongside people in poorer countries in order to share skills, build capabilities and promote international understanding and action, in the pursuit of a more equitable world. Placements are in education, health, natural resources, technical trades, engineering, business, communications and social development. Over 1,750 volunteers work in 57 countries.

VTSC Growers Association
53 York Place
Perth
PH2 8EN
Tel: 01738 622305
Fax: 01738 623188
Contact: Hugh B Edmond, Honorary Secretary
Founded: 1972
Membership: 77

Profile: The Virus Tested Stem Cutting Association was set up in 1972 as the representative body in Great Britain for specialist potato growers who were responsible for producing new seed potato stocks from pathogen free tubers. The association's functions are to engage in any matter relevant to the production, marketing and publicity of VTSC seed potatoes and to represent the interests of the membership by: representing raisers' interests with the government, PMB and other organisations; promoting healthy seed potatoes; promoting dialogue in the industry including an annual conference; disseminating information and statistics; and, promoting the adoption of new agronomic and storage methods.

Wales Craft Council / Cyngor Crefft Cymru Cyf
7 High Street
Welshpool
Powys
SY21 7JP
Tel: 01938 555313
Fax: 01938 556237
Contact: Janet Edwards, Office Manager
Founded: 1977
Membership: 150
Publications: Trade fair catalogues relating to The Wales Fair and Wales Spring Fair
Profile: A membership organisation for professional producers of crafts, gifts and textiles in Wales. WCC owns and organises two annual trade shows in Wales – the Wales Fair each October in Builth Wells and Wales Spring Fair every January in Llandudno.

Wales Tourist Board
Brunel House
2 Fitzalan Road
Cardiff
CF2 1UY
Tel: 01222 499909
Fax: 01222 475321
Contact: Gillian Berntsen, UK Marketing Manager
Founded: 1976
Publications: Wales Magazine
Profile: The board seeks to develop and market tourism in ways which will yield optimum economic and social benefit to the people of Wales. Implicit with this objective is the need to sustain and promote the culture of Wales and the Welsh language and to safeguard the natural and built environment. In order to achieve its aims, the board works in partnership with statutory agencies, local authorities, the private sector and other bodies.

Wales Trekking and Riding Association
Standby House
9 Nevill Street
Abergavenny
Monmouthshire
NP7 5AA
Tel: 01873 858717
Fax: 01873 858717

Wales Wildlife and Countryside Link
Bryn Aderyn
The Bank
Newtown
Powys
SY16 2AB
Tel: 01686 629194
Fax: 01686 622339
Contact: Rosie Walker, Link Officer
Founded: 1989
Membership: 26
Publications: Annual Reports; newsletter
Profile: Wales Wildlife and Countryside Link unites voluntary bodies whose primary aims include the conservation, protection or quiet enjoyment of landscape, wildlife or amenity in Wales. It enables joint discussion and collaboration between its member organisations, continues to develop relations with government and other statutory bodies and encourages joint action on environmental issues when appropriate.

Walford College
Walford
Baschurch
Shrewsbury
Shropshire
SY4 2HL
Tel: 01939 260461
Fax: 01939 261112
Contact: Mr KW Dann, Principal
Founded: 1949
Publications: Prospectus
Previous names: Walford Farm Institute until 1979; Walford College of Agriculture until 1984
Profile: The college was established in 1949 as a centre for agricultural education and training located in the very pleasant surroundings of Walford Estate, seven miles to the north west of Shrewsbury. The estate comprises of 238 ha of farmland and 21 ha of woodland offering a wide range of practical facilities. Over the years the college has expanded its range of courses to cover the full spectrum of land-based/related education and training, for which it has gained a national reputation.

Warren Farm Centre

West Oxfordshire College
Warren Farm
Horton Cum Studley
Oxford
OX33 1BY
Tel: 01865 371794
Fax: 01865 358931
Contact: David Stone, Director
Founded: 1953
Previous names: Oxfordshire Agricultural
Education Centre until 1990
Profile: Warren Farm Centre was set up to
provide first class education and training
resources in most land-based industries:
agriculture, horticulture, horse management,
game management, floristry, agricultural
mechanics and rural skills. The farm is run as a
commercial unit covering some 107 ha of
grassland, crops and woodland. Enterprises
include 120 breeding ewes, 80 commercial
Friesian dairy cows, beef cattle, a range of
cropping and an equestrian centre. There is a
comprehensive range of modern machinery and
well equipped workshops. An excellent
horticultural unit has been developed.

Warren Spring Laboratory

Gunnels Wood Road
Stevenage
Hertfordshire
ST1 2BX
Profile: We have been unable to contact this
organisation. The details given are unconfirmed.

Warwickshire College – Royal Leamington Spa and Moreton Morrell

Moreton Morrell
Warwick
CV35 9BR
Tel: 01926 651367
Fax: 01926 651190
Contact: Bryan Jarvis, Head of Centre (Moreton
Morrell)
Founded: 1949
Previous names: Warwickshire College for
Agriculture, Horticulture and Equine Studies until
August 1996
Profile: Warwickshire College, Moreton Morrell
is Britain's award winning leader in conservation
and the countryside. It is also recognised as the
world's leading horse college. It is set on a
superb campus close to Stratford upon Avon and
Royal Leamington Spa and enjoys a wealth of
excellent facilities. In August 1996 it merged
with Mid-Warwickshire College, Leamington Spa
to become one of the largest further education

providers in the country offering a tremendous
range of subjects and courses to its students.
There is excellent accommodation for over 200
students and an extensive transport network
operating over a 30 mile radius.

Waste Food Feeders Association

National Farmers' Union
Hall Lane Farm
Little Warley
Brentwood
Essex
CM13 3EN
Tel: 01277 811242
Contact: David Ramsey, Chairman
Founded: 1973
Membership: 300
Publications: Ad hoc newsletter
Profile: Members are livestock farmers licensed
by MAFF to process food wastes for animal feed.
The organisation provides the first line of contact
with the food industry. It is a voluntary group
working closely with the livestock section of the
NFU.

Waste Management Information Bureau

AEA Technology
National Environment Technology Centre
E4, Culham
Abingdon
Oxfordshire
OX14 3DB
Tel: 01235 463162
Fax: 01235 463004
Email: wmib@aeat.co.uk
Contact: Heather Cholerton, Manager
Founded: 1974
Publications: WasteInfo (online and CD ROM
database); Waste and Environment Today;
reading lists
Profile: The WMIB is the national referral centre
for information and advice on all aspects of
waste management, supported by the
Department of the Environment. Short enquiries
are answered free of charge. A list of charges is
available for longer enquiries, searches of
WasteInfo and searches of online databases.
Visitors are welcome to the dedicated waste
management library.

Waste Watch

Gresham House
24 Holborn Viaduct
London
EC1A 2BN
Tel: 0171 248 0242
Fax: 0171 248 1404
Contact: April Groves, Information Officer

Founded: 1987
Membership: 250
Publications: Publications list available
Profile: Waste Watch is the national agency promoting action on waste reduction and recycling. It works with local authorities, businesses, community groups and educational establishments across the country. The Waste Watch Wasteline information service answers enquiries from all sectors of the community on waste and recycling issues. Wasteline can be contacted on 0171 248 0242 10am–5pm Monday to Friday.

Water and Land Directorate
Department of the Environment
Room A423
Romney House
423 Marsham Street
London
SW1P 3PY
Tel: 0171 276 8259
Fax: 0171 276 8639
Contact: Mr Neil Summerton, Director
Publications: Publications list available from the Department of the Environment Library
Previous names: Water Directorate until 1995
Profile: The directorate deals with all policy matters relating to the aquatic environment including water supply, collection and treatment of wastewater, the structure within which the industry operates; and the co-ordination of UK marine environmental policies. It ensures that the system of water legislation and regulation works in an effective manner, that adequate supplies of good quality water are available at an acceptable cost and that marine pollution is reduced. It also deals with contaminated land and environmental liabilities policy, including implementation of the Environment Act 1995, technical guidance, the contaminated land research programme and supplementary credit approvals.

Water Appeals Commission (Northern Ireland)
87–91 Great Victoria Street
Belfast
BT2 7AG
Tel: 01232 244710
Contact: Mrs M Hempton, Secretary
Founded: 1973

Water Companies Association
1 Queen Annes Gate
London
SW1H 9BT
Tel: 0171 222 0644

Fax: 0171 222 3366
Contact: Mrs Valerie Homer, Deputy Director
Founded: 1885
Membership: 18
Publications: Fact Book; Water News
Profile: The Water Companies Association represents water supply companies in England and Wales. It provides a collective voice for these companies in water industry matters and encourages improvement and co-operation between its members. It also monitors matters in the EU and makes representations to the European Commission.

Water Research Centre Scotland
Unit 16 Beta Centre
Stirling University Innovation Park
Stirling
Central Scotland
FK9 4NF
Profile: We have been unable to contact this organisation. The details given are unconfirmed.

Water Service
Department of the Environment for Northern Ireland
Northland House
Frederick Street
Belfast
BT1 2NR
Tel: 01232 244711
Fax: 01232 354888
Contact: Mr H R F Plester, Chief Executive
Publications: Framework Document; Corporate/Business Plan; Charter Standard Statement
Profile: The Water Service is the sole water and sewerage authority in Northern Ireland and is an executive agency within the Department of Environment for Northern Ireland. It supplies and distributes drinking water and treats waste water to high quality and environmental standards.

Water Services Association
1 Queen Annes Gate
London
SW1H 9BT
Tel: 0171 957 4567
Fax: 0171 957 4666
Contact: Jackie Conn, Press and Research Officer
Founded: 1989
Membership: 9
Publications: Publications list available
Profile: The WSA's role is to promote and protect the common interests of its member companies in dealings with UK Government, the EU and other regulatory bodies and to ensure that the

expertise and experience of the water industry are able to influence policy and regulatory initiatives on water issues by governmental and other agencies, both national and international. The WSA is governed by a council of its members.

Watercourse Management Division Headquarters
Department of Agriculture for Northern Ireland
4 Hospital Road
Belfast
BT8 8JP
Tel: 01232 253355
Fax: 01232 253455
Contact: Mr Danny McSorley, Chief Executive
Previous names: Drainage Division until 1991, to become an Executive Agency in October 1996
Profile: The division fulfils the parent organisation's role as flood protection, sea defence and river drainage authority for Northern Ireland, as inland navigation authority for Lough Erne and the lower River Bann, and as the body responsible for the control of water levels in Lough Neagh and Lough Erne (in conjunction with the Electricity Supply Board in the Republic of Ireland), and for the development of water recreational facilities for use by the public throughout the province. In the execution of this role, the division has a commitment to the integration of environmental protection, and where appropriate, rehabilitation or enhancement measures into the design and execution of all its activities.

Watercress Association
Agriculture House
Knightsbridge
London
SW1X 7NJ
Profile: We have been unable to contact this organisation. The details given are unconfirmed.

Waterway Recovery Group
Inland Waterways Association
114 Regent's Park Road
London
NW1 8UQ
Tel: 0171 586 2510
Fax: 0171 723 7213
Contact: Neil Edwards, Director
Founded: 1970
Membership: 2,000
Publications: Navvies; numerous technical publications
Profile: WRG has, for over 25 years been co-ordinating the efforts of volunteers to restore Britain's canals. WRG is run entirely by volunteers, with projects based all over the country.

Weed Resistance Action Group
IACR Rothamsted
Harpenden
Hertfordshire
AL5 2LQ
Tel: 01582 763133
Fax: 01582 760981
Contact: Dr S R Moss, Secretary
Founded: 1989
Membership: 50
Publications: Publications list available
Profile: WRAG's objectives are: to provide a forum for information exchange between people actively involved in research into herbicide resistance; to discuss strategies to avoid resistance or to manage resistant populations or to achieve both; to define research methods; to discuss test methodology and agree standards; to agree statements for the media, whether in response to queries or as unsolicited news releases; to maintain communication with similar groups which have been established successfully in other countries.

Welsh Agricultural Organisation Society Ltd
PO Box 8
Brynawel
Great Darkgate Street
Aberystwyth
Ceredigion
SY23 1DR
Tel: 01970 624011

Welsh Beekeepers Association
Trem y Clawdd
Fron Isaf
Chirk
Wrexham
LL14 5AH
Tel: 01691 773300
Contact: BD Rowlands, General Secretary
Founded: 1943
Membership: 1,500
Publications: Newyddlen
Profile: Promoting bee keeping in Wales.

Welsh Black Cattle Society
13 Bangor Street
Caernafon
Caernarfonshire
LL55 1AP
Tel: 01286 672391
Fax: 01286 672022
Contact: Mrs S Evelyn Jones, Secretary

Founded: 1904
Membership: 800
Publications: Annual herd book; Annual Breed Journal
Profile: Breed society for the Welsh Black breed of beef cattle. With the Welsh Black, quality comes naturally. As Britain's premier beef dam breed, linking quality beef production with ease of calving, outstanding mothering ability and hardiness, the Welsh Black is ideally suited to modern farming conditions where ease of management and low inputs are the key to profitable beef production.

Welsh Bleu Sheep Producers Association

c/o WAOS Ltd
PO Box 8
Brynawel
Great Darkgate Street
Aberystwyth
Ceredigion
SY23 1DR
Tel: 01970 624011
Fax: 01970 624049

Welsh College of Horticulture

Northop
Mold
Clwyd
CH7 6AA
Tel: 01352 840861
Fax: 01352 840731
Contact: GA Limb, Principal
Founded: 1955
Publications: Prospectus
Profile: A residential land-based specialist college (FE) offering courses in horticulture, floristry, agricultural and horticultural engineering, environment and conservation, landscape science and equine studies.

Welsh Cycling Union

15 Palmera Gardens
Prestatyn
Clwyd
LL19 9NS
Tel: 01745 888754
Fax: 01745 888754
Contact: Rae Hughes, Secretary
Founded: 1973
Membership: 700
Publications: Bimonthly newsletter
Profile: The Welsh Cycling Union is charged with the administration and control of cycle racing within Wales. It is the only grant funded cycling body recognised by the Sports Council for Wales and is responsible for sending cycling teams to each Commonwealth Games.

Welsh Development Agency

Pearl House
17th Floor
Greyfriars Road
Cardiff
CF1 3XX
Tel: 01433 845500

Welsh Federation of Young Farmers Clubs

Wales YFC Centre
Llanelwedd
Builth Wells
Powys
LD2 3NJ
Tel: 01982 553502
Fax: 01982 552979
Contact: Arwyn Davies, Chief Executive
Founded: 1936
Membership: 6,000
Publications: Quarterly magazine
Profile: Wales YFC seeks to meet the needs of rural young people in Wales through educational, training and social programmes which encourage community involvement and concern for our environment. The movement operates within a framework consisting of 180 clubs and 12 county federations, giving opportunities for personal development of the members. Wales YFC seeks to meet its objectives through a range of programmes which the members have the responsibility for designing and management of the delivery.

Welsh Food Promotions Ltd

Cardiff Business Technology Centre
Senghennydd Road
Cardiff
CF2 4AY
Tel: 01222 640456
Fax: 01222 640048
Contact: Ms Barbara Pounder, Speciality Food Group Executive
Founded: 1992
Membership: 4,000
Publications: Taste of Wales Quarterly Magazine; Taste of Wales Food Map; Directory of Food and Drink Producers
Previous names: Welsh Lamb Enterprise and Welsh Beef Promotions merged to form Welsh Food Promotions Ltd in 1996
Profile: Welsh Food Promotions Ltd is a company which acts as a one stop shop for all food enquiries, whether for developing marketing or even producing a food product in Wales. WFPL can help those in farming and food processing unravel the red tape, and maximise employment and profit opportunities. WFPL is

working towards creating a very high profile for Welsh food through its marketing strategy. WFPL can also offer advice and guidance on food processing development, can provide detailed information on export opportunities and maintains a comprehensive centralised information service.

Welsh Halfbred Sheep Breeders' Association Ltd
Bryn Teg
Penygarnedd
Llanrhaeadr ym Mochnant
Powys
SY10 0AW
Tel: 01691 860336
Fax: 01691 860571
Contact: Mrs Gill Napper, Secretary
Founded: 1955
Membership: 500
Profile: The association was established to promote and market the Welsh Halfbred. Ewes and ewe lambs are sold at five annual official sales in Wales (at Builth Wells, Ruthin and Welshpool). All sheep are inspected before sale.

Welsh Hill Speckled Face Sheep Society
Morris Marshall and Poole
10 Broad Street
Newtown
Powys
SY16 2LZ
Tel: 01686 625900
Fax: 01686 623783
Contact: Gwyndaf Roberts

Welsh Institute of Rural Studies
University of Wales Aberystwyth
Llanbadarn Fawr
Aberystwyth
Ceredigion
SY23 3AL
Tel: 01970 624471
Fax: 01970 611264
Email: wirwww@aber.ac.uk
Contact: Jane Guest, Marketing Coordinator
Founded: 1878
Publications: Publications list available
Previous names: Welsh Agricultural College until 1995
Profile: The Welsh Institute of Rural Studies was established in 1995 as a result of the merger of the Welsh Agricultural College and the Department of Agricultural Sciences at Aberystwyth. It is unique in providing land-based education from National Diploma to PhD level. There are opportunities to study courses in a range of agricultural disciplines, countryside

management, rural resource management and equine studies. The teaching reflects the latest research and business conditions. The research activities of the institute encompass all aspects of agricultural, environmental and countryside management, rural economics and policy development, marketing and agri-business.

Welsh Mountain Sheep Society – Hill Flock Section
c/o WAOS Ltd
PO Box 8
Brynawel
Great Darkgate Street
Aberystwyth
Ceredigion
SY23 1DR
Tel: 01970 624011
Fax: 01970 624049
Contact: Moss Jones, Secretary
Founded: 1908
Membership: 646
Previous names: Welsh Mountain Sheep Society evolved into two sections in the 1970s
Profile: The society represents the interests of members in the development of the improved breeding of Welsh Mountain sheep, promoting the breed's attributes to a wider circle and organises breed sales of rams and draft ewes. Flock inspections help maintain breed characteristics but the society does not record details of individual sheep be they rams or ewes, but of the overall flock performance.

Welsh Mountain Sheep Society – Pedigree Section
Erw Myrddin
52 Ffordd Celyn
Dinbych
Denbighshire
LL16 5UU
Tel: 01745 814289
Contact: Mr Meurig Voyle, Secretary
Membership: 90
Publications: Annual flock book
Profile: The society encourages the breeding and improvement of Welsh Mountain sheep, the native breed of Wales' uplands. The ewes are excellent mothers, quick to lamb, good milkers and both the pure and crossbred Welsh lamb is renowned for its high quality. The society promotes the wool quality, which compares favourably with lowland breeds. The annual pedigree sale is held in September, with the society supporting breed classes at various shows and exhibitions. The society publishes a flock book each year with registered animals and publicity material.

Welsh Mule Sheep Breeders Association

c/o WAOS Ltd
PO Box 8
Brynawel
Great Darkgate Street
Aberystwyth
Ceredigion
SY23 1DR
Tel: 01970 624011
Fax: 01970 624049
Contact: Moss Jones, Secretary
Founded: 1978
Membership: 1,124
Profile: The association promotes the sale of Welsh Mule sheep, which are a cross between the Blue-faced Leicester ram and ewes from one of the traditional Welsh hill breeds – the Welsh Mountain, the Welsh Hill Speckled Face or the Beulah. Over 60,000 ewes are marketed throughout the autumn to farmers throughout the UK.

Welsh National Poisons Unit

Ward West 5
Llandough Hospital
Penarth
South Glamorgan
CF64 1XX
Tel: 01222 709901
Fax: 01222 704357
Email: 101346.3325@compuserve.com
Contact: Mrs Gloria Aldridge, Manager
Founded: 1963
Publications: Publications list available
Profile: The unit was established during 1963 in response to the increasing frequency of episodes of deliberate self-harm in the community. Since then it has provided a 24 hour service to doctors and other health care professionals in Wales. In 1988 it was transferred to Llandough Hospital and since then the work of the service has increased rapidly so that during 1995 a total of 11,311 enquiries were received. This represented a 20% increase in activity compared with 1994. In addition to its information role the unit acts as a resource for undergraduate and postgraduate education and for research in clinical toxicology and gives toxicological advice to health authorities and the Welsh Office.

Welsh Office

Cathays Park
Cardiff
CF1 3NQ
Tel: 01222 825111
Fax: 01222 823797

Contact: Mr Richard Keveren, Head of Rural Policy Team
Publications: A Working Countryside for Wales – rural white paper, published March 1996 (ISBN – 0 10 131802 2)
Profile: The Welsh Office was established on 1 April 1965. Over the years ministerial functions have been devolved to the Secretary of State. Today the Welsh Office is a multi-functional department administering and implementing a wide range of government policies. A white paper setting out the Government's vision for rural Wales was published on 13 March 1996. A Welsh Office team has been established to follow up the paper and put together an action plan. The key aim of the paper is to bring together and enhance the key factors that give rural communities their strength in order to safeguard their future.

Welsh Office Agricultural Department

Crown Offices
Cathays Park
Cardiff
CF1 3NQ
Tel: 01222 825111
Fax: 01222 823352/823562
Profile: The Welsh Office Agriculture Department (WOAD) ensures that the interests of Welsh agricultural and fisheries industries are taken into account in the development and application of European Community and domestic agricultural policy. It aims to operate agricultural support schemes in an effective way and fosters the environmental dimension within Welsh agriculture by helping farmers to maintain efficient farming systems and conserve the countryside and its wildlife. WOAD also supports measures to help maintain and improve farm animal health and welfare. WOAD operates regionally within Wales through five regional offices, the details may be obtained by contacting WOAD Headquarters.

Welsh Orienteering Association

44 Whitethorn Place
Sketty Park
Swansea
SA2 8HR
Tel: 01792 280631
Contact: Jane Selward, Secretary
Founded: 1970
Membership: 400
Publications: Y Ddraig (bimonthly newsletter)
Profile: The WOA is the governing body of the sport of orienteering in Wales, responsible for promoting and regulating the activity.

Orienteering events are normally organised by its member clubs, but the WOA promotes certain major, multi-day competitions. The association concerns itself with fostering good relations with landowners, tenants and commoners, and with the environmental agencies; the sport's 'arena' is the countryside.

Welsh Ornithological Society
Crud Yr Awel
Bowls Road
Blaenporth
Cardigan
Ceredigion
SA43 2AR
Tel: 01239 811561
Contact: John Green, Secretary

Welsh Pony and Cob Society
6 Chalybeate Street
Aberystwyth
Ceredigion
SY23 1HS
Tel: 01970 617501
Fax: 01970 625401
Contact: Anna Jenkins, Secretary
Founded: 1901
Membership: 8,500
Publications: Annual Stud Book; annual journal; bi-annual newsletter
Profile: The Welsh Pony and Cob Society was established in 1901 and continues to encourage the breeding and improvement of Welsh animals. The society currently registers approximately 9,000 animals a year, both nationally and internationally. There are 24 area associations and approximately 20 overseas societies. There is also a Welsh Part Bred Register for animals with more than 25% registered Welsh blood in their parentage.

Welsh Sheepdog Society/Cymdeithas Cwn Defaid
Cymraeg
Cefn Coch
Rhos y Garth
Llanila
Aberystwyth
Ceredigion
Tel: 01974 241593
Contact: John Davis
Founded: 1997
Profile: The society has been established to save the remaining 30 pure-bred dogs and encourage the development of the breed, keeping owners and breeders in contact with each other through the circulation of a newsletter.

Welsh Wildlife Trusts Ltd, The
Upper Hurdley
Church Stoke
Powys
SY15 6DY
Tel: 01588 620112
Fax: 01588 620112
Contact: Robin Cross, Executive Director
Founded: 1995
Membership: 11,000
Publications: Welsh Wildlife Trusts Reviews
Profile: The organisation has been set up to co-ordinate the conservation of the seven Welsh Wildlife Trusts, thereby enabling them to share resources and work more effectively. Welsh Wildlife Trusts Ltd is also responsible for fundraising at a national level for all the trusts. The collective and individual aim of the trusts is to protect Welsh wildlife. They do this by creating and managing nature reserves, and by campaigning locally and nationally.

Welsummer Club
Lasswade
Forest Row
East Sussex
RH18 5EF
Tel: 01342 823302
Contact: Mrs FMC Rogers, Secretary
Profile: A society to promote the Welsummer breed of poultry.

Wensleydale Longwool Sheep Breeders' Association
Old Hall
Hunton
Bedale
Yorkshire
DL8 1QJ
Tel: 01677 450579
Contact: Frank Pedley, Honorary Secretary
Founded: 1890
Membership: 185
Publications: Annual flock book

Wensleydale Sheep Society
Wyresdale
Camforth Hall Lane
Whittingham
Preston
Lancashire
PR3 2AS
Tel: 01772 865872
Profile: We have been unable to contact this organisation. The details given are unconfirmed.

Wessex Water plc

Wessex House
Passage Street
Bristol
BS2 0JQ
Tel: 0117 929 0611
Fax: 0117 929 3137
Contact: Anne Sharp, Senior Company
Secretarial Assistant
Founded: 1989
Publications: Annual Report; Environmental
Report
Previous names: Wessex Water Authority
1974–1989
Profile: Wessex Water plc, which has its
headquarters in Bristol, comprises a holding
company and a principal operating subsidiary,
Wessex Water Services Ltd. With its associated
company of Wessex Waste Management Ltd,
the company provides a total capability for water
and waste water work and waste management
worldwide.

Western Horsemens Association of Great Britain

Zara Training Centre
Highleigh Road
Sidlesham
Chichester
West Sussex
PO20 7NR
Tel: 01243 641662
Contact: Captain RG Ware, Treasurer
Founded: 1968
Membership: 250
Publications: Newsletter
Profile: To provide a representative body for all
people interested in the American western way
of horseriding. To set standards for riders and
instructors and hold examinations. To provide a
show rule book and a panel of judges and to
stage shows and other events connected with
western riding.

Wetlands International

Slimbridge
Gloucester
GL2 7BX
Tel: 01453 890634
Fax: 01453 890697
Previous names: International Waterfowl and
Wetlands Research Bureau until 1996

White Face Dartmoor Sheep Breeders Association

13 West Street
Ashburton
Devon

EX13 5XB
Contact: Secretary

White Park Cattle Society

Wimpole Home Farm
Old Wimpole
Royston
Hertfordshire
SG8 0BN
Tel: 01223 208987
Contact: Mrs Shirley Hartshorne, Secretary
Profile: We have been unable to contact this
organisation. The details given are unconfirmed.

White Wyandotte Club

The School Bungalow
St Peters Way
Menston
Ilkley
Yorkshire
LS29 6NY
Tel: 01943 414759
Contact: Mr J Lockwood, Secretary
Profile: A society to promote the White
Wyandotte breed of poultry.

Whitebred Shorthorn Association Ltd

High Greenhill
Kirkcambeck
Brampton
Cumbria
CA8 2BL
Tel: 016977 48228
Contact: Mrs R Mitchinson, Breed Secretary
Founded: 1962
Membership: 66
Publications: Herd book
Profile: Breed society for the Whitebred
Shorthorn Cattle Society.

Whitefaced Woodland Sheep Breeders Group

Rare Breeds Survival Trust
2 Biddlesden
Brackley
Northamptonshire
NN13 5TR
Tel: 01280 850677
Contact: Carole Muddiman, Secretary/Treasurer
Founded: 1986
Membership: 60
Publications: Members newsletter; breed leaflet
Profile: Their aim is the preservation and
promotion of Whitefaced Woodland sheep as a
distinctive and economically viable breed.

Wild Flower Society

68 Outwoods Road
Loughborough

Leicestershire
LE11 3LY
Tel: 01509 215598
Contact: M Walpole, Administration Secretary
Founded: 1886
Membership: 900
Publications: The Wild Flower Magazine
Profile: The central and distinctive activity of the society is based on recording the plants found, in an annual diary, which is also the basis of various competitions. Members are grouped into regional branches and field meetings are organised during the summer. Mainly a hobby organisation rather than a scientific group, but their aim is to educate in field botany and professional botanists and conservationists are amongst the membership.

Wildfowl & Wetlands Trust, The
Slimbridge
Gloucestershire
GL2 7BT
Tel: 01453 890333
Fax: 01453 890827
Contact: Kim Stiles, Head of Public Relations
Founded: 1946
Membership: 68,000
Publications: Wildfowl and Wetlands; Wildfowl (journal); Wetland News; Wetlands, Industry and Wildlife Manual
Previous names: Severn Wildfowl Trust until 1954; The Wildfowl Trust until 1989
Profile: WWT is a conservation charity which works to save wetlands for wildlife and people. It runs eight centres, open to visitors in Britain and Ireland and will open one in London in 2000. Six of its centres have wildfowl from around the world. Two are managed as reserves for wild birds. It runs extensive research programmes in many aspects of wildfowl and wetland biology.

Wildlife and Countryside Link
246 Lavender Hill
London
SW11 1LJ
Tel: 0171 924 2355
Fax: 0171 924 5761
Contact: Stephanie Hilborne, Principal Officer
Founded: 1979
Publications: Publications list available
Previous names: Wildlife Link until 1993
Profile: Wildlife and Countryside Link is a liaison service for all major non-governmental organisations in the UK concerned with the protection of wildlife and the countryside. Link facilitates debate and promotes joint positions on policy issues in order to influence key decision

makers, particularly in government and in the statutory conservation sector. Joint meetings, letters and reports provide a conduit for views of members to be conveyed more powerfully.

Wildlife Habitat Trust
Marford Mill
Rossett
Wrexham
LL12 0HL
Tel: 01244 570881
Fax: 01244 571678
Contact: Tony Laws, Secretary
Founded: 1986
Profile: The Wildlife Habitat Trust is the UK's sporting shooting organisation fund. It assists the acquisition, management and creation of wildlife habitats for the benefit of conservation and shooting. It is an investment in the future of both our wildlife resources and our sporting heritage.

Wildlife Section
The British Library
National Sound Archive
29 Exhibition Road
London
SW7 2AS
Tel: 0171 412 7402
Fax: 0171 412 7441
Email: Richard.Ranft@bl.uk
Contact: Richard Ranft, Curator, Wildlife Section
Founded: 1969
Publications: Publications list available
Previous names: British Library of Wildlife Sounds until 1994
Profile: The wildlife sounds section of the British Library National Sound Archive was established in 1969 as the British Library of Wildlife Sounds. Today it is the largest collection of its kind in Europe and possibly the most comprehensive in the world, with more than 80,000 recordings of all classes of sound-producing animals from every zoogeographical region. It is an important international resource for anyone interested in wildlife sounds. Recordings are scientifically organised and documented and are widely used by specialists in the field of bioacoustics and related behavioural and zoological disciplines. It is also an invaluable resource for naturalists, teachers, museums and zoos, and for providing sound effects for the broadcasting and film industries.

Wildlife Sound Recording Society
The British Library
National Sound Archive (Wildlife Section)
29 Exhibition Road
London
SW7 2AS

Contact: Dr Alan Burbidge, Honorary Secretary
Founded: 1968
Membership: 300
Publications: Wildlife Sound – the journal of the Wildlife Sound Recording Society
Profile: The society was formed in 1968 and now has over 300 members in Britain and throughout the world. Its objects are to encourage the recording of wildlife sounds and to support projects which aim at furthering the knowledge of bioacoustics, the techniques of recording natural history sounds and other allied subjects. In addition to the Annual General Meeting and Society Spring Meeting, field and local meetings are held throughout the country from time to time. The society publishes Wildlife Sound twice a year and a circulating tape of members' work four times a year.

Wildlife Trusts, The
The Green
Witham Park
Waterside South
Lincoln
LN5 7JR
Tel: 01522 544400
Fax: 01522 511616
Email: wildlifersnc@cix.compulink.co.uk
Contact: Andrea White, Head of Communications
Founded: 1912
Membership: 260,000
Previous names: SPNR until 1976, SPNC until 1981, RSNC until 1990, RSNC The Wildlife Trust Partnership until 1994
Profile: The Wildlife Trusts are a nationwide network of local trusts which work to protect wildlife in town and country. Through their care of 2,000 nature reserves, the Wildlife Trusts are dedicated to the achievement of a UK richer in wildlife, managed on sustainable principles. Sharing this goal and making a vital contribution to its attainment are the junior branch Wildlife Watch and the urban wildlife groups around the country. Using their specialist skills in the fields of conservation and education, The Wildlife Trusts strive to win public recognition that the achievement of their aims is essential for a healthy environment and continued human existence.

Wildlife Watch
The Wildlife Trust
The Green
Witham Park
Waterside South
Lincoln
LN5 7JR

Tel: 01522 544400
Fax: 01522 511616
Email: wildlifersnc@cix.compulink.co.uk
Contact: Mrs Mary Cornwell, Director of Education
Founded: 1971
Membership: 20,000
Publications: Watchword (newsletter); Rockwatch (newsletter)
Profile: Wildlife Watch is the junior branch of the Wildlife Trusts. It is a club for young people concerned about the environment (8 upwards). Individuals, families or school/institutions can join and there are over 1,000 local groups for members to attend. Wildlife Watch also runs Rockwatch, a 'sister' club for budding geologists, and national educational projects which are open to everyone.

Wiltshire Horn Sheep Society
Fairwater Farm
Hawchurch
Axminster
Devon
EX13 5XB
Tel: 01297 678539
Fax: 01297 678539
Contact: JRN Thwaites, Secretary
Founded: 1923
Membership: 120
Publications: Annual flock book; History of the Breed
Profile: The society promotes the breeding of Wiltshire Horn sheep, to the breed standards, at home and abroad and maintains the purity of the breed.

Women's Farm and Garden Association
175 Gloucester Street
Cirencester
Gloucestershire
GL7 2DP
Tel: 01285 658339
Contact: Patricia McHugh, Organiser
Founded: 1899
Membership: 275
Publications: The Hidden Workforce
Profile: The Women's Farm and Garden Association is a voluntary organisation for all women and men whose livelihood is connected in any way with the land, in agriculture, horticulture or allied industries. The association acts as a channel through which members have a voice at national and international levels on all matters concerned with agriculture and horticulture.

Women's Farming Union
NFU National Office
The National Rural Enterprise Centre
National Agricultural Centre
Stoneleigh Park
Warwickshire
CV8 2LZ
Tel: 01203 693171
Fax: 01203 693181
Contact: Mrs Meg Stroude, National Chairman
Founded: 1979
Membership: 600
Publications: Annual Review; numerous
pamphlets
Profile: The Women's Farming Union is a
voluntary national organisation founded in 1979.
It is committed to taking a comprehensive view
of the food chain from production to marketing,
for the benefit of British producers and
consumers and has become an authoritative
voice, respected by all sectors: consumer
groups, retailers and government.

Womens' Environmental Network
Aberdeen Studios
22 Highbury Grove
London
N5 2EA
Tel: 0171 354 8823
Fax: 0171 354 0464
Email: WENUK@gn.apc.org
Contact: Clare Hillyard Melia, Information
Co-ordinator
Founded: 1988
Membership: 4,000
Publications: Publications list available
Profile: WEN educates, informs and empowers
women to take positive environmental action, by
focusing on environmental issues from a
women's perspective. Current campaigns
include waste prevention, air pollution, forests
and paper, and breast cancer. Further information
available.

Wood Energy Development Group
Ingerthorpe Hall Farm
Markington
Harrogate
North Yorkshire
HG3 3PD
Tel: 01765 677887
Profile: We have been unable to contact this
organisation. The details given are unconfirmed.

Woodland Trust
Autumn Park
Dysart Road

Grantham
Lincolnshire
NG31 6LL
Tel: 01476 74297
Fax: 01476 590808
Contact: Mrs Hilary Allison, Public Affairs
Manager
Founded: 1972
Membership: 150,000
Publications: Broadleaf – The Newsletter of the
Woodland Trust; Annual Review; various leaflets
and pamphlets
Profile: The Woodland Trust is Britain's largest
organisation concerned with the conservation of
the heritage of broadleaved trees and woods.
The trust seeks to protect woods by acquiring
them and managing them in perpetuity. The trust
also acquires areas of bare land for tree planting.
The trust currently owns and manages over 750
individual sites covering over 25,000 acres.

Worcestershire College of Agriculture
Hindlip
Worcester
WR3 8SS
Tel: 01905 451310
Fax: 01905 754760
Contact: Mr R Brighton, Principal
Founded: 1959
Publications: Producing and Marketing Organic
Food
Profile: A college of agriculture and equine
studies with a specialist portfolio of organic
agriculture and permaculture courses. Also
provides a unique course in cider making which
supports the local industry. The smallest and
most personal land-based industries college in
the UK.

Working Horse Trust, The
The Estate Office
Sham Farm
Eridge Green
Tunbridge Wells
Kent
TN3 9JA
Tel: 01892 750105
Fax: 01892 750105
Contact: Jo Ambrose, Director
Founded: 1989
Membership: 250
Publications: Horse and Harness (members
newsletter)
Profile: The Working Horse Trust is a practical
group of conservation volunteers, formed to
champion the sympathetic use of heavy, working
horses in countryside management. The trust
actively demonstrates and promotes the use of

working horses in small scale sustainable farming and in the conservation of environmentally sensitive areas, including woodlands. The trust's work is focused on the restoration of ForgeWood Farm at Eridge, East Sussex.

Working Party on Pesticide Residues
c/o Pesticides Safety Directorate
Mallard House
Kings Pool
3 Peasholme Green
York
YO1P 3JR
Tel: 01904 455751
Fax: 01904 455733
Email: p.s.d.information@psd.maff.gov.uk
Contact: Mr R McIntosh, Administrative Secretary
Founded: 1977
Publications: Annual Report of the Working Party on Pesticide Residues (since 1988); three yearly summary available from 1977 (both from HMSO)
Profile: The WPPR advises the Advisory Committee on Pesticides and government departments as appropriate on the scope and nature of surveys for analysis of samples for pesticide residues, and considers the results of any surveys. The WPPR has an independent chairman and its membership is drawn from MAFF, the Department of the Environment, the Department of Health, the Scottish Office Agriculture and Fisheries Department, the Health and Safety Executive, the Laboratory of the Government Chemist, the Association of Public Analysts and a consumer representative.

World Arabian Horse Organization
32 Limerston Street
London
SW10 0HH
Tel: 0171 351 4900
Fax: 0171 351 4422
Contact: Kathy Powell, Executive Secretary
Founded: 1972
Membership: 2,000
Profile: The objects of WAHO are: to preserve, improve and maintain the purity of the blood of the Arabian horse; to promote public interest in the Arabian horse; to further the science of breeding the Arabian horse; to educate the public about the Arabian horse; and, to promote the knowledge in all countries of the history of the Arabian horse.

World Association for Transport Animal Welfare and Studies
32 The Gardens
Brookmans Park
Hatfield
Hertfordshire
AL9 7UL
Tel: 0171 701 5742
Fax: 0171 701 5742
Contact: Clive D Woodham, Secretary
Founded: 1989
Membership: 50
Publications: Members newsletter; Proceedings of Annual Seminar
Profile: The World Association for Transport Animal Welfare and Studies was founded in 1989 to promote improved management, health and welfare of transport and draught animals throughout the world by use of scientific method and humane practice. TAWS representatives are able to undertake projects and consultancies and provide information concerning management of transport animals and systems depending on their use.

World Jersey Cattle Bureau
Wuthering Heights
St Lawrence
Jersey
Channel Isles
Tel: 01534 861572
Fax: 01534 865569
Contact: Derrick I Frigot, Honorary Secretary/ Treasurer
Founded: 1951
Membership: 460
Publications: World Jersey Bulletin; World Jersey Newsletter
Profile: The World Jersey Cattle Bureau is an international organisation composed of National Jersey Associations, individuals and other organisations working co-operatively to improve the profitability of the Jersey cow and to ensure members receive a return on investment. The bureau offers young people the opportunity to travel on the WJCB International Youth Exchange Programme. WJCB organise an international conference every 3 years and regional conferences annually.

World Owl Trust
The Owl Centre
Muncaster Castle
Ravenglass
Cumbria
CA18 1RQ
Tel: 01229 717393

Fax: 01229 717107
Contact: Jenny Thurston, Executive
Administrator
Founded: 1972
Membership: 1,500
Publications: The Release of Captive Bred Barn
Owls as an Aid to Wild Declining Populations
Previous names: British Owl Breeding and
Release Scheme until 1993
Profile: The World Owl Trust is the only
organisation working on owl conservation on a
global scale. The centre serves as a focal point
for owl enthusiasts all over the world and is
involved with owl conservation projects in
countries such as the Philippines, Belize and
Ethiopia. Education is paramount with the WOT
and is carried out by means of talks, tours,
courses and displays. Conservation and
restoration of habitat are also part of the WOT's
objectives together with the release of birds
where possible.

World Pheasant Association
PO Box 5
Lower Basildon
Reading
Berkshire
RG8 9PF
Tel: 01734 845140
Fax: 01734 843369

World Small Animal Veterinary Association
Royal Veterinary College
Hawkshead Lane
Hatfield
Hertfordshire
AL9 7TA
Tel: 01707 55486
Fax: 01707 52090
Contact: Professor PGC Bedford, President
Founded: 1970
Membership: 30,000
Publications: Annual World Congress
Proceedings
Profile: The association's primary purpose is to
advance the quality and availability of veterinary
medicine and surgery relating to small animals.
WSAVA fosters the exchange of scientific
information within the international veterinary
community and furthers international
relationships between all veterinarians dealing
with small animal health and welfare.

World Society for the Protection of Animals
2 Langley Lane
London
SW8 1TJ

Tel: 0171 793 0540
Fax: 0171 793 0208
Internet: http://www.waynet/wspa
Contact: K Cooper, Marketing Director
Founded: 1981
Membership: 100,000
Publications: Animals International Magazine;
Campaign News
Profile: The society aims to promote the
protection of animals, to prevent cruelty to
animals, and to relieve animal suffering in every
part of the world. WSPA aims to promote
humane education programmes to encourage
respect for animals and responsible stewardship,
and laws and enforcement structures and
provide legal protection for animals.

World Veterinary Poultry Association
World Veterinary Association
Institute for Animal Health
Compton Laboratory
Compton
Newbury
Berkshire
RG20 7NN
Tel: 01635 578411
Fax: 01635 577237
Contact: Dr LN Payne, President
Founded: 1959
Membership: 1,300
Publications: Avian Pathology (journal); Aerosols
(newsletter)
Profile: The objectives of the association are: to
organise meetings for studying diseases and
conditions related to avian species; to encourage
research in this field; to promote the exchange of
information and material for study between
individuals and organisations interested in the
avian species; to establish and maintain liaison
with other bodies with related interests.
Membership is open to veterinarians interested
in avian science and non-veterinarians holding a
recognised scientific qualification.

Worlds Poultry Science Association UK Branch
Roslin Institute
Roslin
Midlothian
EH25 9PS
Tel: 0131 440 2726
Fax: 0131 440 0434
Contact: Dr PM Hocking, Secretary
Founded: 1946
Membership: 300
Publications: World's Poultry Science Journal
Profile: The objects of the WPSA are the
advancement of scientific knowledge and public

education and training in the agricultural use of
the avian species.

Worshipful Company of Butchers
Butchers Hall
87 Bartholomew Close
London
EC1A 7EA
Tel: 0171 606 4106
Fax: 0171 606 4108
Contact: FJ Malloy, Chairman of Education
Committee
Founded: 975
Membership: 1,800
Publications: Members newsletter
Previous names: Administers Institute of Meat
Educational/Professional/Membership Function
Profile: A City of London livery company. It
engages in educational/training activities for meat
industry professionals.

Worshipful Company of Coachmakers and Coach Harness Makers
149 Banstead Road
Ewell
Epsom
Surrey
KT17 3HL
Tel: 0181 393 5394
Fax: 0181 393 5394
Contact: Major WH Wharfe, Clerk
Founded: 1677
Membership: 400
Profile: City livery company.

Worshipful Company of Farmers
Pel House
35 Station Square
Pettswood
Kent
BR5 1LZ
Tel: 01689 891238
Fax: 01689 838258
Contact: Margaret Winter, Clerk
Founded: 1952
Membership: 300
Profile: A city livery company (no. 80 in order of
precedence) whose aim and objective is the
stimulation of the development of agricultural
education, through educational courses, travel
bursaries, etc.

Worshipful Company of Farriers
White Garth Chambers
37 The Uplands
Loughton
Essex
IG10 1NQ
Tel: 0181 508 6242
Fax: 0181 502 5237
Contact: HWH Ellis, Clerk and Registrar
Founded: 1356
Membership: 375
Publications: Publications list available
Profile: The company has its origins in 1356 and
was incorporated as a City of London company
after receiving its first Royal Charter in 1674. The
company has specific responsibilities for the
well-being of the craft of farriery in the interest of
equine animal welfare under The Farriers
(Registration) Acts 1975 and 1977. The
regulation of the craft is the responsibility of the
Farriers Registration Council. The company is the
examining body for farriery and promotes
seminars for the education of farriers in fulfilment
of its statutory responsibilities. The company
received its supplemental charter in 1983, which
updated the original charter to modern day
farriery requirements.

Worshipful Company of Fruiterers
Denmead Cottage
Chawton
Alton
Hampshire
GU34 1SB
Profile: We have been unable to contact this
organisation. The details given are unconfirmed.

Worshipful Company of Loriners
9 Rayne Road
Braintree
Essex
CM7 2QA
Tel: 01376 320328
Contact: Dr James W White, Senior Examiner
Founded: 1261
Membership: 300
Profile: City of London livery company dealing
with civic affairs and trade (bits, stirrups, spurs,
saddle trees etc.)

WRc plc
Henley Road
Medmenham
Marlow
Buckinghamshire
SL7 2HD
Tel: 01491 571531
Fax: 01491 579094
Contact: Ellen Knight, Corporate Relations
Founded: 1974
Publications: Publications catalogue available
Previous names: Water Research Centre until
1989

Profile: A leading European research and consultancy organisation, WRc works in the areas of water, wastewater and the environment. Independent and staff controlled, WRc operates from major science and technology centres at Medmenham and Swindon with regional offices in the UK and overseas. WRc provides R and D, consultancy and technical services under contract to the water industry, other industrial sectors, government departments, regulatory agencies, local government, the European Commission and international organisations.

Writtle College
Writtle
Chelmsford
Essex
CM1 3RR
Tel: 01245 420705
Fax: 01245 420456
Email: Postmaster@Writtle.ac.uk
Contact: David L Bebb, Director External Relations
Founded: 1893
Previous names: Essex Institute of Agriculture 1893–1978; Writtle Agricultural College until 1978
Profile: One of the UK's oldest and largest university sector colleges specialising in education, research, consultancy and training services in support of land and related industries. Higher education courses in agriculture, commercial horticulture, amenity horticulture, rural environmental management, equine studies, landscape design, agricultural engineering and leisure management. Further education courses include agriculture, commercial and amenity horse studies, service engineering, small animal care, veterinary nursing and floristry.

WWF-UK
Panda House
Weyside Park
Catteshall Lane
Godalming
Surrey
GU7 1XR
Tel: 01483 426444
Fax: 01483 426409
Contact: Gail Murray, Countryside Officer
Founded: 1961
Membership: 220,600
Publications: Publications list available
Previous names: World Wildlife Fund until 1988
Profile: WWF conserves nature in the UK and throughout the world for the benefit of all life on

Earth. By stopping, and eventually reversing, the degradation of our natural environment, they strive for a future in which people and nature can live together in balance.

WWOOF (Willing Workers on Organic Farms)
19 Bradford Road
Lewes
East Sussex
BN7 1RB
Tel: 01273 476286
Contact: Don Pynches, Co-ordinator
Founded: 1971
Membership: 2,000
Publications: Bimonthly newsletter
Profile: WWOOF is an exchange; in return for their work on organic farms, gardens and smallholdings (full time and quite hard!) workers receive meals, accommodation, the opportunity to learn and, if necessary, transport to and from the local station.

Wyandotte Bantam Club
93 Steam Mill Lane
Ripley
Derby
Derbyshire
DE5 3JR
Tel: 01773 744690
Contact: Miss J Newton, Secretary
Profile: A society to promote the Wyandotte Bantam breed of poultry.

Wye College University of London
Wye
Ashford
Kent
TN25 5AH
Tel: 01233 812401
Fax: 01233 813320
Email: J. Prescott@wye.ac.uk
Internet: http://www.wye.ac.uk
Contact: Professor JHD Prescott, Principal
Founded: 1894
Publications: Publications list available
Profile: Wye College is the rural faculty of the University of London and is one of the leading centres for rural research and teaching in the UK. It has some 800 internal students and a further 800 external students linked to its prestigious distance learning programme (postgraduate). Research and teaching cover a wide range of topics from advanced farm management/ business studies to plant/animal science and microbiology. Teaching and research in the environmental sciences is also a major part of the work of the college.

Yorkshire Agricultural Society
Great Yorkshire Showground
Hookstone Oval
Harrogate
North Yorkshire
HG2 8PW
Tel: 01423 561536
Fax: 01423 531112
Contact: RT Keigwin, Chief Executive
Founded: 1837
Membership: 10,000
Publications: Quarterly society newsletter; annual programmes, catalogues, etc. for the Great Yorkshire Show
Profile: A regional agricultural society for Yorkshire and the North East, responsible for the Great Yorkshire Show held in the second week of July. Active charity year-round in the promotion of agriculture and allied industries and in associated education, research, environmental and charitable matters. Showground facilities used throughout the year for a wide variety of agricultural and commercial functions through Yorkshire Agricultural Enterprise.

Yorkshire Dales National Park
North Yorkshire County Council
Colvend
Hebden Road
Grassington
Skipton
North Yorkshire
BD23 5LB
Tel: 01756 752745
Fax: 01756 752748

Yorkshire Dales Society
The Civic Centre
Cross Green
Otley
West Yorkshire
LS21 1HD
Tel: 01943 461938
Contact: Fleur Speakman, Joint Secretary
Founded: 1981
Membership: 2,000
Publications: The Yorkshire Dales Review; The Dales Digest
Profile: The Yorkshire Dales Society is a registered charity and is concerned to protect and enhance the unique environment of the Yorkshire Dales and to encourage appropriate forms of economic activity, including small business development, environmentally sensitive transport and tourism and traditional hill farming. It works for the retention of essential rural services that thriving communities need and is keen to promote the cultural heritage of the

Dales. A varied programme of events including walks, lectures, visits and social functions is offered throughout the year.

Yorkshire Water plc
West Riding House
67 Albion Street
Leeds
West Yorkshire
LS1 5AA
Tel: 0113 244 8201
Fax: 0113 244 3071
Contact: Miles Foulger, Conservation and Recreation Manager
Founded: 1990
Publications: Annual Conservation and Recreation Report; Annual Environmental Report; numerous leaflets and pamphlets
Previous names: Yorkshire Water Authority
Profile: A regional water supply and sewage disposal company with large upland catchments in the Pennines.

Young Farmers Club of Ulster
475 Antrim Road
Belfast
BT15 3BD
Tel: 01232 370713
Fax: 01232 777946
Contact: Mrs Pamela Robinson, General Secretary
Founded: 1929
Membership: 3,000
Publications: Year Book; Dispatch (members newsletter)
Profile: The objects of the association shall be by way of open clubs to advance the education of young members of the public at large in agriculture, home crafts, country life and related subjects and in the interests of the social welfare of such members to provide, and promote the provision of facilities for recreation and other leisure time occupations, being facilities which will improve their conditions of life and will assist in the development of their spiritual and mental capacities, self reliance and individual responsibility so that they may grow to full maturity as individuals and members of the community.

Youth Hostels Association (England and Wales)
Trevelyan House
8 St Stephens Hill
St Albans
Hertfordshire
AL1 2DY

Tel: 01727 855215
Fax: 01727 844126
Contact: Mr John Kingsbury, National
Countryside Officer
Founded: 1930
Membership: 247,000
Publications: Triangle (members newsletter);
YHA News; Annual Handbook; numerous
posters and leaflets
Profile: YHA is a registered national charity
founded in 1930 whose principal aim is 'to help
all, especially young people, of limited means to
a greater knowledge, love and care of the
countryside, particularly by providing Youth
Hostels or other simple accommodation for them
in their travels, and thus to promote their health,
rest and education'. YHA run a network of 240
Youth Hostel properties, recreation activities,
environmental education, residential experience
and special interest holidays.

Youth Hostels Association of Northern Ireland
22–26 Donegal Road
Belfast
BT12 5JN
Tel: 01232 324733
Fax: 01232 439699
Contact: WJK Canavan, General Secretary
Founded: 1931
Membership: 3,777
Publications: Accommodation Guide
Profile: The Youth Hostel Association for
Northern Ireland was formed in 1931. Its aims
are: to encourage a greater knowledge, love and
use of the countryside; to provide hostels or
other accommodation for its members on their
travels; to take any action possible to preserve
the beauties of the countryside; and, to obtain or
maintain access across rights of way.

Acronyms

2LUS	Second Land Utilisation Survey of Britain
AAB	Association of Applied Biologists
AATA	Animal Transportation Association
ABRS	Association of British Riding Schools
ACA	Anglers' Conservation Association
ACAS	Advisory, Conciliation and Arbitration Service
ACC	Association of County Councils
ACDP	Advisory Committee on Dangerous Pathogens
ACERT	Advisory Council for the Education of Romany and other Travellers
ACES	Association of Chief Estates Surveyors and Property Managers in Local Government
ACIG	Animal Cruelty Investigation Group
ACNFP	Advisory Committee on Novel Foods and Processes
ACP	Association of Cheese Processors
ACPAT	Association of Chartered Physiotherapists in Animal Therapy
ACPNB	Association for Crop Protection in Northern Britain
ACRE	Advisory Committee on Releases to the Environment
ACRE	Action with Communities in Rural England
ACTS	Advisory Committee on Toxic Substances
ADA	Association of Drainage Authorities
AEA	AEA
AEC	Association of Environmental Consultancies
AERDD	Agricultural Extension and Rural Development Department
AES	Agricultural Economics Society
AEU	Agricultural Economics Unit (Exeter)
AGMA	Amenity Grass Marketing Association
AGMED	Institute of Agricultural Medicine and Rehabilitation
AHOEC	Association of Heads of Outdoor Education Centres
AHS	Arab Horse Society
A.I.D.	Animals in Distress
AIFM	Association of Independent Forest Managers
ALANI	Association of Local Authorities of Northern Ireland
ALF SG	Animal Liberation Front Supporters' Group
ALLCU	Association of Librarians in Land-based Colleges and Universities
ALTs	Agricultural Land Tribunals
AMB	Ancient Monuments Board for Scotland
AMC	Agricultural Mortgage Corporation plc
AMCA	Amateur Motor Cycling Association
AMS	Agricultural Manpower Society
AMTRA	Animal Medicines Training Regulatory Authority
ANC	Association of Noise Consultants, The
ANPA	Association of National Park Authorities
ANPCVN	Association of National Park and Countryside Voluntary Wardens
APF	Association of Professional Foresters of Great Britain
APMO	Association of Private Market Operators
APRS	Association for the Protection of Rural Scotland

ARA	Applied Rural Alternatives
ARC	Arthur Rank Centre
ARC	Arable Research Centres
ARET	Allerton Research and Educational Trust
ARIA	Arable Research Institution Association
ASAB	Association for the Study of Animal Behaviour
ASDSFB	Association of Scottish District Salmon Fishery Boards
ASGFM	Association of Stillwater Game and Fishery Managers
ASPI	Animals (Scientific Procedures) Inspectorate
ASSG	Association of Scottish Shellfish Growers
AST	Atlantic Salmon Trust
ATA	Alternative Technology Association
AVA	Association of Veterinary Anaesthetists
AWB	Agricultural Wages Board for England and Wales
AWDC	All Wheel Drive Club
AWS	Anglian Water plc
BABFO	British Association for Biofuels and Oils
BACMI	British Aggregate Construction Materials Industries
B.A.C.S.	Blue Albion Cattle Society
BACS	British Association for Chemical Specialities
BAFSAM	British Association of Feed Supplement and Additive Manufacturers
BAGCD	British Association of Green Crop Driers Ltd
BAGMA	British Agricultural and Garden Machinery Association
BAHS	British Agricultural History Society
BAHVS	British Association of Homeopathic Veterinary Surgeons
BALI	British Association of Landscape Industries
BANC	British Association of Nature Conservationists
BAPSH	British Association for the Pure Bred Spanish Horse
BAS	British Arachnological Society
BASA	British Association of Seed Analysts
BASC	British Association for Shooting and Conservation
BASD	Beef & Sheep Division
BASIS	BASIS (Registration) Ltd
BBA	British Bison Association
BBAC	British Balloon and Airship Club
BBB	British Belgian Blue Cattle Society
BBKA	British Bee-Keepers Association
BBSRC	Biotechnology and Biological Sciences Research Council
BBWA	British Bavarian Warmblood Association
BCCA	British Cyclo-Cross Association
BCDTA	British Chemical Distributors and Traders Association Ltd
BCE	British Cereal Exports
BCGA	British Carrot Grower's Association
BCIS	British Chicken Information Service
BCPC	British Crop Protection Council
BCT	Bat Conservation Trust
BCTGA	British Christmas Tree Growers Association
BCVA	British Cattle Veterinary Association
BDFA	British Deer Farmers Association
BDG	Bioregional Development Group
BDS	British Dragonfly Society
B.D.S.	British Driving Society
BEIC	British Egg Industry Council
BEMB	British Egg Marketing Board (now disbanded)
BEPA	British Egg Products Association
BEPA	British European Potato Association
BES	British Ecological Society
BETA	British Equestrian Trade Association
BFD	Bees for Development
BFSS	British Field Sports Society
BGLA	British Growers Look Ahead
BGS	British Geological Survey
BGS	British Grassland Society

BHA	British Horseball Association
B.H.C.	British Herdsmans Club
BHPS	British Hedgehog Preservation Society
BHRC	British Harness Racing Club
BHS	British Horse Society
BHTA	British Herb Trade Association
BIAC	British Institute of Agricultural Consultants
BIBBA	British Isles Bee Breeders Association
BIFGA	British Independent Fruit Growers Association
BLA	British Lime Association
BLS	British Lichen Society
BMC	British Mountaineering Council
BMHS	British Miniature Horse Society
BMHS	British Morgan Horse Society
BMMA	British Meat Manufacturers Association
BMS	British Mule Society
BMS	British Mycological Society
B.N.C.S.	British Normandy Cattle Society
BNF	British Nutrition Foundation
BOBMA	British Oat and Barley Millers Association
BOF	British Orienteering Federation
BOT	Barn Owl Trust
BOU	British Ornithologists Union
BPA	British Pig Association
BRFI	BRF International
BRISC	Biological Recording in Scotland Campaign
BSAIF	British Sports and Allied Industries Federation
BSAS	British Society of Animal Science
BSBI	Botanical Society of the British Isles
BSD	British Society of Dowsers
BSG	British Stickmakers Guild
BSJA	British Show Jumping Association
BSPP	British Society for Plant Pathology
BTA	British Tourist Authority
BTCV	British Trust for Conservation Volunteers for Wales
BTFRA	British Trout Farmers Restocking Association
BTLIA	British Turf and Landscape Irrigation Association
BTMA	British Timber Merchants' Association
BTO	British Trust for Ornithology
BVA	British Veterinary Association
BVHA	British Veterinary Hospitals Association
BWBA	British Wild Boar Association
BWEA	British Wind Energy Association
BWPA	Black and White Pig Association (Berkshires)
CAAV	Central Association of Agricultural Valuers
CAB International	Centre for Agriculture and Biosciences
CAF	Charities Aid Foundation
CAFRE	Centre for Agricultural, Food and Resource Economics
The Caley	Royal Caledonian Horticultural Society
CAPM	Centre for Aquatic Plant Management
CARE	Cottage and Rural Enterprises Ltd
CAS	Centre for Agricultural Strategy
CAT	Centre for Alternative Technology
CAT Network	Countryside In and Around Towns Network
CBHS	Cleveland Bay Horse Society
CCAH	Cambridgeshire College of Agriculture and Horticulture – Milton
CCFG	Continuous Cover Forestry Group
CCFRA	Campden and Chorleywood Food Research Association
CCTA	Carmarthenshire College of Technology and Art Agriculture Department
CCW	Countryside Council for Wales
CEA	Confederation of European Agriculture
CEBIS	Centre for Environment and Business in Scotland
CEDaR	Centre for Environmental Data and Recording

CEDAR	Centre for Dairy Research
CEE	Council for Environmental Education
C.E.F.I.C.	European Chemical Industry Council
CEI	Centre for Environmental Interpretation
CELTS	Centre for Environment and Land Tenure Studies
CEM	College of Estate Management
CFA	Commonwealth Forestry Association
CHA	Commercial Horticultural Association
CIWEM	Chartered Institution of Water and Environmental Management
CIWF	Compassion in World Farming
CMA	Countryside Management Association
CNCC	Council for Nature Conservation and the Countryside
CNP	Council for National Parks
CoastNET	CoastNET (Coastal Heritage Network)
COC	Committee on Carcinogenicity of Chemicals in Food, Consumer Products and the Environment
COM	Committee on Mutagenicity of Chemicals in Food, Consumer Products and the Environment
COM COM	Commons Commissioners
COMA	Committee on Medical Aspects of Food Policy
CORT	Consortium of Rural TECs
COSQUEC	Committee for Occupational Standards and Qualifications in Environmental Conservation
COT	Committee on Toxicity of Chemicals in Food, Consumer Products and the Environment
CPBS	Connemara Pony Breeders Society
CPOS	County Planning Officers Society
CPRE	Council for the Protection of Rural England
CPRW	Campaign for the Protection of Rural Wales
CPSA	Clay Pigeon Shooting Association
CPSE	Committee on Plant Supply and Establishment
CRDT	University of Wolverhampton Centre for Rural Development and Training
CREM	Countryside Recreation and Environmental Management Research Group
CRN	Countryside Recreation Network
CROWC	Central Rights of Way Committee
CRS	Centre for Rural Studies
CRUC	Christian Rural Concern
CSA	Council for Scottish Archaeology
CSCAW	Catholic Study Circle for Animal Welfare
DAC	Defence Animal Centre
DANI	Department of Agriculture for Northern Ireland
DANI(FS)	Northern Ireland Forest Service
DANI Science	Science Service
DBRW	Development Board for Rural Wales
DBS	Donkey Breed Society
DFA	Drinking Fountain Association – The Metropolitan Drinking Fountain & Cattle Trough Association
DICE	Durrell Institute of Conservation and Ecology
DIF	Dairy Industry Federation Ltd
DOE	Department of the Environment
DOE(NI)	Department of the Environment for Northern Ireland
DSWA	Dry Stone Walling Association of Great Britain
DTI	Department of Trade and Industry
E.A.A.	European Adjuvant Association
EARA	Environmental Auditors Registration Association
ECO Journalists	Environmental Communicators' Organisation
ECO TRUST	Eco Environmental Information Trust
EEAA	Environmental Education Advisers Association
EFRC	Progressive Farming Trust Ltd
EGBA	English Goat Breeders Association
EHL	English Hops Limited
EIC	Environmental Information Centre
ELF	Environmental Law Foundation

EngC	Engineering Council
ENPA	Exmoor National Park Authority
EPNS	English Place Name Society
ERU	Energy Research Unit
ETA	Environmental Transport Association
ETB	English Tourist Board
ETO	Environmental Training Organisation
ETSU	ETSU
EVA	English Vineyards Association Ltd
F&ERC	Food and Energy Research Centre
FAB	Feline Advisory Bureau
FABBL	Farm Assured British Beef and Lamb
FAC	Food Advisory Committee
FAC	Federation of Agricultural Co-operatives (UK) Ltd
FASTCo	Forestry and Arboriculture Safety and Training Council
FAWC	Farm Animal Welfare Council
FCA	Forestry Contracting Association Ltd
FCA	Fencing Contractors Association
FEC	Farm Energy Centre
FF	Forests Forever Campaign
FFI	Fauna and Flora International
FFVIB	Fresh Fruit and Vegetable Information Bureau
FHAGBI	Friesian Horse Association of Great Britain and Ireland Ltd
FMA	Fertiliser Manufacturers Association
FOSFA	Federation of Oils, Seeds and Fats Association Ltd
FRA	Farm Retail Association
FRAC	Fungicide Resistance Action Committee
FSBI	Fisheries Society of the British Isles
FSC	Field Studies Council (Cymru)
FSC	Field Studies Council
FWAG	Farming and Wildlife Advisory Group
FWN	Farmers World Network
GA	Geologists' Association
GAFTA	Grain and Feed Trade Association
GF	Genetics Forum
GGA	Guernsey Growers Association
GHC/ACW	Gwartheg Hynafol Cymru/Ancient Cattle of Wales
GSID	Grants and Subsidies Inspection Division
GVS	Goat Veterinary Society
HAAC	Harper Adams Agricultural College
H&CTA	Horticultural and Contractors' Tools Association
HAPPA	Horses and Ponies Protection Association
HBC	Historic Buildings Council for Northern Ireland
HCC	Horticultural Correspondence College, The
HDC	Horticultural Development Council
HDRA	Henry Doubleday Research Association
HEA	Horticultural Exhibitors Association
HGCA	Home-Grown Cereals Authority
HHA	Historic Houses Association
HIF	Highlands and Islands Forum
HMC	Historic Monuments Council
HMI	Horticultural Marketing Inspectorate
HRA	Horticulture Research Association
HRI	Horticulture Research International
HSA	Council of Justice to Animals and Humane Slaughter Association
HSA	Health and Safety Agency for Northern Ireland
HSA	Hunt Saboteurs Association
HSA	Humane Slaughter Association
HSBA	Herdwick Sheep Breeders Association
HSL	Heritage Seed Library
HTA	Horticultural Trades Association
IACR	Institute of Arable Crops Research
IACR-LARS	Institute of Arable Crops Research – Long Ashton Research Station

IAEA	International Agricultural Exchange Association
IAgrE	Institution of Agricultural Engineers
IAT	Institute of Animal Technology
IAWQ	International Association on Water Quality
IBRA	International Bee Research Association
ICCE	International Centre for Conservation Education
ICF	Institute of Chartered Foresters
ICID	International Commission on Irrigation and Drainage (British Section)
ICUC	International Centre for Underutilized Crops
IEA	Institute of Economic Affairs (Environment Unit)
IEEM	Institute of Ecology and Environmental Management
IEEP	Institute for European Environmental Policy
IEM	Institute of Environmental Management
IERM	Institute of Ecology and Resource Management
IES	Institution of Environmental Sciences
IFEP	International Farm Experience Programme
IFIS	International Food Information Service
IFM	Institute of Fisheries Management
IFOMA	International Fishmeal and Oil Manufacturers Association
IFR	Institute of Food Research
IFST	Institute of Food Science and Technology
IGC	International Grains Council
IGD	Institute of Grocery Distribution
IGER	Institute for Grassland and Environmental Research
IH	Institute of Hydrology
IHSGB	Icelandic Horse Society of Great Britain
IIBC	International Institute of Biological Control
IIDS	Institute of Irrigation and Development Studies
IIED	International Institute for Environment and Development
ILAM	Institute of Leisure and Amenity Management
ILPH	International League for the Protection of Horses
IMA	International Mohair Association
IMI	International Mycological Institute
IMO	Institute of Market Officers
IOA	Institute of Aquaculture
IOH	Institute of Horticulture
IPPS	International Plant Propagators Society
IPSS	Institute of Professional Soil Scientists
ISDS	International Sheep Dog Society
ISO	International Sugar Organization
ISVA	Incorporated Society of Valuers and Auctioneers
ITE	Institute of Terrestrial Ecology
ITF	International Tree Foundation
IVEM	Institute of Virology and Environmental Microbiology
IWA	Inland Waterways Association
IWM	Institute of Waste Management
JAGB	Jockeys Association of Great Britain Ltd
JCCBI	Joint Committee for the Conservation of British Invertebrates
JFU	Jersey Farmers Union
JIC	John Innes Centre and Sainsbury Laboratory
JIMA	John Innes Manufacturers Association
JMT	John Muir Trust
JNCC	Joint Nature Conservation Committee
KES	King's Environmental Services
LAA	Livestock Auctioneers Association
LACS	League Against Cruel Sports Ltd
LASSA	Licensed Animal Slaughterers and Salvage Association
LCE	London Commodity Exchange
LDWA	Long Distance Walkers' Association
LDWPA	Lake District National Park Authority
LEAF	Linking Environment And Farming
LFRA	Leatherhead Food Research Association
LGC	Laboratory of the Government Chemist

LGU	Ladies' Golf Union
LMC	Livestock and Meat Commission for Northern Ireland
LSBA	Lonk Sheep Breeders Association
LTA	Land Trusts Association
LVRPA	Lee Valley Regional Park Authority
MAFF	Ministry of Agriculture, Fisheries and Food
MBR	Monuments and Buildings Record
MDC	Milk Development Council
MDHA	Masters of Deerhounds Association
MEA	Medical Equestrian Association
MHA(UK)	Morgan Horse Association (UK)
MLC	Meat and Livestock Commission
MLURI	Macauley Land Use Research Institute
MMMA	Milking Machine Manufacturers Association
MOLARA	Motoring Organisation's Land Access and Rights Association
MPEP	Milk, Pigs, Eggs and Poultry Division
MRC	Mountain Rescue Council
MSGB	Manorial Society of Great Britain
NABIM	National Association of British and Irish Millers
NABMA	National Association of British Market Authorities
NACM	National Association of Cider Makers
NAEE	National Association for Environmental Education
NAFAC	National Association of Fisheries and Angling Consultatives
NAFS	National Association of Farms for Schools
NAFSO	National Association of Field Studies Officers
NALC	National Association of Local Councils
NALOO	National Association of Licensed Opencast Operators
NAMB	National Association of Master Bakers
NAOE	National Association for Outdoor Education
NAPAEO	National Association of Principal Agricultural Education Officers
NAPGC	National Association of Public Golf Courses
NASPM	National Association of Seed Potato Merchants
NASS	National Association for the Support of Small Schools
NAT	National Association of Teleworking
NATTA	Network for Alternative Technology and Technology Assessment
NBU	Central Science Laboratory National Bee Unit
NCA	National Cattle Association
NCC	National Caravan Council Ltd
NCC	National Consumer Council
NCDA	National Compost Development Association
NDA	National Dairymens' Association
NDC	National Dairy Council
NEMAL	National Egg Marketing Association Ltd
NEMSA	North of England Mule Sheep Association
NERC	Natural Environment Research Council
NFA	National Food Alliance
NFAS	National Field Archery Society
NFBG	National Federation of Badger Groups
NFBU	National Federation of Bus Users
NFCF	National Federation of City Farms
NFO	Natural Fibres Organisation
NFST	Nuffield Farming Scholarships Trust
NFU	National Farmers' Union, The
NFWI	National Federation of Women's Institutes
NFWS	National Ferret Welfare Society
NGC	National Gypsy Council
NGDA	National Game Dealers Association
NHETC	National Horse Education and Training Company Ltd
NIAB	National Institute of Agricultural Botany
NIAPA	Northern Ireland Agricultural Producers Association
NIBA	Northern Ireland Birdwatchers' Association
NICSA	Northern Ireland Countryside Staff Association
NIDA	Northern Ireland Dairy Association

NIEL	Northern Ireland Environment Link
NIGC	Northern Ireland Goat Club
NIHPBS	Northern Ireland Horticulture and Plant Breeding Station
NITB	Northern Ireland Tourist Board
NLS	Environment Agency: National Laboratory Service
NOAH	NOAH
NOEA	National Outdoor Events Association
NPS	National Pony Society
NPTC	National Proficiency Tests Council
NREC	National Rural Enterprise Centre
NRI	Natural Resources Institute
NSA	National Sheep Association
NSALG	National Society of Allotment and Leisure Gardeners Ltd
NSCA	National Society for Clean Air and Environmental Protection
NSQA	Natural Slate Quarries Association
NSWA	National Small Woods Association
NTS	National Trust for Scotland, The
NWTC	National Wind Turbine Centre
OAS	Organic Advisory Service
ODA	Offa's Dyke Association
OFF	Organic Food Federation
OFFER	Office of Electricity Regulation
OFGAS	Office of Gas Supply
OFI	Oxford Forestry Institute
OFWAT	Office of Water Services
OLF	Organic Living Association
OLMC	Organic Livestock Marketing Cooperative
OS	Ordnance Survey
OSNI	Ordnance Survey of Northern Ireland
OSTS	Official Seed Testing Station for Scotland
PANI	Poultry Association of Northern Ireland
PAR	Pagan Animal Rights
PCHP	Pembrokeshire Coast National Park Authority
PDA	Potash Development Association
PEGS	Pesticide Exposure Group of Sufferers
P.G.C.	Pygmy Goat Club
PGRO	Processors and Growers Research Organisation
PHSI	Plant Health and Seeds Inspectorate
PMB	Potato Marketing Board
PPA	Potato Processors Association
PSD	Pesticides Safety Directorate
PTDS	Pig Technology and Development Service
PTES	People's Trust for Endangered Species
PUSG	Pesticide Usage Survey Group
PV-UK	British Photovoltaic Society
PVGA	Processed Vegetable Growers Association Ltd
QKOA	Quarantine Kennel Owners Association UK
RAAAC	Rural and Agricultural Affairs Advisory Committee
RABDF	Royal Association of British Dairy Farmers
RABI	Royal Agricultural Benevolent Institution
RAC	Royal Agricultural College, The
RACMSA	RAC Motorsports Association
RASE	Royal Agricultural Society of England
RBGE	Royal Botanic Garden Edinburgh
RBST	Rare Breeds Survival Trust
RCA	Racecourse Association Ltd
RCAA	Royal Cornwall Agricultural Association
RCAHMS	Royal Commission on the Ancient and Historical Monuments of Scotland
RCEP	Royal Commission on Environmental Pollution
RCHME	Royal Commission on the Historic Monuments of England
RCVS	Royal College of Veterinary Surgeons
RDA	Riding for the Disabled Association
RDBA	Rural Design and Buildings Association

RDC	Rural Development Council for Northern Ireland
RDD	Rural Development Division (DOE)
RDD	Rural Development Division (DANI)
REDA	Rural Education and Development Association
RFS	Royal Forestry Society of England, Wales and Northern Ireland
RGS	Royal Geographical Society (with the Institute of British Geographers)
RHASS	Royal Highland and Agricultural Society of Scotland
RHS	Royal Horticultural Society
RHT	Rural Housing Trust
RICS	Royal Institution of Chartered Surveyors, The
RLAS	Royal Lancashire Agricultural Society
RNAA	Royal Norfolk Agricultural Association
ROA	Racehorse Owners Association Ltd
ROSPA	Royal Society for the Prevention of Accidents
RSABI	Royal Scottish Agricultural Benevolent Institution
RSGS	Royal Scottish Geographical Society
RSPB	Royal Society for the Protection of Birds
RSPCA	Royal Society for the Prevention of Cruelty to Animals
RSS	Remote Sensing Society
RTBTB	Racing Thorougbred Breeding and Training Board
RTDA	Rural Training Development Association
RURAL	Society for the Responsible Use of Resources in Agriculture and on the Land
RVC	Royal Veterinary College, The
SAB	Society for Applied Bacteriology
SAC	SAC
SAFE Alliance	Sustainable Agriculture, Food and Environment Alliance
SAMB	Scottish Association of Master Bakers
SANA	Scottish Anglers National Association
SAOS	Scottish Agricultural Organisation Society Ltd
SASA	Scottish Agricultural Science Agency
SBA	Scottish Beekeepers Association
SBREC	Sugar Beet Research and Education Committee
SBS	Saanen Breed Society
SCI	Society of Chemical Industry
SCMA	Stilton Cheese Makers' Association
SCOPA	Seed Crushers and Oil Processors Association
SCP	Scottish Conservation Projects Trust
SCPA	Scottish Cashmere Producers Association
SCRA	Scottish Countryside Rangers' Association
SCRI	Scottish Crop Research Institute
SCTA	Scottish Corn Trade Association
SCU	Scottish Crofters Union
SEAC	Spongiform Encephalopathy Advisory Committee
SEF	Scottish Environmental Forum
S.E.P.R.A.	Scottish Egg Producer Retailers Association
SERC	Scottish Endurance Riding Club
SETA	Scottish Egg Trade Association
SFACET	Scottish Farm and Countryside Educational Trust
SFGB	Stone Federation of Great Britain
SFMTA	Scottish Federation of Meat Traders' Associations (Inc.)
SFT	Society of Feed Technologists
SFV Ltd	Scottish Farm Venison Ltd
SGGB	Showmens Guild of Great Britain
SLF	Scottish Landowners' Federation
SOAEFD	Scottish Office Agriculture, Environment and Fisheries Department
SPIB	National Poisons Information Service (Edinburgh)
SPVS	Society for Practising Veterinary Surgeons
SQBLA	Scotch Quality Beef and Lamb Association
SRI	Silsoe Research Institute
SSB	Scottish Salmon Board
SSBA	Shropshire Sheep Breeders Association and Flock Book Society
SSC	Scottish Sports Council
SSF	Scottish School of Forestry

SSLRC	Soil Survey and Land Research Centre
SSPCA	Scottish Society for the Prevention of Cruelty to Animals
SSPDC	Scottish Seed Potato Development Council
STB	Scottish Tourist Board
S.T.R.I.	Sports Turf Research Institute, The
STSF	Scottish Target Shooting Federation
SWAN	Society for Wildlife Art of the Nations
SWLG	Scottish Wild Land Group
SWT	Scottish Wildlife Trust
SYHA	Scottish Youth Hostels Association
T.A.G.	Towpath Action Group
TAPS Centre	National Centre for Toxic and Persistent Substances
TAWS	World Association for Transport Animal Welfare and Studies
TBA	Thoroughbred Breeders' Association
TCA	Telework, Telecentre and Telecottage Association
TCPA	Town and Country Planning Association
TDB	Technical Development Branch
TFA	Tenant Farmers' Association
TGA	Timber Growers Association
TRADA	Timber Research and Development Association
TRSS	Trekking and Riding Society of Scotland
TSA	United Kingdom Land and Hydrographic Survey Association
TTF	Timber Trade Federation
UAOS	Ulster Agricultural Organisations Society Ltd
UFAW	Universities Federation for Animal Welfare
UKAFMM	United Kingdom Association of Fish Meal Manufacturers
UKASTA	United Kingdom Agricultural Supply Trade Association Ltd
UKDA	United Kingdom Dairy Association
UKELA	United Kingdom Environmental Law Association
UKEPRA	UK Egg Producers Association
UKFN	UK Forests Network
UKIA	United Kingdom Irrigation Association
UKPTF	United Kingdom Provision Trade Federation Ltd
UKROFS	United Kingdom Register of Organic Standards
UTDA	Ulster Tourist Development Association Ltd
VDS	Veterinary Deer Society
VIRSA	Village Retail Services Association
VLA	Valuation and Lands Agency
VLA	Veterinary Laboratories Agency
VMD	Veterinary Medicines Directorate
VOA	Valuation Office
VPA	Vegetable Protein Association
VSO	Voluntary Service Overseas
VTSC	Virus Tested Stem Cutting Association
WAHO	World Arabian Horse Organization
WAOS	Welsh Agricultural Organisation Society Ltd
WCB	Worshipful Company of Butchers
WCC	Wales Craft Council / Cyngor Crefft Cymru Cyf
WCL	Wildlife and Countryside Link
WEN	Womens' Environmental Network
WFGA	Women's Farm and Garden Association
WFPL	Welsh Food Promotions Ltd
WFU	Women's Farming Union
WJCB	World Jersey Cattle Bureau
WLD	Water and Land Directorate
WMD	Watercourse Management Division Headquarters
WMIB	Waste Management Information Bureau
WOA	Welsh Orienteering Association
WOAD	Welsh Office Agricultural Department
WOT	World Owl Trust
WPA	World Pheasant Association
WPPR	Working Party on Pesticide Residues
WPSA	Worlds Poultry Science Association UK Branch

WRAG	Weed Resistance Action Group
WRG	Waterway Recovery Group
WSA	Water Services Association
WSAVA	World Small Animal Veterinary Association
WSPA	World Society for the Protection of Animals
W.S.R.S.	Wildlife Sound Recording Society
WVPA	World Veterinary Poultry Association
WWCL	Wales Wildlife and Countryside Link
WWF-UK	WWF-UK
WWOOF	WWOOF (Willing Workers on Organic Farms)
WWT	Wildfowl & Wetlands Trust, The
YFC	National Federation of Young Farmers' Clubs
YHA	Youth Hostels Association (England and Wales)
YHANI	Youth Hostels Association of Northern Ireland

Subject Index

Subject Index

W

FARMING PRESS BOOKS & VIDEOS

Below is a sample of the wide range of agricultural and veterinary books and videos we publish. For more information or for a free illustrated catalogue of all our publications please contact:

Farming Press Books & Videos
Farming Press, Miller Freeman plc
Wharfedale Road, Ipswich IP1 4LG, United Kingdom
Telephone (01473) 241122   Fax (01473) 240501

Beef Breeds of Britain
Presented by JOE HENSON

Joe discusses famous native British beef breeds and looks at how several of these have developed in North America. He also covers continental breeds that have become familiar in Britain recently.

Birds of Prey: management and training   BRYAN PATERSON

An introduction to keeping hawks and falcons and to learning to fly them successfully.

Directory of Courses in Land-based Industries 1997–1998
NICHOLAS BOND

A comprehensive annual guide to full-time and sandwich courses offered by agricultural and horticultural colleges and related institutions in the United Kingdom.

Free-range Poultry   KATIE THEAR

Non-intensive poultry keeping for both small-scale and larger-scale units.

Harnessed to the Plough (VHS video)
ROGER AND CHERYL CLARK with PAUL HEINEY

Roger and Cheryl Clark demonstrate a year of contemporary horse-drawn cultivations and harvesting on their Suffolk farm. Additional commentary by Paul Heiney.

Keeping Ducks: beautiful, comical things (video)   TOM BARTLETT

Shows the beginner all aspects of duck keeping, from choice of breed to egg incubation and showing.

New Hedges for the Countryside
MURRAY MACLEAN

Gives full details of hedge establishment, cultivation and maintenance for wind protection, boundaries, livestock containment and landscape appearance.

Peers, Peasants and Pheasants
JUDY VOWLES

The experiences, challenges and pleasures of a family as they begin working at a racing stud on an estate in south-west England in the 1980s.

Practical Accounting for Farm and Rural Enterprise   BEN BROWN

Covers the full range of accounting needs from data collection through profit and loss to analysis of results.

Seven Centuries of the English Windmill   DAVID BENT

Shows many of the windmills of the Midlands, East Anglia and southern England, and provides an insight into the dignified and often dangerous world of windpower over the seven centuries of the English windmill.

Sheep of the Hills presented by
JOE HENSON

A number of British upland sheep breeds are shown in their attractive upland environments. Joe Henson explains how the breeds evolved and looks at how the British sheep industry is organised to produce prime lamb and wool.

Sheep of the Vales presented by
JOE HENSON

This video takes a look at native downland and lowland sheep, and covers well-known as well as rarer breeds. It was filmed in Britain and America and shows breeds recently imported from the continent.

Farming Press is a division of Miller Freeman plc which provides a wide range of media services in agriculture and allied businesses. Among the magazines published by the group are *Arable Farming*, *Dairy Farmer*, *Farming News* and *Pig Farming*. For a specimen copy of any of these please contact the address above.